ALSO BY JOSEPH WHEELAN

Midnight in the Pacific:
Guadalcanal—The World War II Battle That Turned the Tide of War

Their Last Full Measure:
The Final Days of the Civil War

Bloody Spring:
Forty Days That Sealed the Confederacy's Fate

Terrible Swift Sword:
The Life of General Philip H. Sheridan

Libby Prison Breakout:
The Daring Escape from the Notorious Civil War Prison

Invading Mexico:
America's Continental Dream and the Mexican War, 1846–1848

Mr. Adams's Last Crusade:
John Quincy Adams's Extraordinary Post-Presidential Life in Congress

Jefferson's Vendetta:
The Pursuit of Aaron Burr and the Judiciary

Jefferson's War:
America's First War on Terror 1801–1805

BLOODY OKINAWA

THE LAST GREAT BATTLE
OF WORLD WAR II

JOSEPH WHEELAN

hachette
BOOKS
NEW YORK

Hachette Books
Hachette Book Group
1290 Avenue of the Americas, New York, NY 10104
HachetteBooks.com
Twitter.com/HachetteBooks
Instagram.com/HachetteBooks

Printed in the United States of America

First Edition: March 2020

Hachette Books is a division of Hachette Book Group, Inc.
The Hachette Books name and logo are trademarks of Hachette Book Group, Inc.

The Hachette Speakers Bureau provides a wide range of authors for speaking events. To find out more, go to www.hachettespeakersbureau.com or call (866) 376-6591.

The publisher is not responsible for websites
(or their content) that are not owned by the publisher.

Print book interior design by Trish Wilkinson.

Library of Congress Cataloging-in-Publication Data has been applied for.

ISBNs: 978-0-306-90322-9 (hardcover); 978-0-306-90321-2 (e-book)

LSC-C

10 9 8 7 6 5 4 3 2 1

Contents

List of Maps

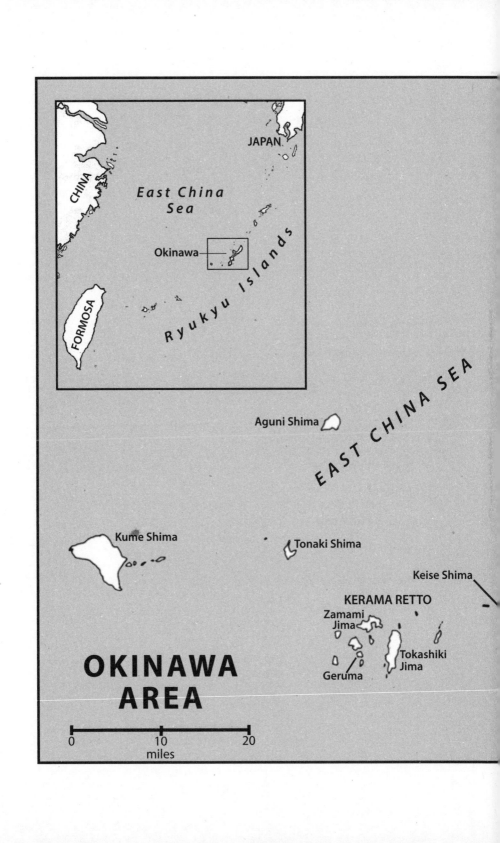

JAPAN

CHINA

East China
Sea

Okinawa

Ryukyu Islands

FORMOSA

EAST CHINA SEA

Aguni Shima

Kume Shima

Tonaki Shima

Keise Shima

KERAMA RETTO

Zamami
Jima

Tokashiki
Jima

Geruma

OKINAWA
AREA

0   10   20
miles

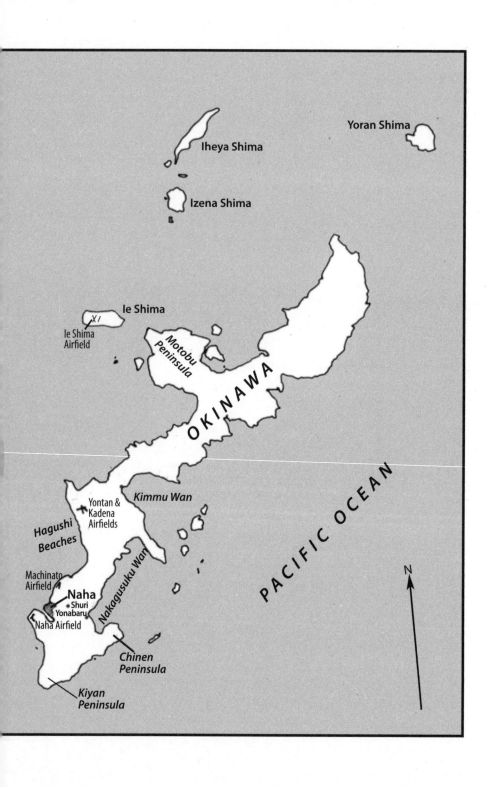

Yoran Shima

Iheya Shima

Izena Shima

Ie Shima

X 1

Ie Shima
Airfield

Motobu
Peninsula

OKINAWA

Kimmu Wan

Yontan &
Kadena
Airfields

Hagushi
Beaches

Nakagusuku Wan

Machinato
Airfield

Naha
• Shuri
Yonabaru
Naha Airfield

Chinen
Peninsula

Kiyan
Peninsula

PACIFIC OCEAN

N

Prologue

The only course left is for Japan's one hundred million
people to sacrifice their lives by charging the enemy to make
them lose the will to fight.

—IMPERIAL JAPANESE HEADQUARTERS WAR JOURNAL, 1945[1]

WITH SIXTY-NINE PLANES AND TWENTY-SIX hundred crewmen, the
USS *Franklin* had recently joined Admiral Marc Mitscher's Fast Carrier
Task Force, TF-58, in the Pacific Ocean waters between Okinawa and Japan
to begin air operations against Japan on March 18.

The modern Essex-class carrier was launched in 1943, and in 1944 she
participated in the Peleliu and Philippines campaigns. On October 30, near
Leyte Gulf, a kamikaze crashed her flight deck. The Japanese plane's 550-
pound bomb exploded in a ready room, wiping out a battle-dressing station. Fifty-six men died. After repairs at the Puget Sound Naval Shipyard in
Bremerton, Washington, *Franklin* returned to the Pacific.[2]

"Big Ben," as her crewmen fondly called her, had a new skipper, Captain
Leslie Gehres, and at Pearl Harbor, she acquired a new chaplain, the Rever-
end Joseph O'Callahan, a Catholic priest.

O'Callahan celebrated Mass for *Franklin*'s sailors on Saturday,
March 17—Saint Patrick's Day—giving general absolution to twelve hundred men. TF-58's pilots and sailors would have no time for Mass on Sunday, when carrier planes would begin attacking airfields on Kyushu, Japan's
southernmost island.

The Fast Carrier Force's objective was to neutralize the airfields in southern Kyushu that were the staging areas for enemy suicide planes, or kamikazes. This was vitally important, because on April 1, the Pacific war's largest amphibious campaign, Operation Iceberg, would begin at Okinawa.

On schedule, March 18, hundreds of warplanes from TF-58's seventeen carriers attacked Kyushu's fifty-five airfields and their hangars and the shipyards on the Inland Sea with bombs, rockets, torpedoes, and machine-gun fire. They destroyed hangars and parked aircraft, pitted airstrips with bombs, and damaged seventeen Japanese ships in the Inland Sea, and at Kobe and Kure.

The Japanese deployed five submarines to sink the carriers, but US destroyers and dive-bombers, by now well schooled in hunting down subs, sank them all.

With better prospects for success, Admiral Matome Ugaki, commander of the 5th Air Fleet at Kyushu, dispatched 193 aircraft, including 69 suicide planes from his "Special Attack Unit," on March 18. Ugaki's pilots bombed the *Enterprise*, *Intrepid*, and *Yorktown*. Seven sailors died, but damage to the carriers was minimal and the ships were able to continue operations.[3]

The Japanese suicide squadrons were a desperate expedient adopted in October 1944, as Allied forces prepared to invade the Philippines, to address the yawning disparity between American and Japanese air and naval strength. In the ensuing months, the kamikazes had become a pillar of Japanese air strategy as other options had vanished in a blizzard of American bomb attacks. Conscripts now filled many of the cockpits because of the shrinking number of kamikaze volunteers.[4]

THE FAST CARRIER TASK FORCE was 55 miles from Kyushu at dawn on March 19 when Big Ben launched forty-five of her planes, while twenty-two other aircraft were being fueled on *Franklin*'s hangar deck. Mitscher's task force had edged closer to Kyushu so that its squadrons of Hellcats, Corsairs, and Wildcats could more easily strike the enemy warships berthed beyond Kyushu at Kobe and Kure.

Franklin's radar screens were free of bogeys at 7 a.m. when Captain Gehres scaled back her readiness level from General Quarters to Condition III, allowing his men to go to the mess hall for their first hot meal in three days. Within minutes, hundreds of hungry sailors were queued up on the hangar deck for breakfast, waiting to descend the ladder to the galley one deck below.

March 19 was the nineteenth birthday of Elden Rogers, a sailor who worked on the hangar deck. In a letter that he had written home three days earlier, he lamented his recent failure at Pearl Harbor to reconnect with friends. "I guess luck can't be with me always," he wrote. "So long for now. Don't be worrying about me. Things are peaceful out here now."[5]

At 7:08 a.m., without any warning, a dive-bomber displaying the Rising Sun "meatball" insignia flashed out of the base of a low cloud 1,000 yards ahead of *Franklin* and made a mast-level bombing run. In the blink of an eye, it released two 550-pound bombs and escaped before gunners could find its range.[6]

Both bombs crashed through the flight deck, exploding nearly simultaneously in the hangar space below. Fed by fuel vapor, a chain of explosions roared through the armed Avengers, Corsairs, and Hellcats on the hangar deck, rocking the ship. Idling Corsairs burst into flame, and their whirling propellers slashed adjacent planes and men. All but two of the more than five hundred men in the hangar deck area—crewmen either standing in line for breakfast or servicing planes—were instantly incinerated, among them Elden Rogers.[7]

"I saw guys flying through the air" from the explosions, said Seaman 1/c Ralph Packard, who was on the nearby destroyer *Hunt*. "I saw men running around on fire, just flaming torches." Electrician Mate Al Cole watched sailors jump off the flight deck into the sea, "drowning right and left."

On *Franklin*'s flight deck, Seaman 2/c George Sippel grabbed the arm of a man running in terror toward him, "hollering and screaming," and the man's arm came off in Sippel's hand. "It was just like a turkey leg," he said. "It was cooked right through." Horrified, Sippel threw the arm overboard.[8]

The hangar deck was "just a mass of orange and white flames," said Aviation Machinist's Mate Glenn Davis. The ship burned so fiercely that steam rose from *Franklin*'s wake. Radioman George Black was shocked by what he saw when he reached the hangar deck. "There were several hundred bodies," he said. "None of them were wearing clothing. It was just arms, legs, hands, heads, and what have you." Firefighters groped through the choking smoke to play the fire hoses on the flames as pitch bubbled between the flight deck's planks.[9]

Meanwhile, the high-pitched shriek of streaking 1,200-pound 11.75-inch "Tiny Tim" rockets that had been mounted on the wings of the burning planes added a dimension of terror to a scene of nearly indescribable carnage. The rockets flashed by in "great orange streaks a few feet over our

heads," wrote a Marine lieutenant. *Franklin*'s executive officer, Commander Joe Taylor, described it as "one of the most awful spectacles a human has ever been privileged to see." *Franklin* lost power and her forward momentum slowed until she was dead in the water.[10]

THE NEW CHAPLAIN, FATHER O'CALLAHAN, a thirty-nine-year-old Irish-Catholic priest from Boston's Roxbury district, had taught physics at Boston College and Holy Cross before becoming the first Jesuit to become a Navy chaplain; he was aboard the carrier *Ranger* during the North Africa landings in October 1942.

Upon awakening March 19, he remembered that it was the Feast of Saint Joseph—his namesake and the patron saint of a "happy death." A short time later, as he was eating breakfast in the officers' wardroom, he heard a loud "bang" and the sound of breaking glass. The officers dove under the table. O'Callahan told himself, "This is it."[11]

In the inky blackness that engulfed *Franklin*'s lower decks with her power gone, the priest groped along a fire-blackened passageway to the junior aviators' bunkroom, where corpsmen were treating injured pilots. O'Callahan administered viaticum, or last rites, to the dying; some of them perished in his arms.

Then, he led a group of men single file up a ladder to the flight deck, now a scarred slab covered with burned, mangled bodies. Spotting a pile of 5-inch shells glowing dangerously from the heat of the raging fires, the priest enlisted some sailors to help him hose them down, manning the nozzle himself. "He went right into the fires," said Marine Tech Sergeant Ray Larson of VMF-452. Conspicuous in his helmet with a white cross, O'Callahan helped roll a blistering-hot live bomb out of a darkened gun turret and pushed it off the deck. He then trundled blackened corpses up ladders from belowdecks.

Commander Stephen Jurika, who was *Franklin*'s navigator and standing beside Captain Gehres on the bridge, was awed by O'Callahan's actions. O'Callahan was "a soul-stirring sight," he wrote. "He seemed to be everywhere . . . doing everything he could to save the ship."

"I never saw a man so completely disregard the danger of being killed," said Gehres, who recommended the priest for a Congressional Medal of Honor. O'Callahan received the award in January 1946, becoming the first Navy chaplain so honored.

Also awarded the Medal of Honor was Lieutenant Donald Gary, a *Franklin* engineering officer who led three hundred men to safety during

three harrowing trips from a smoke-filled mess hall on Deck 3. Gary also organized a party that splashed through pitch-black passageways clogged with floating bodies to light a boiler and get the ship's screws turning again so that she could be towed.[12]

Despite the towering flames, exploding ammunition, and billowing smoke, Captain Gehres and the 704 crewmen who were still aboard and able to perform their duties saved their ship. Eight hundred seven men died, 487 were wounded, and 1,000 others left the ship or were blown overboard.

By 11 a.m. *Franklin* was making 15 knots. She limped into Ulithi Atoll, the Navy's major western Pacific staging and repair station, 360 miles southwest of Guam in the Caroline Islands.

A memorial service was held for the dead before *Franklin* embarked on an epic, 12,000-mile journey to New York. When *Franklin* stopped at Pearl Harbor, fifty Navy WAVES who had given *Franklin* her sendoff a month earlier burst into tears when they saw the mangled ship and her skeleton crew.* *Franklin* was the most heavily damaged US carrier to survive the war, and never saw combat again.[13]

TWO MINUTES AFTER *FRANKLIN* WAS hit, miles away another enemy dive-bomber swooped down on the carrier *Wasp*, cruising 52 miles off Shikoku Island east of Kyushu, and dropped a bomb on the flight deck. The *Wasp* had dispatched two-thirds of her planes on bombing missions against enemy airfields and shipyards. The bomb crashed through the flight deck and exploded in the galley, killing the cooks and mess attendants preparing breakfast.

Unlike *Franklin*'s sailors, *Wasp*'s crewmen had not yet queued up for breakfast, sparing her the staggering casualties sustained by *Franklin*; even so, *Wasp* reported 101 men killed or later succumbing to wounds, and 268 wounded—of a crew of about 2,500. *Wasp*'s crewmen were able to quickly control the fires that erupted, and within an hour she was landing planes. *Wasp* continued combat operations with TF-58 for the next few days before sailing to Ulithi. The stench of burned flesh permeated the ship for weeks as she continued on to Bremerton, Washington, for major repairs.[14]

---

* Captain Gehres filed desertion charges against the 1,000 crewmen who had left the ship either voluntarily or were blown into the water. The sailors were sequestered at Pearl Harbor. The charges were later dropped, but the anger and hard feelings inspired by Gehres's vindictiveness endured for decades.

WHEN TF-58'S FOUR DAYS OF March raids ended, the Fast Carrier Task Force was down five carriers—*Franklin* and *Wasp*, out of action for months or more; and *Intrepid, Enterprise,* and *Randolph,* all undergoing minor repairs at Ulithi. *Randolph* had been crashed at Ulithi on March 11 while riding at anchor.[15]

During the March raids, American pilots reported having destroyed 528 planes in the air and on the ground. While undoubtedly an inflated figure, US fliers had still dealt a major setback to the Japanese plan to disrupt the April 1 Okinawa landings with waves of warplanes. Many Japanese planes, men, and repair facilities, however, had escaped the American onslaught in hangars hidden inside hills adjacent to the airfields. Japan's air fleets could still deliver a big punch.[16]

A MASSIVE AMERICAN INVASION FORCE was poised in the western Pacific to strike Okinawa, the largest of the 600-mile-long Ryukyu Islands chain that arced from Kyushu to Formosa. Okinawa was the Ryukyu capital, and the southernmost of Japan's forty-seven prefectures.

For the first time, US forces would attempt to capture a populous Japanese home territory, inhabited by 450,000 civilians. Operation Iceberg would be a dress rehearsal for the dreaded future invasion of the Japanese homeland.

Okinawa's capture would place US squadrons within 350 miles of Kyushu and establish a forward naval base for the amphibious assault on Japan. Bombing missions against Tokyo were currently staged from the Mariana Islands, and only the B-29 Superfortress possessed the fuel capacity for the 3,000-mile round-trip flights. From Okinawa, however, US medium bombers and even fighters and dive-bombers could easily strike Japan.[17]

The Japanese Thirty-Second Army on Okinawa fully anticipated an amphibious assault and was prepared to fight to the last man. A message from the commander of the Okinawa Area Special Naval Force that was intercepted on March 31 said, "There is no better time than today for giving one's life for one's country." The Japanese had a name for this kind of battle: "Tennozan." Mount Tennozan was where a 1582 battle between feudal lords had been fought.

Its name denoted a final showdown battle.[18]

The Enemy's Doorstep

The chips are down. No holds barred. It's your wits, your training, your strength, your courage against the tough, tricky, resourceful little yellow bastards who were responsible for Pearl Harbor. They asked for it. Let's give it to them.

—MARINE GENERAL ROY S. GEIGER,
III AMPHIBIOUS CORPS COMMANDER, BEFORE L-DAY[1]

AFTER US FORCES CAPTURED SAIPAN, Tinian, and Guam in the Mariana Islands in mid-1944, the next objective became the Philippines, conquered by the Japanese in the spring of 1942. The Philippines were indispensable to Japan's survival, commanding the sea routes over which rubber and petroleum flowed to Japan from Borneo and Sumatra, colonial subjects of Japan's so-called Greater Asia Cooperation Sphere.

In October, with planning in the final phases for the invasion of Leyte in the Philippines by General Walter Krueger's two-hundred-thousand-man Sixth Army, senior US military leaders were debating what would come next. Should American forces attack Luzon, the largest Philippine island and the seat of the capital, Manila—or invade Formosa?

General Douglas MacArthur, who had escaped from the Philippines in 1942 before it fell to the Japanese, pushed for Luzon. Admiral Ernest King, the chief of naval operations, favored Formosa. Weeks of debate culminated in the San Francisco Conference, September 29 to October 1, 1944, at the Navy's Western Sea Frontier headquarters, attended by Admirals King,

Chester Nimitz, and Raymond Spruance, and Army Generals Simon Bolivar Buckner Jr. and Millard Harmon. Nimitz, commander-in-chief of the Pacific Ocean Area Forces, endorsed Luzon, pointing out that nine divisions would be needed to invade Formosa—divisions that were unavailable until after the European war ended. Spruance, Harmon, and Buckner sided with Nimitz in preferring Luzon to Formosa, whose capture, Nimitz said, would come at a price of fifty thousand US casualties.

King argued that Formosa would make an ideal base for blockading Japan, but he later came around to Luzon, which would be quickly followed by two more operations—for a total of three campaigns in less than three months. After invading Luzon on December 20, Iwo Jima and Okinawa would follow, edging US forces ever nearer to Japan.

The Fifth Fleet would cover both of these campaigns, while the Seventh Fleet would support MacArthur in the Philippines.

Nimitz submitted a memorandum outlining the campaigns. It said that Iwo Jima, a volcanic speck in the Bonin Islands, would be assaulted first on January 20. Once the sulfurous volcanic island was captured, B-29s from Saipan could use it for emergency landings, and it would also serve as a base for their fighter escorts.

The memorandum said the third target would be Okinawa, 760 miles northwest of Iwo Jima in the Ryukyu or Nansei Shoto island chain, which dangled between southern Japan and Formosa like a necklace. Just 350 miles from Japan, Okinawa could be developed into the primary air and naval base for launching the invasion of Japan's home islands, hosting 780 medium bombers and excellent fleet anchorages. Okinawa's invasion date was tentatively scheduled for March 1, six weeks after the Iwo Jima landing.[2]

On October 2, Admiral King recommended to the Joint Chiefs of Staff the invasions of Luzon, Iwo Jima, and Okinawa, and the chiefs the next day ordered the operations to proceed. Once detailed planning began, the timetables for the campaigns were pushed back two to four weeks: the invasion of Luzon to begin on January 9, Iwo Jima on February 19, and Okinawa on April 1, with the hope that the strong northerly winds and gales common in the Ryukyus between October and March would have subsided. Formosa was shelved for the time being.[3]

The Joint Chiefs of Staff still had to decide whether the Army, under General Douglas MacArthur, or the Navy, under Admiral Chester Nimitz, would command the US land forces that would invade Japan. Under

the present Pacific theater command structure, it would probably be Nimitz, because MacArthur's South West Pacific Area realm extended only to Luzon. The Army, however, proposed consolidating all Army units under one commander and suggested that a supreme commander be named for the entire Pacific. No decision was made.[4]

The United States, hard-pressed to support just twenty thousand marines on Guadalcanal in 1942, was now fully mobilized, and her millions of uniformed servicemen were racking up victory after victory over two powerful enemies two oceans apart. For the three Pacific campaigns approved in October by the Joint Chiefs of Staff, more than nine hundred thousand men would be committed—more than five hundred thousand for Okinawa alone.

In just three years, America had become a world-striding goliath wielding astonishing power.

JAPAN, UNSURE OF THE ALLIES' intentions, had vacillated between preparing for landings on Formosa and Okinawa. The Japanese understood that the capture of either island would put American bombers within 350 miles of Kyushu; Okinawa lay that distance, too, from China and Formosa. Japanese strategists recognized that Okinawa would provide generous anchorages for the US Pacific Fleet, while Formosa lacked good ports. Formosa, however, would give the Allies an oceanic pathway to China.[5]

Okinawa's two east-side bays—Nakagusuku Wan and, to its north, Kimmu Wan—had helped convince American senior officers to choose it over Formosa. Nakagusuku and Kimmu would make ideal advanced naval bases for the invasion of Japan; they were deepwater and partly protected by small islands and barrier reefs on the Pacific Ocean side of the island. The two bays lay across Okinawa's midsection from its western Hagushi beaches, which were lapped by the East China Sea.[6]

Antoine-Henri Jomini, who was Marshal Ney's chief of staff during the Napoleonic Wars and later a Russian general, wrote in his classic *Art of War* that when an army wishes to cross a large body of water, its commanders should deceive the enemy as to the landing place and prepare the way with artillery fire. Deception and heavy preparatory gunfire were pillars of the evolving Okinawa campaign: Operation Iceberg.[7]

AS THEY ANALYZED POTENTIAL BEACHHEADS, Operation Iceberg's planners initially considered "Plan Baker," consisting of two amphibious

landings two days apart. This was a possibility only because Iceberg was flush with manpower, the first Central Pacific amphibious operation that would land an actual field army of more than one hundred eighty thousand assault troops in two corps. Plan Baker proposed putting ashore III Amphibious Corps—the 1st and 6th Marine Divisions—on Okinawa's southeast coast, between Chinen Point and Minatoga.

Two days later, XXIV Corps, the Army's 7th and 96th Divisions, would storm the Hagushi beaches. Then, after the Marines secured the high ground behind its landing beaches, they would march north to Yonabaru on Okinawa's east coast, unite with XXIV Corps, and drive westward across the island.

Plan Baker was rejected because there were few good beaches on Okinawa's southeastern coast, and nearby islands might interfere with naval gunfire support. Moreover, Japanese ground forces could mass on the high ground and prevent a union of the Marine and Army units.

But Iceberg planners decided that the southeastern Okinawa coast could fulfill another purpose, one that would have pleased the clever strategist Jomini: it would serve as a point of deception. Marines would approach the coast as if to land there, but would not go ashore.[8]

IN THE SPRING OF 1944, the US government began interviewing scholars and specialists about the history, culture, politics, and economics of the Ryukyu Islands, anticipating an invasion in the future. An eighty-year-old conchologist, Ditlev D. Thaanum, related what he knew about the Hagushi beaches, where he had collected shells before the war. An elderly colleague of Thaanum's, Daniel Boone Langford, described the venomous habu snakes that inhabited Okinawa.[*] In November 1944, the Office of the Chief of Naval Operations published two volumes, *Civil Affairs Handbook: Ryukyu (Loo Choo) Islands* and *The Okinawans of the Loo Choo Islands—a Japanese Minority Group*.[9]

Okinawa, with about four hundred fifty thousand civilians, would be the most populous island to be invaded during the Pacific war by the Allies.

---

[*] It turned out that the habu danger was exaggerated. It was poisonous, but not lethally so: just three confirmed habu bites, none fatal, were reported during the campaign. Late in the campaign, some Marines grew so fed up with their rations that they killed and cut up a habu into filets, and fried and ate it.

About 65 miles long from north to south, its breadth ranged from 5 to 25 miles. The island's population density was greatest in the south: 2,700 people per square mile, four times that of Rhode Island.

The island's history and its people's ancestry were unique. "Liuchiu" was an ancient Chinese name for the islands that include Okinawa, which became known as the "Great Lew Chew." Some have speculated that the name "Ryukyu" stemmed from the Japanese inability to pronounce *l*'s. The chain of 140 islands—30 large enough to support people—arcs 790 miles between Kyushu and Formosa and forms a boundary between the East China Sea and the Pacific.[10]

Due to the "Japan current" flowing from the south, Okinawa is subtropical and humid, but its climate is more temperate than any other Pacific island invaded by the United States. It receives an average of 80 inches of rainfall annually. It is located in the middle of the so-called typhoon belt of the East China Sea; three to six typhoons a year directly impact Okinawa, generally between April and October.[11]

Okinawans are an admixture of Chinese, Malayan, Micronesian, and Ainu—the latter ancestry shared with the Japanese. Darker and smaller than the Japanese, Okinawans raised and largely subsisted on sweet potatoes—also distilled into alcohol—as well as sugarcane, barley, beets, and cabbage. Every acre of arable soil was cultivated on terraced hills.

With the exception of the cities of Naha, Shuri, Itoman, and Yonabaru, three-fourths of Okinawans lived in southern villages of one hundred to one thousand people for the most part, connected by single-track dirt roads and trails. A narrow-gauge railroad linked Naha in the west with Yonabaru on the east coast and other towns. Okinawans lived in frame houses with red-tiled roofs, or in thatched huts, each with a garden and stone wall.

The native religion was a synthesis of indigenous Okinawa religions and Shintoism, Taoism, and Buddhism. The islanders revered their ancestors, placing urns containing their bones in large, stone burial tombs built flush against the hillsides. The distinctive tombs, which faced in the general direction of China, were a signature architectural feature of Okinawa.

From 1187 to 1879, the year that Okinawa and the Ryukyus were annexed by Japan after Japan's Meiji Restoration, the island was ruled by five monarchical dynasties. Throughout the Middle Ages, the monarchs paid tribute to China, the Okinawans' primary cultural ancestor. To demonstrate fealty to China, Okinawa's ancient castles at Shuri, Zachini, and Nakagusuku, like the hillside tombs, were all built facing west.

The island people spoke a dialect called "Luchuan," and were stoical, easygoing people known for their courtesy, gentleness, and their strong rice brew, awamori. Racially distinct from the Japanese, Okinawans were regarded as second-class Japanese citizens.

This was no anomaly; the Japanese in fact looked down upon all other races, believing that their origin was divine and that they were preordained to rule the world. This belief rested on their conviction that Emperor Hirohito was the 124th descendent of the goddess Amaterasu, the mother of Japan's first emperor, Jimmo Tenno, whose reign began in 660 BCE.

George Orwell, who wrote World War II broadcasts for the BBC, said the Japanese had for centuries espoused "a racial theory even more extreme than that of the Germans." For reasons of racial superiority, said Orwell, Japanese soldiers believed that it was their prerogative to slap other Asians in conquered territories, and to similarly abuse Anglo war prisoners.

By the summer of 1945, Okinawans' problems related to their inferior status would seem trivial compared to their dreadful privations and soaring death toll, which would surpass anything seen by other Pacific islanders during the war.[12]

TWENTY-SIX YEARS BEFORE JAPAN ANNEXED the Ryukyu Islands in 1879, Commodore Matthew Perry's squadron, en route to Japan to make a historic trade agreement with the isolated feudal kingdom, sailed into Naha's harbor. Okinawans presented gifts, which were spurned by the Americans.

With a Marine escort, Perry and his party went ashore on June 6, 1853, and paraded 4 miles from Naha to the royal palace at Shuri Castle, the ancient seat of the Ryukyu king. Perry rode in a sedan chair carried by natives as bands played and American cannons boomed in an emphatic display of US power that awed islanders.

Ryukyu royalty were absent when Perry's party reached the palace. Perry demanded that the United States be permitted to establish a coaling station at Naha, so that commercial US steamships could refuel on their way to China and Japan. When the Okinawans politely demurred, Perry threatened to forcibly seize Shuri Castle. Reluctantly, the Okinawa officials gave in to Perry's demand and consented to permit the coaling station; to supply wood and water at reasonable prices to all US vessels entering any Ryukyu harbor; and to rescue and care for any American shipwreck victims—also a provision in the Treaty of Kanagawa that Perry would sign with Japan on March 31, 1854, that opened two Japanese ports to US vessels.

Returning to Okinawa in July 1854, Perry and the Ryukyu prince regent signed "A Compact between the United States and the Kingdom of Lewchew," which strongly favored US interests. After being ratified by the US Senate in 1855, the Ryukyu compact was quickly forgotten. For the next ninety years, there was little or no contact between Okinawa and the United States.[13]

FOR THREE HUNDRED YEARS, JAPAN'S Meiji emperor had been a figurehead under the Tokugawa Shogunate. But Perry's visit in 1853–54 kindled aspirations among progressive Japanese to break out of the straitjacket of tradition and acquire Western technology. The result was the Meiji Restoration of 1868, which returned to the emperor the ancient authority wielded for centuries by the feudal shoguns.

Both China and Japan coveted the Ryukyus—Japan's Meiji regime for expansionist reasons, China to deny Japan use of them as stepping-stones to Korea. Relations soured between the two countries, and war threatened. In 1875, Japan invaded the Ryukyus and ordered the kingdom to break off all trade with China. Hostilities appeared to be imminent.

In 1879, former US president Ulysses S. Grant arrived in Peking during his hugely publicized around-the-world tour. Fearing that China and Okinawa officials would persuade Grant to intervene in the dispute over the Ryukyus, Japan declared the Ryukyus to be a Japanese prefecture and deposed Okinawa's Shuri monarch. Japanese troops occupied the Shuri palace.

The last Okinawa king was exiled to Tokyo, where he was given the title of marquis. In 1894–1895, Japan defeated China in the First Sino-Japanese War and acquired Formosa. The Shuri palace, its grounds, and the mansions of Shuri noblemen—many of whom had fled to China—succumbed to disrepair and neglect.

The Japanese settled into their new role as Okinawa's overlord. New civil administrators were sent to Okinawa for training before being moved elsewhere in Japan. Unhappy with their new status as a subject people in their own country and having to bow to Japanese soldiers, thousands of Okinawans immigrated to Hawaii.[14]

ALLIED AIR ATTACKS ON OKINAWA began in October 1944, days after military strategists elected to invade Iwo Jima and Okinawa instead of Formosa. Early on October 10, seventeen carriers and escort carriers, five battleships, fourteen cruisers, and fifty-eight destroyers from Admiral Marc

Mitscher's Fast Carrier Task Force arrived off Okinawa with over one thousand warplanes. Shortly after dawn, waves of carrier planes roared over the island. The first attack hit the airfields at Yontan, Kadena, Ie Shima, and Naha, destroying about eighty aircraft on the ground and cratering the runways; a score of other Japanese planes was shot out of the sky. Subsequent attacks targeted Naha's harbor and munitions with bombs, rockets, machine guns, and torpedoes.

A total of 1,356 strikes were carried out on October 10, and more than 500 tons of bombs fell. The last sorties plastered Naha with incendiary bombs, destroying nearly 90 percent of the capital city of sixty-five thousand. Sunk were twenty cargo ships, a destroyer, a minesweeper, and scores of smaller vessels. Naha warehouses filled with millions of rounds of ammunition and three hundred thousand sacks of rice went up in flames. An estimated six hundred soldiers and civilians were killed, and another nine hundred were wounded.

"They were flying so low I could see the pilots' faces," said Horikawa Kyoyu, a student at Shuri. A Japanese soldier in a sea-raiding unit presciently noted in his journal, "The enemy is brazenly planning to destroy completely every last ship, cut our supply lines, and attack us."[15]

In November, Army intelligence men in B-29s photographed Okinawa for the first time. More aerial photo missions followed in January, February, and March. Mitscher's carrier task force carried out raids on Okinawa during the months preceding landing day. After one of them, a Japanese superior private wrote, "What kind of bastards are they? Bomb from 0600 to 1800!"[16]

ADMIRAL RAYMOND SPRUANCE, THE CENTRAL Pacific Task Force commander, was nicknamed "the electric brain" early in his career because of his grasp of electricity. But the epithet later referred to his quick, calm decision-making in times of crisis, such as his leadership during the battles of Midway and the Philippine Sea. But Spruance also had the misfortune of being a sailor prone to seasickness in heavy seas. The vulnerability had dogged him since his midshipman days, when the Naval Academy newspaper *The Lucky Bag* reported that Spruance was "a faithful supporter of the lee rail on all summer cruises."

The admiral issued his operations plan for the Okinawa invasion on January 3; Admiral Richmond Kelly Turner, the Joint Expeditionary Force commander, released his on February 9; and on March 5, Admiral Chester

Nimitz, commander-in-chief of the Pacific Ocean Area Forces, and his operations officer Admiral Forrest Sherman presented their Iceberg plan to the Joint Chiefs of Staff in Washington. The chiefs accepted the plan and agreed on a timetable for invading Japan.[17]

Nimitz, who undoubtedly had one of the world's most stressful jobs, during the Guadalcanal campaign developed a tremor that his doctor said was due to nervous tension. His doctor suggested that the admiral, who had grown up in the Texas hill country hunting and fishing, take up target shooting. Nimitz set up a pistol range outside his Pearl Harbor office and practiced with a .45 automatic that had been modified to fire .22-caliber ammunition. He would balance a half-dollar on the barrel and slowly squeeze off rounds without the coin falling off. The doctor's prescription calmed the Pacific Ocean naval commander, and the tremor vanished, but Nimitz continued to target-practice.[18]

In February, Nimitz proceeded with the invasion of Iwo Jima, an 8-square-mile volcanic island midway between Saipan and Japan. More than seventy thousand Marines from the 3rd, 4th, and 5th Divisions and soldiers from the Army's 147th Regiment went ashore beginning February 19. About twenty-two thousand Japanese resisted furiously from caves and bunkers, and from inside hills honeycombed with tunnels.

The flag-raising atop 556-foot Mount Suribachi depicted in the iconic Associated Press photograph February 23 marked the completion of only the first phase of one of the bloodiest battles in Marine Corps history. The island was finally secured March 26, after 6,821 Americans had been killed in action.

As at Peleliu, no banzai attacks were made on Iwo Jima, and the initial landings met minimal opposition. General Holland Smith, the operation's ground commander, was puzzled that "every man, every cook, baker, and candlestick maker" had not attacked the Americans on the beaches. But the Japanese were following a new strategy, first tested on Peleliu: fighting from well-prepared defenses instead of attacking the invaders at the water's edge. Later during the Iwo Jima battle, Smith conceded, "I don't know who he is, but the Jap general running the show is one smart bastard."[19]

FIGHTING STILL RAGED ON IWO JIMA in mid-March, when seven Army and Marine divisions held rehearsals for Operation Iceberg on beaches from Guadalcanal to Leyte Gulf, and from Espiritu Santo to Saipan. The multitude of locales reflected the enormity and complexity of the Okinawa

offensive, which pulled together infantry divisions, logistical assets, warships, and air squadrons from all over the Pacific.

In the Philippines, XXIV Corps commander General John Hodge and Tenth Army commander General Simon Bolivar Buckner watched the practice landings of the 7th and 96th Divisions, which had recently helped capture Leyte. Hodge lent Buckner Volume 2 of Douglas Southall Freeman's *Lee's Lieutenants*, and Buckner gave Hodge a quart of scotch.[20]

Also in March, the British Pacific Fleet joined hands with the Fifth Fleet. President Franklin Roosevelt, British prime minister Winston Churchill, and the Combined Chiefs of Staff had agreed at the Octagon Conference in Quebec in September 1944 that the British Fleet would participate in operations against Japan in 1945. The British Fleet, designated as Task Force 57 for Iceberg, would protect the "left flank" against threats from Formosa and the Sakishima Islands, while Admiral Mitscher's TF-58 cruised east of Okinawa. TF-57 consisted of 4 aircraft carriers, 2 battleships, 5 cruisers, and 15 destroyers.

The British carriers carried fewer planes than American carriers, their guns did not track targets automatically, and their computers could not process information quickly. Their chief advantage was their 3-inch-thick steel flight decks, which absorbed kamikaze crashes better than American carriers' wooden flight decks. Wooden flight decks were lighter weight and enabled the flattops to carry more planes, but were easier for kamikazes and bombs to penetrate.[21]

Amid these preparations for Operation Iceberg, America's XXI Bomber Command shocked Tokyo with a massive B-29 raid during the night of March 9–10; it was without precedent in the Pacific war.

SAIPAN'S CONQUEST BY US FORCES in July 1944 marked a tectonic shift in the Pacific war. Perceptive Japanese leaders believed Saipan's loss and the capture of Guam and Tinian, also in the Mariana Islands, assured Japan's doom. It meant that long-range B-29s could now bomb the homeland, and that it was just a matter of time before there would be an Allied invasion of Japan, resulting in an Asian Götterdämmerung.

Prince Naruhiko Higashikuni, commander of Japan's Home Defense Headquarters, confided to aides after Saipan's fall, "If we cannot stop the B-29s from coming over Japan, we can do nothing. We have nothing in Japan that we can use against such a weapon." Indeed, in March 1945 the consequences so dreaded by Japan began unfolding in a rain of incendiary bombs.[22]

At dusk on March 9, 334 B-29s from the XXI Bomber Command rose from the airstrips on Saipan, Tinian, and Guam for the 1,500-mile flight to Tokyo, a densely populated city of more than 4 million people. Each plane carried 184 napalm and incendiary bombs—2,000 tons in all, or ten times what the Luftwaffe dropped on London on December 29–30, 1940, during the so-called Second Great Fire of London. The B-29s' cargo was designed to cause maximum damage and casualties: 8,519 incendiary bomb clusters would break apart and release 496,000 bomb cylinders.[23]

Tokyo was a tinderbox of wood-and-paper houses built inches apart that covered 200 square miles. Kerosene lamps and electricity flowing through low-hanging power lines provided lighting and heating. Meals were cooked over charcoal or natural gas that entered the homes in shallowly buried pipes. Had Tokyo been constructed for the express purpose of exploding in flames it could not have been more combustible than it was in March 1945.

Amid the residences were concrete office buildings and cinder-block factories—as well as the Ueno Park Zoo. In 1943, the city public park director had ordered the destruction of the zoo's lions, bears, leopards, snakes, and other potentially dangerous animals as a precaution against an Allied bombing that might unleash them on the populace. Tokyo's vulnerability to fire had been amply demonstrated in September 1923 when the 9.0-intensity Great Kantō earthquake ignited firestorms that killed nearly 100,000 people.[24]

This was not the first B-29 raid on the Japanese capital—there had been others beginning in November 1944—but the earlier sorties were "precision" bombing missions from 30,000 feet. While antiaircraft guns and Japanese fighters were usually unable to bring down Superfortresses flying at that high altitude, the bombers usually failed to hit their targets too. The light damage inflicted by those air strikes lulled the Japanese into a false complacency.

After an ineffective raid on March 4, General Curtis LeMay, commander of the XXI Bomber Command, announced a radical change of tactics. Bombers would henceforth strike at night from 5,000 to 8,000 feet, thereby improving accuracy, while admittedly risking higher casualties from ground fire. The bombers would carry fewer crewmen and no machine guns, so that more bombs could be loaded. Although the bombing missions would still target war industries, a secondary objective was to also sow terror in the populace.[25]

Code named Operation Meetinghouse, the March 9–10 raid was aimed at a 10-square-mile mixed industrial-residential area between the Sumida and Ara Rivers, where war munitions were produced and where 400,000 people lived.

Coast watchers alerted civil and military officials minutes before the air strike that waves of enemy bombers were barreling toward the city at low altitudes. But there was too little time to mount an adequate air defense, or for people to take shelter; Tokyo lay at the mercy of the bombers. Even worse, gale-force winds boomed through the city that night.

At midnight, pathfinder bombers dropped clusters of 70-pound napalm bombs to form a fiery X marking the objective for the Superfortresses following them.

From atop Sophia University hill, Father Gustav Ritter, a Jesuit priest, saw "a silver curtain falling." Within minutes, winds gusting to more than 60 miles per hour whipped the flames from the incendiary bombs into a roaring conflagration that began devouring downtown Tokyo's paper-and-wood buildings and all that lay in its path.

People spilled into the streets from the burning buildings, only to be transformed into torches and run screaming with their skin hanging from their arms. Many jumped into the canals to escape the flames and were boiled alive. Anguished shrieks pierced the roar of the consuming flames. The firestorm destroyed two hundred fifty thousand homes within 16 square miles. The scale of the fires overwhelmed Tokyo's fire department, destroyed ninety-six of its fire engines, and killed at least eighty-eight firemen, with others listed as missing.

"We were in Hell," wrote Funato Kazuyo, a sixth-grade schoolgirl. "All the houses were burning, debris raining down on us."

"People's clothes were on fire," said Masuko Harino, a factory worker whose hostel was hit by firebombs. "Some people were writhing about in torment and no one had time to help them. . . . We ran. . . . The road on both sides was full of people's possessions burning up."

In one of the city's few air-raid shelters, Masatake Obata, an air-raid warden, arrived after having been knocked unconscious for over an hour by an incendiary bomb cluster that landed near him. When he awoke, he saw that flames had burned his shoes, melted his toes, and blackened his hands and arms. In the shelter, Obata examined other people's injuries and admonished them not to fall asleep. They chanted Buddhist prayers together to stay awake.

At daybreak, blackened corpses clogged the riverbanks and bridges, and the streets and alleyways. The raid, lasting more than two hours with bombs coming down "like raindrops," was the deadliest air raid in history and Japan's worst disaster since the 1923 earthquake.

Captain Shigenori Kubota, commanding an Army medical rescue unit, toured the stricken area in a truck with twenty-four men and reported seeing "mountains" of blackened corpses.

More than one hundred thousand Tokyo residents died, among them the schoolgirl Funato's mother and two siblings. Another million people were left homeless. General LeMay's raiders lost fourteen B-29s.[26]

AFTER BOMBING TOKYO, THE XXI Bomber Command carried out low-level raids against Nagoya, Osaka, and Kobe during the following week, targeting an aircraft engine factory, railroads, and shipworks. The death toll from the three raids totaled ten thousand, well below those of the Tokyo raid; the relatively low number was due to the absence of the strong winds that had lashed Tokyo when it was bombed.[27]

The B-29 raids and the sorties by Admiral Mitscher's fast carriers off the mainland shocked Japanese officials, but the government's reaction was to vastly intensify the suicidal resistance begun in the Philippines the previous fall with the advent of the Special Attack kamikaze squadrons. More kamikaze pilots were recruited, conscripted, and trained; new squadrons were formed.

Japanese leaders urged all citizens to participate in a monstrous demonstration of resistance to the death that they called "The hundred million as a Special Attack Force." After the fall of the Marianas in 1944, Imperial Japanese Headquarters had acknowledged in its war journal, "The only course left is for Japan's one hundred million people to sacrifice their lives by charging the enemy to make them lose the will to fight." The very idea sent chills down the spines of US military leaders planning Japan's invasion.[28]

BUT OKINAWA WOULD COME FIRST. Its invasion would be the acme of twenty years of strides in amphibious warfare doctrine and improvements in naval warplanes and warships. Progressive theories on amphibious warfare and naval aviation had received, at best, just passing notice in the Navy until well into the 1930s. Even then, senior naval officers discouraged promising young officers from pursuing careers in naval aviation. Battleships—the man-of-wars that had ruled the oceans for centuries—remained the

Navy's backbone as late as 1942. The stodgier old-timers believed that flattops and carrier planes would never replace battleships as the Navy's predominant weapon.

The rise of naval air power during the 1930s was in step with innovations in amphibious warfare doctrine developed by the Marine Corps, which began preparing a war plan for Japan in the early 1920s. This included a prophetic eighty-page document, "Advanced Base Operations in Micronesia." Written by Marine intelligence operative Lieutenant Colonel Earl "Pete" Ellis, it boldly predicted that Japan would start the war, and that the Navy's Pacific Fleet would win it, aided by Marine landing forces capturing Japanese-occupied islands.*[29]

Along with advances in amphibious-warfare doctrine and improvements in naval aircraft, flattops were evolving too. In the early days, seaplane carriers used cranes to lower pontoon planes into the water for takeoff and then hoisted them back aboard after they made water landings. The 1922 Washington Naval Treaty's strict limits on battleship and battle cruiser tonnages encouraged the major powers to convert many capital ships to flat-decked aircraft carriers. At the same time, new aircraft carriers built from scratch began emerging from shipyards during the mid-1920s. The first US fleet carrier, *Saratoga*, was commissioned in 1927.

Notable exceptions to the dismissive attitude of most senior naval officers toward carrier warfare were Admirals William Halsey and Marc Mitscher and Japanese Admiral Isoroku Yamamoto. Mitscher was one of the first thirteen students to attend the Navy's flight school in Pensacola, Florida, in 1916. For his first flight, he flew a plane made of wood, wire, and canvas. Mitscher's commander in the Pacific, Chester Nimitz, described him as "the most experienced and most able officer in the handling of fast carrier task forces who has yet been developed."

Halsey, who commanded the Pacific Third Fleet, learned to fly in 1935 at the age of fifty-two—the oldest person in the Navy to do so—after being assigned to duty on *Saratoga*. He believed naval officers in future wars should thoroughly understand aviation.

Yamamoto had closely watched the early development of air power while on assignment in the United States after World War I. In the early

---

* Shadowed by Japanese agents, Ellis, an alcoholic, died in the Palau Islands in May 1923 after a bout of heavy drinking.

1930s he oversaw the rapid buildup of Japan's air fleet in the belief that air power would win the next war. In helping to plan the attack on Pearl Harbor, Yamamoto demonstrated carrier planes' superiority to capital ships, midwifing a new age in naval warfare. The Combined Fleet commander was killed at Bougainville in April 1943 when American P-38s shot down his plane in a surgical strike.[30]

A WEEK BEFORE THE SCHEDULED April 1 landing on Okinawa, the Army's 77th Infantry Division carried out the first amphibious landings of Operation Iceberg—in the small islands of Kerama Retto and Keise Shima off Okinawa's west coast.

The 77th had a proud history. First activated in World War I, its ranks were filled mainly by men from New York City, Brooklyn, and Jersey City, and it was known as the "Statue of Liberty" division. The 77th fought at Château-Thierry in France in 1918. Seven of its companies comprised the unlucky "Lost Battalion," which was surrounded by Germans in the Argonne Forest in October 1918 and reduced to one-third of its original number before relief arrived. Reactivated in World War II, the 77th fought with distinction in 1944 on Guam and at Ormoc on Leyte.

Admiral Richmond Kelly Turner, commander of Task Force 51, the Joint Expeditionary Force, had insisted upon creating a semiprotected fleet base on Kerama Retto's four central islands for Operation Iceberg. While some senior officers argued that Kerama Retto was too close to Okinawa, and was therefore vulnerable to land-based Japanese aircraft, those concerns were overridden and plans were laid for its invasion six days before L-Day.[31]

Admiral Morton Deyo's Gunfire and Covering Force moved into the mineswept waters off Okinawa on March 25 and went to work on its targets with 9 battleships, 10 cruisers, 32 destroyers, and 177 gunboats. In Deyo's force were the first rocket ships sent into action by the US Navy—a dozen LSM(R)s, or medium landing ships converted to fire rockets and provide close-in support for amphibious operations. In the seven days before landing day, Deyo's Covering Force fired 27,000 shell rounds, 33,000 rockets, and 22,500 mortar rounds, as Mitscher's carrier planes flew 3,100 sorties. Most of the naval gunfire fell around the Hagushi beaches and on the nearby airfields with little effect; the Japanese defenders were in fortifications inside ridges miles away. By March 27, all of the Iceberg ground assault forces were at sea, converging on Okinawa.[32]

TF-58 ROVED 100 MILES EAST of Okinawa, its aircraft repeatedly hitting Okinawa and Kerama Retto. At the same time, underwater demolition
teams (UDTs) destroyed barriers planted by the Japanese along the beach
approaches to those islands.

In the waters off Okinawa's Hagushi landing beaches on March 29,
UDT swimmers, painted silver for concealment in the water and equipped
with a knife, fins, and mask, left their landing ships in rubber boats. They
swam the last mile and a half to shallower waters to map Okinawa's fringing coral reef and other obstacles. The Navy had learned the hard lesson at
Tarawa about the consequences of amphibious craft getting hung up on
reefs. Abandoning their marooned landing craft on Tarawa's reef, the Marines had to wade 100 yards through waist- and chest-deep water to shore
while braving heavy machine-gun fire; Japanese gunners cut hundreds of
them to ribbons. Six months later at Saipan, underwater teams blasted gaps
in the reef to clear paths for the landing craft.

As the UDT swimmers advanced toward Okinawa's beaches, they secured one end of a spool of fishing line at the outer edge of the reef and
gradually unwound it. It was knotted at 25-yard intervals, and at each knot
they dropped a small leaded line to measure the water depth, noting it with
a stylus on sandpapered Plexiglas sheets wrapped around their forearms.
They also took note of coral knobs and other obstacles, and the locations
of navigable channels. The swimmers drew light, scattered enemy fire, and
when they returned to their ship, they reported that the beach could support amtracs, and that there were just a few places where the water would
be deep enough at high tide for landing craft.

The swimmers found twenty-nine hundred stakes embedded in the reef,
5 feet apart in rows. Formidable barriers to the Hagushi beaches, the posts
were 4 to 8 feet tall and 6 inches in diameter, some of them driven into
coral, others set in concrete.

The next day, March 30, the "frogmen" used explosives that they carried in haversacks to blow up all but two hundred of the posts, while
warships shelled the beach. One of the frogmen, Petty Officer 2/c Arthur
Kaplan, said sailors described him and his mates as "half fish, half crazy."
The frogmen were forbidden to discuss with anyone outside their unit
what they did.

Minesweepers from Admiral Alexander Sharp's Mine Flotilla, Task
Group 52.2, cleared 3,000 square miles around Okinawa, destroying 257
mines in a half dozen minefields—some of them off Okinawa's southeast

coast—to reinforce the deception that landings were planned there. In an unswept area, the destroyer *Halligan*, screening bombardment units 12 miles west of Naha, struck a mine and sank.[33]

THE DOZEN OR MORE SPARSELY populated islands 15 miles west of Naha known as Kerama Retto would provide a sheltered anchorage where the Fifth Fleet could rearm, refuel, resupply, and undergo emergency repairs, and from which Navy patrol bombers could conduct anti-submarine and search-and-rescue operations. Especially attractive was a natural anchorage—12,000 yards long and 6,000 yards wide—bordered on the east by Tokashiki, the largest island, and on the west by Zamami, Aka, Geruma, and Hokaji.

Keise Shima, 8 miles west of Naha and 11 miles southwest of the Hagushi beaches, was seen as a platform from which American 155mm guns would support the landings and hit the enemy deep in southern Okinawa. The Fleet Marine Force Amphibious Reconnaissance Battalion scouted Keise Shima's four coral islets on March 26 without meeting any enemy troops or civilians. The scouts green-lighted its occupation by XXIV Corps's artillery.[34]

As they had done at the Hagushi beaches, frogmen slipped into the sea to take soundings, map the Kerama reef bottom, and assess whether the beaches could support landing vehicles and light trucks. They could. After the swimmers returned to their ship, their data embroidered a chart of the islands that would be used when the 77th Division landed the next morning.[35]

KERAMA RETTO WAS THE OKINAWA base of a Japanese Special Attack Unit that operated bomb-laden, 28-foot-long plywood speedboats designed to attack and destroy US transports and landing craft. At Lingayen Gulf in the Philippines, the suicide boats had sunk one US landing craft and damaged three others. There were more than 350 of these so-called Shin-yos, or "ocean-shakers," dispersed throughout the Kerama Retto islands. A total of 2,335 Japanese troops were assigned to build and maintain the sea-raiding bases.

Improbable though it seemed, the speedboats were the Japanese Navy's main line of defense on Okinawa; their sole mission was to ram US ships and detonate an explosive charge. Some carried the charges in the bow, others as depth charges. Each explosive had a five-second fuse that

theoretically gave the skipper time to escape, but any hope of survival was chimerical.[36]

DURING THE FIRST US LANDINGS of the Pacific war on Japanese home soil, five battalion landing teams from the 77th Division went ashore simultaneously on March 26 on five of Kerama Retto's islands: Aka Shima, Zamami, Geruma, Hokaji, and Yakabi. Geruma, Hokaji, and Yakabi fell quickly, but hundreds of Japanese troops defending Zamami and Aka Shima resisted. More landings were carried out March 27–28 on other islands, including Tokashiki; fifteen Kerama islands would eventually be stormed.[37]

The first attacks caught the Japanese flat-footed. US assault troops captured the bases used by three sea-raiding squadrons and seized nearly three hundred suicide speedboats before they could be deployed from Aka Shima, Zamami, and Tokashiki. On Aka Shima, Japanese naval troops and Korean laborers stubbornly resisted the 306th Infantry's Company I—the first company to land in the Ryukyus—from caves and bunkers before being overcome. On Zamami, several hundred Japanese soldiers and Korean laborers launched nine attacks during the night of March 26–27. They were all repulsed after fierce hand-to-hand fighting that left the ground strewn with sixty Japanese bodies.[38]

"Kerama" means "islands filled with good and happiness." But the name turned out to be tragically ironic during the four-day invasion in March. Geruma was the first Kerama island where US troops beheld the ghastly sight of civilians who had taken their own lives rather than be captured, or had been shot by retreating Japanese troops. The countryside was covered with the bloody, mangled bodies of women, children, and elderly men.[39]

THE CIVILIAN DEATHS AT KERAMA RETTO culminated of years of relentless government propaganda demonizing Americans. From the outset of the Pacific war, Japanese propagandists in lurid strokes had portrayed Americans as brutish killers who delighted in murdering, torturing, and raping captive soldiers and civilians. In 1942, Japanese troops fighting on Guadalcanal were warned that if they were captured they faced torture, dismemberment, or worse, such as being staked to the ground and crushed by steamrollers. Better to die in a banzai attack or by suicide, they were told.

On Saipan, US troops had seen the poisonous effects of years of anti-American propaganda: the suicides of up to ten thousand civilians who

hurled themselves and their families from cliffs, drowned themselves in the sea, or killed themselves with knives and grenades.

After imperial forces lost Saipan, Guam, and Tinian in the Marianas in the summer of 1944 and Japanese cities suddenly lay within range of American B-29 bombers, astute Japanese naval leaders recognized that defeat was inevitable. Soon afterward, four hundred thousand schoolchildren were moved from Japanese cities to the countryside, and anti-American propaganda was intensified.

One broadside pronounced Americans to be no better than beasts, and "the more of them that are sent to hell, the cleaner the world will be." Japanese propagandists also explicitly described atrocities carried out in the United States against African Americans and American Indians. The XXI Bomber Command's low-level raids in March stoked the Japanese hatred of Americans, "who left an indiscriminate trail of blackened corpses of babies and grandmothers among the wreckage of war," wrote journalist Masuo Kato.[40]

NOW, AT KERAMA RETTO, 77TH Division soldiers were forced to bear witness to the poisonous fruits of the brainwashing campaign. On Tokashiki, Japanese soldiers had distributed two grenades to each member of an island youth organization and instructed them to throw one at the Americans and kill themselves with the other. Japanese soldiers and Okinawa Home Guard troops rounded up about one thousand people from hamlets all over the island. Garrison commander Yoshitsugu Akamatsu ordered them to hand over their food to the army and commit suicide.

Some villagers detonated grenades; others killed themselves with razors, sickles, ropes, and rocks. Sixteen-year-old Kinjo Shigeaki watched a village elder beat his wife and children to death. Shigeaki and his older brother then killed their mother and two younger siblings with rocks and sticks. "We wailed in our grief," he said.

Toyoko Azama, a schoolgirl, said about four hundred people from her village were ordered to take refuge on Mount Nishi in the center of the island. Local defense officials distributed grenades, and people began blowing themselves up. A man killed his family with a hatchet; a woman hacked open her daughter's belly with a hoe; a doctor killed his family with a knife, and then disemboweled himself.

Toyoko's uncle detonated a grenade while surrounded by family members. A baby's head was blown off, and Toyoko's sister-in-law, her sister, and two children died.

Shigeaki, his brother, and some other boys resolved to die by attacking the Americans. But before they did, they encountered groups of Japanese soldiers who clearly did not intend to take their own lives. Wracked by guilt over having been manipulated by the Japanese to kill their siblings and mother, the boys abandoned the idea of sacrificing themselves.[41]

During the night of March 27, soldiers of the 77th Division's 306th Regiment, bivouacked on Tokashiki's northern end, heard explosions and "the screaming of a mass of women and children" in the distance. In a "pretty little valley" the next morning, March 28, they found about 250 dead and dying civilians. The shocked Americans offered the survivors food and medicine.

Three hundred twenty-nine civilians died on Tokashiki; another 234 suicides were reported on Zamami; and others died on Geruma. Several civilian men in American custody on Geruma, embittered because Japanese soldiers had persuaded them to kill members of their families, attempted to murder a Japanese prisoner.[42]

KERAMA RETTO WAS PRONOUNCED SECURED late March 28, with the exception of a few hundred Japanese soldiers in Tokashiki's hills who refused to surrender. Under an unofficial truce, the Japanese refrained from further attacks and the Americans did not disturb them. More than eleven hundred civilians were rounded up, fed, and given medical care before the 77th Division's departure on March 30. The enemy holdouts remained on Tokashiki until the end of the war. On August 23, after receiving confirmation of Japan's surrender, 216 of them surrendered to American troops.

Engineers and Seabees immediately began transforming Kerama Retto into an important roadstead with space at the two main anchorages in the center of the island group for forty-four ships, a large repair base, radar installations, facilities for restocking ships with provisions and ammunition, and a seaplane anchorage. Admiral Allan Smith, who commanded a cruiser division, wrote that Kerama "gave a firmness to the Okinawa tactical situation. . . . We were there to stay, with a place to tow damaged ships, look after survivors, replenish and fuel, drop an anchor."

The 77th Division, claiming to have killed 530 Japanese and to have captured 121 more, had lost 31 killed and 81 wounded. The Navy reported 124 sailors dead or missing after kamikaze crashes on three vessels, including battleship *Nevada*, with 11 killed, and destroyer *O'Brien*, with 50 men

killed or missing, and 76 wounded. In the days before L-Day, kamikazes also damaged destroyers *Dorsey*, *Kimberley*, and *Porterfield*, and six other American vessels.[43]

Minus a battalion left behind for security on Zamami, the 77th reembarked on transport ships March 30. It would not participate in L-Day; its next target was Ie Shima. The 12-square-mile island lay 3.5 miles west of northern Okinawa and 20 miles north of the Hagushi beaches. About 3,000 Japanese troops and fifteen hundred armed civilians defended its three airfields.[44]

On March 31, the day before Operation Iceberg's infantry divisions assaulted the Hagushi beaches, the Army's 420th Field Artillery Group began unloading its twenty-four 155mm guns on Keise Shima's coral inlets—in plain sight of the Japanese atop Okinawa's jagged hills south of Hagushi. By dawn on L-Day, the artillerymen would be ready to lend fire support to the American invaders. General Mitsuru Ushijima, annoyed by the Americans' brazenness, ordered his artillerymen to shell Keise Shima at midnight. The shelling caused no damage or casualties.[45]

ADMIRAL MARC MITSCHER, THE ASCETIC-LOOKING commander of TF-58, the Fast Carrier Force, was a veteran of Pacific campaigns dating to Midway. He looked older than his fifty-eight years, and his code name was "Bald Eagle" because of his lack of hair; he habitually wore a long-billed ball cap; "the Mitscher cap" would later become Navy-authorized shipboard attire. Mitscher commanded the *Hornet* during the Doolittle Raid in April 1942. During the Battle of the Philippine Sea in 1944, Mitscher switched on his ship's deck lights and searchlights to guide his pilots home from their missions after nightfall—an extremely rare, risky demonstration of his solicitude for his flyers.

As a naval commander experienced in Pacific island amphibious operations, Mitscher had no illusions about what lay ahead. The invading force, he said, faced "a very tough job" on Okinawa, honeycombed as it was believed to be with caves, tunnels, and gun emplacements.

General Roy S. Geiger, commander of the III Amphibious Corps, agreed, although in a memorandum to his staff he appeared to relish the challenge. "The chips are down. No holds barred. It's your wits, your training, your strength, your courage against the tough, tricky, resourceful little yellow bastards who were responsible for Pearl Harbor. They asked for it. Let's give it to them."

On the eve of the Okinawa landings, General Simon Bolivar Buckner Jr., the Tenth Army's commander, noted in his journal, "Tomorrow is Easter Sunday, my father's birthday and the day of my first battle. I hope that I shall be able to look back upon it with the same degree of enthusiasm with which I anticipate it." Buckner's father, Simon Bolivar Buckner Sr., was a well-known Civil War general who led Confederate troops in three battles. Buckner Jr. had commanded US forces in Alaska for three years, but lacked combat experience.[46]

Aboard a transport ship with Marines in the East China Sea the evening before the landing, syndicated newspaper correspondent Ernie Pyle contemplated the upcoming campaign. Pyle had come ashore with US troops in the European theater—at Normandy, Sicily, and other places—but never in the Pacific. "Anybody with any sense is nervous on the night before D-day," he wrote. "You feel weak and you're trying to think of things but your mind stubbornly drifts back to the awful thought of tomorrow."[47]

Before the landings, Radio Tokyo broadcast "Going Home," a song set to the haunting melody of the second movement of Antonin Dvořák's Ninth Symphony, "The New World." Radio Tokyo warned American soldiers bound for Okinawa, "Enjoy it while you can, because when you're dead you're a long time dead. . . . Let's have a little jukebox music for the boys and make it hot. . . . The boys are going to catch hell soon, and they might as well get used to the heat."[48]

Indeed, things were going to get a lot hotter for everyone.

L-Day

The approaching landing waves possessed something of the color and pageantry of medieval warfare, advancing relentlessly with their banners flying.

—ADMIRAL MORTON L. DEYO,
COMMANDER OF THE GUNFIRE AND COVERING TASK FORCE[1]

The carnage . . . was wonderfully and beautifully not there.

—NEWSPAPER CORRESPONDENT ERNIE PYLE[2]

AS FAR AS THE EYE could see, Admiral Richmond Kelly Turner's mammoth Task Force 51—more than fourteen hundred combat ships, auxiliary vessels, and landing craft—blanketed the calm waters of the East China Sea off Okinawa on this bright Easter Sunday morning of April 1. Five to 7 miles from shore, three hundred landing craft in eight transport squadrons were getting into position in the mild 75-degree weather. Aboard were four infantry assault divisions of ninety-four thousand men waiting with trepidation to splash onto the Hagushi beaches on Okinawa's western shore. The shock troops comprised a little more than half of the 182,112 soldiers, Marines, and sailors in Operation Iceberg's landing force, and a fraction of the 548,000 men assigned to the operation.

The broad Hagushi beaches lay just below the island's narrow waist and opposite the Yontan and Kadena Airfields. The Tenth Army hoped to seize

them quickly so that land-based aircraft could aid carrier planes in fending off enemy air attacks.

Heard no more aboard the ships were the lighthearted shipboard songs sung during the journey from Ulithi to Okinawa: "Tarawa Boom-de-ay," "Goodbye, Mama, I'm off to Okinawa," and others. The landing troops completed their final preparations with a sense of grim fatalism.

Windlasses rattled loudly as they swung out and lowered amphibious vehicles into the sea. Green, red, blue, yellow, purple, orange, white, and brown banners fluttered from them in the light breeze. They would guide similarly color-coded landing craft to the assembly points from which they would storm four Hagushi landing beaches spanning 8 miles. The 1st and 6th Marine Divisions of General Roy Geiger's III Amphibious Corps would land on the two northern beaches. The Army's 7th and 96th Divisions of General John Hodge's XXIV Corps would come ashore alongside the Marines to the south.[3]

It was by far the largest amphibious operation of the Pacific war. In terms of assault troop numbers, transport ships, and supply totals, Operation Iceberg rivaled even Operation Overlord—the Normandy landing ten months earlier—and was one of the largest invasions in history. The troops and 747,000 tons of cargo had been assembled for the operation at Eniwetok, Ulithi, Saipan, and Leyte after having been loaded at ports spanning thousands of miles, from the West Coast and Oahu to Guadalcanal, New Caledonia, and Espiritu Santo. The supply line feeding into Okinawa was the war's longest, stretching 6,000 miles across the Pacific, and including eleven ports of call.[4]

No other US naval officer better understood the dangers and complexities of landing troops and supplies on remote, hostile Pacific islands than "Terrible Turner," as Admiral Richmond Kelly Turner's subordinates had nicknamed him because of his abrasiveness and explosive temper. As had been the lean, beetle-browed admiral's practice while commanding joint expeditionary forces at every major battle of the Pacific war beginning at Guadalcanal in 1942, at 4:06 a.m. on April 1, L-Day, Turner, from his flagship, *Eldorado*, signaled the commencement of the attack with the words, "Land the landing force!"[5]

The immediate effect of Turner's order was to unleash a stupendous naval bombardment of the landing beaches, and the bluffs and hills behind them, continuing the Navy's three-day air and sea onslaught on the landing zone. For an hour and a half, 10 battleships, 9 cruisers, 23 destroyers, and

177 gunboats plastered the Okinawa coastline with 44,825 shells of 5 inches or larger; 33,000 rockets, fired by LSM(R) rocket gunboats; and 22,500 mortar shells. The avalanche of metal was described as the largest amount of naval gunfire ever expended in support of an amphibious assault. Soon, the island was partially obscured by an umbrella of smoke.

The troops would not go ashore, however, until 8:30 a.m., in synchronicity with high tide, when landing craft would have sufficient water clearance to pass over parts of Okinawa's fringing coral reef. Armored amphibious craft would support the troops once they reached shore.

Most of the battleships firing at the Okinawa shoreline had been deemed obsolete—too slow to keep up with the fast carriers—and they had been refitted for shore bombardment. Their huge 12-to-16-inch turret guns fired high-explosive shells weighing 1,200 to 1,800 pounds apiece, capable of pulverizing enemy bunkers and pillboxes, even on reverse slopes.

"The power of the thing was ghastly," wrote Ernie Pyle, who was aboard an assault transport. "Great sheets of flame flashed out from a battery of guns, gray-brownish smoke puffed up in a huge cloud, then the crash of sound and concussion carried across the water and hit you."

The Navy gunners paused at times so that scores of Navy and Marine Hellcats and Corsairs from Admiral Mitscher's Fast Carrier Task Force off Okinawa's east coast could fly low over the beaches and hit them with bombs, napalm, rockets, and machine-gun fire. The planes' gunfire sounded like "a gigantic cotton sheet being ripped apart."[6]

The Bisha River, which bisected the Hagushi beaches, was crowded with Japanese landing craft and motor torpedo boats. Aerial photos showed that bluffs overlooking the beaches were riddled with caves and tunnels hardened to resist bombing and naval gunfire. They afforded machine-gunners enfilading fire along the beaches. Behind the beaches rose 6-to-10-foot-high seawalls that threatened to slow the advance and become a deathtrap for the landing troops. Naval gunfire directors targeted all of them.[7]

AMERICAN INTELLIGENCE OFFICERS WERE IN fact unsure just how many Japanese troops were on Okinawa—or their whereabouts. In February, after analysts learned that the Japanese 9th Infantry Division had been transferred from Okinawa to Formosa, 37,500 enemy soldiers were believed to be on Okinawa. But by April 1, the estimate was changed to 75,000 regulars. Only sketchy information existed about Korean and Okinawan

labor auxiliaries, or the Okinawa guardsmen, the Boeitai, of whom there were roughly thirty thousand.

Because of cloud cover, aerial reconnaissance flights south of the landing areas failed to detect the large Japanese buildup in the Shuri Castle area. The hornets' nests of overlapping defenses infesting that area would be an ugly surprise for the Tenth Army.[8]

THE ASSAULT TROOPS, ROUSTED FROM a restless sleep at 2 a.m. for a breakfast of steak and fresh eggs, were edgy, grim, and resigned to being met by a fusillade of steel at the beach—the overture to so many Pacific island landings. Navy crewmen joked that the troops reminded them of condemned men eating a last meal. Second Lieutenant Robert Crowten of the 1st Marine Division wrote that as he and his men went to their landing craft, a chaplain met them at the ramp with tears in his eyes. "I thought this was kind of a negative way to go," he wrote.[9]

It was still dark when the troop ships dropped anchor off the western coast of Okinawa in calm waters. Crews offloaded landing craft, and the assault troops began boarding the diesel smoke–spewing tracked amphibious landing vehicles, or LVTs.

About 6 a.m., gray dawn crept into the eastern sky over Okinawa's hills, and the shadowy outlines of hundreds of ships, around which milled the amphibians and landing craft, could be seen off the Hagushi beaches. No enemy opposition had yet materialized, except for a few warplanes that were quickly driven away or shot down. Grunting under the weight of their gear, the soldiers and Marines clambered down the nets hanging from the troop ships into the gently rocking amphibians.

A haze of yellow cordite smoke from the battleship guns filled the air, pierced by the guns' flash and roar. Rockets crashed onto the shore with a "c-r-r-rack, like a monstrous lash."

At 7:59 a.m., the first assault craft left the line of departure 4,000 yards from shore and moved toward the beaches. The amphibians formed up in waves, eighteen in all, each nearly 7 miles long. As H-Hour neared, a line of small ships dropped anchor at the line of departure to direct traffic. The control crafts' mission was to guide the landing craft to their color-coded beaches. To simplify identification, each of them flew a pennant matching the beach color and the color painted on landing vehicles under its care.

Three years of assaulting enemy-held Pacific islands had helped American planners to nearly perfect the art of amphibious landings. Saipan was

OKINAWA LANDING BEACHES

April 1, 1945

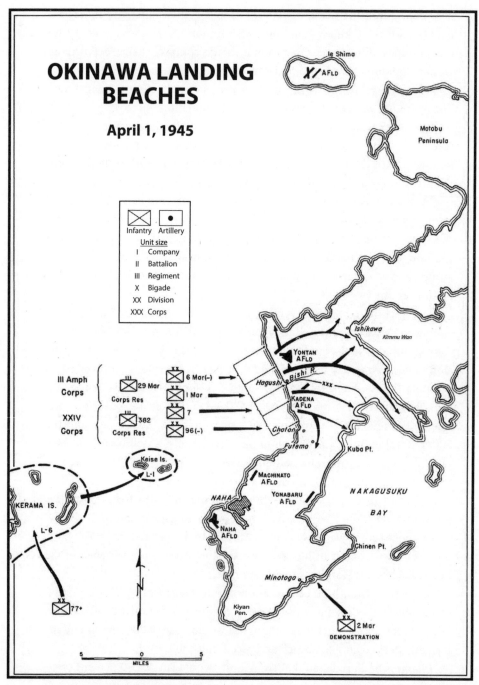

Map adapted from Okinawa: The Last Battle *by Roy E. Appleman, et al.*
(Center for Military History, 1948)

now considered the acme of successful island invasions, and it was the template for the Okinawa landings, with minor alterations to account for topographical differences. Operation Iceberg's comprehensive, detailed operational plan included reconnaissance, minesweeping, frogmen, logistics, preparatory gunfire, air strikes, and the actual assault, among other things. The operation was equal parts choreography and blunt force.[10]

Onlookers watched in awe. "The approaching landing waves possessed something of the color and pageantry of medieval warfare, advancing relentlessly with their banners flying," wrote Admiral Morton Deyo, commander of the Gunfire and Covering Task Force.[11]

"A marvelous sight it is, these waves of landing craft extending parallel to the coast as far as the eye can see," wrote Captain Samuel Eliot Morison, the Navy's World War II historian. Morison watched the spectacle from the bridge of the battleship *Tennessee*, flagship of Task Force 54, Deyo's gunfire and covering group. Morison counted "the incredible figure of 700" landing craft.

"No finer military spectacle could be seen in the entire war," wrote Morison, who had also witnessed the Normandy and North Africa landings.[12]

Amphibious tanks landed in the first wave at 8:30 a.m., with the mission of destroying any beach pillboxes in their path. Infantrymen splashed ashore a minute later; units of the 96th Division arrived first, using ladders to scale the 10-foot seawall, partly demolished by naval gunfire. The 96th's demolition teams blasted bigger holes in the seawalls and the 780th Amphibious Tank Battalion and six-wheeled amphibious trucks—DUKWs—carrying mortars poured through, advancing 3,000 yards inland. Subsequent assault waves arrived at ten-minute intervals.[13]

"We had three beautiful rainbows coming in," said Corporal Roger Spaulding of the 6th Marine Division. "Boy, that's a good omen."[14]

A smoke screen was laid down in the hills to the east to blind the enemy, but only a few rounds of Japanese mortar and artillery fire splashed in the beach shallows, and sniper fire was sporadic.

The assault troops, braced for a murderous hailstorm of enemy gunfire, came ashore standing up. They relaxed; some grinned at their good fortune. "I've already lived longer than I thought I would," said a 7th Division infantryman after crossing the beach and ascending a hill.[15]

Planners had predicted that some units would sustain 80 percent casualties, but only 28 men were reported killed in action, and 105 wounded. Second Lieutenant Crowten, who had prayed on his way to shore, was elated when he landed and "nothing happened."

"The Japanese pulled an April Fool's Day joke on us," said Jim Anderson of the 1st Marine Division. Another 1st Division Marine, Private First Class E. B. Sledge, wrote, "Jubilation over the lack of opposition to the landing prevailed, particularly among the Peleliu veterans."[16]

Anticipating heavy casualties, a senior medical officer had converted an LST into a floating hospital after the assault troops boarded the amtracs. Rows of cots and bottles of plasma were readied. Just one casualty appeared: a man whose buddy had accidentally shot off the tip of one of his fingers.

Marine Corporal David Macpherson of the 1st Armored Amphibious Battalion said the amazed invaders repeatedly declared in disbelief, "Why, this is just like one of MacArthur's landings. We don't even have to crawl!" "Happy Easter!" some Marines cheerfully called to one another.[17]

General Pedro del Valle, who commanded the 1st Marine Division, found the weak resistance "a source of astonishment."

Ernie Pyle, who had participated in numerous amphibious landings in the European theater, marveled at the ease of this one. "Never before have I seen an invasion beach like Okinawa—there isn't a dead or wounded man in our whole sector of it. Medical corpsmen were sitting among their sacks of bandages and plasma and stretchers with nothing to do. . . . The carnage . . . was wonderfully and beautifully not there."

Time magazine correspondent Robert Sherrod, who had memorably reported on the bloody Tarawa landing, wrote that the Okinawa invaders faced "slightly more opposition than they would have had in maneuvers off the coast of California. To say merely that they were bewildered is to gild the lily of understatement."[18]

Admiral Raymond Spruance, commander of the Fifth Fleet, wrote to his wife, Margaret, "Our landings on Okinawa have gone better than our wildest dreams have led us to expect." Yet he realistically expected the Japanese to soon "put up a stiff fight and have to be killed."

The day before the landings, Spruance had a brush with Japanese aviators eager to sacrifice their lives: his flagship, the heavy cruiser *Indianapolis*, was crashed by a kamikaze. Its bomb exploded under the ship, and nine sailors died. Spruance transferred his flag to the battleship *New Mexico*.[19]

AMAZINGLY, BY 9:30 A.M., SIXTEEN thousand troops were ashore, and by the end of the day, sixty thousand Americans were advancing swiftly inland to objectives that they had hoped to reach, if lucky, after three days

of hard fighting. General Buckner said it was "as beautiful a piece of team-work as I have ever seen."

Glitches were remarkably few: four artillery pieces sank when DUKWs foundered in the surf; several Sherman tanks were temporarily stranded on the reef. A 1st Marine Division battalion spent the night in ships' boats off-shore for lack of tracked landing vehicles to transfer them to smaller craft at the reef. "It was very cold out there," said a stranded Marine from the 3rd Battalion, First Regiment.[20]

THE DECEPTIVELY EASY LANDING DAY was an unsolicited gift from the Japanese. The Thirty-Second Army's commander, General Mitsuru Ushi-jima, and his staff had elected to mount only a token defense of the land-ing beaches. This reflected a revolution in Japanese strategic thinking from the offensive to the defensive. The shift began after the battles for Saipan, Guam, and Tinian in the Marianas in mid-1944—when perceptive leaders recognized that Japan was losing the war. "Our war was lost with the loss of Saipan. It meant [the United States] could cut off our shipping and at-tack our homeland," said Vice Admiral Shigeyoshi Miwa. "When we lost Saipan, hell was upon us," acknowledged Fleet Admiral Osami Nagano, supreme naval adviser to Emperor Hirohito.[21]

Through the invasion of the Marianas, the Japanese had defended the landing beaches from inside pillboxes and bunkers, and by launching mas-sive banzai attacks to drive US forces into the sea. On Saipan, three thou-sand to four thousand Japanese troops, some of them swathed in bandages, on crutches, and unarmed, had hurled themselves at the American lines. The losing battle for the Marianas was the last time the Japanese attempted to defend the beaches, or launched mass attacks.

The loss of the Marianas changed the dynamic for Okinawa, which Im-perial Japanese Headquarters had believed would be secure behind the so-called Tojo Line, the supposed impregnable barrier of the Marianas. When the line was breached and the Japanese fleet was destroyed during the Bat-tles of the Philippine Sea and Leyte Gulf, senior officers in Tokyo urged the Thirty-Second Army, established in March 1944, to defend the Ryukyus, build airfields, and strongly fortify Okinawa.

The new Japanese strategy, the so-called defense in depth, was first seen at Peleliu and Leyte the previous fall, and at Iwo Jima in February. An important feature was the construction of mutually supporting for-tifications in caves, cliffs, and hills where Japanese infantrymen waited,

as mortars and artillery pounded the Americans at a distance until they reached machine-gun range. Conventional counterattacks by mobile reserves supported by tanks replaced the headlong banzai charges that figured prominently in the Japanese defense of Guadalcanal, Tarawa, and Saipan.

The aim was to inflict maximum casualties, grind down the enemy, and break his will—a strategy summed up by the Thirty-Second Army's slogan: "One plane for one warship/One boat for one ship/One man for ten of the enemy or one tank."[22]

At Imperial Japanese Headquarters in Tokyo, however, many diehards refused to concede an inch of territory to the invaders. They had insisted that Ushijima fight the Americans at the Hagushi waterline and stop them from capturing Yontan and Kadena Airfields. But in December, after Imperial Headquarters transferred Ushijima's 9th Division to the 40th Army on Formosa, even the diehards could see that the Thirty-Second Army lacked the manpower to defend the Okinawa beaches.[23]

Consequently, Ushijima and his staff planned to employ only delaying tactics at the presumed landing sites. The preponderance of their forces would be reserved for a massive defensive battle in southern Okinawa's complex terrain of caves, hills, and escarpments carved up by valleys, rivers, ravines, and gorges.

With few exceptions, the ridges and gorges around Shuri Castle, where Ushijima chose to make his fight, were anathema to tanks. The broad green flanks of Mount Shuri concealed the Thirty-Second Army's large headquarters cave and an astonishing network of smaller caves and tunnels, manned by ten thousand troops. Carefully selected fighting positions—from simple dugouts to pillboxes and bunkers, to caves where artillery could be rolled out on railroad tracks and then retracted—covered all of the approaches.

A small delaying force, armed with only rifles, machine guns, and a smattering of heavier armament, would literally be sacrificed in the futile defense of the landing beaches and the two airfields. The 3,473 defenders were airfield service troops and Boeitai—the home guard—some of whom were in their middle teens. They had been hastily fused into the so-called 1st Specially Established Regiment four days before the landings. Fewer than half of them even had rifles. The rest of the regiment's total arsenal consisted of fifty-five light machine guns, eighteen grenade launchers, ten heavy machine guns, and five 20mm dual-purpose machine cannons.

The regiment was ordered to destroy the airfields when the Americans landed, to blow up bridges, and to build tank obstacles before retreating

south to the main defensive line. The delaying force accomplished only part of its mission and damaged but did not destroy Yontan and Kadena Airfields.

The 1st Specially Established Regiment was summarily crushed by the veteran US combat troops. The survivors fled into the hills of northern Okinawa.[24]

A DOZEN MILES SOUTH OF the Hagushi beaches, the Thirty-Second Army's commanders watched the landings through binoculars from atop the Shuri Heights. The observers included General Ushijima; General Isamu Chō, Ushijima's fiery chief of staff; Colonel Hiromichi Yahara, the Thirty-Second Army's analytical operations officer; and Ushijima's staff officers. To conceal their unease, the officers smoked cigarettes and bantered about the waste of so much ordnance on an undefended coastline.

Yahara joked that the American onslaught was like "a blind man who has lost his cane, groping on hands and knees to cross a ditch." However, a note of disquiet crept into the officers' conversations when they began to realize that the Special Attack planes—kamikazes—that were to have disrupted the invasion had not appeared as promised.

The Thirty-Second Army's headquarters cave complex beneath Shuri Castle was the largest and most fully developed on Okinawa. The island's rugged limestone and coral hills and ridges lent themselves to defensive fortifications, honeycombed as they were with natural and man-made caves. The Japanese had improved upon nature by digging into the clay that lay 30 to 60 feet under the coral and limestone shell to hollow out fortifications and living quarters.

The headquarters complex could hold more than one thousand people. Its tunnels, rooms, offices, and sleeping and eating quarters for Japanese soldiers, auxiliary troops, laborers, and female office workers were 50 to 160 feet underground. North to south, the complex stretched 425 yards, with a multitude of side chambers.

But the Thirty-Second Army's great achievement—surpassing even the defensive network's efficacy—was that its 60 miles of underground fortifications in southern Okinawa were practically invisible to US aerial reconnaissance, and virtually immune to US naval and aerial bombardment.

General Chō's name for the headquarters complex was "Heaven's Grotto Battle Headquarters," although it was hot, humid, and with the passage of time, odoriferous.

The access shafts into the Thirty-Second Army tunnel featured wooden ladders and landings every dozen feet. Concrete pillars and ironwood beams taken from the forests in the mountainous north supported the walls, which were lined with wood paneling. Officers had desks, chairs, and electricity, and there was a 72-foot-long kitchen at one end of the main tunnel. The headquarters was amply supplied with food and liquor. Chō, a gourmand, had brought with him a chef and a pastry chef.

Besides being an engineering marvel, largely constructed with shovels and entrenching tools (there were just two bulldozers on the entire island), it had been completed in just three months. To the west lay the 5th Artillery Command's 200-yard tunnel. To the east, the 62nd Division headquarters operated from a 300-yard-long complex.[25]

General Chō had studied strongpoint defenses with the Russians and adapted them to Okinawa for active and static cave defenses. In the bloody days, weeks, and months ahead, the Tenth Army would come to dread the brilliant lethality of the Thirty-Second Army's defensive network.

IN A BUNKER NEAR THE Shuri Heights, a Japanese soldier watching the landings was impressed by the "wealth of supplies the like of which we had not seen in years." He wrote that "our orders were unambiguous; we were to lie low, to wait. . . . We stayed in our bunker and watched the huge army come ashore."

A radioman with the 5th Harbor Base Unit wrote in a diary found later, "It's like a frog meeting a snake, just waiting for the snake to eat him."

The Thirty-Second Army's battle instructions called for it to lure the Americans "into a position where he cannot receive cover and support from the naval and aerial bombardment," so that it could be "wiped out."[26]

UNTIL L-DAY, USHIJIMA AND HIS staff were unsure whether the Hagushi beaches would be the Americans' objective. The Minatoga Peninsula on Okinawa's southeastern coast was also considered a credible landing site—so much so that the 24th Division, part of the 44th Independent Mixed Brigade, and artillery units were deployed there.[27]

The Tenth Army's strategists played to the enemy's expectations to the last minute on L-Day by lunging toward Minatoga with the 2nd Marine Division, the Tenth Army's reserve, while the main force assaulted the Hagushi beaches. The 2nd Division Marines climbed down cargo nets into Higgins boats that advanced toward the beach before circling back to the

ships, where the Marines climbed the cargo nets on the ships' seaward sides, and then repeated the charade by again descending the cargo nets. "I think I must have made that trip eight or ten times," said Marine Charles Pase. "Very tiring." The feint received more attention than the actual landings. The 2nd Division, which had fought at Guadalcanal, Tarawa, Saipan, and Tinian, did not go ashore.

Before turning back to Saipan, the 2nd Division sustained the first casualties of L-Day when a kamikaze crashed *LST-884*, which had three hundred Marines aboard. The explosion and fire killed twenty-four Marines and sailors. A second suicide plane smashed into the transport *Hinsdale*, claiming sixteen more lives.

The instant Admiral Jerald Wright of Demonstration Group "Charlie" learned that the main landing force was on the Hagushi beaches, his ships reversed their engines and withdrew under a smoke screen. Wright's Task Group 51 feinted again on April 2, but without casualties.[28]

AFTER THE LANDING FORCE CROSSED the undefended Hagushi beaches, and the men's adrenaline had subsided in the relieved aftermath, they saw that they were in a rural, intensely cultivated countryside of small fields rising gradually from the sea. Instead of palm trees and swamps as in the tropical South Pacific, there were hardwood trees and some pines, and fields planted in cabbage, beans, and radishes. "It didn't look at all unlike Indiana in late summer when things have started to turn dry and brown," observed Ernie Pyle, a native Hoosier who might have been a little homesick. "I think most of us were surprised at how pretty it was." A Marine who had spent months in the tropics told Pyle, "This weather feels more like American weather than anything since I left home."

At dusk, three Japanese planes flew over them, headed toward the beach. "In a moment all hell cut loose from the beach," Pyle wrote. "Our entire fleet and the guns ashore started throwing stuff into the sky. . . . As one of the Marines said, there were more bullets than there was sky." The three planes were shot down.

That night, Pyle and his countrymen were introduced to Okinawa's tenacious mosquitoes. "I've never been so tortured by them," Pyle wrote. Repellant did no good, and when he woke up at 2 a.m., his nose, upper lip, and one eye were swollen from bites; he slept the rest of the night entirely covered by a blanket. In the morning, Pyle took the antimalarial drug Atabrine for the first time. When the Tenth Army became better established on

Okinawa, aerial spraying of DDT was begun, targeting the anopheline mosquito larvae, and scores of men were assigned to malaria-control units.[29]

The Americans landed at the end of Okinawa's mild subtropical winter, and before the onset of the May rains and the hot weather of summertime. In terms of weather, this was the ideal time to be on the island, although this particular early April was chilly. George Peto of the 1st Marine Division complained that the Marines' summer-weight dungaree jackets failed to keep them warm. "We shivered as we moved on." Peto even claimed, possibly facetiously, to have seen snowflakes one evening. The Marines' long acclimatization to tropical heat had thinned their blood, he conceded.[30]

BY 10 A.M. ON LANDING day, 7th Infantry Division units were crossing Kadena Airfield—much like they had seized Dulag Airfield on October 20 on the first day at Leyte—after easily pushing through scattered sniper fire and some stiffer opposition from caves and tombs. Captain Warren Hughes's 17th Regiment company flushed twenty Okinawa Boeitai home guardsmen from a cave and killed them all after they threw grenades that injured several Americans. At Kadena, Hughes saw "their [Japanese] dummy planes on the shell-pocked strip [and] their actual planes, shot full of holes, parked in their revetments."

The 6th Marine Division's 4th Regiment swept across Yontan Airfield at 1 p.m. Two other Okinawa airfields, Naha and Machinato, lay to the south; the Japanese had begun work on a fifth airstrip at Yonabaru, but had then abandoned it.

Iceberg planners had not expected to capture the airfields until L+3. By nightfall on L-Day, Seabees and Marine engineers had cleared the Yontan runways and filled the holes. Kadena Airfield was ready for emergency landings, and the front lines were nearly 3 miles inland.

So quickly did the airfields change hands that the pilot of a Zero landed at Yontan after dark on April 1, unaware that the Americans now possessed it. "When he stepped out on the wing, they hit him with a bunch of search lights and they riddled him," wrote Bill McClellan of the 1st Marine Division. "He didn't have a chance."

By the second day, April 2, artillery observation planes were taking off and landing at Yontan while Seabees and Marine engineers continued to patch up the runways.[31]

On the same day, the 7th Division's 17th Regiment chopped Okinawa in half at its waist, seizing the highlands that overlooked Nakagusuku Bay

on the eastern, Pacific Ocean side of the island. Japanese units in northern Okinawa were now cut off from the principal forces in the south. Patrols sent to the 1,000-yard-wide coastal flatland below the high ground reported that civilians told them that the Japanese had abandoned the central part of the island.

III Amphibious Corps's 1st Marine Division pushed straight east toward the coastline, impeded only by scattered defenders, infiltrators, and the rugged terrain. General del Valle, the division commander, told reporters during the afternoon of April 2, "I don't know where the Japs are, and I can't offer you any good reason why they let us come ashore so easily."

The 6th Marine Division turned north. Marching into the foothills northwest of the Hagushi beaches, the Marines wiped out 250 Japanese at two strongpoints.[32]

HIDING IN CAVES NEAR THE landing zone were terrified Okinawa civilians, brainwashed by the Japanese into believing that the Americans were going to torture and slaughter them. The civilian population would present a disturbing set of problems to the invaders. The Japanese Thirty-Second Army had conscripted thirty-nine thousand Okinawans between the ages of eighteen and forty-five on January 1 to serve the Japanese as soldiers, auxiliaries, and laborers. Seventeen thousand to twenty thousand male Okinawans were integrated into the Thirty-Second Army, while the others served in reserve units or as laborers.

One result of the wholesale draft of Okinawa men into Japanese service was that nearly all of the civilians encountered by the Americans were women, children, and old men. Most of them refused to leave the caves when exhorted to by American soldiers, and others committed suicide rather than surrender.

In peacetime, Okinawans lived in clusters of thatched huts in villages, drew water from communal wells with a bucket on a rope, and traveled to their fields in two-wheeled carts pulled by small, shaggy horses that resembled Shetlands. An open sewer channeled human waste. But these were not normal times, and many civilians had gone into hiding.

Mike Monroe and his comrades from the 96th Division's 382nd Regiment burst into a hut where a group of old men, women, and children cowered in a corner, passing around a teapot and drinking. To the Americans' horror, "within minutes, they were all dead," Monroe said. They had been drinking poisoned tea. "Their minds had been poisoned by the Japs."[33]

The first civilian captives were moved into evacuated villages in peaceful areas. Service troops began building military government compounds, each designed to hold twenty-five hundred to ten thousand civilians. Stoical and docile, the interned civilians were fed, clothed, and housed in the temporary camps. They appeared happy to be free of the Japanese, who had beaten them, expropriated two-thirds of their crops, and forced them to build fortifications without pay.[34]

The natives were vegetarians who subsisted on sweet potatoes, beets, barley, and sugarcane. Americans were taken aback by their diminutive stature—many of the women and elderly men were barely 4 feet tall.

Foreseeing that Okinawa's more than four hundred thousand civilians would present a problem unique in the annals of the Pacific war, plans for Iceberg included a Military Government Section of the Okinawa Island Command to manage civilians while the combat troops campaigned. Initially, they expected to care for thirty thousand civilians. But by the end of April, one hundred twenty-six thousand civilians were under the Military Government Section's control. The section eventually expanded to a force of five thousand that included specialists and translators who attempted to persuade islanders to turn themselves in.[35]

OKINAWA SCHOOLS HAD BECOME INCREASINGLY nationalistic after military training was introduced in 1939. Each day, students were required to recite the Imperial Rescript to Soldiers and Sailors, pledging fealty to Emperor Hirohito. Japanese Army marching songs replaced school songs; math problems focused on calculating tank, ship, and bullet quantities; in physical education class, boys learned how to throw grenades and plunged bayonets into straw effigies of Winston Churchill and Franklin Roosevelt. Beginning in June 1944, when the Thirty-Second Army's first units arrived, military instruction intensified: schoolchildren were taught how to march and to fire a rifle. They "volunteered" to help build fortifications, runways, and shelters, and they raised vegetables. Girls studied nursing.[36]

During candlelight ceremonies held during the night of March 27, teenage boys and girls graduated from the First Prefectural Middle School and the Shuri Girls School amid distant explosions of US naval gunfire. Japanese Army officers watched Nakanishi Yukiko and her classmates sing the school song. "Halfway through, everybody started to cry and you couldn't hear the words. We all felt that there was just no hope," said Hoshino Masako.

The next day, the girls were assigned to the 62nd Infantry Division Hospital Cave as members of the Shuri Girls Nursing Corps. The officer in charge told them when they arrived, "You girls will all die with me in battle." Indeed, thirty-three of them—more than half—would perish from wounds and disease.[37]

Nearly a hundred boys also graduated that night from the First Prefectural Middle School. During the ceremony, an American naval shell landed near them with a thump. The frightened students were preparing to scatter when the Japanese officer attached to the school shouted, "Don't move! Nobody is to move!" Nobody did. The boys were inducted into the Blood and Iron for the Emperor Corps. They wrote goodbye letters to their parents and grandparents, enclosing nail clippings and locks of hair.[38]

At Okinawa Normal School in Shuri, after the new graduates received their certificates, 386 students and staff members took the Blood and Iron oath. The students received military orders along with the rank of private second class. Two hundred twenty-four of them would be killed in action.

About seventeen hundred young men from Okinawa's middle schools served in Blood and Iron units, mostly as runners or guerrillas. Six hundred senior middle school girls were sent to basic nursing training.[39]

BY THE END OF APRIL 3, the Tenth Army had reached the objectives set for April 15. Heartened by the astonishingly easy gains, General Buckner and his Tenth Army staff lifted restrictions on his divisions' advances after attempting to stop III Amphibious Corps and XXIV Corps at the Day 10 objective, which had been reached on the second day.

"These first four days had been too easy for us," wrote Private First Class Sledge, a veteran of Peleliu. He and his comrades were "confused as to what the Japanese were doing," and Sledge worried that "the new men were lulled into a false sense of well-being."

A teenager in the 4th Marines complained that "none of us in our unit have had any chance to shoot yet." Lieutenant Colonel J. Broiler, deputy commander of the 12th Marines artillery regiment, sent a request to a supply officer: "Please send us a dead Jap. Our men have not seen any of them. We'll bury the corpse for you."[40]

THE 1ST MARINE DIVISION CONSOLIDATED its position in the island midsection on April 3, and the 6th Marine Division pushed north, while the 96th and 7th Divisions of XXIV Corps wheeled to the right toward southern Okinawa. There the real battle for the island would be fought.[41]

Japan officially acknowledged the Okinawa invasion on April 2, dampening the following day's traditional celebration of Emperor Jimmu Day. The holiday commemorated the beginning of Japanese expansion two thousand years earlier when Jimmu conquered Yamato, a province of Honshu.

In Tokyo, Prime Minister Kuniaki Koiso, who had replaced Hideki Tojo after the Japanese defeat at Saipan in July 1944, vowed that the Americans would be driven from Okinawa and Saipan. Two days later, Koiso resigned under pressure, blamed for the losses on Leyte, Luzon, and Iwo Jima. Emperor Hirohito replaced him with seventy-seven-year-old Admiral Kantarō Suzuki, a former imperial grand chamberlain.

Although there was no immediate change in Japan's determination to fight to the bitter end, despite the ruin visited on scores of cities by US bombers, Hirohito was concerned about what was happening on Okinawa.

"If this battle turns out badly, the army and navy will lose the trust of the nation," the emperor said. His anxiety deepened when American troops captured Kadena and Yontan Airfields. "Why doesn't the field army go on the offensive?" he plaintively asked Army Chief of Staff Yoshijirō Umezu. On the second day of the invasion, the emperor wrote, "Nothing is going the way it was supposed to."[42]

The First Defensive Line

The low whine changing to a louder and louder scream . . .
it seemed that a pair of rubber gloves filled with ice cubes
had grabbed your stomach and flipped it over.

—CAPTAIN WARREN HUGHES OF THE 7TH DIVISION,
DESCRIBING THE SENSATION OF BEING SHELLED[1]

When we got there, there was an army up there, all right, but
it wasn't the 383rd Regiment. . . . Our men came tumbling
down, their rifles falling.

—PRIVATE FIRST CLASS DICK THOM OF THE
96TH DIVISION, DESCRIBING AN UNSUCCESSFUL
ATTEMPT TO CAPTURE KAKAZU RIDGE[2]

Infantry, old fashioned and direct and bloody and full of casualties, is the only way to overrun them.

—SERGEANT WILLIAM BECKMAN OF THE
96TH DIVISION ON THE VIRTUAL INVULNERABILITY
OF JAPANESE DEFENSES TO AIR ATTACKS[3]

THE TENTH ARMY WAS ENJOYING an unanticipated interlude of big gains
against light resistance, and some men were daring to hope that Okinawa
would be an easy campaign. Lieutenant Bob Green, serving as a liaison between the 763rd Tank Battalion and 96th Infantry Division, said there was

"an air of fierce optimism" at both headquarters. Some staff officers now believed that the Army divisions would quickly sweep aside the Japanese as they moved south. Their optimism would prove to be premature.[4]

Admiral Richmond Kelly Turner, who commanded the expeditionary force, was eager to begin utilizing two bays on the island's eastern, Pacific Ocean coastline to augment the landings of supplies and vehicles under way on the Hagushi beaches. Moreover, the bays would help fulfill Iceberg's objective of making Okinawa the advance naval base for mainland Japan's conquest. Before Turner could begin using the bays, Chimu Wan and Nakagusuku Wan, the six small islands located near the bays' mouths had to first be secured.

The Fleet Marine Force Amphibious Reconnaissance Battalion scouted the islands and reported that just one of them, Tsugen Shima, off Nakagusuku Wan, appeared to be heavily defended. It could not be bypassed, because it lay directly opposite the mouth of Nakagusuku Wan.

Minesweepers plied the waters of the harbors for a week as frogmen removed landing craft obstacles. A battalion of the Army's 27th Infantry Division, the Tenth Army's reserve along with the 2nd Marine Division, prepared to capture Tsugen Shima. On the morning of April 10, the 3rd Battalion of the 27th's 105th Infantry landed on the 3,000-yard-long island's south beaches with amphibious tanks and tractors.

They met little opposition at the beaches. However, two hundred to three hundred Japanese soldiers occupied Tsugen Town, which sat on a high ridge, and two nearby knobs. Tunnels, caves, and pillboxes overlooked low ground sown with antitank mines. Despite the relatively small number of defenders, it took all four of 3rd Battalion's companies to silence them over two days. When the battalion reembarked on LSTs on April 11, its ranks were thinner by ninety-two men. The 239 Japanese who died were all wearing full dress uniforms that displayed their decorations.

The successful operation meant that shipments of food and ammunition could now be brought into the eastside bays. Seabees immediately began landing construction equipment on the Chimu Wan beaches.[5]

MORALE WAS HIGH AMONG THE enemy soldiers waiting for the Tenth Army a dozen miles south of the landing beaches. Beginning in the summer of 1944, the Japanese had carefully prepared defenses that would inflict high casualties when the Americans marched south. They finished the job by March 1945 after several months of punishing excavation work, nearly all of it done with shovels and other hand tools.

Building tunnels and mutually supporting firing positions had forged a strong bond among the men of the Thirty-Second Army, formed a year earlier out of units sent to Okinawa from across Asia; it had never fought as a field army. Their fortifications were now ready, and amply stocked with food, water, ammunition, and medical supplies. The Japanese soldiers patiently waited for the US 7th and 96th Divisions to come to them.

About seventy-seven thousand Japanese Army regulars and thirty thousand Okinawa Boeitai were assigned duties on Okinawa. Some manned the caves, tunnels, bunkers, pillboxes, and trenches concealed inside Okinawa's tortuous coral and limestone ridges, steep valleys, and deep ravines. Others were assigned to tank platoons; antiaircraft and artillery batteries; antitank, shipping, and engineering units; communications and mine-laying sections; and ground crews at the airfields.

About five thousand men from sea-raiding battalions were reassigned to infantry units after building the suicide-boat installations at Kerama Retto. Men from support units would be reassigned to frontline duty as casualties thinned the ranks. There was a ten-thousand-man naval force commanded by Admiral Minoru Ōta—the so-called Naval Base Force—that was deployed at Naha Harbor and nearby Oroku Peninsula, but just one-third of them were Japanese Navy troops; the rest were recent conscripts, Boeitai, and civilian employees. Twelve thousand Korean laborers and "comfort women" accompanied the Thirty-Second Army.

A small, poorly trained garrison had defended Okinawa until the fall of the Mariana Islands in June and July 1944. Realizing that Okinawa was going to become an Allied invasion target because of its proximity to the Japanese mainland, the Japanese high command reinforced the island with nine infantry and three artillery battalions. Throughout the summer, artillerymen, infantrymen, and support and service troops poured into Okinawa. They included the 9th, 24th, and 62nd Divisions and the reconstituted 44th Independent Mobile Brigade.

The original 44th IMB was destroyed before it could reach Okinawa when the submarine *Sturgeon* torpedoed *Toyama Maru* on June 29, 1944, and sent it to the ocean bottom with fifty-six hundred soldiers, of whom just six hundred survived. Two months later, the 44th IMB was rebuilt with men from other units.

In December 1944, Imperial General Headquarters abruptly withdrew the twenty-five-thousand-man 9th Division from Okinawa and sent it to Formosa in the belief that Formosa was General Douglas MacArthur's next objective after Leyte. But the Japanese were incorrect: the US Sixth Army

invaded Luzon instead. Consequently, the 9th Division idled away the rest of the war on Formosa. Colonel Hiromichi Yahara, the Thirty-Second Army's chief operations officer and architect of Okinawa's defenses, described the departed 9th Division as "the cream of the Okinawan defense force."

Okinawa was promised two divisions to replace the 9th Division, but the promise was not kept. When the 28th Division arrived at Okinawa, it was immediately shunted to the Sakishima Gunto islands. Another division ticketed for Okinawa, the 84th, was not sent because of the rising American submarine threat. The Thirty-Second Army's commander, General Mitsuru Ushijima, was forced to make the best of the manpower on hand.[6]

Soft-spoken, dignified, physically imposing, and respected by his troops, Ushijima had succeeded General Masao Watanabe, the Thirty-Second Army's first commander, in August 1944 when Watanabe became ill and was recalled to Tokyo. The fifty-seven-year-old Ushijima had commanded the 36th Infantry Brigade in China in 1937. The brigade was with the Japanese forces that invaded Shanghai and captured Nanking, where up to 300,000 civilians and war prisoners were massacred.[7]

Ushijima was shrewd and pragmatic, and he did not embrace the Japanese Army's Bushido philosophy, revived at the beginning of the Meiji Restoration to help cultivate a spirit of ultranationalism. During the Pacific war's early years, Bushido's adherents believed that spiritual power alone could compensate for the enemy's many material advantages. Ushijima disagreed. "Do not depend on your spirits overcoming this enemy," he cautioned his officers. "Devise combat methods based on mathematical precision: then think about your spiritual power."[8]

Ushijima studied recent Pacific war campaigns: Tarawa, Saipan, Peleliu, and Leyte. He paid particular attention to the strategy adopted by General Tadamichi Kuribayashi in defending Iwo Jima with twenty-two thousand men against an invasion force many times greater. Outnumbered and without hope of receiving reinforcements, Kuribayashi had elected to not contest the Americans' beach landings but to instead wage an attritional battle.

Faced with a similar situation, Ushijima adopted a similar strategy.[9]

Colonel Yahara, Ushijima's forty-two-year-old operations officer, was a cerebral tactician and talented engineer whose nickname was "Sobersides." He had attended a planning conference in Tokyo as the Marianas were being invaded and the so-called Tojo Line of defense was being shattered, to help plan the defense of Formosa and the Ryukyus. During the conference, Yahara convinced senior officers of the logic of husbanding the

Ryukyus' military resources on Okinawa, which he identified as the island chain's keystone.

In the hope that a "protracted defense" of Okinawa would persuade the Allies to enter negotiations rather than risk a bloodbath by invading Japan, Imperial Headquarters issued new tactical guidelines, published as "Essentials of Island Defense." Prolong the fighting for as long as possible, the guidelines said, and erode the enemy's fighting ability so that he could be defeated in a decisive battle.

"We should attack the enemy from 'underground'" was Yahara's prescription for implementing the guidelines' principal tenet. It meant fighting a largely passive defensive battle from tunnels and caves, a tacit admission that the Japanese could no longer match the enemy's strength at sea, in the air, or on the ground.

With that in mind, most of the Thirty-Second Army was committed to defending the southern third of the island—a strategy described by Yahara as *jikyusen*, or "war of attrition." Yahara said units should operate and attack at night, and not during the daytime when they would be at the mercy of Allied artillery, air strikes, and naval gunfire.

New suicide tactics were adopted for destroying tanks. Soldiers would attack them with satchel charges; volunteers would be promoted three ranks, but would not live to enjoy their advancement.[10]

Chief of Staff Chō chafed at waging an attritional campaign. He relished taking the fight to the enemy, and not waiting for the enemy to come to him. Colonel Yahara described Chō as a "ruthless nationalist" who had had a leading role in the Nanking massacre. While at Imperial General Headquarters in Tokyo during the 1930s, Chō belonged to a right-wing extremist group involved in several unsuccessful coup attempts to establish a military dictatorship.[11]

The Thirty-Second Army's staff had concluded that because northern Okinawa lacked the southern island's strategic assets—mainly airstrips and harbors—it merited defense by only part of the 44th IMB. The region was sparsely populated and mountainous, and its most prominent feature was Mount Yae-Take on the Motobu Peninsula.

The remainder of the 44th IMB had been sent to positions overlooking the Minatoga beaches to guard against an American landing on the southeast coast. Also posted there was the 24th Division, the Thirty-Second Army's largest tactical unit and originally organized to fight Russian mechanized forces in Manchuria. Neither the 44th IMB nor the 24th Division was battle-tested.[12]

Japan's 10th Area Army, headquartered in Taipei, was the Thirty-Second Army's hierarchical superior, and it initially objected to the plan to not defend Okinawa's beaches. It demanded that General Chō explain the decision. When Chō reminded his superiors that shoreline defenses had failed in the past and, if employed on Okinawa, would ensure the Thirty-Second Army's swift destruction, they dropped their objections. They also conceded that their removal of the 9th Division from Okinawa in December justified the Thirty-Second Army's decision, and they threw their support behind the plan.[13]

At a meeting in January at Imperial General Headquarters in Tokyo that resulted in adoption of the "Outline of Army and Navy Operations" for defending Okinawa, Iwo Jima, Formosa, Shanghai, and South Korea, Chō was enjoined not to fire on "blue shipping" during the American landing; shore battery fire would give away Japanese positions. Chō was assured that air strikes, including kamikazes crashing warships, would destroy the US naval forces.[14]

The Thirty-Second Army was giving up airfields that it had laboriously built mainly with human muscle. In 1944, Imperial Japanese Headquarters had envisioned Okinawa becoming an air defense center. But by early 1945 it was apparent that an acute shortage of planes and pilots meant that their contribution to Okinawa's defense would be minimal—and that the Japanese had in fact built airfields for the Americans to use. On March 10, the Japanese began destroying what they had laboriously built. Ushijima and Yahara were under no illusions that the destruction would be lasting; they believed that within the first ten days of the American invasion, enemy warplanes would be operating from Yontan and Kadena Airfields.[15]

That left Ushijima and Yahara to hope that Japanese kamikazes would destroy the US fleet and isolate the invasion force, and that a "defense in depth" along a 5-mile belt spanning southern Okinawa would prove impossible for American ground forces to breach.

The defensive core was the ancient home of Okinawan kings, Shuri Castle. Two airfields anchored the defensive line's western and eastern flanks: Machinato Airfield on the western coast and Yonabaru Airfield on the eastern side. A third airstrip, Naha Airfield, lay south of Machinato and the capital city of Naha.

THE THIRTY-SECOND ARMY'S DEFENSE IN depth was unique to the Pacific war. It began at the northern edge of the Machinato-Yonabaru line and extended 4 miles south to Shuri Castle. The Japanese had transformed

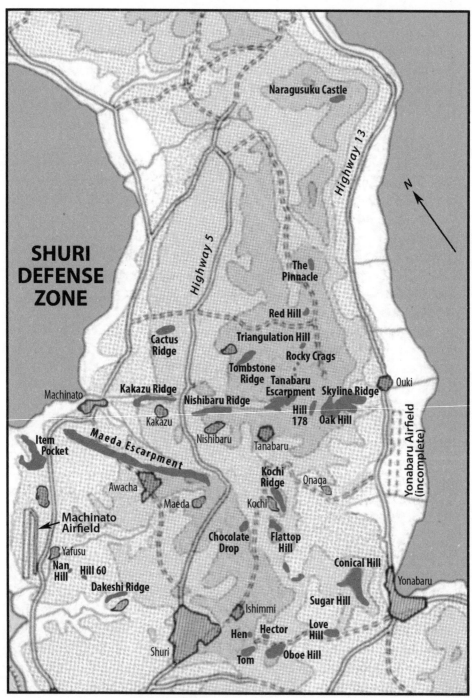

Map adapted from Okinawa: The Last Battle *by Roy E. Appleman, et al.*
(Center for Military History, 1948)

20 square miles of ridges, escarpments, valleys, and gorges into a chain of linked underground positions carved out of the area's jumbled terrain features. Concrete and rebar being in short supply, they often reinforced their positions with local materials, such as coral, limestone, and coconut and hardwood logs. Boxes that had contained rations and ammunition were filled with sand, as were empty rice bags. When concrete was used, it was often substandard because the cement had been mixed with seawater, and coral or shells were used as aggregate instead of gravel.[16]

Every hollowed-out ridge and escarpment harbored a network of tunnels with multiple entrances, making it relatively easy to move troops from position to position for counterattacks, with minimal exposure to enemy fire. These strongpoints bristled with mortars, light and heavy machine guns, 37mm and 47mm antitank guns, and 50mm grenade launchers—"knee mortars" that could lob a beer can–size explosive more than 700 yards. The defenses included fortified tombs and guns in pillbox embrasures from which artillery might be rolled out on railroad tracks hidden behind sliding steel doors.

Each fortification supported others nearby with mortars, machine guns, and artillery. Attacking one hill would provoke fire from gunners entrenched in neighboring hills. An order to the 44th IMB read, "It must be borne in mind that one's own fire power plays an important part in the defense of the neighboring positions and vice versa."[17]

The 27th Tank Regiment's small force of twenty-seven light and medium tanks reflected the Thirty-Second Army's philosophy that tanks would be of little use in its "fixed position defenses" scheme. Although it had the technological capability to provide both, the Thirty-Second Army lacked bazookas, and radio contact was nonexistent between small units on the front line and the impressive array of artillery batteries in the rear.

ALMOST SERENDIPITOUSLY, THE THIRTY-SECOND ARMY possessed more big guns and abundant ammunition than were available to Japanese artillerists during any previous Pacific battle: 287 large- and medium-caliber guns and howitzers; 296 smaller artillery; and 24 so-called spigot mortars. The latter were 320mm fieldpieces with a 1-mile range whose 660-pound shell, visible in flight, resembled "a garbage can with fins"; it was nothing less than an instrument of terror.

It was the first time during the Pacific war that Japanese artillery units served under a unified command. Credit for the concentration of heavy

guns belonged to Colonel Yahara, Ushijima's operations officer, who took the rare step of placing them under the 5th Artillery Command, led by General Kosuke Wada, an artillerist of high repute.

The Thirty-Second Army also possessed fifty-two 47mm and twenty-seven 37mm antitank guns; ninety-six 81mm mortars; and eleven hundred knee mortars. Like the spigot mortar, the Japanese "rocket mortar" with a 1,500-pound warhead was another unpleasant novelty for Americans on the receiving end. It made "a whooshing sort of rocket sound. . . . It slammed into the ground about a quarter mile away with a tremendous detonation that rumbled the earth," wrote George Peto, a forward observer for a Marine mortar squad. Fortunately for the Americans, it was used sparingly.

Many of the guns had been destined for the Philippines, but ended up on Okinawa for want of shipping. General Wada had the equivalent of nine artillery battalions at his disposal; these were in addition to the division guns.

The big guns would add a dimension of terror for American infantrymen and contribute to Iceberg's epidemic of battle-fatigue cases.[18]

IT WENT WITHOUT SAYING THAT the Japanese troops were expected to fight until everyone was dead—known as *gyokusai*, or "smashing the jewel." Captivity was dishonorable because it implied that self-preservation was more important than one's country; suicide was preferable. Japanese soldiers were conditioned to embrace this absolute from the day they began recruit training, a brutal rite of passage during which they were routinely beaten; forced to endure extreme cold, heat, exhaustion, hunger, and thirst; and required to memorize the "Imperial Rescript to Soldiers and Sailors," whose recitation lasted fifteen minutes. They were drilled day and night in bayonet fighting.[19]

Despite the unbroken string of defeats beginning with Guadalcanal in 1942–43, Japanese soldiers still blindly clung to the belief that Japan would eventually triumph—"victory disease," it was called. It was a testament to the power of propagandists' lies about phantom Japanese victories. The myth of invincibility endured even in the spring of 1945, when a core tenet of the Thirty-Second Army was that sacrificing one's life to inflict attritional losses would lead to a negotiated peace favorable to Japan.[20]

And yet Yahara and his fellow officers also recognized that each American division had five to six times the firepower of a Japanese division. When the numbers were worked out on a larger canvas, the disparity was

staggering. To counteract the onset of pessimism, Yahara wrote a pamphlet titled "The Road to Certain Victory," which enumerated the Thirty-Second Army's defensive advantages: fighting from fortifications, tunnels, and caves, and employing "sleeping tactics"—a byword for permitting the enemy to draw near, pinning him down, cutting him off from reinforcements, and destroying him.[21]

GREEN HILLS AND RIDGES ROSE in ranks before the American infantrymen as they marched south through the countryside—the 96th Division on the right, the 7th on the left. At first, resistance was minimal, and to some soldiers who had never been in combat it seemed possible that the campaign might soon be over. Combat veterans, however, did not believe the Japanese would give up Okinawa without a fight, and they were wary of a trap.

The 96th Division's infantrymen were nicknamed "Deadeyes" because marksmanship was emphasized by the division assistant commander, General Claudius Easley, a former captain of the Army's rifle and pistol teams. The 96th's soldiers would very soon appreciate Easley's insistence on accurate shooting.

On April 4, the Deadeyes' honeymoon ended when, without warning, heavy antitank, machine-gun, and sniper fire suddenly converged from every direction on a patrol of the 96th Reconnaissance Troop. The well-concealed Japanese had allowed the patrol to advance into a valley "and then hurled volley after volley of deadly accurate fire," said Staff Sergeant Don Eaton. Eleven soldiers died and thirty-four were wounded, and antitank rounds left three of the patrol's five vehicles blazing wrecks. The advance paused while explosives experts cleared 1,000 yards of roadway saturated with mines.[22]

The next day, April 5, the 96th struck the outer ring of the Japanese Shuri Line defenses. A torrent of artillery and mortar fire greeted the Deadeyes at Cactus Ridge, striking cold terror into the marrow of soldiers who had never been under fire. Bob Jackson of the 382nd Infantry screamed as he flattened himself into the hillside. "I tried to dig my way to the center of the earth," he said.[23]

Left of the 96th, the 7th Division ran into a buzzsaw too. The 7th, nicknamed the "Hourglass Division" because its emblem was two juxtaposed 7's forming an hourglass, faced a 475-foot ridge capped by a 30-foot coral spike, dubbed "the Pinnacle." The spike, believed to be the

place where Commodore Matthew Perry had raised the American flag in 1853, was a Japanese watchtower that provided an excellent view of the surrounding area.

Defending it were 120 men of Lieutenant Seiji Tanigawa's 1st Company of the Japanese 14th Independent Battalion. Tanigawa had carefully selected their positions, and they were dug into caves, rifle pits, underground pillboxes, and tunnels, and armed with eight light and two heavy machine guns, and seven 50mm knee mortars. Barbed wire and minefields guarded the Pinnacle's likely approaches. Although the defenders were not plentiful, their ferocious resistance halted the forward progress of the 7th Division's 184th Infantry.

Two companies from the 184th's 1st Battalion launched a frontal assault on April 6. Staff Sergeant Pete DePallo and some Company B comrades reached the base of the Pinnacle. He climbed partway up it and began dropping grenades into the cave entrance at the spike's southern base. Two NCOs behind DePallo threw grenades up to him that he then threw down into the cave. The aroused defenders fought back with knee mortars, satchel charges, and hand grenades and repulsed the assault after fifteen minutes of fighting. A second attack that morning also failed.

In a third attack, Colonel Daniel Maybury, the 1st Battalion's commander, sent Company C up a draw on the Japanese flank, and it reached the top without a single casualty. When Staff Sergeant Walter Peters saw a Japanese soldier poke his head from a cave, he scorched him with his portable flamethrower. Peters and his comrades then killed nearly one hundred of the defenders with flamethrowers and white-phosphorus grenades.[24]

That night, a jittery tank gunner opened up with his .30-caliber machine gun when he heard noises in the dark. The torrent of gunfire was followed by silence, and then by the sound of a baby crying. At daybreak, Sergeant Porter McLaughlin and some men investigated and found two young women and a small boy shot dead. Nearby lay a two-year-old girl who had been shot through the groin but was alive. "She was one of the most beautiful children I ever saw," said McLaughlin. At the aid station, the medic said the child could not survive her wound and gave her a shot of morphine; she died a few minutes later.

A week later, after the Americans had become inured to the death that was all around them, a crying baby near the perimeter of the 96th's 382nd Infantry evinced a different reaction. During the early hours of April 13, edgy troops fired on movement along the perimeter, and when it ended

they heard "a baby howling." The crying lasted fifteen minutes, stopped, and then resumed. "Then there was a long burst of fire from one of our machine guns and silence," said Private First Class Donald Decker, an assistant gunner with a mortar squad. "No more crying was heard." In the morning, the soldiers found the baby's body strapped to the back of his dead mother.[25]

The enemy's gritty willingness to die fighting earned the grudging respect of some 7th Division troops. Lieutenant Donald Fitzgerald of the 184th said the enemy's "defense tactics were termed 'fanatical' by our forces. But in reality, the behavior of the enemy was the way Americans would have acted in similar circumstances, except that we would have called it 'heroism.'" The Pinnacle provided a splendid, if sobering, view of the enemy strongholds nearby, dashing any lingering hopes for a quick, easy campaign.[26]

During these first clashes with Ushijima's army, the Americans experienced the variegated terrors of being under artillery attack, "the low whine changing to a louder and louder scream . . . it seemed that a pair of rubber gloves filled with ice cubes had grabbed your stomach and flipped it over," wrote Captain Warren Hughes of the 7th Division's 17th Infantry.[27]

Because of the accuracy of the artillery fire, many American soldiers initially doubted that Japanese artillerymen were firing the guns. The gunners had to be Germans, they believed. So it had also been early in the war when Americans were convinced that Japanese pilots could neither fly at night nor conduct successful air-to-ground attacks. Indeed, old biases regarding Japanese abilities died hard.[28]

THE 96TH DIVISION CAPTURED CACTUS RIDGE on April 7 in storming attacks through fusillades of Japanese knee-mortar fire. Staff Sergeant Francis M. Rall of the 383rd Infantry wrote, "We figured that the way to get out of that knee mortar fire was to get to where it was coming from. So we stood up in waves, firing everything we had and throwing hand grenades by the dozen, and charged the Jap position."

The blunt tactic silenced Cactus Ridge, wiping out one hundred fifty defenders and at least fifteen pillboxes, but it pushed the 96th into a more lethal killing zone where Tombstone, Nishibaru, and Kakazu Ridges converged.

"Every defensive position is covered by murderous cross fire," said Staff Sergeant William Beckman Jr. of the 382nd Infantry. His Company F

crawled, ran, and dove in attempting to escape the deadly machine-gun, mortar, and artillery fire pouring down from the escarpments all around. That night, white-phosphorus shells drifted slowly to earth, illuminating the rugged terrain in a chilly chiaroscuro light. "I hear, again, the screams of one of our men caught under a short falling shell, his body burning," Beckman said.[29]

The 382nd Infantry's 1st Battalion took aim at Tombstone Hill, named for three prominent tombs on its western slope. It guarded the way to the Japanese outer defensive line of ridges and escarpments that extended across most of the southern island. Kakazu Ridge marked the barrier's western terminus. Next to it was Nishibaru Ridge, and east of Nishibaru was Tanabaru Escarpment, straddling the 96th and 7th Division boundary. In the 7th's sector, Tanabaru encompassed Skyline Ridge, Ouki Hill, and Hill 178.

Tombstone, 800 yards long and oriented northeast to southwest, was defended by Japanese infantrymen, and also protected by a curtain of artillery fire from Nishibaru and Kakazu. Although dive-bombers pummeled Tombstone, precise Japanese mortar fire pinned down the advancing US troops, set fire to an ammunition dump on an adjacent hill, and plastered an 81mm mortar squad and a command post.[30]

On April 10, all three of the 382nd's battalions, advancing in a line from the north, assaulted Tombstone as rain steadily fell. The Japanese fiercely resisted. Tanks accompanying the soldiers bogged down in the mud, and heavy mortar, machine-gun, and 47mm antitank fire drove back the 3rd Battalion on the left. The 1st Battalion attempted to seize the hill's northwest nose in a combination frontal and flanking attack.

After lying quiet as the Americans got into position, the Japanese pounded them with mortar and artillery fire, then launched a swarming ground attack from caves, trenches, and pillboxes. Machine guns opened up on the Americans at nearly point-blank range, and flamethrowers deployed by both sides incinerated soldiers as massive spigot mortars burst around the hill. Lieutenant Robert Bolan, a company commander, was shot in the shoulder and a dud mortar round broke his collarbone, but he continued to lead his men.

The 382nd was forced to withdraw, and Tombstone remained in Japanese hands.

"The enemy still held his commanding ground," wrote Lieutenant Jess Rogers, "and despite all efforts to reduce his positions by fire, he was able to

register at will upon any given spot from flank to flank, and to reach back a considerable distance into the rear areas. For the front line soldier, it was a matter of sitting tight and taking it."

Stalled by continual shelling, machine-gun fire, and counterattacks, the 382nd attempted no more attacks for over a week. The Japanese took full advantage of its control of the high ground. "Always, always, regardless of where I go or where I am or what I am doing, I am always under fire," wrote Sergeant Beckman.[31]

THE JAPANESE 62ND DIVISION ENTRENCHED on the outer defensive line had carefully selected positions that supported one another. For the American soldiers, dislodging the defenders would be a slow, bloody process, but nowhere would it more exasperating than at Kakazu Ridge.

It was just 300 feet high, and a deep coral gorge choked with brush and trees traced Kakazu's northern base. Behind Kakazu lay the Urasoe-Mura Escarpment, which US commanders regarded as a more important objective.

Kakazu, however, proved to be the month of April's bloodiest battleground. Colonel Munetatsu Hara's men had devoted months to excavating and fortifying Kakazu's underground defenses. In some places, they were 150 feet below the surface, embedded in solid rock, well camouflaged, and nearly impervious to US naval and artillery fire.

The gorge, serving much like a castle moat, was both a natural tank obstacle and an aiming point for the numerous artillery pieces, mortars, and machine guns in Kakazu's caves, tunnels, trenches, and passageways. In its reverse slope positions, shielded from attackers, even more guns were zeroed in on the hill's approaches.

On Kakazu Ridge's western flank, a cut separated the hill from its 250-yard-long continuation, nicknamed Kakazu West. The same gorge that protected Kakazu also guarded Kakazu West's northern approaches. Its formidable defenses rivaled Kakazu's, and defenders on both hills could readily direct heavy fire at American soldiers attacking either of them.

At 5 a.m. on April 9, Companies A and C from Colonel Ed May's 383rd Infantry assaulted 700-yard-long Kakazu Ridge, and with surprising ease reached the ridge crest. Then, the Japanese awakened to the danger. From their tunnels and holes they flailed the attackers with a thunderous artillery barrage, rifle and machine-gun fire, and volleys of grenades, satchel charges, and sticks of dynamite.

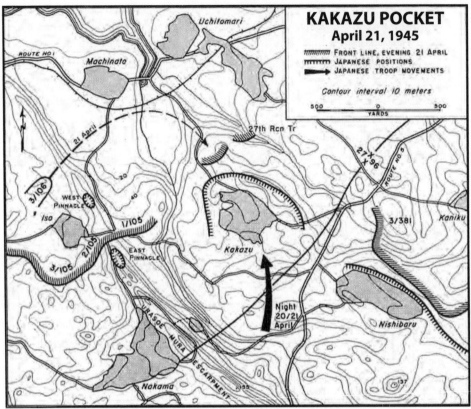

Map from Okinawa: The Final Battle *by Roy E. Appleman, et al*
(Center for Military History, 1948)

The Japanese counterattacked through their own mortar fire. In vicious hand-to-hand fighting, they drove May's assault troops into gullies, saddles, and pockets along the ridge. May dispatched Company G from the 383rd's 2nd Battalion, but it was pinned down by artillery before reaching the ridge. Litter parties were shot down.

May ordered the companies clinging to the ridge crest to "hold at all costs." "If the battalion commander is jumpy, have the Exec. O. take over command," he said.[*] His exhortations were unavailing; Companies A and C were forced to withdraw under a smoke screen. At the gorge, able-bodied

---

[*] Exec. O. is the executive officer, the second-in-command.

survivors and men from Company B that had managed to cross the open ground between the American line and the gorge were ordered to renew the attack. Captain John Van Vulpen, Company B's commander, led forty-six men up the gorge's south bank—and into a volcano of mortar and machine-gun fire. Seven men were hit instantly and were dragged on ponchos back to the gorge, and the other attackers followed them. The artillery fired all of the smoke rounds that it possessed. When they were gone, Captain Hugh Young radioed Lieutenant Leo Ford from headquarters, "God bless you, Leo."

Ford persuaded his men to leave the gorge by telling them, "It's safe to come out now. Smoke will be coming soon and we can make a break for it," reported John Beaufort of the *Christian Science Monitor*. "But there was no smoke, only the terrible fire of machine guns, rifles, and mortars from the Japanese on the ridge three hundred yards away."

That night, the battered survivors made their way to the rear in twos and threes.

Correspondent Gordon Cobbledick of the Cleveland *Plain Dealer* described the withdrawal of wounded men who had hidden in Kakazu's caves after the failed attack. "Four were half crawling, carrying and dragging a makeshift litter on which lay the most seriously wounded survivor. Two other wounded men were crawling on their bellies."

During the initial attack, Private First Class Edward Moskala had knocked out two Japanese machine guns with grenades and his automatic rifle. With seven other soldiers, he helped cover the withdrawal; together they killed more than twenty-five enemy troops. Three times, Moskala went back to retrieve wounded comrades and was killed during his last trip. The 383rd's 1st Battalion lost one-half of its men on April 9.[32]

DURING THE 1ST BATTALION'S FUTILE attack on Kakazu, May's 3rd Battalion was assaulting Kakazu West. Lieutenant Willard "Hoss" Mitchell, a former Mississippi State University football and basketball player, led one of the two companies, Company L, over the gorge before the Japanese reacted. Mitchell's "lardasses," as he affectionately called his men, defied heavy enemy fire to reach the Kakazu West crest in the predawn darkness. With satchel charges, Mitchell and Private First Class Joseph Solch destroyed a 320mm spigot mortar rolled from a cave on rails and killed nine men. Five of Solch's comrades were wounded, and he acted as a rearguard while four of them crawled away; he carried the fifth man on his back.

Company L braced itself in a saddle between two knolls to meet waves of Japanese counterattacks. During one of them, Solch killed fifteen enemy soldiers with his Browning automatic rifle (BAR). Mitchell rescued two of his men trapped by enemy machine-gun fire. "Here comes the Hoss and God's on the Hoss's side!" he shouted, according to *Chicago Tribune* correspondent Tom Morrow. "Whereupon he sprinted out into a sheet of mortar, machine-gun and sniper fire, gathered up his charges, and fetched them to safety."

Company L repulsed four frontal assaults before being compelled to withdraw under a smoke screen and artillery barrage with just three of its original eighty-nine attackers unwounded and their ammunition nearly gone. In one day, May's 383rd Infantry had suffered a shocking 326 casualties.[33]

Nonetheless, the next day, April 10, the 96th Division ordered the attacks to be renewed on the two Kakazus, utilizing both the 381st and 383rd Infantry. Air strikes, an artillery barrage, and gunfire from the battleship *New York* preceded the stark frontal assault by three thousand men from four battalions in the pouring rain. The Japanese pounded the assault troops with artillery and mortar fire. Somehow, the 381st managed to reach the Kakazu West ridge crest.

The 383rd found the other Kakazu ridge teeming with enemy troops who had emerged from their caves and tunnels the instant the bombardment ceased. "We blew the hell out of the place before we went up, but it didn't do much good," said Private First Class Francis Lambert. The enemy's subsequent counterattack nearly annihilated Company K of the 383rd and drove survivors off the ridge.

Dick Thom, one of the reinforcements sent to assist Company K, said, "When we got there, there was an army up there, all right, but it wasn't the 383rd Regiment. . . . Our men came tumbling down, their rifles falling." The fighting raged until the next day, April 11, when the 383rd was withdrawn from Kakazu.[34]

The nightmare appeared to be without end. On April 11, the 381st's 1st Battalion clawed its way to within yards of the Kakazu's crest before being stopped by two Japanese counterattacks. Tech Sergeant Alfred "Chief" Robertson, armed with a BAR, grenades, a bayonet, and a trench knife, single-handedly destroyed two machine guns and killed twenty-eight defenders, and then commandeered a radio to direct mortar fire. "Just a good day for the Chief," drily remarked a comrade.[35]

The next day, the battalion attacked Kakazu four times in one hour, charging across the saddle from Kakazu West. Enemy mortar fire falling at an astonishing rate of one to two rounds per second smothered every attack. A 320mm shell hit an aid station, killing two medical officers and ten men.

The 383rd's summary report on the Kakazu attacks said, "We were greatly handicapped at Kakazu by the impossibility of using tanks and by heavy enemy artillery and mortar fire."[36]

Meanwhile, the 382nd Infantry on the 96th Division's eastern flank was stopped cold at Tombstone Ridge.

PLANNING HAD BEGUN FOR THE largest US offensive of the Pacific war, scheduled to kick off April 19. XXIV Corps would attack southward with the 7th and 96th Divisions, and with its floating reserve, the 27th Division, which was now entering the western end of the battle line. Over several days, the 27th would replace units of the 96th while the Deadeyes shuffled eastward to the center of the line. The changeover began April 12 when a battalion of the 27th's 106th Infantry relieved a battalion of the 96th.

In due time, the Kakazus would become the 27th Division's responsibility. The 96th had paid dearly for meager gains against the two tenaciously defended fortresses, having lost 603 men killed and 1,401 wounded. But the division dished out more than it got, killing 4,663 Japanese soldiers.[37]

THE 7TH DIVISION'S 184TH AND 32nd Infantry had edged southward down Okinawa's eastern coast. At first, they encountered only light opposition. Then, on April 4, the regiments reached the base of Castle Hill, named for a castle built on the heavily wooded ridge four hundred years earlier, and now a crumbled ruin with only its thick walls remaining. Japanese units atop the eminence stopped the advancing American troops with machine-gun, mortar, and artillery fire. As the Americans prepared to launch a full-scale assault, the defenders slipped away, and the 184th occupied Castle Hill on April 5.[38]

Red Hill, so named because of its treeless red summit, was tougher, and not even the main objective; Hill 178 was, 2,000 yards beyond Red Hill. Entrenched in a formidable array of caves and connecting trenches, an enemy force estimated at up to 1,000 soldiers threw back the 184th's initial frontal attack on Red Hill on April 7. The Americans had attempted to cross a 1,000-yard exposed flatland of rice and bean fields under heavy fire. A second attack, supported by ten medium and five light tanks, also failed when

mines and satchel charges destroyed three tanks. A torrent of machine-gun and mortar fire drove away the Hourglass infantrymen, and the Japanese swarmed the remaining tanks with satchel charges and flaming rags. Two medium tanks held off the attackers and the rest escaped.

While the Japanese congratulated themselves on the success of their tactic of separating US infantrymen from supporting armor, the 184th's 3rd Battalion launched a flanking attack and quickly seized Red Hill at a cost of just two casualties. Army officers had discovered that Japanese defenders, intensely focused on repulsing frontal attacks, sometimes could be surprised by well-executed flank assaults.[39]

The 184th captured Triangulation Hill on April 8, and then lost it to Japanese soldiers boiling out of holes and caves. A counterattack by Company K of the 184th dissolved under withering artillery fire, but a second attempt to recapture the hill succeeded later on April 8.

That same day, while approaching nearby Tomb Hill—so named because the reinforced concrete pillbox on its crest resembled a burial tomb—the 184th's Companies F and G were caught in the open in a cabbage patch by Japanese shellfire, and casualties soared; one round killed seven men and wounded five more. The next day, enemy 150mm guns drove back two other assault companies to Triangulation Hill. A pair of fresh 184th companies seized Tomb Hill later on April 9 after two bloody attacks.[40]

The Hourglass Division had now reached the Shuri fortified zone. The village of Ouki lay on a ridge that split into two narrow fingers—the longer of them Skyline Ridge.

APRIL 9 WAS THE FIRST day since L-Day that rain fell on Okinawa. It was the beginning of the episodic rains that typically preceded the monsoon season in May and June. Cold rain soaked 7th Division's 32nd and 184th Infantry, and the misery was compounded by a furious mortar and artillery barrage and buzzing Nambus. That night, April 9–10, Japanese artillery pummeled the division with fifteen hundred rounds, its heaviest bombardment yet.

An attempt to steal around the Japanese right flank was thwarted by another Japanese artillery barrage on April 10. Attacks on Ouki and Skyline Ridge failed. The division withdrew and dug in, remaining idle for the next eight days.[41]

The 7th needed a breather. It had just three days' worth of 105mm and 155mm shells on hand, and there was a critical shortage of 81mm mortar shells because of heavy usage during the advance and the loss of two

ammunition ships. The converted "Victory" ships *Hobbs Victory* and *Logan Victory* were sunk by kamikazes at Kerama Retto.

General John Hodge, the XXIV Corps commander, realized from his experiences on Guadalcanal, Bougainville, and Leyte that he must obtain more shells before any major offensive such as the one planned for April 19. Army and Navy transport planes airlifted 117 tons of replacement 81mm shells to Okinawa from Guam and other supply depots.[42]

During its first ten days on Okinawa, the 7th Division had suffered 1,119 casualties, including 120 battle deaths and 13 men missing in action. Japanese shelling was blamed for 290 cases of battle fatigue. Lieutenant Donald Fitzgerald of the 7th's 184th Infantry said just four combat-capable men remained in his platoon; the rest were casualties.[43]

The Japanese, however, were hemorrhaging men even more rapidly. The 7th Division claimed to have killed 2,236 Japanese troops, although many of them belonged to the delaying force wiped out near the landing beaches during Iceberg's first days. The Japanese 12th Independent Infantry Battalion reported just 475 effectives by April 12, a little more than one-third of its original strength.[44]

The 7th Division's idle period did not exempt it from enemy shelling altogether, but the bombardments' duration dropped sharply to just half an hour before dawn and another half hour after sunset. Unlike the Americans, the Japanese could not replenish their dwindling artillery stocks, and they conserved whenever possible.

American casualties mounted anyway. From April 11 to 19, the 7th Division reported 825 casualties, half of them due to battle fatigue or other non-combat causes. Navy ships and aircraft from Yontan and Kadena periodically bombarded suspected Japanese positions, leaving the sky smudged by pillars of smoke.[45]

PRE-INVASION RECONNAISSANCE HAD NOT PREPARED XXIV Corps for the wasps' nest that the Americans encountered north of Shuri in the outer defensive zone. Aerial photos of southern Okinawa, when not impeded by thick clouds, had revealed only rugged green hills that divulged little or nothing of the brilliant interlocking defenses inside and around them.

Now XXIV Corps was learning through hard experience that Castle Hill, Pinnacle, Red Hill, and Kakazu were the northernmost layers of a strongly fortified, miles-deep defensive system whose focal point was Shuri Castle. This defensive line linked Skyline Ridge, the village of Ouki,

and the Hill 178 complex in the east to blood-drenched Kakazu Ridge in the west.[46]

Sergeant Beckman of the 96th Division's 382nd Infantry saw for himself the difficulty of dislodging the enemy when he ordered an air strike on caves at Kakazu, where two large howitzers were firing on his men. As he watched, accurate rocket fire apparently destroyed the caves. But minutes later, the same two howitzers emerged from the same cave, fired, and retreated into it. Beckman concluded that the Japanese defenses were virtually invulnerable to air attacks.

"Infantry, old fashioned and direct and bloody and full of casualties, is the only way to overrun them," he said.[47]

While the 27th and 96th Divisions moved into their new positions and the 7th Division rested prefatory to XXIV Corps's offensive, the enemy was poised to launch the campaign's first major counteroffensive.

ON APRIL 3, EMPEROR HIROHITO, dissatisfied with what was happening on Okinawa, had directed the Thirty-Second Army to mount a counteroffensive and drive the Americans into the sea, or to make a counterlanding that would dramatically alter the strategic situation.

Hirohito might have seemed a remote demigod to most of his subjects, but he in fact was deeply involved in military matters. On the second day of the Allied invasion of Okinawa, the emperor worried aloud that "if this battle turns out badly, the army and navy would lose the trust of the nation." By the third day, Hirohito could no longer simply watch from the sidelines. When the emperor's order to counterattack reached General Ushijima, he could only obey. "All of our troops will attempt to rush forward and wipe out the ugly enemy," Ushijima replied.[48]

Planning began immediately for a mass nighttime infiltration of the US lines all along the Kakazu-Nishibaru-Yonabaru front. The ebullient General Chō, the Thirty-Second Army chief of staff, was delighted by the opportunity to at last take the initiative. Some staff officers strongly objected—most prominently, Colonel Yahara, the Army's operations officer. They advocated sticking to the Thirty-Second Army's original attritional strategy.

The counteroffensive's primary objectives after breaking through the American lines would be Yontan and Kadena Airfields. Admiral Matome Ugaki, commander of the 5th Air Fleet and former Combined Fleet chief of staff, wrote that it was essential to "nullify the enemy's use of those airstrips."

The attack was initially set for the night of April 6, but was moved back to April 8, and then postponed a second time because the Japanese feared

an Allied landing on Okinawa's southern beaches that night. The counter-offensive was rescheduled for the night of April 12.

The 272nd Independent Infantry Battalion of the 62nd Division would lead the attack on the 96th Division in the Kakazu area, and the 22nd Infantry Regiment of the 24th Division would attempt to break through the American 7th Division in the east. Carrying 110-pound packs and bags of food, the 22nd marched for two days through the rain from Naha to the east coast, where it was to strike the Hourglass lines.

The infiltrators were to pass swiftly and silently through the American XXIV Corps positions in a "sinuous eel line" and conceal themselves in caves and tombs north of the battle lines. By daybreak, they were to be in camouflaged hiding places. At a predetermined time, they would strike the Allies' rear and the two airfields. "The secrecy of our plans must be maintained to the last," the Japanese instructions said.[49]

Colonel Yahara believed that the plan would squander the lives of hundreds, if not thousands, of frontline troops. After losing the argument, Yahara acted to reduce the Thirty-Second Army's inevitable losses by quietly trimming the number of battalions committed to the operation from six to four. In so doing, he ensured that the operation would fail.[50]

Thirty minutes before the attack began, Japanese artillery fired three thousand rounds, concentrating on the western battle line, where the 272nd Infantry Battalion hoped to breach the Deadeyes' positions at Kakazu and Kakazu West. It was the heaviest Japanese barrage of the Pacific war.

The Americans responded with deafening volleys of gunfire from four battleships and two destroyers. Star shells interspersed with explosive rounds brightly illuminated the battlefield and exposed the attacking Japanese soldiers. The opportunity to shoot scores of enemy troops in the open elated many XXIV Corps troops, frustrated by days of being under fire from an invisible enemy.[51]

At Kakazu and Kakazu West, sixty enemy troops nearly broke through the 383rd Infantry's Company G, which momentarily mistook the Japanese for Americans. Company G killed fifty-eight attackers and stopped the attempted infiltration.

Finally able to turn the tables on the Japanese streaming out of their fortifications into the open, the Deadeyes punished them with the kind of intensive mortar, artillery, and machine-gun fire that they themselves had endured for a week.

The Japanese continued to attack even when badly wounded. Some of them charged ahead with tourniquets on their legs, groins, and arms, said Private First Class Charles Moynihan, a radio operator liaison between an artillery unit and the 381st Infantry. Shot down by the score, they were soon "stacked up like a bunch of worms," he said.[52]

"We were pinned down by concentrated mortar fire before we could cross the hill," wrote a Japanese soldier in the 272nd Battalion, which bore the withering fire until dawn, when it withdrew after having suffered heavy casualties. "Only four of us [in his platoon] . . . were left . . . the Akiyama Tai [1st Company, 272nd] was wiped out while infiltrating." Another company that suffered massive casualties literally disintegrated while it was attempting to withdraw, the soldier said.[53]

The counteroffensive at Kakazu failed in large part because of the frenzied resistance of Americans such as Tech Sergeant Beauford Anderson of the 381st Infantry—still on the Kakazu line, which the 27th Division was in the early stages of taking over.

Anderson had wound up in a cave in the saddle between Kakazu and Kakazu West with fifteen unfired Japanese mortar shells, but without a mortar to fire the shells. He solved the problem by transforming himself into a launching device: tearing the mortar shells from their casings, pulling the safety pins, rapping them against a rock to activate them, and then hurling them like footballs into a draw teeming with approaching enemy soldiers. When he ran out of Japanese mortar rounds, he threw mortar shells from his own light mortar section.

The next morning, after the echoes from the last explosions had faded, Anderson counted twenty-five bodies, seven knee mortars, and four machine guns among the debris in front of his position.* Three hundred seventeen enemy dead were reported in the 96th Division area.[54]

The Japanese counteroffensive made no inroads in the 7th Division sector on the eastern battle line. The 184th Infantry's 2nd Battalion repulsed two attacks on their positions at Tomb Hill, north of the Tanabaru Escarpment. About thirty Japanese were killed each time. Small infiltration parties that penetrated the American lines were wiped out, one by one. Colonel Yahara believed the attacks failed in the east because the terrain was

---

* Anderson was later awarded the Congressional Medal of Honor for his heroics.

unfamiliar to the Japanese 22nd Infantry, which had marched across the island from Naha.

The counterattack met the same result the next night when, illuminated by naval star shells, the Japanese were once more repulsed. By dawn on April 14, about half of the Japanese who participated in the counteroffensive, 1,594 men, had died. Fewer than 100 Americans were killed.[55]

While the Tenth Army briefly savored its brief respite from high casualties, terror and death continued to hurtle from the skies at the Fifth Fleet.

The Kamikazes

The men who can save the country are not the military or political leaders. The salvation of Japan lies in the young people of twenty-five to thirty-five—or even younger—in their body-hitting spirit.

—ADMIRAL TAKIJIRŌ ŌNISHI,
FOUNDER OF THE SPECIAL ATTACK CORPS[1]

Put forth everything you have. All of you come back dead.

—JAPANESE SQUADRON COMMANDER
TO PILOTS BEFORE TAKEOFF[2]

THE JAPANESE NAVAL PILOTS STOOD at attention around a long table as their planes warmed up on the runway. Everyone at the small air base off the southern coast of Japan had turned out to honor the departing men, members of the Special Attack Corps. They were about to embark on Kiku-sui No. 1—*kikusui* meaning "chrysanthemums on flowing water," with the chrysanthemum symbolizing Japan.

The pilots would not return from this mission, and this was their last meal. The table, covered by an immaculate white cloth, offered an array of victuals: sake, dried cuttlefish, seaweed, dried chestnuts, and balls of rice with red beans.

The kamikaze pilots were dressed in clean clothes, and wore white head-bands adorned with the rising sun, and "thousand-stitch" belts—made

by random Japanese women who had each added one stitch, along with a prayer. The belt ostensibly protected its wearer from harm, but years of war had disabused the Japanese of this belief, and the belts now signified national unity, if even that. The pilots also carried various personal objects on their final missions, ranging from good-luck dolls that hung from their belts to ceremonial swords to family heirlooms to silk Japanese flags signed by friends in India ink. Some wore white robes; some carried the ashes of comrades killed in battle.

Before climbing into their cockpits, the pilots raised their sake cups in a final toast to the emperor and sang their battle song:

> *The airman's color is the color of the cherry blossom.*
> *See, oh see, how the blossoms fall on the hills of Yoshino.*
> *If we are born proud sons of the Yamato race, let us die,*
> *Let us die with triumph, fighting in the sky.*[3]

During a similar ceremony at Kanoya Air Base on Kyushu, Admiral Matome Ugaki, commander of the 5th Air Fleet, presided in his dress whites. "We shall meet in Minatogawa," he said, lifting his sake cup. The Minatogawa Shinto shrine in Kobe commemorates a 1336 battle of the Kenmu Restoration period, the last time the emperor possessed any power until the Meiji Restoration five centuries later. The pilots shouted three "banzais" and boarded their planes to drum rolls.[4]

THE FALLING CHERRY BLOSSOM WAS the totem of the Special Attack Corps pilots. The Corps came into being in October 1944 as a result of the crushing Japanese naval and air defeat at the Battle of the Philippine Sea on June 19–20—nicknamed the "Great Marianas Turkey Shoot" by Americans. Three Japanese fleet carriers were sunk, and more than four hundred planes were destroyed, and with them many of Japan's remaining veteran pilots.

The Imperial Japanese Navy was now hopelessly overmatched against the US Navy, which had grown into a colossus since the dark days of Guadalcanal in 1942; during that campaign's nadir, just one American aircraft carrier plied the South Pacific. Now, in Admiral Marc Mitscher's Task Force 58 alone, there were seventeen aircraft carriers and many hundreds of planes—Corsairs, Hellcats, and other advanced warplanes that had replaced the antiquated Wildcats and Dauntless dive-bombers of the Pacific war's early days.

In air combat, the Grumman F6F Hellcat had established its overwhelming superiority to any Japanese fighter plane in the air—a reversal of the situation in 1942 when the Zero outperformed every US warplane. "The Hellcats were fully as agile as our own planes, much faster, and able to out-climb and out-dive us," wrote famed Japanese ace Saburō Sakai. If more experienced pilots had flown the Hellcats, he said, "every Zeke [Zero] would have been shot down in less than a minute."[5]

Meanwhile, Japan's production of warplanes and ships was ebbing because US submarine attacks on ships carrying raw materials from Southeast Asia—along with strategic bombing—were choking Japan's supply line and causing an acute fuel shortage. Because of limited fuel supplies, the testing of new naval technology was restricted to the Inland Sea, and warplane prototypes could not be thoroughly vetted. "Our air forces suddenly found themselves fighting against impossible odds," Captain Rikihei Inoguchi and Commander Tadashi Nakajima, who were staff officers for Japan's air fleets, wrote in *The Divine Wind*. "The supply even of Zeros was insufficient to fill half the requirements of the fighting fronts."[6]

The Zero, however—or "Zeke," as it was often called—remained a formidable adversary if competently flown. Corsairs were 48mph faster at sea level and 80mph faster at 25,000 feet, and could climb and dive at greater speeds than Zeros. But Zeros were more maneuverable and could "turn inside" a Corsair's turning radius.[7]

Japan could not train good pilots or build planes and ships fast enough to avert the looming disaster, so in desperation leaders turned to suicide planes. "One plane for one ship" became the mantra of the Special Attack Corps.

ON OCTOBER 13, 1944, THE Japanese Imperial Navy sent a top-secret message announcing the creation of "*shinpu* [Special Attack] units" to raise the morale of the armed forces and the Japanese people.[8]

Two days later, Admiral Masafumi Arima, commander of the 1st Air Fleet's 26th Air Flotilla, climbed into a dive-bomber and crashed into an American ship while leading ninety-nine fighters and dive-bombers on a mission in the Philippines. Radio Tokyo celebrated his sacrifice.[9]

Admiral Takijirō Ōnishi, commander of the 1st Air Fleet, paid an unexpected visit to Mabalacat Airfield in the Philippines on October 19 to promote the new Special Attack Corps. Known for his radicalism and abrasiveness, Ōnishi was drummed out of the Naval War College for slapping a Geisha. In 1942, when he was asked to share his views at a gathering of

Japanese luminaries, he accused the prime minister, the Planning Board, and Army and Navy leaders of having contributed nothing to the war effort. They should resign immediately, he declared. He further riled the assemblage by advocating scrapping the Imperial Navy's battleships and using the materials to build more warplanes.[10]

Standing before officers of the 201st Air Group during his surprise appearance at Mabalacat, Ōnishi said the Special Attack Corps would deliberately crash planes armed with 500-pound bombs into enemy ships. Captain Inoguchi, the 1st Air Fleet's senior staff officer, conceded that a Japanese flier sent on a conventional mission to bomb an American aircraft carrier had a "very slim" chance of returning alive anyway. "If one is bound to die, what is more natural than the desire to die effectively, at maximum cost to the enemy?" Inoguchi said. He later elaborated: "We Japanese base our lives on obedience to Emperor and country. On the other hand, we wish for the best place in death, according to Bushido. Kamikaze originates from these feelings. . . ."

The 201st Air Group was now a "crash-dive unit." When the group leader explained the new mission to the pilots, "in a frenzy of emotion and joy," the arms of every pilot shot up in approval, said Inoguchi. Admiral Ōnishi told them, "Thus, on behalf of your hundred million countrymen, I ask of you this sacrifice, and pray for your success." He added, "You are already gods, without earthly desires." The first twenty-six kamikaze pilots snipped locks of their hair to leave behind for their relatives and sang "Going Out to Sea," the so-called Hymn of the Dead, before taking off on October 21, but they found no targets. That would change.[11]

THE CONCEPT WAS REVOLUTIONARY: WHILE Japanese pilots had sometimes deliberately crashed their planes into ships throughout the Pacific war, never before (or since, for that matter) had an aviation unit been formed for that express purpose. Because of Japan's ancient tradition of absolute patriotic devotion, carefully preserved and further cultivated during the nineteenth-century Meiji Restoration, the idea of en-masse suicide plane attacks was easily accepted. The Japanese Army's tradition of *gyokusai*—"smashed jewel"—had been established in May 1943 by the twenty-five-hundred-man Attu garrison's decision to fight to the last man. It was a short step to applying this concept to aerial warfare.

The "divine wind," or kamikaze, was renowned in Japanese history and legend because of the fateful typhoon of August 1281 that destroyed

a thirty-five-hundred-ship Sino-Mongol invasion fleet under Kublai Khan before it could land in Japan. Had it not been for the storm, Japan, rent by civil war, would likely have succumbed to the invaders.[12]

AT 7:45 A.M. ON OCTOBER 25, 1944, kamikazes went into action to thwart the US invasion of Leyte. One Japanese commander reportedly told his pilots before their departure, "Put forth everything you have. All of you come back dead." Twelve kamikazes scored hits on three carrier escorts in the San Bernardino Strait area. One of them struck *St. Lo* and exploded; the flattop sank minutes later, at 11:25 a.m. Carrier escorts *Santee* and *Kikun Bay* were damaged, but survived. Killed in the attacks were 131 Americans and the 12 Japanese pilots. "The men who can save the country are not the military or political leaders," Ōnishi wrote. "The salvation of Japan lies in the young people of twenty-five to thirty-five—or even younger—in their body-hitting spirit."[13]

During the period beginning October 25 at Leyte and ending at Lingayen Gulf in January 1945, kamikazes sank 22 Allied ships and damaged 110 others. On February 21, the only suicide attack of the Iwo Jima campaign—by 25 kamikazes and 15 conventional aircraft—sank the carrier escort *Bismarck Sea*, and damaged the carrier *Saratoga*, the carrier escort *Lunga Point*, and three other ships. Kamikazes and their escort fighters and dive-bombers killed more than two thousand Americans between October and March. Crash-diving Japanese pilots were posthumously promoted two ranks.[14]

ABOARD SIX WARSHIPS OFF OKINAWA, radio intelligence units monitored the airwaves around the clock for coded Japanese messages, and forwarded their intercepts to ULTRA cryptanalysts. US naval intelligence had become adept at breaking the Japanese code, which was changed on the first day of every month. The Allies first began to make progress in breaking the code in 1942, but the code-breaking usually proceeded too slowly to affect events. However, by 1945 analysts were breaking the code on the second or third day of each month, even as the ciphers became more complex.[15]

On April 4, ULTRA cryptanalysts sent a warning to the Okinawa naval task forces: "Evidence afternoon 3rd that X-Day for Kikusui No. 1 will be the 5th." A subsequent message sent on April 5 said, "X-Day may be 6 rather than 5 April."[16]

This was the much-anticipated Operation Ten-Go, which the Japanese air fleets had planned to launch against the Americans on L-Day. Task Force 58's intensive carrier raids targeting enemy airstrips on Kyushu and shipping in the Inland Sea had disrupted the Japanese timetable and forced postponement of Ten-Go until April 6.

Radar-equipped destroyers surrounded Okinawa; they alerted the combat air patrols (CAPs), the first line of defense against the Japanese intruders. The CAPs were composed of fighter squadrons from Admiral Marc Mitscher's carriers and, later, air units from Yontan and Kadena Airfields. Enemy pilots who penetrated the CAPs next faced 5-inch medium-range antiaircraft fire from the picket ships. From closer range, 40mm and 20mm AA guns in multimount "gun tubs" joined in trying to knock down the enemy craft.

Early on April 6, ULTRA cryptanalysts deciphered an intercepted Japanese request for fuel oil for "the 2nd Fleet sortie," heretofore unknown and now an object of intensive curiosity. At 1:05 p.m., another decryption outlined the timetable for the 2nd Fleet sortie, as well as its route—emerging from Japan's Inland Sea via Bungo Channel and proceeding to Okinawa. US submarines and aerial observation units in the area were alerted. Soon, reconnaissance-plane reports began to trickle in; they focused everyone's attention.[17]

LEADING THE TASK FORCE WAS the superbattleship *Yamato*, the flagship of the 2nd Fleet, with 3,233 crewmen. *Yamato* and her sister, *Musashi*, launched in February 1942, were the largest battleships ever built. Each was armed with nine 18-inch guns whose shells weighed 3,200 pounds apiece and had a maximum range of 22 miles. Whenever *Yamato* was about to fire her massive guns, a bugle was sounded so crewmen could cover their ears. Eight hundred sixty-three feet long, with a 35-foot draft, the two battleships had a cruising speed of 25 knots and were graceful in appearance, with streamlined masts and smokestacks, and unbroken flush decks from stem to stern. They were built to surpass state-of-the-art British, German, and US battleships, but even as they were being built during the 1930s, progressive-minded naval officers like Admiral Isoroku Yamamoto were asserting that the battleship era had passed and that the naval air power age had begun.[18]

Musashi was sunk October 24 at the Battle of Leyte Gulf, shredded by waves of US dive-bombers and torpedo bombers. Three bombs hit *Yamato*,

but because she was the most massively armored ship ever built, she shook off the damage and survived the battle.[19]

The name Yamato bore great historical significance; it was a seventh-century poetic name for Japan; appropriately enough, the battleship *Yamato*'s enormous superstructure resembled a pagoda. Navy men regarded *Yamato* with a feeling akin to religious devotion, and their faith in the 72,000-ton vessel grew when she returned from Leyte after her sister ship was sunk there.

During the 2nd Fleet sortie, *Yamato* would be accompanied by the 2nd Destroyer Squadron—eight destroyers led by the light cruiser *Yahagi*. Some of the last remaining operational ships in the once-mighty Imperial Japanese Navy were now part of Operation Ten-Go.[20]

Emperor Hirohito's keen interest in achieving victory on Okinawa led to the addition of the *Yamato* task force to Operation Ten-Go. At a meeting on March 29 at the imperial palace, Hirohito urged Admiral Koshirō Oikawa to "leave nothing to be desired" in defending Okinawa. The battle's outcome would "decide the fate of our empire."

Oikawa assured the emperor that two thousand Imperial Japanese Navy aircraft, a good portion of them kamikazes, stood at the ready.

"Is that all?" the emperor reportedly asked. Oikawa replied that fifteen hundred Japanese Army planes would join the onslaught.

"But where is the navy?" Hirohito asked. "Are there no more ships? No more surface ships?"[21]

Consternation prevailed when the emperor's comments reached Imperial General Headquarters. Stung by what it interpreted as an imperial reproach and an implicit suggestion that it utilize its scarce surface vessels, the high command drew up a plan to send *Yamato* on a mission that in a bygone era would have been described as a "forlorn hope."[22]

Without exception, the officers of the *Yamato* task force opposed the plan as a waste of men and materiel. Imperial Japanese Navy Headquarters, realizing that it must apply "personal persuasion" to ensure the mission's success, dispatched Admiral Ryūnosuke Kusaka, the Combined Fleet's chief of staff, by seaplane to the *Yamato* to win over Admiral Seiichi Itō, the 2nd Fleet's commander.

Itō, a tall, stooped fifty-four-year-old, had served as a staff officer for most of the war, and he and Kusaka had been classmates at the naval academy at Etajima decades earlier. During the meeting aboard the *Yamato* with Itō and the 2nd Fleet's staff, Kusaka declared that Ten-Go would

prolong Japan's survival and that its sailors, officers, and pilots would "die gloriously, heralding the deaths of 100 million Japanese who prefer death to surrender." Itō argued vigorously against the mission, but grudgingly consented to it in the end. Ten-Go would be Itō's first sea battle, and most likely his last.[23]

Admiral Keizō Komura left the meeting to break the news to his subordinate commanders of the 2nd Destroyer Squadron on his flagship *Yahagi*. The eight destroyer captains unanimously denounced the plan as futile and wasteful—a rare act that would have normally been regarded as mutinous.

Komura returned to the *Yamato* and candidly shared the opinions of his destroyer captains with Itō and Kusaka, adding that he agreed with them. It did no good. He was told the mission would be a decoy for Kikusui No. 1—although the *Yamato* task force would in fact sail after Kikusui No. 1 had already begun. Senior officers wanted to see the *Yamato* in action, Kusaka said.

In explaining the higher-ups' rationale to his destroyer commanders, Komura said that the mission would provide "an appropriate chance to die." Attempting to lift the downcast commanders' spirits, Captain Tameichi Hara, the *Yahagi* captain, told them they were not "sheep whipped to a sacrificial altar. We are lions released in the arena, to devour the enemy gladiators. . . . You are not to commit suicide. You are to beat the enemy." The destroyer commanders reluctantly accepted their mission.[24]

AFTER SUNRISE ON APRIL 6, Japanese fighters warmed up on airstrips on the outlying islands south of Kyushu. Of the 699 planes committed to the first *kikusui*, 355 were kamikazes. The other 344 were conventional warplanes whose job was to shield the kamikazes and to dive-bomb American ships.[25]

"Dear Parents," wrote Flying Petty Officer 1/c Isao Matsuo on the eve of the mission, "please congratulate me. I have been given a splendid opportunity to die. This is my last day. The destiny of our homeland hinges on the decisive battle in the seas to the south where I shall fall like a blossom from a radiant cherry tree."[26]

The heavily censored farewell letters to loved ones included locks of hair, fingernail clippings, sometimes even part of a finger—tokens that could be cremated and then added to the family shrine.[27]

Later, during an interrogation by his American captors, General Torashirō Kawabe somewhat disingenuously claimed that Special Attack

Force pilots did not set out to commit suicide. "He looked upon himself as a human bomb which would destroy a certain part of the enemy fleet . . . [and] died happily in the conviction that his death was a step toward the final victory."[28]

In addition to crash-diving ships, kamikaze pilots were instructed to ram enemy planes, but to not attempt to engage their more skillful adversaries. Those that reached their targets intact, though, turned to their toolkit of tactics. They broadcast "window"—strips of cut metal, foil, or wire—to baffle radar. If they approached at high altitude, they hid in the clouds until they were able to dive at a steep angle, aiming for amidships between the stack and bridge. If diving on a carrier, they targeted the elevators. Bow-on attacks were recommended to minimize exposure to ship gunfire. Kamikazes sometimes approached at nearly wave height, hoping to strike amidships just above the waterline, while evading radar and the ship's big guns, which could not hit such low-flying targets.

The kamikaze training manual said pushing the elevator control forward would increase speed, warning that "it is essential at this time not to miss the target because of shutting one's eyes for a moment." But the most effective strategy was for several planes at one time to swarm a ship from multiple angles to prevent its gunners from concentrating their fire on a single plane.[29]

There had never been such a large-scale airborne suicide attack. In the Philippines, the kamikazes' first battleground, the suicide planes had come in groups of three to six. On Okinawa, sporadic kamikaze attacks had occurred since L-Day, when five ships were damaged and sixty sailors and Marines were killed. The spurt of small-scale kamikaze attacks had continued on April 2, when eleven planes hit the US anchorage on Okinawa's eastern side, crashing several transports and causing 133 deaths.[30]

So, when destroyer radar screens began to fill with bogeys on April 6, there were exclamations of surprise at the size of the attack, but not at the attack itself; radio intelligence intercepts and ULTRA cryptanalysts had warned the Pacific naval command to expect "large scale air attacks"— many of them kamikazes—early April 6.[31]

SIXTEEN RADAR-EQUIPPED PICKET SHIPS WERE stationed around Okinawa at distances ranging from 20 to 75 miles from "Point Bolo," near the Hagushi beachhead. Destroyers, minelayers, minesweepers, and destroyer escorts manned the picket stations, accompanied by Landing Craft

Support gunboats—nicknamed "mighty midgets" because their three twin 40mm guns were deadly against Japanese suicide planes. They patrolled around the clock at 15 knots within a 5,000-yard radius of the center of their stations.

By the end of Operation Iceberg in late June, 36,422 men would serve on 206 destroyers and support craft at the picket stations. They were known collectively as Task Group 51.5, commanded by Captain Frederick Moosbrugger.

The picket stations north of Okinawa were prime targets because Japanese pilots encountered them first. Radar Picket Station No. 1, located 50 miles north of the beachhead, was ground zero for the first *kikusui* attacks.

Aboard the leading picket ship at each station was a "fighter director" team. When radar detected incoming enemy planes, the fighter director contacted the combat air patrol—usually four fighter planes assigned to cruise above his sector, and alerted the other picket ships. When the combat air patrol intercepted the Japanese planes, more American warplanes converged on the scene.[32]

By the fourth year of the Pacific war, most of Japan's best pilots were dead or unable to fly. Hastily trained and inexperienced aviators now occupied the cockpits of the fighters and bombers, giving the more skillful Marine and Navy fighter pilots a great advantage. Unless numerically overwhelmed or facing an air-combat veteran, an American pilot usually was able to shoot down his attackers.

Yet, some *kikusui* pilots managed to penetrate the fighter shield, and then it fell to the ship's captain to maneuver and expose the attacker to the ship's beam and its array of 40mm, 20mm, and 5-inch guns fired by adrenaline-pumped crews fighting for their lives. Proximity-fused 5-inch antiaircraft shells that exploded beside the plane appeared to work best.[33]

THE APRIL 6 ATTACKS BEGAN around 3 p.m. and lasted five hours. The first wave of twenty-seven fighters attempted to lure the American CAPs to higher altitudes. They were followed by forty Army fighters running interference for the two hundred Army and Navy kamikazes from the 5th Air Fleet and 6th Air Army.[34]

Sailors quickly learned to discern which picket-ship guns were firing in order to assess the danger level. The firing of 5-inch guns meant that kamikazes were still a distance away. When the 40mm Bofor auto-cannons joined in, a kamikaze was targeting the sailors' ship, and the sound of the 20mm guns was the signal to take cover.[35]

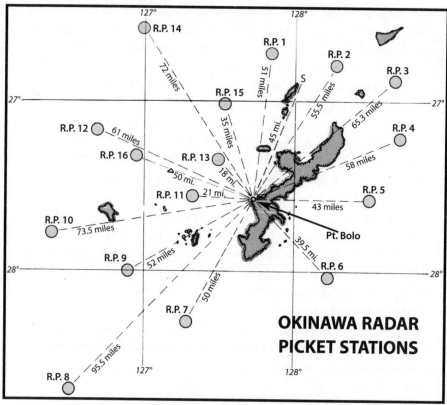

Map adapted from US Navy Bulletin COM PHIBS OP PLAN A1-45

The first ship crashed was the destroyer *Bush*, swarmed by forty to fifty planes at Radar Picket Station No. 1. The bandits orbited before diving on *Bush*. "We got several of them, but . . . one hit the bridge . . . [it] exploded and fire went everywhere and over our number two mount," said Gunner's Mate Floyd Ford. A bomber crashed amidships, its bomb exploding in the forward engine compartment and killing everybody there. An oily column of smoke rose from the stricken destroyer, and she listed to port. Flooding shorted out the emergency generators, instantly shutting down her 5-inch guns and 40mm Bofors. As the fire raged around Ford's Number 2 turret, he and his mates dropped through the discharged shell chute to the deck, and escaped on a life raft.[36]

At the same time, two combat air patrols assigned to *Bush's* picket station had run low on fuel and departed after shooting down several planes.

Navy fighter squadrons VF-82 and VMF-112 were dispatched from the carrier *Bennington*, and VF-30 and VF-45 lifted off from light carriers *Belleau Wood* and *San Jacinto*. "A general melee" ensued; at the end of the day, the American pilots claimed one hundred kills.

Major Herman Hansen Jr. and Lieutenant George Murray of VMF-112 jumped on an enemy fighter darting among the clouds. It attempted to shake the Corsair pilots by executing a "split S" inverted half-roll maneuver. Hansen stayed with his quarry, but his guns jammed and he nearly flew into the Japanese plane. Murray, however, was able to close and pepper the enemy plane with machine-gun fire; when Murray was just 25 feet away, his adversary burst into flames and crashed into the sea.

The enemy plane's attempt to elude his pursuers with a split S suggested that he was a conventional pilot, and not from the Special Attack Corps. VF-82's report noted that the Japanese suicide pilots' lack of maneuvering reflected their minimal training and experience. "Of all the enemy [suicide] planes encountered, not one returned fire; all remained on course, bearing in toward the surface vessels."[37]

Bush reported that she was sinking and summoned *Colhoun* from Radar Picket Station No. 2. *Colhoun* found the stricken ship down by the stern and with the "remains of what appeared to be a Betty plastered on her starboard side amidships."

With a dozen bogeys circling like vultures, the *Colhoun* attempted to interpose herself between the predators and *Bush* while assuming control of the picket station's combat air patrol.

But the Japanese pilots smelled blood. At 5:30 p.m., a Zero dove into *Bush*'s main deck on the port side, nearly cutting the destroyer in two and igniting a large fire. Fifteen minutes later, another Zero crashed the forward part of the ship, wiping out a wardroom where casualties were being treated. Flames enveloped the forecastle. Then, a fourth suicide plane struck the destroyer. With a loud tearing noise, she came apart amidships, folded in two, and sank at 6:30 p.m.—the first US ship sunk on picket duty off Okinawa. Ninety-four sailors died.[38]

While defending *Bush*, *Colhoun* had made herself a target. Shortly after 5 p.m., a Zero in flames smashed into the main deck, and its bomb detonated in the after fire room. Minutes later, another Zero crashed into the forward fire room; the explosion of its bomb broke the keel, pierced both boilers, and tore a 20-foot-long hole in the starboard side below the waterline. From the main deck railing of the *Colhoun*, Marine lieutenant Junie

Kohan watched the destruction of his ship in horror, rooted to his spot while his shipmates scattered.

Flooding shut down *Colhoun*'s power, but firefighters controlled all the fires within eleven minutes by using 120 cans of foam extinguisher. Two more suicide planes slashed another hole below the waterline and crashed the port beam. With two below-waterline holes and no way to staunch the flooding, *Colhoun* was abandoned, and sunk later that night by *Cassin Young*. Thirty-five deaths were reported.[39]

Gunboats converged on *Bush* and *Colhoun* to pluck survivors from the cold, heavy seas before they drowned or succumbed to their wounds. "We picked up more dead than alive," said Lieutenant Bob Wisner, *LCS(L)-37*'s communications officer. "We piled all the dead people on the fantail." At sunrise the next morning, the sea "was just filled with people . . . sagging in their jackets . . . a terrible sight."[40]

The radar picket ships were Kikusui No. 1's chief targets, but not the only ones. Off Ie Shima just west of Okinawa, one of the early Special Attack waves arrived over destroyer *Hyman*, and an attacker crashed between her two stacks. Crewmen put out the fire. Electrician Mate 2/c Jon Warren Jones Jr., who was helping tend to the wounded, found two dead shipmates with their clothes all blown off and their bodies crusted with third-degree burns. The skull of one of them was riddled with .30-caliber bullets, and "his stomach [was] ripped open and intestines lying all over the deck and a big piece of plane through his chest and sticking out both sides." The two were among the eleven crewmen who were killed.[41]

The high-speed minesweeper *Emmons*, supporting Sweep Unit 11 east of Ie Shima, witnessed a swirling dogfight overhead when fifty to seventy-five attackers clashed with several CAP units. *Emmons*'s after-action report noted the same phenomenon reported by VF-82: "It appeared the enemy did not choose to engage our aircraft but was more intent on making an attacking run on surface craft."

CAP pilots claimed fifty kills, but some kamikazes slipped through, and *Emmons* was struck by five warplanes, causing massive explosions and fires. The minesweeper's gunners, who knocked down six other kamikazes, kept shooting even as fire crews vainly tried to contain the blazes raging around them. The last straw was a "heavy hit aft [that] shook the whole ship," reported Water Tender 3/c James Korney. The crew was ordered to abandon ship, and a sister ship later sunk her. *Emmons* reported sixty-one deaths.[42]

Newcomb was crashed five times, but the destroyer survived, with 43 men killed or missing. The destroyer *Leutze*, while attempting to render aid, was struck by the fifth *Newcomb* kamikaze when it skipped across *Newcomb*'s deck into *Leutze*. Eight *Leutze* sailors died. The minesweeper *Defense* picked up fifty-two *Newcomb* sailors in life rafts. When one badly injured sailor was being hauled aboard *Defense*, "all the flesh came off his arm, he was burned so bad," wrote James Boswell.[43]

Twenty-two kamikazes penetrated CAP defenses and sank six ships on April 6; eighteen others were damaged. The first day of Kikusui No. 1 claimed more than 350 American lives. TF-51 and TF-58 pilots claimed to have shot down more than three hundred enemy planes. As usual, the Japanese grossly exaggerated the damage done to the American fleet, declaring that sixty-nine ships were sunk or damaged, including two battleships and three cruisers.

A kamikaze pilot who parachuted from his smoking plane was picked up from a red life raft by American sailors and made a prisoner. Admiral Marc Mitscher said the pilot wore a silk scarf bearing the inscription, "Kamikaze Special Attack Unit 3." A college graduate and flight instructor, the pilot was, Mitscher said, "now matriculating in [the] *Hornet*."[44]

General Simon Bolivar Buckner Jr., who was commanding the Tenth Army from the amphibious force command ship *Eldorado*, described the kamikaze onslaught in a letter to his wife, Adele: "I have had thrills in duck blinds but none comparable to that of seeing an enemy plane shot down when it was heading directly at our ship."[45]

Operation Ten-Go resumed April 7, but without the intensity of April 6's attacks and with fewer planes. Nonetheless, shortly after noon, a Judy dive-bomber suddenly appeared over the carrier *Hancock*, whose planes were away, hunting for the *Yamato* task force near Kyushu. From an elevation of 50 feet, the Judy dropped a bomb that plowed through the flight deck and exploded on the hangar deck, destroying several planes. The force of the explosion caused the Judy to cartwheel into a row of planes on the flight deck. Sixty-four men died, and seventy-three other crewmen were blown overboard and picked up by destroyers. Twenty planes were destroyed.

As a testament to the efficiency of *Hancock*'s damage-control teams, four hours after she was attacked, her flight deck was landing planes that were low on fuel and circling the ship.[46]

WHILE THE WAVES OF TEN-GO attacks crashed against the American picket stations surrounding Okinawa, *Yamato* and her escort ships were weighing anchor in the Inland Sea.

Clearly, "Operation Ten-ichi-gō," as this adjunct to Ten-Go was code named, was launched for the sole purpose of satisfying the emperor's wish that the Japanese surface fleet participate in Kikusui No. 1. Rather than acknowledge this fact, naval staff officers insisted that the mission's purpose was to draw away US interceptors from the massive Japanese kamikaze attack, increasing its chances for success. If *Yamato* and her escorts reached Okinawa, they would charge into the enemy anchorage at daybreak on April 8 and run aground; the survivors would fight as soldiers.

The officers assigned to carry out the mission, however, knew that it was suicide, pure and simple, and they had protested. Even General Ushijima on Okinawa opposed it. "Sincere thanks for your cooperation," he telegraphed Admiral Itō. "But this is not a good opportunity. Please postpone mission."

The Combined Fleet, unwilling to squander its scarce fuel on a doomed mission, allotted only enough fuel—2,000 tons—for the *Yamato* to reach Okinawa, but not enough for it to return. For the same reason, the mission was denied air support. However, fleet staff officers scraped up another 2,000 tons of fuel for Yamato's return trip and made certain that the escort ships also had enough fuel for a round-trip.

Although he had opposed the mission from the beginning, Admiral Ugaki of the 5th Air Fleet could not allow it to sail without any air cover. Ugaki allotted fifteen fighters to support the *Yamato* task force during the first part of its mission.[47]

Before weighing anchor, a dozen or so ill *Yamato* sailors and some older men who had families at home were selected to remain behind. Fifty new naval academy graduates aboard *Yamato* were also sent ashore, over their protestations. "We couldn't bear to take them along on an expedition into certain death," wrote Ensign Mitsuru Yoshida, an assistant radar officer. "Moreover, fifty newcomers would diminish our fighting strength, not augment it." Yoshida composed a farewell letter that exhorted his mother to "rejoice . . . if I am lucky enough to die a death of which I need not be ashamed."[48]

Before they sailed, *Yamato*'s officers and men indulged in a night of drinking. The men quaffed ceremonial sake, and the officers broke out

scotch looted four years earlier from the British at Singapore. There were many toasts. The ship's cooks served delicacies such as sekihan, a red bean paste; akashiratsuki; sea bream; and extra rations that had been saved for emergencies.[49]

As the *Yamato* "Surface Special Attack Force" under Admiral Itō glided over the Inland Sea on the mild, sunny morning of April 6, the crewmen could see cherry trees in bloom along the shore. Leading the column was the cruiser *Yahagi*, followed by destroyers *Isokaze*, *Hamakaze*, *Yukikaze*, and *Fuyutsuki*; battleship *Yamato*; and destroyers *Suzutsuki*, *Asashimo*, *Kasumi*, and *Hasushimo*.

A message from the Combined Fleet's commander was read to all hands: "The fate of the empire today rests on this one action," it said, echoing Admiral Heihachirō Tōgō's exhortation before Japan's major victory over the Russian fleet at Tsushima Strait in 1905. The message raised spirits, and crewmen bowed in the direction of the emperor, sang the national anthem, and shouted "banzai!" three times.[50]

DURING THE NIGHT OF APRIL 6–7, the task force passed out of the Inland Sea through Bungo Strait. The strait was a favorite hunting ground for American submarines, which had sunk thousands of tons of Japanese shipping there.

At 2:45 a.m. on April 7, the US submarines *Hackleback* and *Threadin* picked up the task force on radar off the southeast coast of Kyushu. The Japanese ships turned west, skirting southern Kyushu, evidently with the idea of giving Mitscher's task force a wide berth and attacking Okinawa that evening.[51]

Hackleback's contact message to the US Fifth Fleet resulted in Admiral Raymond Spruance being awakened on the battleship *New Mexico*. After examining a map displaying the relative positions of Itō's and Spruance's task forces, the lean-faced, taciturn admiral instructed his radioman to direct Admiral Marc Mitscher and his Fast Carrier Task Force, TF-58, to handle the situation for the moment. Spruance then returned to bed and slept for a few hours more.[52]

At dawn, Mitscher's carriers launched search aircraft to locate the approaching enemy task force. Mitscher was a gaunt man who, like Spruance, weighed little more than 100 pounds. "Bald Eagle," as he was code named, smoked up to two packs of cigarettes a day while perched in his tall swivel chair on the bridge, facing aft to keep the wind out of his face.

The admiral had become ill overnight, having possibly suffered a minor heart attack, and his chief of staff, Commodore Arleigh Burke, had taken over for Mitscher on the flagship *Lexington*. Burke was a renowned destroyer commander that the Navy had paired with the aviator Mitscher to command the fast carriers; both officers initially bridled at the arrangement, but they later warmed to each other.

Burke ordered TF-58's four task groups to assemble northeast of Okinawa, holding his strike planes until search results were in. Later in the day, Mitscher, although pale and weak, returned to the "flag plot" and resumed command.[53]

As the rest of the Fifth Fleet began to gather north of Okinawa, Admiral Mort Deyo's six-battleship TF-54 formed a battle line to block Japanese ships from reaching the Iceberg anchorage. Deyo and the "black shoe" ship commanders—whose footwear set them apart from Mitscher's "brown shoe" naval aviators—yearned to meet the Japanese task force on the high seas, realizing that this might be one of their last chances to engage enemy ships in an important surface battle.

The fast carrier squadrons had been assigned the job of warding off the Kikusui No. 1 air attacks, which continued on April 7, but on a smaller scale than the previous day. Yet, TF-58's sailors and pilots were as eager as Deyo's to claim the prize and were counting on the search planes to reveal the enemy task force's position so that Mitscher's air squadrons could have a crack at it.

At 8:23 a.m., a TF-58 search plane spotted the *Yamato* group southwest of Kyushu, on a westward course. The report said that *Yamato* was screened by destroyers and in the center of a diamond-shaped formation that was zigzagging at 24 knots. The destroyer *Asashimo* had fallen behind with engine trouble.

"We hope you will bring back a nice fish for breakfast," Deyo's immediate superior, Admiral Richmond Kelly Turner, had cheerily written to Deyo. The battleship group commander had just begun to compose a reply, "Many thanks, will try to . . ." when a message reporting the enemy task force sighting came in, and Deyo finished his response with the words, "if the pelicans haven't caught them all."[54]

TF-58 sent up sixteen fighters at 9:15 a.m. to continue tracking the enemy task force. Around 10 a.m., twelve US carriers began launching 386 Hellcats, Corsairs, Helldivers, and Avenger torpedo bombers from 240 miles away from the *Yamato*'s last reported position.[55]

TF-58's commanders tensely awaited the news that their warplanes had reached their target. It came just after noon. Lookouts on the *Yamato* spotted the American attack planes at 12:32 p.m.

Indeed, the pelicans had caught the fish.[56]

Sinking the Battleship *Yamato*

A veritable circle of fire closes in on us: from above, from all points of the compass, glistening.

—ENSIGN MITSURU YOSHIDA, DESCRIBING THE MASSIVE
US AIR ATTACKS ON THE SUPERBATTLESHIP *YAMATO*[1]

Laffey circled madly like a wounded fish, black smoke coiling above her like trailing viscera.

—LIEUTENANT FRANK MANSON, AFTER KAMIKAZES HAD
BOMBED AND CRASHED THE DESTROYER, JAMMING HER RUDDER[2]

ABOVE THE *YAMATO* **TASK FORCE,** American pilots encountered a 3,000-foot cloud ceiling with rain squalls all around. "Our training instructions, to dive steeply from 10,000 feet or higher, proved useless," wrote Lieutenant Thaddeus T. Coleman, a Fast Carrier Force pilot. Moreover, the chaotic arrival of the four carrier groups' strike planes and their lack of coordination produced what Coleman described as the "most confusing sea-air battle of all time."

"Bomber pilots pushed over in all sorts of crazy dives, fighter pilots used every maneuver in the book, torpedo pilots stuck their necks all the way out, dropped right down on the surface and delivered their parcels so near the ships that many of them [the bombers] missed the ships' superstructures by inches," said Coleman. So many carrier planes crowded the skies around *Yamato* that they got in one another's way.[3]

But the low clouds also provided concealment for the attackers until they were ready to pounce, while their prey was clearly visible.

Captain Tameichi Hara, in charge of *Yamato*'s destroyer screen, was just as frustrated as Coleman. "All our practice and training—with homing torpedoes, proximity fuses, and radar-controlled gunfire—had been of no use in this day's action against hundreds of planes. Everything we did seemed to be wrong. This very operation itself, without aerial protection of any kind for the ships, was a grotesque mistake."[4]

The task force's token air support had turned back, and the superbattleship, which normally carried six Zero seaplanes, had left five of them at Kure; the sixth was catapulted earlier in the morning and sent back to base, as were the last two seaplanes remaining on *Yahagi*. "In accordance with operational orders, the sky above the task force holds no friendly aircraft to defend us," wrote Ensign Mitsuru Yoshida.[5]

Lieutenant Francis Ferry, a VB-82 dive-bomber pilot, thought it "strange" to find no planes defending the enemy task force. "There was no Japanese air cover for the Japanese fleet."[6]

Nine minutes after arriving over the *Yamato* task force, the first of four waves of US carrier planes struck. "When you start to dive the world seems very small," said Navy pilot Edward Sieber. Two bombs struck *Yamato*, one of them planted on *Yamato*'s forward turret by Second Lieutenant Kenneth Huntington, flying from the carrier *Bennington* with VMF-112. Four minutes later, a torpedo plowed into the superbattleship.

Lieutenant Ferry was one of the three dive-bombers in his eleven-plane group who was able to make a run on *Yamato*. He released all of his rockets and bombs at once at 300 to 500 feet. *Yamato* gunners were "shooting everything they had at us," except the massive, 18-inch guns, which could not aim low enough to hit them. "I think it was probably the most difficult flight that I ever had."

Hamakaze, one of *Yamato*'s destroyer escorts, was hit simultaneously by a bomb and a torpedo and sank a minute later, bow first. Also sent to the bottom was *Asashimo*, which had lagged 5 miles behind the rest of the task force because of engine problems. After being strafed and bombed, *Asashimo* was hit by two torpedoes, one of them exploding in the engine room. She quickly sank and, while going down, was wracked by another explosion underwater that blew her to pieces. All 326 crewmen died.

The destroyers violently corkscrewed and zigzagged to avoid the attackers as bombs exploded on the ships and burst around them. "The spectacle was at once thrilling and terrifying," said Hara.

Twelve minutes into the one-sided battle, three American bombs and two torpedoes left Hara's flagship *Yahagi* dead in the water. More bombs and another torpedo hit *Yahagi*, and the carrier planes kept coming. Hara's crew dumped *Yahagi*'s torpedoes so they wouldn't explode and add to the destruction. "A few guns barked as their burned and blood-soaked crews still manned their posts," he said. "My proud cruiser was but a mass of junk, barely afloat."[7]

Then came the second wave of American carrier planes. Within minutes the water was foaming with up to twenty torpedoes. Three struck *Yamato*'s port side.

"A veritable circle of fire closes in on us: from above, from all points of the compass, glistening," wrote Ensign Yoshida. "An avalanche" of planes descended on the Japanese task force, "swooping about like swallows" and difficult to hit because they changed directions so quickly. Five more torpedoes hit the port side, and bombs rained down on the battleship's gun turrets. "One after another, turrets fly up in the air," Yoshida wrote, leaving "a scene of carnage" and staggering casualties.[8]

Besides fighting back with its antiaircraft and 5-inch turret guns, *Yamato* tried to bring down her attackers with her massive 18-inch guns, firing incendiary shells that exploded in cones of shrapnel. However, the big guns were not designed for fast firing and were only marginally effective.[9]

Two more torpedoes slammed into *Yamato*'s port side from a third wave of attackers, whose bombs hit near the funnel. Starboard flooding was ordered to correct *Yoshida*'s alarming list to port, but the tactic succeeded only in drowning several hundred sailors belowdecks.[10]

More than 150 planes piled in during a fourth wave of attacks that desolated the battleship's immaculate unbroken topside deck, struck by at least ten more bombs. From the bridge, Ensign Yoshida watched the American planes coming straight at him, machine guns winking. Sailors and officers fell around and on top of him; their bodies protected Yoshida from bullets and flying shrapnel. Torpedo bombers carved out several more belowwaterline holes, and *Yamato*'s list increased.[11]

Lieutenant Bill Delaney was completing a low-altitude attack in his Avenger torpedo bomber when an explosion on *Yamato* set his plane on fire. Delaney bailed out and climbed into his yellow life raft; his two crewmates struggled with their parachutes and drowned.

Two Martin PBM Mariners—the big "flying boats" nicknamed "Dumbos" for the Disney flying elephant—spotted Delaney. While one of them

distracted a nearby Japanese destroyer, the other made a water landing. Delaney dove off the raft and swam to the flying boat. Crewmen snagged Delaney with a boat hook, and the Dumbo flew him to Yontan Airfield on Okinawa.[12]

Lieutenant Commander Herb Houck, leader of *Yorktown*'s strike group, led twenty Hellcats in a strafing run on *Yamato* to distract the battleship's gunners from the torpedo bombers in their train. He saved his 500-pound bomb for another target—and found it in the *Isokaze*, hitting it amidships. The destroyer sank minutes later.

Houck then swooped down on and strafed survivors in the water, and the other Hellcats followed suit.[13]

Throughout the debacle, Admiral Itō, who had forcefully opposed "Operation Ten-ichi-gō," sat silently in his bridge chair, arms folded as if silently protesting the squandering of his task force, while everyone around him was killed or wounded by machine-gun fire.[14]

When the fifth wave of attackers approached at 2 p.m., *Yamato* was dead in the water. Its antiaircraft and secondary guns were silent; only a handful of machine guns remained in action.

With *Yamato* doomed and swarms of US warplanes annihilating her task force, Itō countermanded his orders and canceled the entire operation. He directed the six surviving escort ships to return to port after rescuing whomever they could. The order came too late for Hara's light cruiser *Yahagi*. A dozen bombs and seven torpedoes sent it to the bottom at 2:05 p.m. Clinging to a log in the oily water, Hara saw "scores of planes swarming about [*Yamato*] like gnats."

After giving the order to abort the mission, Itō rose from his chair, saluted his chief of staff, shook hands with his few surviving staff officers, and retired to his cabin, where he shot himself.[15]

Admiral Aruga Kōsaku, *Yamato*'s captain and nicknamed "Gorilla" because of his size and bald head, lashed himself to a binnacle on the bridge and, eating a biscuit given to him by one of the lookouts, went down with his ship when it rolled over and sank at 2:23 p.m., about 180 miles southwest of Kyushu.

As the behemoth took the plunge, there was a deep, thunderous explosion as battery shells stored belowdeck detonated, followed by a bright flash of light and a 6,000-foot pillar of fire that resembled a volcanic eruption. It could be seen 200 miles away. A shower of debris and shrapnel killed scores of men in the water. Smoke rose in a 4-mile-high mushroom

cloud visible in Kyushu. *Yamato* broke in two and went to her saltwater grave 1,200 feet below.[16]

The superbattleship's massive oil slick attracted American pilots, who strafed the survivors in the water for twenty minutes, killing many of them. They scrambled for places in scarce lifeboats, so overloaded they were in danger of sinking; coxswains and petty officers kicked away men trying to board, or hacked off their hands with swords to keep the boats afloat—"a scene of living hell," wrote Ensign Yoshida.

After the warplanes left, sailors from the destroyer *Fuyutsuki* attempted to pluck *Yamato* crewmen from the water; a few hundred were picked up, many of them badly wounded and dying. Taken to the destroyer's sick bay with a head wound, Ensign Yoshida said the dispensary reeked of blood. "In one corner of the room a great mound of corpses reaches up to the ceiling," Yoshida wrote.[17]

Subaltern Sakae Kogomo had slid down the side of *Yamato* into the water with his air-raid repair team. They made a raft with salvaged lumber and were rescued by *Yukikaze*. Kogomo offered a cigarette to a badly wounded crewman, "but he could not take it. He was completely armless and legless." The mangled sailor died on the *Yukikaze*.[18]

The 2nd Fleet was decimated. The task force had lost six of its ten ships and a total of 3,665 men in what would prove to be the last major sea-air battle of World War II. Fewer than 300 *Yamato* crewmen survived from a ship's company of 3,332.

During the lopsided battle, Japanese antiaircraft fire brought down just ten American planes, with twelve crewmen lost.

One of the surviving Japanese destroyers, *Suzutsuki*, had to sail backward to Kyushu because her bow had been destroyed.[19]

"Now the naval tradition only lives in spirit, having no ships at hand. What shall we do?" wrote Admiral Ugaki, commander of the 5th Air Fleet.[20]

While struggling to stay afloat after *Yahagi* went down, Captain Hara heard voices lifted in song; Japanese sailors were singing "Song of the Warrior," over and over to steel themselves for death: "*If I go to sea/I shall return a corpse awash . . .*"[21]

ADMIRAL ISOROKU YAMAMOTO, THE LATE Combined Fleet commander, had gotten it right years earlier when he had pronounced the battleship era finished, eclipsed by the rise of carrier-based air-strike forces. A dozen or so torpedo strikes had doomed *Yamato*. Yamamoto had

memorably written, "The fiercest serpent can be overcome by a swarm of ants." No new ships of the line were built after World War II.[22]

The day after the annihilation of the *Yamato* task force, Admiral Turner sent a jubilant message to Admiral Chester Nimitz: "I may be crazy but it looks like the Japs have quit the war, at least in this section."

Nimitz drily replied, "Delete all after 'crazy.'"[23]

ON APRIL 12, AFTER TWO days of weather-related cancelations, Kikusui No. 2 was finally airborne. Three hundred eighty Japanese warplanes, 185 of them kamikazes, hoped to wreak havoc on the US Fifth Fleet's carriers, battleships, and transports.[24]

The day before the mass attack, Japanese suicide pilots, flying in small groups and individually, had struck American capital ships. A Zero crashed the deck of the battleship *Missouri*, causing minor damage and no deaths—except that of the pilot, whose body was recovered from the wreckage and buried at sea in a funeral service performed by a Navy chaplain, angering many sailors. On the same day, two Judy dive-bombers plunged into the *Enterprise*, just returned to the fleet from the Ulithi repair depot. While the damage was minor, it sidelined *Enterprise* for another ten days.[25]

As they had during Kikusui No. 1 on April 6–7, CAPs and radar picket ships would absorb the brunt of Kikusui No. 2. Some Japanese pilots might have thought it was strategically smart to knock out the US fleet's eyes and ears. But it is far more likely that inexperienced kamikaze pilots who did not know a destroyer from a battleship saw the picket ships as convenient targets.

The attacks followed the same template as Kikusui No. 1, with conventional warplanes flying cover as the kamikaze pilots avoided dogfights to focus on crashing ships.

Carrier warplanes and thirty-one Corsairs from Okinawa airfields shot down most of the enemy attackers, with one estimate of Japanese losses totaling 330 aircraft.

Of course, some of the attackers slipped through the air shield. Although American ship losses were lighter than during Kikusui No. 1, kamikazes still inflicted considerable damage—on the carrier *Essex*; battleships *Tennessee*, *New Mexico*, and *Idaho*; light cruiser *Oakland*; and ten destroyers, three destroyer escorts, three minesweepers, two gunboats, and a landing ship. Hundreds of American sailors died, ninety-three of them when kamikazes crashed the minelayer *Lindsay* and destroyer *Whitehurst*.[26]

Kikusui No. 2 sent two US ships to the bottom—the gunboat *LCS(L)-33*, hit by a "Val" dive-bomber while at Radar Picket Station No. 1, and the destroyer *Mannert L. Abele.*

On the *Tennessee*, Lieutenant Charles Burrows watched a smoke-billowing kamikaze dive on his ship, missing his gun director by a hair's breadth. "I felt the wind of it," he said. The plane sped by the bridge and beneath the starboard yardarm, smashed into two 40mm mounts and several 20mm guns, and finally crashed on the quarterdeck.

"To the uninvolved observer . . . it is like sitting in the middle of a railroad track and watching the locomotive come at 200 miles per hour. You're certain it's curtains," said Burrows.

Marine Corporal W. H. Putnam was blown overboard. He surfaced near a life raft and climbed in—next to the headless torso of the kamikaze pilot.[27]

Japanese pilots routinely exaggerated the damage that their mass attacks wreaked on the American fleet. After Kikusui No. 2 on April 12, they claimed to have sunk one carrier, two cruisers, and two unidentified vessels, and to have set a battleship on fire. "The United States Navy's losses were extremely heavy, so if it continues like this it will result in a tragic end within two weeks," predicted Admiral Ugaki.

Ugaki later became skeptical of his pilots' reports after doing the arithmetic. "There can't be so many undamaged carriers still operating, even if they were decoys," he wrote. "Every day we try to finish the enemy task force, and yet they can't be finished." After months of being weighed down by guilt over sending so many young men to their deaths, in April Ugaki resolved to one day follow their example. "I was glad to see that my weak mind, apt to be moved to tears, had reached this stage."[28]

In retaliation for the April 12 attack, Admiral Spruance moved TF-58 north and sent hundreds of carrier planes on missions against Japanese air bases on southern Kyushu.[29]

DURING KIKUSUI NO. 2, THE *Mannert L. Abele* became the first US ship sunk by a Japanese Ohka attack aircraft. Before the Ohka hit the destroyer, a Zero plunged into her engine room, where its 500-pound bomb exploded, leaving the ship dead in the water. A short time later, the Ohka, or "cherry blossom"—a one-seat, manned suicide craft propelled by three rockets and armed with a 2,600-pound warhead—slammed into the destroyer at high speed. The massive explosion broke her keel, and she sank minutes later, claiming the lives of seventy-nine sailors. Two enemy planes then strafed

and bombed the survivors in the water, a bomb landing close enough, said, Ensign David Adair, "to lift me out of the water. I heard several around me scream from pain caused by the blast." The men chased away approaching sharks by splashing the water with their feet.

It was the first time that the Japanese had deployed their new, top-secret weapon in combat. Twin-engine "Betty" bombers carried eight of them into Kikusui No. 2. The Ohka pilots rode inside their bombers while approaching the target, and then climbed through the bomb bay into the Ohka's small wooden cockpit, where they pulled a release handle to break free.

Shooting across the sky at speeds of up to 600mph, Ohkas were rarely seen in flight, and were practically impossible to hit when they were spotted. Lieutenant Hamilton McWhorter III happened to glimpse one from his Hellcat, describing it as "a small dark shape streaking downward at very high speed."

Besides the one that sank *Mannert L. Abele*, another pierced the hull of the destroyer *Stanley* at Picket Station No. 2, but did not explode until it had exited the other side. Two other destroyers had close calls, but were not hit. Gunner's Mate 3/c Hank Kalinofsky said the one that missed his zigzagging destroyer escort looked like "a fighter plane loaded with dynamite, with wings. The fellow sat there with a sort of joy stick driving that thing down."[30]

Before the Okinawa campaign, the Japanese manufactured 750 Ohkas—derisively nicknamed "*bakas*," or "fools," by the Americans. Six hundred volunteers recruited from Japanese naval units beginning in August 1944 became members of the new Ohka unit, the 721st Naval Air Corps, known as the "Thunderbolt Corps."

The bulky Ohkas, 19 feet long with a 16-foot wingspan, dramatically slowed a Betty's air speed from its usual 265mph to 184mph, making the bomber relatively easy to shoot down—the fate of most of the Betty hosts and their payloads.[31]

During an attack by forty-eight warplanes on Admiral Mitscher's carrier force off Kyushu on March 21, sixteen Bettys carried Ohkas into combat with a fifty-five-fighter escort, but fifty American warplanes intercepted and destroyed all of them about 60 miles from their targets. Some jettisoned their Ohkas before they went down, but none hit American ships.[32]

On L-Day, Marines discovered fifteen Ohkas hidden in the bushes near the Hagushi beaches. They were photographed and carefully examined because nothing like them had been seen before in the Pacific theater.[33]

THE *KIKUSUIS* OF APRIL 6–7 and April 12 had given American pilots and "tin can" sailors at Okinawa a harrowing introduction to Japanese kamikaze warfare. Crewmen on the radar picket destroyers nicknamed the area between Kyushu and Okinawa "kamikaze alley" and patrolled it with mingled fear and defiance.[34]

However, advances in firefighting technology and new methods of training crewmen were enabling more ships than before to survive catastrophic damage from bombs and crashed planes. Innovations in firefighting equipment included the "fog nozzle," which issued a fine spray that extinguished fires quicker than a stream of water; fire-smothering foam; portable gas-powered "hand billy" water pumps, needed when a ship's electrical system failed; and breathing apparatus, cutting torches, and standard-size hoses and couplings. The Navy was generous in supplying its ships with the latest damage-control tools.

Navy Lieutenant Harold Burke, former deputy chief of the New York Fire Department, was credited with introducing a new philosophy for training firefighter crewmen: "get the fear of the fire out of the sailor." By 1943, Burke had trained 260 firefighting instructors, who in turn imparted Burke's lessons to thousands of men at Navy schools across the country.[35]

LIEUTENANT HAMILTON MCWHORTER III WAS sitting in the cockpit of his Hellcat on the carrier *Randolph*'s flight deck on Friday, April 13, when over the ship's loudspeaker came news of President Franklin Roosevelt's death: "Attention, all hands. President Roosevelt has died. I say again, President Roosevelt has died. Our Supreme Commander is dead."

The announcement was met by shock and silence. For many young sailors, Roosevelt had been their president since they were in grade school. On the attack transport *Montrose*, Boatswain E. F. Stuckey said, "Few of us spoke, or even looked at each other. We drifted apart, seeming instinctively to seek solitude. Many prayed, and many shed tears."

That same day, April 13, the Navy ended its news blackout on Japanese kamikaze attacks. The embargo had been in place since late 1944, when Special Attack Squadrons first went into action in the Philippines. Navy censors in the Pacific expurgated news reports about the attacks, and editors and publishers in the United States were asked to observe the blackout—ostensibly so that the Japanese could not assess the kamikazes' effectiveness. The British Admiralty believed that the censorship went too far.

But now, with the advent of the *kikusuis* and the Japanese media wildly inflating US losses, the Navy had decided to lift its veil of silence. Its first official statement on the subject April 13 said, "While the scale of suicide attacks increases, effectiveness is diminishing daily." Admiral Chester Nimitz, commander-in-chief of Pacific forces, added that the attacks had had "negligible success" and would not stop the United States from winning the Pacific war.[36]

In actuality, the onslaught was sapping the morale of picket-ship officers and men. Commander Frank Johnson of the destroyer *Purdy*, where thirteen men were killed and fifty-eight were wounded when it was crashed at Radar Picket Station No. 1 on April 12, was pessimistic. "The prospects of a long and illustrious career for a destroyer assigned to radar picket station duty is below average expectancy," he wrote. "That duty is extremely hazardous, very tiring, and entirely unenjoyable."[37]

Bert Cooper, a Navy corpsman who helped treat burn victims in an Okinawa hospital, said one patient was the sole survivor from a gun tub hit by a kamikaze, and "the only thing pink you could see was where his lips were . . . he was just covered with black burns all over." The dying gunner summoned Cooper to his stretcher. "Doc," he said, "I'm an orphan. Who is going to remember me?" Cooper replied, "I'll remember you. I'm going to remember you every day of my life." Cooper had made the same promise to a dying Marine gunnery sergeant. After the war, every night when he went to bed Cooper asked himself if he had remembered "the Sarge and the Gunner's Mate" that day. Usually he had, but if he had not, "I would go to sleep saying, 'I thought of you guys.'"[38]

THE USS *LAFFEY* SAILED FROM Kerama Retto and relieved destroyer minelayer *J. William Ditter* at Radar Picket Station No. 1, 50 miles north of the Hagushi beaches, during the afternoon of April 14. *Laffey*'s crew was fully aware of what this meant. Quartermaster Ari Phoutrides informed his brother in a letter that they were at "the hottest station of them all." Of all the pitched battles between picket ships and kamikazes, the coming ordeal of the *Laffey* would be the most memorable of them all.[39]

The destroyer's crewmen were experienced combat veterans. *Laffey* had served at Utah Beach on D-Day, battled kamikazes in the Philippines the previous fall, and had recently been at Iwo Jima. Commander Frederick Julian Becton reassured his men that they possessed the requisite skills for thwarting suicide planes—gunnery and maneuverability—and that "they are going to go down, but we aren't."[40]

April 15 passed quietly at Station No. 1, but *Laffey*'s crew was on edge. During the night, enemy planes flew just outside the range of *Laffey*'s 5-inch guns, forcing the sailors to repeatedly go to general quarters. They could not help but feel that they were being sized up for an attack.[41]

At dawn April 16, after bad weather had delayed its scheduled start the previous day, Kikusui No. 3 commenced beneath sunny skies. About 165 kamikazes and more than 300 conventional attack and escort planes lifted off from airfields at Kyushu, Tokunoshima, and Taiwan to assault ships off Okinawa and airfields on the island. Kamikaze pilots planned to swarm American warships to distract their gunners so that they could score more hits.[42]

Laffey's combat air patrol arrived around dawn: three divisions from VF-10, the "Grim Reapers" from the carrier *Intrepid*. The CAP was immediately diverted to the north to meet the incoming waves of Japanese aircraft. After the CAP had departed, a Zero crashed *Intrepid*'s after deck, and its bomb penetrated to the hangar deck, where it exploded and burned forty planes. Nine sailors died. Three hours later, after repairs were made, *Intrepid* began landing planes.[43]

Consequently, *Laffey* was without fighter protection when fifty bogeys appeared on her radar screen. Recognizing the destroyer's vulnerability, the Japanese pounced.

Beginning at 8:27 a.m. and for the next eighty minutes, *Laffey* was subjected to sustained attacks by twenty-two kamikazes. "Planes approached from all directions and all elevations," wrote Commander Becton.

"Everywhere you turned, you could see them coming in," said Torpedo's Mate 2/c Fred Gemmell. "All our guns were blazing as fast as they could do."[44]

Laffey's gunners shot down the first eight attackers, but then four Val dive-bombers bore in. Two attacked from the port side and two from starboard. "You know he's [the kamikaze pilot] going to die—you pray he won't take you with him," said Lieutenant Frank Manson.

Two of the attackers crashed *Laffey*, one after dropping a bomb that damaged the starboard side. The landing gear of a third Val snagged on some gun mounts, and it spewed burning gasoline across the deck before going overboard and exploding. The fourth Val dropped a bomb that pierced the deck and exploded in a 20mm ammunition magazine. The explosion knocked out *Laffey*'s radar and jammed the rudder; she began sailing in circles.

"*Laffey* circled madly like a wounded fish, black smoke coiling above her like trailing viscera," said Lieutenant Manson.[45]

Wounded and dead men were sprawled all over the fantail. One man had been burned to a crisp with his hands covering his face. A 20mm gunner was still alive, but his legs were gone. He died while begging to be freed from his gun straps.[46]

Then, two planes crashed the aft deckhouse seconds apart, killing several men and igniting new fires.

Forty-five minutes into the ordeal, FM-2 Wildcats and Corsairs from the *Intrepid* appeared on the scene. Counting at least twenty Japanese planes hovering predatorily over *Laffey* while waiting their turn to crash-dive the destroyer, the Grim Reapers swooped down on the attackers.

Ensign Alfred Lerch shot down seven; Lieutenant Commander Wally Clarke and his wingman, Ensign Jack Ehrhard, splashed three. By day's end, the Grim Reapers claimed thirty-three kills while defending *Laffey*.[47]

Two of the last eight attackers dropped bombs on the fantail and the forward 20mm gun mount before being shot down. The other six were destroyed before they could cause major damage.

After the twenty-second attacker was splashed, twenty-four Wildcats and Corsairs circled overhead, shielding *Laffey* from further harm, as surface craft raced to her aid.

The sight of *Laffey*'s shredded, debris-strewn after deck shocked nineteen-year-old Seaman Andrew Martinis. It was "almost like shipyard workers were still working on her." Worse were the pieces of bodies scattered everywhere, even in the gun mounts.

Her rudder was jammed, she was down by the stern, and she had just four 20mm guns still operable, yet *Laffey* had miraculously survived being crashed six times and bombed four times. Moreover, her gunners had shot down nine kamikazes. Thirty-two crewmen had been killed; seventy-two were wounded.[48]

Towed to Hagushi Beach for initial repairs, *Laffey* would sail under her own power to Saipan, Pearl Harbor, and the Seattle shipyards for more extensive refitting.

An Army truck transported the dead *Laffey* crewmen to the 6th Marine Division cemetery overlooking the Hagushi beachhead. A chaplain conducted a graveside rite for the dead sailors, and their bodies joined hundreds of others that lay under shrouds in four long columns, awaiting interment.[49]

DURING *LAFFEY*'S ORDEAL AT PICKET Station No. 1, the destroyer *Pringle*, her counterpart 40 miles to the west at Picket Station No. 14, was

also under attack. It didn't last long. At 9:10 a.m., a Val struck the base of *Pringle*'s No. 1 stack, and the plane's 1,000-pound bomb exploded in the fire room, breaking the destroyer's keel. *Pringle* sank five minutes later.

Pringle Sonarman 1/c Jack Gebhardt, heeding the order to "abandon ship," dove into the water and saw his broken ship's bow and stern pointed sharply upward. Japanese planes strafed survivors in the water, and sharks were drawn to the scene, but gunners on nearby ships drove off both. Sixty-five sailors died, and 110 were wounded.[50]

At 9:50 a.m., minesweeper *Harding* was sailing from her anti-submarine screening station to aid *Pringle*'s survivors when two Vals attacked her on opposite beams; one crashed alongside her, and the other struck the bow near the No. 1 and No. 2 guns and exploded, flooding the forward engine room. *Harding* limped to Kerama Retto under her own power, having lost twenty-two men, killed or missing.

The destroyer *Bryant*, dispatched from Radar Picket Station No. 2 to aid *Laffey*, was attacked by three Zeros around 9 a.m. The combat air patrol splashed two of them, but the third Zero, smoking heavily, plowed into *Bryant*'s port side beneath the bridge, and its bomb exploded. The bridge was engulfed in flames, and communications to the rest of the ship was lost. After firefighters extinguished the fires, *Bryant* headed for Kerama Retto for repairs. Thirty-four crewmen had died, and thirty-three were wounded.

In addition to *Laffey*, *Intrepid*, and *Harding*, eight other ships were damaged on April 16 during Kikusui No. 3. *Pringle* was the only ship sunk.[51]

US pilots reported shooting down 270 Japanese planes. Nearly all of the participating Japanese Army Special Attack planes were destroyed. Replacement planes would have to be sent to Kyushu from Japan's northern bases.

Between the *kikusuis*, smaller groups of kamikazes and individual pilots continued to target American ships.

On April 22, a Val slammed into *LCS(L)-15*, its bomb exploded, and the gunboat went down in three minutes, taking fifteen crewmen with her. Radioman 3/c Harold Kaup was in the radio room when he heard the explosion. He jumped overboard, clinging to a potato locker as his ship sank stern-first.

On the same day, a kamikaze crashed the destroyer *Isherwood* while she was on anti-submarine patrol, and ignited her depth charges. Forty-two crewmen died in the explosions and fires.[52]

But in the skies above the Fifth Fleet on April 22, seven "Death Rattlers" from VMF-323 enjoyed an epic day, shooting down twenty-five low-flying

Val dive-bombers in twenty-five minutes. Lieutenant Jerry O'Keefe of VMF-323 got five of them, including one that turned toward him head-on, flames licking the fuselage. O'Keefe kept firing until they were 50 feet apart and the Val rolled away, crashed into the sea, and exploded. "It was one of the most exhilarating, brief moments of my life," he said. Major George Axtell also destroyed five Vals, and Major Jeff Dorroh got six.[53]

That day too, Lieutenant John Leaper of VMF-314 had expended all of his ammunition in shooting down two Betty bombers—one carrying an Ohka—when a Zero attacked Leaper's wingman. Determined to take down the enemy plane even with his ammunition gone, Leaper attempted to saw off the Zero's tail with his propeller, but failed. Leaper tried a new approach, maneuvering his Corsair above the Zero and then crashing down on top of it.

His propeller sawed into the front of the Zero's cockpit. The radical maneuver worked, and the Zero went down, just as Leaper's right auxiliary tank exploded, ripping off his right wing. His plane began spinning violently, and Leaper bailed out. His chute split top to bottom when it opened and broke two shroud lines. Then, to avoid a Zero that was diving on him, Leaper jerked on one of the intact shroud lines and his chute collapsed.

He dropped like a rock for 4,000 feet until he managed to reopen the chute. Leaper floated to the water, where a destroyer picked him up an hour and a half later.[54]

ALTHOUGH HIS WARPLANE LOSSES WERE mounting steadily, they did not dissuade Admiral Ugaki from launching another mass suicide attack. Kikusui No. 4 commenced on April 27–28, with 115 Army and Navy kamikazes—one-third the kamikazes of Kikusui No. 1—plus hundreds of conventional warplanes.[55]

The attacks damaged nine ships and sank *Canada Victory*, a converted merchant ship that was delivering ammunition to the Hagushi beachhead. She reported twelve killed and seventeen wounded. A kamikaze crashed the transport evacuation ship *Pinckney* amidships, incinerating the hospital ward in a horrific fire that killed thirty-five patients and crewmen.[56]

At 8:41 p.m. on April 28, a lone kamikaze crashed the hospital ship *Comfort* as she was transporting wounded men from Okinawa to Guam. *Comfort*, one of the six hospital ships assigned to Iceberg, was fully illuminated, as required by Geneva Convention rules. The suicide pilot flew over *Comfort* almost casually at a low altitude, as though deciding where

to strike her. He circled and dived, smashing into the superstructure. The explosion wiped out the surgery, killing thirty Army nurses, patients, and sailors. Wounded were forty-eight soldiers, sailors, nurses, and patients.[57]

ALTHOUGH JAPANESE PILOTS SEEMINGLY POSED the gravest danger to CAP pilots, it was not always the case. Friendly fire from US ships was often a greater threat. An Air Defense Command report stated, "Our own antiaircraft batteries . . . continually fired on our own planes when taking off and until they were out of range." Even when squadron and division commanders warned ship batteries that friendly planes were taking off, "they continued to fire." Next on the list of hazards was midair collision— with another American plane. They usually occurred when pilots pursuing the same Japanese plane did not see one another; the collision often destroyed both friendly aircraft.[58]

SINCE MARCH 25, MORE THAN half of Ugaki's 5th Air Fleet had been destroyed: an estimated 620 planes shot down or missing, and 80 more shot to pieces on the ground. When all Army and Navy air unit losses were tabulated, the total exceeded 1,000, of which at least 820 had been lost during Kikusui Nos. 1 through 4. Remaining under Ugaki's command were 620 aircraft—but just 370 of them operational.[59]

Ugaki had become discouraged. In his journal, he wrote, "From now on our strength doesn't permit us to carry out more than air guerrilla warfare in both name and reality. Now we have come to the stage that we have expected to reach for some time. We can't do anything at all, with little money remaining in our pocket when it's most needed."[60]

Nevertheless, he fully intended to continue battering the US Fifth Fleet with his air fleet.

Determined to destroy American warships and aircraft by whatever means, the Japanese sent water-borne suicide attackers against US ships in 18-foot boats armed with rockets and explosives; in manned torpedoes— *kaitens*—launched from submarines; and even as swimmers armed with hand grenades. Five suicide boats crashed into US ships, sinking one of them, *LCI(G)-82*, on April 4, with eight men killed. The suicide swimmers were least successful of all, usually detected in the water and killed before they could detonate their grenades next to a ship.[61]

The Japanese saw better results by launching nighttime suicide air raids on the Okinawa anchorage and Yontan and Kadena Airfields. Naval

officers called them "witches on broomsticks." Signalman 3/c Nick Flores of *LSM-120* watched a kamikaze suddenly appear over the Okinawa anchorage around midnight one night "out of nowhere, gliding in low with its engine cut off—like a giant bat." It smashed into a nearby landing ship before anyone could fire a shot, he said.[62]

At Kerama Retto, the Navy each night cloaked the inland basin anchorage with smoke, so that the Japanese pilots could not clearly see the anchored ships, seaplanes, and tenders. Ships with smoke generators were stationed in a line across the anchorage's windward side. During the daytime, antiaircraft guns and combat air patrols were effective in warding off air attacks.[63]

To thwart nighttime kamikaze attacks, land-based F6F-5N Hellcats from VMF(N)-543 began night patrols April 14 over Okinawa and the most vulnerable radar picket stations. Carrier-based night fighters soon joined them.

The night fighters were standard F6F-5s equipped with a 250-pound APS-6 radar; their pilots had twenty-nine weeks of additional training. When a ship's radar detected bogeys, the night fighters were vectored to the area and activated their onboard radar, whose 5-mile range enabled them to locate and shoot down the intruders. The night fighters largely counteracted the Japanese nighttime air attacks.[64]

THE ACCUMULATED AMERICAN SHIP LOSSES from *kikusui* raids alarmed Admiral Chester Nimitz. Kamikazes and conventional Japanese aircraft sank thirteen Allied ships and damaged more than 100 others in April. The Navy that month reported 956 men killed, 2,650 wounded, and 897 missing in action.[65]

So many damaged ships thronged Kerama Retto's emergency repair facilities that help was summoned from Ulithi. Captain A. I. McKee, Service Force Pacific's assistant fleet maintenance officer, and repair crews arrived in a 3,500-ton floating drydock towed by the fleet tug *Jicarilla*. Along with McKee came the repair ship *Nestor*, the tug *Molala*, four support landing craft, and two destroyers. McKee and his men remained at Kerama Retto for a month.[66]

In an attempt to curtail the mass attacks, Nimitz ordered General Curtis LeMay's XXI Bomber Command to refocus its raids on the airfields harboring kamikazes at Kyushu and Shikoku, instead of continuing to firebomb Japan's cities and industries. The most recent incendiary bombing had occurred April 14, when 327 B-29s attacked northwest Tokyo's

industrial district, killing 2,459 people and damaging the Imperial Palace and Meiji Shrine.[67]

LeMay protested Nimitz's order, but the Joint Chiefs of Staff upheld Nimitz. When Nimitz refused to release the B-29s for incendiary raids a week later, LeMay complained to the Army Air Force (AAF) commander, General Henry "Hap" Arnold, that Nimitz was hampering the war effort. Arnold took up the matter with Admiral Ernest King.

Known for his splenetic outbursts, King replied to Arnold that if the AAF would not support the Navy, then the Navy might just let the Army fend for itself on Okinawa. Nothing more was said about LeMay's complaint. From April 17 until May 11, XXI Bomber Command concentrated on crushing Ugaki's Ten-Go program, but the results were mixed.[68]

Grumbling acquiescence was sometimes the best possible outcome when the rival services' priorities collided and exposed old fault lines.

The Drive North and Ie Shima

It was mountain warfare of the most rugged sort. Infantry
combat was at very short ranges.

—6TH MARINE DIVISION DESCRIPTION OF THE
FIGHTING AT MOUNT YAE-TAKE ON THE MOTOBU PENINSULA[1]

It was the most remarkable thing I have ever seen. . . . I
saw troops go through enemy mortar concentrations and
machine gun fire that should have pinned them down. But
instead they poured across the field.

—DESCRIPTION OF THE 77TH DIVISION'S
ASSAULT ON IE SHIMA'S PINNACLE[2]

THE 6TH MARINE DIVISION WAS the only Marine division that was established overseas—and in 1946 it would be deactivated without ever entering the United States. Created in September 1944, it was organized around
the 1st Provisional Marine Brigade that had fought on Guam. Nearly half
of the men in its 4th, 22nd, and 29th Regiments were veterans of various
Pacific campaigns.

The 6th Division's commander, General Lemuel Shepherd, had led the
1st Provision Brigade and had participated earlier in the Cape Gloucester
campaign. As a young officer with the 5th Marines during World War I,
Shepherd was wounded twice at Belleau Wood, where his actions earned
him the Navy Cross.

The 4th Regiment was the division's best-known unit. During the 1920s and 1930s, it served in Shanghai and helped defend the international zone when Japanese troops invaded China. The regiment eventually withdrew to the Philippines, where in 1942 it suffered heavy casualties on Corregidor. After General Jonathan Wainwright surrendered US forces in the Philippines in May 1942, Japanese soldiers force-marched the survivors to prisoner-of-war camps. The 4th Marines disappeared from unit rosters.

On February 1, 1944, the regiment was officially reactivated, and the Marine Corps's four Raider battalions were assigned to fill its ranks. The Raiders' hit-and-run exploits of the early Pacific war under Colonels Merritt "Red Mike" Edson and Evan Carlson no longer had a place in the massive amphibious operations of 1944 and 1945. The 1st, 4th, and 3rd Raider Battalions were transformed into the 1st, 2nd, and 3rd Battalions of the 4th Marines. The 2nd Raider Battalion became the regimental weapons company.

The 4th Regiment's commander was the highly regarded Lieutenant Colonel Alan Shapley, who had led several Raider units. On December 7, 1941, Shapley saved a drowning man at Pearl Harbor after being blown off the *Arizona* while commanding the doomed battleship's Marine detachment. For that, he was awarded the Silver Star.[3]

WHILE XXIV CORPS WAS BATTERING General Ushijima's stout Machinato-Yonabaru line south of the Hagushi beaches, III Amphibious Corps's two Marine divisions had secured the island's midsection with little trouble.

The 6th Marine Division was now marching rapidly up the Ishikawa Isthmus into northern Okinawa. This was terra incognita for the Americans, who knew only that it was a ruggedly mountainous region with few inhabitants.

Just as XXIV Corps had pushed southward insensible to the presence of a large, well-armed Japanese force dug into the coral and clay hills there, so the 6th Division, too, was flying blind. Because of cloud cover and the northern island's dense pine forests, aerial reconnaissance had revealed little about enemy positions or strength.

The 6th Division advanced with such alacrity that it was a struggle for the artillerymen to keep up. Guarding its rear was the 1st Marine Division, which only five months earlier had suffered 6,336 casualties on Peleliu.

The 6th Division's 4th Regiment moved up the main road hugging the east coast, while the 29th Marines marched up the west coast in columns.

Japanese retreating from the landing beaches had sown mines, booby traps, and abatis to slow the Marines' advance, but the mines were shallowly buried and unprotected by enemy covering fire. Tank bulldozers easily toppled the abatis. The barriers barely slowed the division's progress.[4]

The 29th Marines seized the port of Nago, reduced to rubble by naval gunfire. It became the division's resupply portal, obviating the need for transshipments from the Hagushi beaches.

After initially believing that the Japanese had no fortifications in the north, General Shepherd changed his mind when civilians reported on April 7 that the enemy occupied strongholds in the Motobu Peninsula, a sparsely populated area that was as large as Saipan. Subsequent aerial reconnaissance revealed signs of fresh excavation in a cluster of hulking hills in the peninsula's southwest sector, overtopped by 1,200-foot Mount Yae-Take.[5]

III Amphibious Corps had tentatively planned for the 2nd Marine Division, a floating reserve off Okinawa, to make an amphibious landing on Motobu, while the 6th Division sealed the peninsula's base. But on April 9, the 2nd Division returned to Saipan, and the 6th Division became solely responsible for securing Motobu.[6]

Shepherd sent the 29th Marines' three battalions northward through the peninsula in separate columns while the 22nd and 4th Marines held the peninsula base. A war-dog platoon that accompanied the Marines was credited with alerting patrols to Japanese ambushes on many occasions.[7]

Motobu was described in the 6th Marine Division history as "a country in itself," consisting of pinewoods, coral ridges, and "impossible slopes" cultivated by hardy mountain farmers who were poorer than their southern Okinawa counterparts.

On April 10, the 29th's 2nd Battalion seized the port of Unten on the peninsula's northeast coast. There, the Marines discovered twenty-one pens for midget submarines, six wrecked midget subs, and an abandoned torpedo boat base. The 150-man naval garrison had fled into the interior.[8]

Before April 10 ended, all three battalions clashed with Japanese forces in the middle of the peninsula along the east-west road connecting Itomi to Toguchi on the western coast. The enemy put up a passive guerrilla defense, usually engaging only in the late afternoon, when it was too late for the Marines to send reinforcements. South of the road, rendered nearly impassable by roadblocks, mines, and booby traps, lay Mount Yae-Take, surrounded by ranks of smaller hills. The region was a chaotic jumble of cliffs, deep ravines, and caves connected by tunnels.

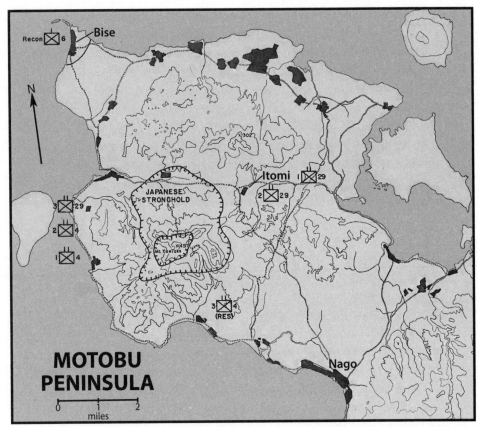

Map adapted from The History of the U.S. Marine Corps during World War II, Volume 5,
by Benis M. Frank and Henry I. Shaw, Jr. (Historical Branch, U.S. Marine Corps, 1968).
Original map by T.L. Russell.

The 6th Reconnaissance Company continued to march north, and on April 12, the division scouts, facing only light opposition, captured Bise Saki on the northern Motobu cape. Admiral Richmond Kelly Turner planned to build a radar station on the cape to ease pressure on the vulnerable picket ships.[9]

DURING THE NIGHT OF APRIL 10–11, the 29th's 1st Battalion, which had marched up the middle of the peninsula while the 3rd Battalion skirted the

west coast, fought off repeated counterattacks lasting until dawn. General Shepherd characterized it as a "particularly bitter fire fight," interspersed with hand-to-hand fighting.

As the Marines began tightening the noose around Mount Yae-Take, the fighting intensified in the nearly roadless wilderness. Company I of the 29th was ambushed April 12 by enemy troops firing mortars, artillery, and automatic weapons. The attack pinned down the Marines for two hours and inflicted nearly seventy casualties before the bloodied company was able to withdraw. Corporal Hubert Welch Sr. was blown off his feet by a mortar round that peppered his face and neck with shrapnel and left him with a concussion; the same round dismembered his best friend.[10]

The twenty-five hundred Japanese defenders who occupied the caves, tunnels, and pillboxes on Mount Yae-Take and an adjacent prominence belonged to the so-called Udo Force. Its nucleus was Colonel Takehido Udo's 2nd Infantry Unit of the 44th Independent Mixed Brigade. Udo Force was composed of two full infantry battalions; artillerists with 150mm and 75mm guns; naval gunners with a pair of 6.1-inch coastal guns; two units of Okinawan reservists and conscripts; and the naval troops from Unten. The Japanese had plentiful mortars and light and heavy machine guns, good radio and telephone communications from a telephone exchange in Udo's Mount Yae-Take command post, and horses to carry supplies up the mountain's steep slopes.[11]

All approaches to the 6-mile-by-8-mile area surrounding the prominence were mined and covered by enemy fire—the same situation faced by XXIV Corps in southern Okinawa, but in miniature. In its report, the 6th Marine Division characterized what ensued as "mountain warfare of the most rugged sort. Infantry combat was at very short ranges." The Marines neutralized enemy caves and pillboxes with flamethrowers and explosives. Tanks and trucks were useless in the vertical terrain, forcing Marines to hand-carry ammunition, water, and supplies to the front lines.

Sergeant William Manchester of the 29th Marines described it as "French and Indian warfare," in which survival depended on knowing "which ravines were swept by Nambu fire and how to avoid them."[12]

Plans were made on April 13 to attack Yae-Take the next day from two sides simultaneously. From the west, Colonel Shapley's 4th Marines and the 29th's 3rd Battalion would push eastward, while the 29th's two other battalions on the east side of Yae-Take drove westward.[13]

"**SHOOT-AND-RUN**" **TACTICS BY MOBILE** Japanese machine-gun squads stopped the two-battalion attack from the east on the Itomi-Toguchi Road on April 14. But in the west, the Marines advanced inland 1,200 yards and seized a 700-foot ridge that was an important stepping-stone to Yae-Take.

The Japanese used guerrilla tactics to unnerve the 4th and 29th Marines and kill their officers. They shot anyone seen looking at a map, directing men with their arms, or carrying a pistol instead of a carbine. Enemy gunners would allow a platoon to pass them without shooting, and then fire on the company headquarters staff. In this manner, Major Bernard Green, a 4th Marines battalion commander, lost his life. His killers disappeared before they could be located.[14]

"It was like fighting a phantom enemy," wrote a Marine officer. Another Marine remarked, "They've all got Nambus, but where are they?"[15]

The 29th's Company G led the 4th Marines' attack the next day against Hill 200, the next objective. Undergrowth concealed Japanese cave positions that erupted in gunfire, inflicting sixty-five casualties on Company G, and claiming three successive company commanders. The 29th's 3rd Battalion attacked Green Hill, and Lieutenant James Green was killed when he rushed the hill while "throwing grenades like baseballs." The 3rd's sister battalions remained bottled-up to the east. The Marines counted 1,120 enemy dead on Yae-Take's western slopes by day's end.[16]

When a sniper on Yae-Take killed four men in Patrick Almond's Company F, 4th Marines, the dead men's companions flushed the enemy soldier with a grenade. To their surprise, the sniper was a twelve-year-old boy. The Japanese had given him a rifle with a broken magazine and ordered him to kill Americans and delay their assault. He could only fire one shot at a time, but "he was a damn good shot, and he did what they left him to do," said Almond. "We shot him right there."[17]

During the night, Colonel Udo, conceding that Yae-Take would fall very soon, sent part of his force to the mountains to the north to prosecute a guerrilla war.[18]

On April 16, two 6th Marine Division regiments launched a full-scale attack up Yae-Take's leg-killing steep slopes, pinioning the Japanese between two 29th Marines battalions and the 4th Marines. "My throat was thick with fear," wrote Sergeant Manchester of the 29th Marines. Initially driven back 100 feet from the crest by knee mortars and grenade volleys, the 4th Marines' 1st Battalion attacked again and Companies A and C reached the top. Six hours later, seventy-five Japanese soldiers launched a banzai attack and were repulsed.

In this attack, Corporal Richard Bush, a squad leader in the 4th Marines' Company C, was hit in both thighs by enemy machine-gun fire and taken to an aid station. There, a live Japanese grenade thudded to the ground near Bush, and he instantly rolled over on it, smothering the explosion with his body and shielding the men near him from injury or death. Amazingly, although he lost three fingers and suffered severe stomach wounds, Bush lived to be awarded the Medal of Honor for sacrificing himself to save his comrades' lives.[19]

An unexpected benefit of the Yae-Take attack was the capture of a paddock of horses that the Japanese had used to carry supplies up the mountain. Until this point, the Marines had toted 5-gallon cans of water on their shoulders and bandoliers of ammunition clips across their chests while ascending the steep slopes.

The horses proved to be of little use, though. Corporal Robert E. Lee Ferrier of the 22nd Marines described them as small, underfed, and weak. Ferrier's comrade loaded one with equipment, and "if it kept moving it was okay, but every time the column stopped, this guy had to get on one side of the poor thing to hold it up so it wouldn't fall over."[20]

With Yae-Take, Motobu's only fortified area, now in American hands, it was a relatively easy matter for the Marines, aided by naval gunfire, to swiftly overrun the lower nearby ridges against scattered resistance. Several hundred Japanese survivors, including Colonel Udo, eluded the 29th Marines' attempt to cut off their avenue of retreat and fled into northern Okinawa.

At Udo's Mount Yae-Take command post, the Americans found a letter of mock sympathy addressed to the 6th Marine Division: "We express our hearty regret with you all over the death of the late President. What do you think was the true cause of the late President's death? A miserable defeat experienced by the US forces in the sea around the island of Okinawa!"[21]

THE 6TH DIVISION COUNTED MORE than 2,500 enemy dead during the Motobu operation and captured 46 prisoners. The division report said that 236 Marines were killed, 1,061 were wounded, and 7 were missing. Colonel Shapley said the Motobu operation was "as difficult as I can conceive an operation to be. . . . It was an uphill fight all the way."

On April 20, the day after the 6th Division began its final drive to the north coast, General Roy Geiger, the III Amphibious Corps commander, declared organized resistance ended in northern Okinawa. The Marines began sending 500 to 1,500 civilians per day to internment camps.[22]

During the division's last push northward, "great gusts" of rain blew in and the ground became sodden. The 4th Marines were met by intensive machine-gun fire from fixed positions that they eliminated with flamethrowers and explosives. In one cave complex, the Marines wiped out seventy-five Japanese soldiers.

Guerrilla raids flared on the western and northern coasts, with Japanese soldiers and partisans damaging Marine water and supply depots and setting fires in the villages. The 6th Division intensified its patrolling to dig out Japanese pockets. On April 22, the 22nd Marines' patrols killed 35 enemy troops in a firefight; the next day, they killed another 50 Japanese while clearing caves and pillboxes.

On April 27, a 4th Marines patrol spotted a two-hundred-man enemy column of Motobu survivors marching to the east coast. The 4th's 3rd Battalion intercepted the column and fought the Japanese for three hours the next day, killing 109 enemy soldiers.[23]

The guerrilla activity and sporadic arson in northern Okinawa compelled the Tenth Army to keep a division in the north for the rest of the campaign.

Armored amphibians on April 21 transported a Marine reconnaissance battalion to Yagachi Shima, one of several small islands lying off the Motobu Peninsula. The Marines met no resistance, but found a leper colony of eight hundred adults and fifty children on the island.[24]

WHILE THE 6TH DIVISION TOILED up rugged Yae-Take, the 1st Marine Division was enjoying a respite from heavy combat. Syndicated newspaper correspondent Ernie Pyle said the division was in a holiday mood, which was reflected in the Marines' eschewal of helmets in favor of an array of civilian hats appropriated from native homes. They wore green twill hats, baseball caps, and panama and felt hats. "For some reason soldiers the world over like to put on odd local headgear," Pyle wrote.[25]

The 1st Division had been assigned to invade Miyako Island in the Sakishima Group north of Formosa, but when the operation was postponed indefinitely, the division became available for operations on Okinawa. The Marines patrolled northern Okinawa, where they destroyed enemy artillery and ammunition dumps, killed snipers, and interned hundreds of civilians.

One day, a platoon went on patrol and failed to return. Another patrol was sent to find it. "Just before the sun came up, we found the whole platoon dead, on top of a ridge," reported Sergeant Jim Moll. Ambushed by

Japanese soldiers, the Marines were caught so completely unawares that they had not even fired their weapons. Nearby, Moll's platoon discovered ten Japanese soldiers cooking breakfast over a fire and killed them all.[26]

THE TENTH ARMY'S NEXT OBJECTIVE was Ie Shima, an 11-square-mile island 3 miles from Motobu's western coast. On the morning of April 16, as the 6th Division was slogging up Yae-Take's summit, the Army's 77th Infantry Division began landing on Ie Shima's southern beaches.

Japanese engineers had built an airfield with three landing strips arranged in an "XI" configuration atop Ie Shima's 165-foot west-central plateau. Two miles to the east lay Ie Town, above which loomed the island's chief geographical feature, the rocky, 600-foot peak known as Iegusugu, but which the Americans nicknamed "the Pinnacle," the same name given to a 475-foot hill near Okinawa's Shuri Line. Ie Shima was roughly shaped like an aircraft carrier, with the Pinnacle resembling its island. When the invasion of Okinawa became increasingly likely, the Japanese forcibly evacuated 3,000 of Ie Shima's 8,000 inhabitants, built fortifications, and began destroying the airstrips.[27]

Army Air Force and Navy strategists planned to transform Ie Shima into a B-29 base and an air-defense system for Okinawa. But it would first have to be wrested from the Japanese.

Aerial reconnaissance of Ie Shima revealed no signs of enemy activity, and some Tenth Army senior officers concluded that the Japanese had evacuated the island. They proposed that the 77th Division land two companies to reconnoiter the island during the daytime.

General Andrew Bruce, the 77th's commander, objected to this plan, pointing to the earlier estimate of 2,500 Japanese troops occupying Ie Shima. The enemy was still there, he believed, but in well-concealed positions.[28]

LED BY GENERAL BRUCE, THE 77th had fought on Guam and in the Philippines, from which it was withdrawn in February—a six-week turnaround without rest before Operation Iceberg. Marine General Holland M. "Howlin' Mad" Smith had watched Bruce and his division in action on Guam and had liked what he had seen. "I was very much impressed by Bruce and his men . . . when the 77th did move, it moved fast."

The 77th was the first division to clash with Japanese troops during the Okinawa campaign, when it invaded Kerama Retto in late March. Now, weeks later, the 77th's 24,000 men were poised to go into action once more.[29]

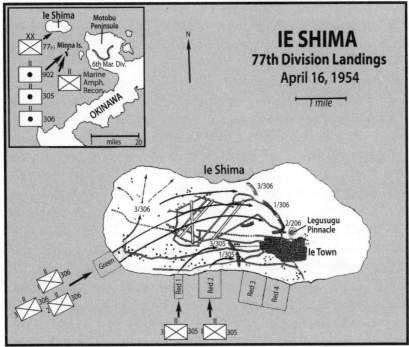

Map adapted from Okinawa: The Last Battle *by Roy E. Appleman, et al.*
(Center for Military History, 1948)

THE DIVISION EMBARKED AT KERAMA Retto on April 2 for the Ie
Shima invasion planned two weeks hence. As the convoy sailed from the
anchorage late that afternoon, eight kamikaze planes attacked without
warning and crashed four ships, with devastating results for the convoy
command and the leadership of the 77th's 305th Infantry.

One hundred thirty-two soldiers and sailors were killed on the destroyer transports *Dickerson*, *Henrico*, *Goodhue*, and *Achernar*, including
the convoy commander and executive officer, and the 305th's commander,
executive officer, and two staff officers. Three hundred eight men were
wounded.

Quick action by Private First Class Max Drucker of the 306th Infantry saved the *LaGrange* from a similar fate. Drucker was on deck near a
20mm antiaircraft gun when a kamikaze dove on the destroyer transport.

He leaped to the AA gun and riddled the enemy plane, causing it to crash into the sea 100 yards from the ship. Drucker's gun was the only one on *LaGrange* that was fired during the attack.

The *Dickerson*, whose bridge was crashed by a "Nick" fighter, reported fifty-four deaths and was later scuttled. The *Henrico*, its bridge pulverized by a Fran attack bomber, lost forty-nine killed. Sent for repairs, *Henrico* was out of commission for the rest of the war. After returning to Kerama Retto with its wounded, the invasion force was reconstituted aboard replacement ships and again weighed anchor for Ie Shima.[30]

In the meantime, Navy underwater demolition teams (UDTs) scouted Ie Shima's reefs and beaches to create tide charts and identify the best landing approaches. Reconnaissance parties roamed the southeast beaches without being fired on, but rifle fire met them on the southern and southwestern beaches.

The scouts shrewdly deduced that the Japanese were attempting to steer them to southeast Ie Shima's gentle beaches, which they strongly suspected would be heavily defended from the caves that overlooked them. Planners shifted the amphibious landings to Ie Shima's southern and southwestern beaches.[31]

Two days before landing day—W-Day, scheduled for April 16—a Marine reconnaissance battalion attached to the 77th seized the islet of Minna Shima 4 miles southeast of Ie Shima without difficulty. The next day, April 15, the 305th, 902nd, and 306th field artillery battalions landed howitzers and gun crews there. By evening, the battalions were ready to support the Ie Shima landings the next morning.[32]

AT DAWN APRIL 16, GUNS of all calibers from two battleships, four cruisers, seven destroyers, twenty-four mortar boats, and six gunboats pounded the Ie Shima beaches. Artillery from Minna Shima and the Motobu Peninsula, 3 miles away, added to the roaring cacophony. US warplanes then bombed and rocketed the island, and dropped napalm. When they had finished, a thick pall of smoke and dust shrouded the Pinnacle. A Japanese soldier wrote in his diary, "Their firepower is so great we dared not show our heads."

Transports and landing ships carrying the 77th Division left the Hagushi anchorage beneath a dense smoke screen at about the time that the Kikusui No. 3 kamikaze attacks on the radar picket ships were beginning. Combat air patrol fighters and picket ships intercepted and shot down

Japanese pilots who targeted the task group. Shipboard gunners splashed seven enemy planes.

Three battalions from the 305th Infantry and two from the 306th landed on Ie Shima at 8:35 a.m. The 306th proceeded to the airfield, capturing it that afternoon, as the rest of the assault force pivoted eastward toward Ie Town, halting at nightfall before reaching the small city.[33]

That night, Japanese soldiers and armed civilians, many of them wearing army uniforms, poured out of underground tunnels and pillboxes near the beach and attacked the 305th's 3rd Battalion. They carried rifles, sharpened bamboo stakes, boxes of mortar shells to be used as satchel charges, and bags of grenades.

Suicide bombers blew themselves up, showering the defenders with body parts; the dismembered leg of one attacker broke the arm of an American soldier. The Japanese were cut down before they could break through the lines, and 152 bodies were counted the next morning.

Major Masashi Igawa, the senior Japanese officer on the island, commanded the 1st Battalion of the 2nd Infantry Unit of the 44th Independent Mixed Brigade. The 2nd Infantry's two other battalions, led by Colonel Takehido Udo, had been sent to defend the Motobu Peninsula. Helping Igawa to defend Ie Shima was the 50th Specially Established Infantry Battalion, formerly the 50th Airfield Battalion, whose mission ended when the last Japanese planes left the island. Igawa had at his disposal more than three thousand troops.

Evidently because of Igawa's persuasive leadership, more than fifteen hundred Ie Shima civilian men and women had volunteered to fight to the death beside the Japanese defenders with small arms, grenades, satchel charges, and crude spears. Nowhere during the Okinawa campaign did civilians resist as strongly as they did on Ie Shima.

When the 305th's Company I resumed its march the next morning toward Ie Town, a grotesque sight met the soldiers: the bodies of three enemy officers with sword blades protruding from their backs. The officers had committed suicide by impaling themselves on their swords after planting their hilts in the ground on a hillside.[34]

That morning, two battalions of the 307th Infantry and part of the 706th Tank Battalion came ashore on Ie Shima's southeast beaches. Light to moderate mortar and machine-gun fire swept the attackers from caves overlooking the beaches that had survived naval gunfire and air strikes. The assault secured the gently sloping southeast beaches, permitting the

landing of tanks and heavy equipment that could not negotiate the more rugged beaches to the west.[35]

Once ashore, the 307th advanced over heavily mined fields and roads to the edge of Ie Town. Inside the ruined town, blasted by naval gunfire and air strikes, the Japanese had erected wire entanglements and mutually supporting pillboxes. They fought from within the rubble that choked the streets and barred the passage of tanks and self-propelled guns.

Nearly every house had been transformed into a pillbox. Only infantrymen willing to engage in the most elemental combat could wrest Ie Town from the Japanese—by fighting house to house, each street a phase line.

The 77th battled yard by yard through the town against the dug-in Japanese. For two days, a dead baby lay in the road; on the third day, a tank crushed the infant's body.

Sergeant Jerry Levin, awarded a Bronze Star on Leyte and wounded on Guam, was sent with three other men to pick up a dead officer's body. They found it where he and two others had been ambushed and killed. On either side of the officer's intact body was a dead soldier, "the bottom half of their bodies gone."[36]

Honeycombed with spider holes, bunkers, pillboxes, and caves—some guarded by sliding steel doors—the Pinnacle north of Ie Town was a jarring visual reminder that the tiny island's conquest would be incomplete until the 600-foot prominence was captured. With its fortified firing positions and dominating height, the Pinnacle invited unhappy comparisons to Iwo Jima's Mount Suribachi.[37]

Before it could assault the Pinnacle, the 77th had to first secure Ie Town, an approach hill nicknamed "Bloody Ridge," and the reinforced concrete building atop Bloody Ridge: Government House. The 307th, aided by the 305th's 1st Battalion, managed to seize most of the open ground below Bloody Ridge on April 18. On the nineteenth, however, a deluge of Japanese mortar and machine-gun fire shattered a four-battalion attack against high ground east of the ridge.[38]

His efforts to seize the Pinnacle from the south and west having come to nothing, General Bruce ordered a ground reconnaissance of the Pinnacle's north side. But heavy artillery, mortar, and machine-gun fire from the Pinnacle frustrated efforts to identify potential approaches, and aerial photos were unhelpful.

So Bruce boarded a Navy control boat and made a personal reconnaissance from the sea of potential northern approaches to the Pinnacle. After

analyzing the information gathered from his scouting foray, Bruce decided to mount the primary attack on the Pinnacle from the north, instead of the south.

On April 20, the 306th Infantry was within striking distance of the Pinnacle's northern slopes. It crossed the minefield guarding the Pinnacle's base, with Sergeant Harold Murray crawling forward under heavy fire to explode the mines with bullets from his submachine gun.

Then, Tech Sergeant LaVerne Northrup led a platoon of M-8 self-propelled howitzers into position at the Pinnacle's base on foot while under fire, and the 306th's infantrymen crossed a gunfire-swept open field to begin their assault. A War Department observer later wrote, "It was the most remarkable thing I have ever seen. . . . I saw troops go through enemy mortar concentrations and machine gun fire that should have pinned them down. But instead they poured across the field."

Starting up the hill while bowed beneath the rain of grenades and satchel charges hurled down from above, the 306th took possession of the Pinnacle's northern side. It then began methodically clearing caves and pillboxes with flamethrowers and grenades. By nightfall, 900 Japanese soldiers lay dead.

On the same day, the 306th's sister regiment, the 307th, fought its way up Bloody Ridge and captured Government House after a furious grenade and bayonet battle. At 4:30 a.m. April 21, the 307th's 2nd Battalion crushed an all-out assault by the Japanese through their own mortar barrage, "seeming to be oblivious to the fact that their ranks were being decimated by the deadly hail of fragments."

The fighting ended at dawn, when 364 enemy bodies were counted. Many had blown themselves up with satchel charges in the hope of killing Americans too. The dead included eight women, one of them armed with a saber and the others with spears.[39]

The last Japanese positions in Ie Town's ruins were destroyed on April 21, the day that the Army declared Ie Shima secured. "The last three days of this fighting were the bitterest I ever witnessed," General Bruce wrote.[40]

During the six-day battle, 4,794 Japanese soldiers and armed civilians were killed, and 179 became prisoners. The 77th Division reported 217 men killed, 876 wounded, and two missing.[41]

The Army removed the approximately four thousand natives who remained on Ie Shima, and transported them to internment camps at Kerama

Retto, where they remained until late 1945. Engineers began repairing two of Ie Shima's airstrips, and by mid-May the Army Air Force's 318th Fighter Group and Marine Air Group 22 were flying missions from them.[42]

ERNIE PYLE WAS THE BEST-KNOWN syndicated war correspondent in America in 1945. His feature columns appeared in nearly four hundred daily newspapers and three hundred weeklies—more publications than those carrying the columns of either Drew Pearson or Walter Winchell. Since 1942, the thin, balding Hoosier had written about ordinary fighting men on the front lines in North Africa, Sicily, Italy, and France. The columns earned Pyle a Pulitzer Prize in 1944.[43]

Pyle left Europe in September 1944 on a home furlough, rejoining his wife, Gerry, at their home in Albuquerque, New Mexico, and visiting his parents in Indiana. But home was no sanctuary from crises; while Pyle was in Albuquerque, Gerry attempted suicide and then underwent electroshock therapy at a mental hospital.

He returned to the battlefront in 1945—for the first time, to the Pacific theater. "I'm going simply because there's a war on and I'm part of it and I've known all the time I was going back. I'm going simply because I've got to—and I hate it."[44]

In a letter from the Pacific, Pyle wrote, "I wouldn't give you two cents for the likelihood of me being alive a year from now." When fellow correspondent Robert Sherwood reminded Pyle that he had said that before previous Allied operations in North Africa, Italy, Sicily, and Normandy, Pyle replied, "Sometime I have got to be right."[45]

He landed at Okinawa with the 1st Marine Division, his first time accompanying Marines into combat. For the next week or so, he dined with the Marines on moldy K rations, surmising that the rations had been growing fungus in a warehouse for three years.

In a column, he wrote of Okinawa, "The countryside is neat and the little farms are well kept," and the climate superb. "The worst crosses to bear were the mosquitoes, the fleas, and the sight of the pathetic people." Yet life in war zones was much the same everywhere, "unchanged by distance or time . . . a pattern so imbedded in my soul that it seemed I'd never known anything else in my life."[46]

Pyle joined the 77th Division on April 17, the day after it landed on Ie Shima. He spent the night at the 305th Regiment's command post. The regiment, said its commander, Lieutenant Colonel Joseph Coolidge,

"anticipated this visit with pleasure and pride and with the hopes of meeting this great little fellow who had portrayed the lot of the doughboy in Europe with such moving simplicity." The famous correspondent was besieged by autograph requests.[47]

On the eighteenth, Pyle was riding to the front in a jeep with Coolidge and three soldiers when a Nambu machine gun opened up on them near the outskirts of Ie Town. The men abandoned the jeep and dove into a shallow roadside ditch.

When Pyle and Coolidge raised their heads to check on the other men, the Nambu began firing again. Coolidge ducked, and he saw Pyle drop back.

Coolidge found Pyle lying on his back. His hands were resting on his chest, holding a knitted cap that he always carried with him. Coolidge saw no bleeding, but then noticed a purplish hole in Pyle's left temple. The bullet had killed him instantly. Patrols from the 305th hunted down and killed the enemy machine-gunner.[48]

Pyle's body was transported to the 77th Division cemetery on Ie Shima and "buried with deep sorrow and reverence." A crude marker was erected that said, "On this spot the 77th Infantry Division lost a buddy, Ernie Pyle, 18 April 1945." Pyle's remains were later reinterred in the National Memorial Cemetery of the Pacific, in Hawaii's Punchbowl.[49]

The April Offensive

It's going to be really tough. There are 65,000–70,000 fighting Japanese holed up in the south end of the island. I see no way to get them out except to blast them out yard by yard.

—GENERAL JOHN HODGE, COMMANDER OF XXIV CORPS,
ON THE EVE OF THE APRIL 19 US OFFENSIVE[1]

So if this line isn't moving within five days, we'll get someone here to move it so we can all get out from under these stupid air attacks.

—A FRUSTRATED ADMIRAL CHESTER NIMITZ
TO GENERAL SIMON BOLIVAR BUCKNER JR.,
TENTH ARMY COMMANDER[2]

They [the Tenth Army] should have thrown a left hook down there in the southern beaches. . . . They had a hell of a powerful reinforced division, trained to a gnat's whisker.

—COLONEL SAMUEL TAXIS, 2ND MARINE DIVISION
OPERATIONS OFFICER, AFTER THE REJECTION OF A PLAN
FOR THE 2ND DIVISION TO OPEN A SECOND FRONT
BY LANDING IN SOUTHEASTERN OKINAWA[3]

IN MID-APRIL, TWO ARMY DIVISIONS—THE 7th and 96th—battered strongly fortified Japanese defenses stretching across southern Okinawa from Machinato Airfield in the west to Yonabaru Airfield in the east.

Casualties rose sharply, and the Americans' nerves began to fray under the hammering of General Kosuke Wada's powerful 5th Artillery Command—the largest Japanese artillery concentration of the Pacific war, with 250 guns of 70mm or larger.

Combat fatigue would become a bête noir of the American soldier on Okinawa. Although sleep deprivation, the brief intervals between campaigns, and frequent close combat contributed to the psychoneurosis, the key trigger was prolonged exposure to mortar and artillery fire. During World War I, the phenomenon was called shell shock when it was observed that intensive artillery bombardments caused the number of cases to soar.

By April 15, combat-fatigue cases in the 96th and 7th Divisions had become so widespread that both divisions established rest camps behind the lines. By the end of April, the Tenth Army had dedicated a field hospital to the treatment of combat fatigue, whose symptoms ranged from dull detachment to sobbing, screaming, and incoherent shouting.[4]

Rifleman George Brooks of the 96th Division's 382nd Infantry said enemy shelling at night "caused more mental breakdown—combat fatigue—than anything else. We lost a lot of men this way." Each round, he said, sounded like it "is coming right into your foxhole." Some men went "yelling off into the woods, or just broke down and cried."[5]

Soldiers sent to the Tenth Army's convalescent camp remained under observation for a week. If they did not show signs of improvement, they were shipped to a hospital on Guam or Saipan. However, 90 percent of the milder cases and 80 percent of the more severe ones were able to return to duty, although often in support units and not on the front line.[6]

Sergeant Benjamin Capaldi of the 7th Division's 32nd Infantry visited a shell-shocked friend at a rest camp, and "I hardly recognized him. His eyes have sunken into his sockets. His face is drawn and skinny. He talks in whispers and the least bit of noise excites him." Capaldi's friend was so fearful of being sent back to the front that "he actually shakes when someone comes in with a paper."[7]

It was now apparent that the stresses of combat could transform trained, seasoned, well-led soldiers into psychiatric patients. Battle-fatigue cases were bound to escalate soon, for XXIV Corps was preparing to mount its first large-scale offensive on Okinawa.

AFTER THE DISASTROUS JAPANESE COUNTEROFFENSIVE at Kakazu, Kakazu West, Tomb Hill, and Tanabaru on April 12–14, the battlefront

had been unusually quiet except for furious, sporadic artillery and mortar exchanges. The reason was that XXIV Corps was preparing for its planned April 19 offensive by stockpiling artillery ammunition, which was at a low point due to hard usage and the sinking of two ammunition ships by kamikazes. Transport planes initially flew needed munitions to Okinawa to address the shortage. But on April 15, with the offensive just four days away, General Buckner submitted a special request for more artillery ammunition, and five LSTs were loaded at Saipan and sent to Okinawa. In the meantime, naval, air, and artillery forward observers were busy identifying potential targets.[8]

The 27th Division, one of the Tenth Army's two reserve divisions, landed on Okinawa on April 9, and on the 15th it displaced the 96th Division on the western line. The 96th shifted into the middle, with the 7th Division on its left.

Supported by the fire of a dozen and a half warships, 324 guns, dozens of tanks, and sorties by 650 planes, three infantry divisions with up to 60,000 assault troops would lunge southward along a 5-mile battlefront.[9]

General Buckner had come ashore April 18 to personally oversee the massive attack after directing the Tenth Army from Admiral Richmond Kelly Turner's flagship *Eldorado* since L-Day. It would be Buckner's first combat operation in a thirty-seven-year Army career.

A West Pointer, Buckner had served as the academy's commandant during the 1930s, and later commanded Army forces in Alaska for three years. Buckner was an outdoorsman who liked to lead his staff on long, grueling hikes. His favorite drink was "bourbon and puddle water," imbibed after he had given his customary toast: "May you walk in the ashes of Tokyo."

Buckner established his headquarters in Uchi, a small village 2 miles southwest of Kadena Airfield. His staff was huge. In ensuring that each service branch was amply represented, Buckner had created a bloated command that numbered in the hundreds. Marine General Oliver P. Smith, the Tenth Army's deputy chief of staff and liaison to III Corps, attempted to address the problem by cutting the staff by one-third. Even so, 340 staff officers still remained, divided into forward and rear echelons, with a liaison detachment at Pearl Harbor.[10]

With a battlefront just 5 miles long and dense Japanese defensive positions extending southward 4 miles, maneuver appeared impossible. General John Hodge, the XXIV Corps commander, understood the difficult

task that his men faced, but believed that a single overwhelming attack could crack the Japanese defenses and save American lives in the long run. In hindsight, Hodge's belief appeared to be akin to the unreasonable optimism that led to Pickett's charge at Gettysburg and Grant's Cold Harbor assault, both debacles.

"It's going to be really tough," Hodge acknowledged. "There are 65,000–70,000 fighting Japanese holed up in the south end of the island. I see no way to get them out except to blast them out yard by yard."[11]

The bludgeoning all-out frontal attack would be the largest land offensive of the Pacific war, and would be devoid of flourishes, feints, or flanking movements. However, there would be opportunities for tactical maneuvering if the XXIV Corps broke through somewhere.

The objective was to seize the east-west highway south of Shuri Castle—the road linking Yonabaru on the east coast with Naha, Okinawa's capital, on the west coast. By so doing, the Tenth Army would surround the bristling Shuri defenses and sever their connection to Okinawa's southern tip. Without access to resupply, reinforcements, or a path for retreat, the defenders could be reduced according to the Tenth Army's timetable.[12]

Across the battle line, the Japanese were bracing for what they knew was coming.

"The enemy is now preparing to advance on all fronts. Our front lines will necessarily be subjected to fierce bombardments," said a 62nd Division order dated April 14. It advised unit commanders to strengthen their positions, and to establish strongpoints in places where their reduction would not hasten the collapse of the line. Special instructions were issued for satchel-charge attacks on American tanks.[13]

THE 27TH DIVISION WAS ORIGINALLY established in 1908 as a New York National Guard unit that became known as "The New York Division." Federalized in July 1917 for the Great War, during the Somme Offensive of September 1918, the 27th suffered more than eight thousand casualties. Reactivated as a federal division in 1940, the 27th fought on Butaritari Island in the Gilberts in November 1943, and Eniwetok in the Marshalls in February 1944.

Marine General Holland "Howlin' Mad" Smith, who had led the campaigns in the Gilbert and Marshall Islands, faulted the 27th Division for being slow and poorly trained. By comparison, Holland Smith's Marines epitomized aggressiveness and sought to capture their objectives as quickly

as possible. The 27th, commanded by the gentlemanly General Ralph Smith, advanced methodically, and relied on its artillery to blast the enemy from its positions and minimize Army casualties.[14]

When the 27th again was assigned to Holland Smith's V Amphibious Corps in the Mariana Islands for the Saipan invasion in June 1944, Holland Smith's discontent with the Army and his counterpart, Ralph Smith, reached the boiling point.

The 27th, sandwiched between the 2nd and 4th Marine Divisions as they marched up Saipan's west and east coasts, had the tough job of crossing broken ground under intensive fire from Japanese gunners in caves. The 27th moved forward slowly and lagged the Marine divisions, which had to slow the pace of their advances to avoid exposing their flanks.

Holland Smith became apoplectic, accusing the 27th of dilatoriness, and of even being "yellow." The climax came on June 24 when Holland Smith fired General Ralph Smith. The Army general was tersely informed of his dismissal in a note delivered to him at the front by an aide. On June 28, General George Griner Jr., a former assistant commander of the 77th Division, was appointed to succeed Ralph Smith, inheriting the daunting job of reviving the discredited 27th Division.

At 4 a.m. on July 7, thirteen days after Smith's firing, an "avalanche of humanity"—between 3,000 and 4,000 Japanese soldiers—poured through a gap in the 27th Division line, overrunning two battalions of the 27th and three Marine artillery batteries. The Americans formed a new defensive line and, after a ferocious four-hour defensive battle, wiped out the banzai attackers. More than 4,000 Japanese were killed. When Saipan was secured July 9, the 27th Division reported losses of 1,053 killed and 2,617 wounded.[15]

The controversy did not die. In a *Time* magazine story in September, correspondent Robert Sherrod denigrated the 27th's performance on Saipan, but many of his facts were questionable or patently false, based on Holland Smith's version of events and secondhand Marine accounts. The article reinforced the Marines' preconceptions about the 27th—and enraged the Army, which sought to revoke Sherrod's press credentials. Outraged 27th soldiers wrote letters to *Time* denying Sherrod's charges, but censors returned most of them because they contained classified information.

General Griner labored to rebuild the dispirited division's morale during its R&R on hot, malarial Espiritu Santo by procuring fresh meat and starting a newspaper, but disillusionment lingered.[16]

The blowup tarnished the 27th's reputation among Marines and soldiers alike. Some men in the 96th Division grumbled when the 27th entered the line beside their division on April 15. "I never saw such an ugly bunch," said Dick Thom, operations officer for the 381st Infantry's 1st Battalion. "Morale was awful. . . . They were the fuckups of the Pacific." Staff Sergeant William Beckman of the 382nd's 2nd Battalion distrusted the division after hearing that it had fought poorly on Saipan, and that "their officers did not fight, provided no leadership . . ."[17]

Yet the 27th was assigned to strike the first blow of Buckner's April 19 offensive.

A CAPTURED JAPANESE DOCUMENT GAVE General Griner the idea for a night attack near Machinato. The document informed Japanese troops, "The enemy generally fires [its guns] during the night, but very seldom takes offensive action."

It was true that during the Pacific war, Americans had rarely fought at night. But during its months of R&R on Espiritu Santo, the 27th Division had practiced night maneuvers, and Griner now decided that he would do the unexpected during the night of April 18–19, hours before the main offensive began.[18]

The frowning Urasoe-Mura Escarpment stretched across the entire 27th Division front, and in fact ran eastward all the way to Skyline Ridge in the 7th Division's sector. In the western part of its zone, the 27th held the north side of Machinato Inlet, a small, 150-foot-wide tidal basin. Immediately east lay a large, open stretch of ground covered with rice paddies and surrounded by high ground. It was nicknamed "Buzz Bomb Bowl" because it apparently had served as a practice range for the notorious Japanese 320mm spigot mortars. Still farther east was the Kakazu hill mass, a series of sharp ridges that ran east and west. The Japanese 62nd Division defended the area.

Griner sent an engineer in a bulldozer down the rutted road leading to the inlet. During the day, the engineer made a show of working—albeit somewhat aimlessly, other than to pull out a stuck jeep or two. After nightfall, however, bulldozer operators industriously repaired the road and extended it to the inlet.

The 27th's operation began at 4 p.m. on April 18 when a platoon-strength force from Company G, 106th Infantry, concealed by a smoke screen, crossed Machinato Inlet by balancing on a pipeline. They were not fired

upon. The soldiers scaled the 75-foot bluffs on the inlet's south side, and began cleaning out enemy outposts around Machinato village.[19]

Around 8:30 p.m., the 102nd Engineers Combat Battalion trundled sections for four bridges—two Bailey bridges, a footbridge, and a pontoon bridge for tanks—to Machinato Inlet. Griner and his staff had decided it was impracticable to repair and use a blown railroad bridge on the inlet's eastern end because it was exposed to fire from the Buzz Bomb Bowl.[20]

Working in darkness, Lieutenant Irving Golden and Company A of the 102nd Engineer Battalion completed the first of the Bailey bridges by 10 p.m. An hour later, they began building a second Bailey bridge 200 yards away, completing it by 3 a.m. Tanks and self-propelled guns began crossing the inlet.

The engineers also finished a 128-foot footbridge that 106th infantrymen began crossing to the inlet's south bank. Company F then edged southward down Route 1 to where it passed through the Urasoe-Mura Escarpment. Climbing a ridge near the cut, Lieutenant Robert Hyland Jr.'s platoon fired on unsuspecting Japanese troops singing around small fires while they prepared breakfast.

Enemy mortar rounds began falling, but the 106th pushed on and seized the west end of Urasoe-Mura, its mission a success. It planned to next strike southeast down the escarpment to unite with the 27th's 105th Infantry, which was about to attack Kakazu Ridge. At 2 a.m., the 106th's 2nd Battalion entered Machinato.[21]

AT 6:40 A.M., AMERICAN SHIPS, artillery, and warplanes unleashed a torrent of metal on the Japanese positions along the Urasoe-Mura Escarpment that barred the Tenth Army's way. It was the greatest bombardment of the Pacific war: twenty-seven artillery battalions, or about one gun allotted for every 30 yards, plastered the enemy strongpoints. The 19,000-round hailstorm lasted forty minutes. The barrage drifted southward like a thunderstorm as the infantry made final preparations for the assault. In addition, 650 warplanes made more than 900 sorties, dropping 482 tons of bombs, firing 3,400 rockets, and expending more than 700,000 rounds of .50-caliber and 20mm ammunition. At Yonabaru, 67 planes dropped napalm; 139 warplanes struck Shuri Castle. "The rolling drumfire of guns echoed through the hills and ravines," wrote a *New York Times* reporter.[22]

Marine General Frederick Henderson, a deputy chief of staff for the Tenth Army, went so far as to say that the aggregation of Army and Marine

artillery, plus the naval gunfire from LVTs, destroyers, and battleships "gave us a guns/mile-of-front ratio on Okinawa that was probably higher than any US effort in World War II." Coupled with the Americans' flexible fire-direction system, which could train all of the guns within range on a single target, US firepower equaled and possibly exceeded that of the Soviet Army, which sought a three-hundred-guns-per-mile concentration during an attack, said Henderson.[23]

Many Tenth Army troops did not believe it possible that anyone could survive the extraordinary onslaught. In truth, though, the Japanese, deep inside the hills and safe in their caves, bunkers, and tunnels, were scarcely touched. "The American artillery was very fierce but, because their fire was spread out over a large area, it did very little damage to our bunkers," a Japanese infantryman wrote.

General Josef R. Sheetz, commander of XXIV Corps's artillery units, later estimated that the barrage killed no more than 190 enemy troops—about one Japanese soldier for every hundred shells fired by Sheetz's artillerymen. Japanese prisoners who were inside the deep caves beneath the Shuri Line at the time later told their captors that the bombardment was not felt.[24]

As it had on L-Day, the Tenth Army simultaneously carried out another water-borne demonstration against Minatoga in the southeast. A battalion of the 77th Division, withheld from the Ie Shima operation, darted toward shore in landing craft and then withdrew. The feint prevented thousands of Japanese troops from reinforcing the Thirty-Second Army's line north of Shuri.[25]

As the American assault battalions surged forward, their supporting fire ebbed, and thousands of Japanese 62nd Division troops emerged from caves, bunkers, and spider holes. They reciprocated with a blizzard of artillery, mortar, and machine-gun fire, and enemy soldiers hurled grenades and satchel charges.[26]

KAKAZU RIDGE WAS THE 27TH Division's main obstacle to the Urasoe-Mura Escarpment, whose western end had been captured by the 106th Infantry.

At the same brush-choked coral gorge that had come to symbolize the 96th Division's impotency before Kakazu Ridge ten days earlier, the 27th's 105th Infantry found itself pinned down on April 19.

With the 1st Battalion stopped, the 2nd Battalion, following close behind, attempted to push ahead but stalled when its commander, Major

Holeman Grigsby, scouting ahead, was wounded four times by machine-gun fire and left for dead (he survived).

General Griner, the 27th's commander, believed that a combined infantry-tank attack could overpower Kakazu's defenders, permitting the 105th to cross over the ridge and enter Kakazu Village beyond it.

Part of the 1st Battalion rose to its feet and again attempted to get over the open ground prefatory to climbing Kakazu, but sheets of machine-gun fire blazing from hiding places in the northern slope forced it to go to ground again.

Then, thirty tanks from the 193rd Tank Battalion's Company A appeared on the battalion's left. They traveled in a column—without the anticipated infantry support—southward down Route 5 toward a saddle that separated Kakazu from Nishibaru Ridge to the east.

Mines destroyed three tanks, and a 47mm antitank gun lurking under a ledge of Nishibaru Ridge knocked out four others, but the rest swept around Kakazu Ridge, entered Kakazu Village, and demolished it.

Except for a platoon that the Japanese had deliberately allowed to pass over the ridge before wiping it out, the 105th's 1st and 2nd Battalions remained pinned by mortar and machine-gun fire on the northern side of Kakazu.

Griner's infantry-tank assault had no infantry component. The result was that in Kakazu Village, the tanks were prey for enemy suicide attack units armed with satchel charges, and 47mm antitank guns. The tank crews fought back furiously amid the explosions, roaring fires, and shrieks of pain, and the Japanese exacted a heavy toll. When ordered to withdraw, just eight tanks were able to return to their lines. Crewmen marooned in the village with their disabled tanks dug pits beneath them and hid there for days before rejoining their units. The destruction of twenty-two tanks was the largest single-day armor loss of the Okinawa campaign.[27]

ORDERED TO SEIZE KAKAZU WEST, the 105th's 3rd Battalion elected to go around it and attack the Urasoe-Mura Escarpment. The battalion was momentarily stalled by enemy machine-gun fire from a pillbox on Kakazu West—until Sergeant Richard J. Bean launched a one-man attack on the position. After plastering it with eight bazooka rounds, Bean snatched up a BAR, stormed the pillbox, and wiped out the defenders.[28] The 3rd Battalion raced to the top of the escarpment and joined the 106th at the western end.

The 105th's 2nd Battalion, which had been stopped at the ravine on Kakazu's north side, followed the 3rd's lead, and then Colonel Walter Winn,
the 105th's commander, withdrew his 1st Battalion from the ravine and sent
it, too, up the Urasoe-Mura. By late afternoon, the 105th had abandoned the
entire northern side of Kakazu Ridge after having suffered 158 casualties.

General Griner believed it wiser to bypass Kakazu than to continue to
lose men trying to capture it, but the hole in XXIV Corps's line made Generals Simon Buckner and John Hodge anxious; they feared that the Japanese would counterattack through the gap.

Colonel Michael Halloran, who commanded the 96th Division's 381st
Infantry at adjacent Nishibaru Ridge, vigorously disagreed with Griner's
decision, offering a somewhat baffling rationale: "You cannot bypass a Japanese because a Jap does not know when he is bypassed."

Griner must have become uneasy, too, about the regiment's precipitous
move, because at nightfall, he sent a company of the 165th Infantry to occupy the abandoned positions on Kakazu's north side.[29]

PART OF THE 96TH DIVISION'S 381st Infantry reached the forward slope
of adjacent Nishibaru Ridge, but ran into volleys of grenades and mortar
and machine-gun fire from multiple positions, including Kakazu Ridge.
The mutually supporting enemy positions were cleverly sited—and lethal.

The 381st's mission was to seize Nishibaru Ridge, held by the Japanese 12th Independent Infantry Battalion, overrun Nishibaru Village on
the other side, and then storm the Urasoe-Mura Escarpment. The 381st's
3rd Battalion swept over Nishibaru's crest and pushed on to the edge
of Nishibaru village before being driven back. In the meantime, American conventional and flame tanks scorched enemy caves and bunkers on
Nishibaru's reverse slope.

On April 21, the 382nd's 3rd Battalion joined the 381st 3rd Battalion
on Nishibaru Ridge and attacked eastward. The Japanese fought back with
knee and spigot mortar fire, bombardments from pre-registered artillery
batteries, and repeated counterattacks. A Japanese company that counterattacked from Nishibaru Village was driven back only after a hard fight in
which the Americans fought with exemplary courage.

Staff Sergeant David Dovel commandeered a heavy machine gun when
the gunner was killed. Firing it from his hip, Dovel roved the ridgeline to
avoid knee-mortar fire. Sergeant John Arend and Lieutenant John Stevens
grabbed automatic weapons and charged through grenade and machine-
gun fire to wipe out attackers.[30]

At one point during the furious fighting on Nishibaru, an odd incident occurred. A Japanese soldier speaking perfect English asked to see the commanding officer. A helpful soldier who thought the inquirer was American led him to the company command post—where the enemy soldier proceeded to try to kill the officer. The Japanese soldier and two companions were killed instead.[31]

The 382nd fared better on Tombstone Ridge—so named because of the burial tombs scattered over the 75-foot-high hill. After charging up Tombstone's western slope, the 382nd clung to the ridge's nose under a lash of enemy fire that inflicted high casualties. As night fell, the ridge's slopes were littered with 240 Japanese dead and eighteen wrecked machine guns and mortars.[32]

AFTER THE PRELIMINARY BARRAGE ENDED on April 19, two battalions of the 7th Division, on the battle line's eastern periphery, advanced south from Tomb Hill toward Hill 178 and Skyline Ridge. Hundreds and then thousands of rounds of American shellfire rained down on the two hills—the 7th's artillerymen had a generous allotment of 30,000 rounds available to fire the first day.

"The shells fell so fast that separate explosions were lost in the roar," a witness said. The battalions parted ways, with the 184th's 2nd Battalion turning right to attack Hill 178, while the 32nd Infantry's 2nd Battalion veered left toward Skyline Ridge. Farther to the east, the 32nd's 3rd Battalion began a pincerlike movement along the length of Skyline toward the village of Ouki at the ridge's tip. It then planned to march back up the ridge to meet its sister battalion on top.[33]

The 32nd's 2nd Battalion advanced 500 yards to Skyline Ridge's crest, at a spot that was so narrow that it barely accommodated a footpath. Japanese soldiers on the reverse slope flailed them with artillery, machine-gun, and mortar fire. Then, 100 to 150 Japanese troops charged through their own exploding mortars, and threw back the Americans.

Tech Sergeant Porter McLaughlin, who saw the Japanese swarm his comrades while his antitank platoon was firing armor-piercing shells into enemy caves, said, "It gave us a terribly sick and hopeless feeling." Enemy troops at one point seized an American flamethrower and turned it on the wounded. Piercing screams and the odor of burning flesh jarred the Americans. At the end of the day, Skyline Ridge remained fiercely contested—with the 32nd clinging to the forward slope, and the Japanese holding the reverse slope.[34]

As would be true all along the battle line, the 184th discovered that to capture Hill 178, it had to first seize Rocky Crags because the strongpoints supported one another. Rocky Crags's 700-yard-long ridge of coral out-croppings overlooked Hill 178's approaches. The two dominating coral heads for which Rocky Crags was named jutted up 30 feet or more, provid-ing the enemy with ideal observation points and firing positions. The hill beneath the coral heads was honeycombed with tunnels and caves stocked with supplies, weapons, and troops, which could be continually replenished and reinforced.[35]

When the 184th attempted to capture the Crags, machine-gun and ar-tillery fire from Hill 178 and nearby Tanabaru Escarpment smothered the assault. No significant progress was made against Rocky Crags on April 19.

Up and down the battle line, the offensive had achieved advances of just 800 to 1,200 yards on April 19, with the much-maligned 27th Division reporting the largest gains. The Japanese lines had held. XXIV Corps re-ported 720 casualties.

"Progress not quite satisfactory," General Buckner wrote in his diary that night. Speed up the advance, Buckner told General Hodge, XXIV Corps's commander.

But ordering it done would not make it so. As a *New York Times* cor-respondent noted, the Japanese defenses were "perhaps the sturdiest that American troops have so far encountered in the war against Japan."[36]

THE OFFENSIVE RESUMED THE NEXT day, April 20, with no slackening of intensity, although the weary Americans' initial optimism about achiev-ing a quick breakthrough had evaporated. The 96th Division's 382nd Infan-try seized the rest of Tombstone Ridge, and the 381st put five companies atop Nishibaru Ridge and fought a savage battle around Nishibaru Village south of the ridge, but withering enemy fire prevented the regiment from entering the town. Further advances were stymied by the large numbers of Japanese dug into Nishibaru's reverse slope and their comrades on neigh-boring Kakazu Ridge. From Kakazu, a large number of huge spigot mortars were trained on the 96th troops; a round landed amidst Company E of the 381st Infantry, killing four men, wounding six others, and leaving a swim-ming pool-size crater.

The next day, April 21, the 382nd's 3rd Battalion marched from Tomb-stone Ridge to Nishibaru Ridge and began pushing eastward along its crest. The Japanese launched multiple counterattacks.

Sergeant Dovel helped repel the first swarm of enemy troops by blasting them with a 62-pound heavy machine gun that he fired from his hip. He badly burned his hands, and his legs were peppered with shrapnel from mortar fire. There were three more counterattacks—all repulsed, with 198 Japanese killed.[37]

Two battalions of the 381st launched a fresh attack on Nishibaru Village, where they became locked in a desperate fight in which the Deadeyes fired their heavy machine guns without tripods. Enemy fire raked them from Nishibaru Ridge's reverse slope, and from Kakazu to the west. The Deadeyes were forced to withdraw under a smoke screen, carrying their wounded on improvised litters.[38]

In its "Notes on the Enemy," the 96th Division reported that the Japanese had become "security minded," evidenced by the lack of dog tags and documents found on dead enemy soldiers. Later, more than five hundred dog tags were found on one ring belonging to the 89th Infantry. Two other rings, each containing more than a hundred dog tags, were recovered later at another site.[39]

Lieutenant Colonel Edward Stare, commander of the 383rd Infantry's 3rd Battalion, was in a foxhole when a Japanese infiltrator who had somehow avoided getting shot while racing through three 96th Division perimeters dived into Stare's foxhole. Stare promptly threw him out, and a soldier shot him. The slain Japanese soldier, they discovered, was laden with booty from the American lines: thirty cases of C rations, five cartons of cigarettes, two boxes of chocolate bars, a bottle of Vitalis hair tonic, and three American trench knives.[40]

ON THE OFFENSIVE'S SECOND DAY, April 20, the 27th Division, on the battle line's western end, attempted to push eastward along the Urasoe-Mura Escarpment to capture its West and East Pinnacles. The division stirred up a hornet's nest of artillery, mortar, rifle, and machine-gun fire from the front and rear. The Japanese 62nd Division's 64th Brigade had just replaced the battered 63rd Brigade on the crest of the escarpment, and in its rear was a spigot-mortar regiment and more infantrymen.

Japanese counterattacks smashed two companies of the 105th Infantry near the East Pinnacle. The 2nd Battalion reported losses of 50 killed and 43 wounded in a short period. At the end of the day, the 27th Division reported 506 casualties, the greatest one-day loss of the campaign by a division.[41]

At the Machinato Inlet, Japanese artillery fire destroyed two of the bridges built by the 27th Division engineers. Engineers quickly replaced the bridges. Enemy artillerists also pounded the Route 1 passageway through the Urasoe-Mura Escarpment, disrupting resupply efforts.[42]

One night, a Japanese soldier carrying a demolition charge on his back and a grenade on his belt approached the inlet's pontoon bridge, unaware that engineers were guarding it. An engineer opened fire, and his first shot detonated the grenade, blowing a large hole in the soldier's belly and killing him. Another engineer drove a stake through the hole, and attached a note to the stake: "Warning! Don't nobody else fuck around with this bridge no more. Signed: 102nd Engineer Battalion." Thereafter, the bridge was left undisturbed.[43]

FROM APRIL 20 TO 23, the American offensive's progress was measured in yards. Despite ceaseless artillery, mortar, and naval gunfire, and air strikes, there were no major breakthroughs. It was intrinsically a bloody infantry-tank battle with frequent hand-to-hand fighting, much like the combat on Iwo Jima and Peleliu. In the places where the raging battle brought XXIV Corps to a standstill, the fighting bore an eerie resemblance to the primordial battles waged in France and Belgium during World War I.[44]

Sometimes a frustrated soldier's brash act opened the way to bigger things. While the 7th Division's 184th Infantry tried to reduce the stubbornly held Rocky Crags with a 155mm gun at close range—a process that took an unbelievable two days—the regiment's attacks continued on Hill 178 with little to show for them. Hill 178 was heavily fortified and laced with interlocking bands of fire, and until it fell, division senior officers did not believe it possible to capture Skyline Ridge.

Then, on April 21, Colonel John Finn's 32nd Infantry, dug in below an embankment on Skyline's north side, received a gift: an unexpected opportunity to clear Skyline, thanks to the furious initiative of one soldier.

Sergeant Theodore MacDonnell was acting as an observer for the 91st Chemical Mortar Company attached to Company E when he saw an enemy gunner in a pillbox kill an Company E soldier. Enraged, MacDonnell left the safety of the embankment and charged the pillbox, throwing grenades. Failing to knock out the pillbox on the first try, MacDonald persisted. After returning to the embankment for more grenades, he twice more assaulted the pillbox single-handedly. Still, the Japanese gunners kept shooting.

On his fourth trip for more grenades, MacDonnell retrieved a BAR. It jammed after one shot, necessitating a fifth trip to his former position. This time, he picked up a carbine, raced back to the pillbox, and killed the three gunners inside. He hurled the enemy machine gun and a knee mortar down the slope. Amazingly, after having braved machine-gun and rifle fire five times, MacDonnell was unscathed.

With the pillbox out of commission, Lieutenant Fred Capp led Company E over the embankment and up Skyline Ridge. Colonel Finn quickly sent Company F as a reinforcement, and the two companies cleared the ridge crest of enemy troops at a cost of just two killed.[45]

Lieutenant Willard "Hoss" Mitchell, who had stormed Kakazu West on April 9 at the head of Company L of the 96th's 382nd Infantry before being driven back with 86 casualties, was now, two weeks later, ordered to open the path to Nishibaru Ridge. His "lardasses," back to full strength with replacements, first captured Hill 7, a stepping-stone to Nishibaru, following a three-hour grenade duel with Japanese on the reverse slope. Then, Mitchell broke the impasse at Nishibaru by rushing over the crest with three grenades and his carbine and destroying a machine-gun nest.

That sparked an hours-long firefight on the reverse slope, where the Japanese fought from pillboxes, caves, and spider holes. Company L prevailed. That night, the 96th held Nishibaru Ridge and Tanabaru Escarpment. The five-day offensive had cost the Deadeyes 118 killed, and 660 wounded.[46]

JAPANESE DEFENDERS AT ROCKY CRAGS continued to throw back determined tank-infantry assaults on April 21 and 22 by Captain Charles Murphy's B Company of the 7th Division's 17th Infantry, aided by the 711th Tank Battalion. On the 21st, Murphy's men appeared to have captured the coral knobs after the captain reached the top of the second crag while tanks pulverized the first crag. But then a burst of enemy gunfire erupted once more from adjacent Tanabaru Escarpment and from the first crag. Japanese soldiers poured out of holes in the second crag, throwing grenades, and the Americans pulled back. The next day, when Murphy's men and the tanks tried again, enemy troops with satchel charges attacked the tanks when they crossed the open area beneath the crags. Infantrymen killed the attackers before they could detonate the explosives, and the Americans again began climbing Rocky Crags. Japanese artillery repelled the attack and set a tank ablaze.[47]

The Army's tank losses so alarmed General Buckner's staff that it summoned the 1st Marine Tank Battalion to the XXIV Corps battle line. But

General Roy Geiger, III Amphibious Corps's commander, objected to the piecemeal commitment of Marine tanks to Army units, and General Pedro del Valle, the 1st Marine Division commander, bridled at breaking up his division's infantry-tank team. Buckner withdrew the order.

The Marines' objections to sending tanks to the Army did not extend to their artillery, however; the 11th Marines provided artillery support to Army units throughout April when the 1st Marine Division, which the 11th normally supported, was inactive in central Okinawa.[48]

While enemy artillery was foiling the attacks on Rocky Crags, it was also bleeding the 27th Division as it attempted to capture the East and West Pinnacles on the Urasoe-Mura Escarpment. Japanese gunfire was so intensive from April 20 to 23 that supplies had to be air-dropped to troops on the escarpment or carried by tanks to the ridgetop.

Then, on April 23, the East Pinnacle fell during a surprise attack by the 105th Infantry's 1st Battalion. Two assault companies had climbed Urasoe-Mura, reaching the top in the midst of more than one hundred startled enemy troops defending the East Pinnacle. During the hand-to-hand melee, the combatants fought with bayonets, clubs, and grenades. Staff Sergeant Nathan Johnson reportedly shot and clubbed to death more than thirty Japanese soldiers.

That night, a Japanese bugler blew a call from inside the West Pinnacle, and about thirty soldiers poured out of it and launched a banzai attack. All of the attackers were killed.[49]

XXIV CORPS'S FIVE DAYS OF frontal attacks had cost the Japanese plenty, although it might not have seemed so to the exhausted, bloodied Americans, punished by the incessant fire of mortars, artillery, and machine guns. The 62nd Division was reeling from the Americans' hammer blows. General Isamu Chō, the Thirty-Second Army's chief of staff, warned that the 62nd would cease to exist unless it was reinforced.

The Japanese's dire manpower situation compelled Ushijima to send to the front lines his last large uncommitted units—the 24th Division and part of the 44th Independent Mixed Brigade. Heretofore, they had been idle at Minatoga, guarding against a possible American amphibious landing on the southeast coast that had never materialized. When the transfer was completed, a 5,500-man rear-area supply force would be the last remaining Japanese unit south of Shuri Castle. Part of the 24th would take over the eastern half of the 62nd's line, while the rest of the division, along with the 44th IMB, would establish a new line 1 mile to the south.[50]

Ironically, just as the Japanese had concluded that the Americans would not open a second front, US leaders were debating that very question. An actual landing behind enemy lines was being considered—and not a feint like the two landing craft runs of April 1 and 19 that had ended with last-minute U-turns.

EVEN BEFORE THE IE SHIMA invasion, General Andrew Bruce, the 77th Division's commander, had proposed that his men land near Minatoga and open a second front. The 77th had surprised the Japanese by coming ashore in December 1944 behind their lines at Ormoc on Leyte, and Bruce believed the same tactic would succeed on Okinawa. In his April 11 diary entry, General Buckner alluded to his subordinate general's idea with a trace of condescension: "As usual [Bruce] is rarin' to try a landing behind the Jap main position in southern Okinawa."[51]

The idea did not die. On April 21, ten days after Buckner's diary entry, Marine Commandant Alexander Vandegrift and General Roy Geiger, III Amphibious Corps's commander, urged Buckner to bring the 2nd Marine Division from Saipan and land it behind the Japanese lines. The Minatoga beaches, once a credible candidate for Iceberg's amphibious landing, were worthy of reconsideration, they argued. Admiral Richmond Kelly Turner, the Iceberg amphibious commander, and XXIV Corps General John Hodge both supported the plan's revival.[52]

However, Buckner was a risk-averse leader who believed that battles were won with superior firepower, not by surprise maneuvers. A second landing, he and his staff warned, might turn into another Anzio, "only worse"—one of the reasons a Minatoga landing was initially rejected during the planning of Iceberg. The January 1944 amphibious landing at Anzio, Italy, became a debacle when the Allies were slow to move off the beachhead and German troops captured the high ground overlooking it. The Germans shelled them for months. A 50-foot cliff fortified with bunkers and guns overlooked the Minatoga beaches.

Buckner and his staff also argued that the beaches were too small to accommodate the supplies that a second front would require. The Tenth Army's supply officer, General David Blakelock, added that not enough ammunition was available.

Buckner instead proposed landing the 2nd Marine Division on Kikai Shima, north of Okinawa, in July. Admiral Forrest Sherman, Admiral Chester Nimitz's chief of staff, sided with Buckner; he thought the Minatoga proposal was "impractical." Sherman said that it would take too long

to load out the 2nd Division, although Vandegrift promised him it could be under way in six hours. While that was surely an exaggeration, the division's ships were still combat-loaded from the feint toward Minatoga.

Colonel Samuel Taxis, the 2nd Division's operations officer, expressed the frustration of many Marines over the rejection of the plan. "They [the Tenth Army] should have a thrown a left hook down there in the southern beaches. . . . They had a hell of a powerful reinforced division, trained to a gnat's whisker." The 2nd Division was battle-hardened from its campaigns on Guadalcanal, Tarawa, and Saipan.[53]

Buckner's caution, however, might have been warranted. The new front would have been beyond the range of Tenth Army's artillery, while the Japanese 5th Artillery Command, much closer at hand, might have easily zeroed in on and pounded the assault troops on the landing beaches. The Japanese 24th Division, only a few miles away and not yet sent to reinforce the 62nd Division, might have stopped the 2nd Division from advancing inland.

But perhaps the decisive factor against opening a second front was Buckner's desire to keep casualties as low as possible. "I must avoid a spectacular hurry in order to save lives," he wrote. In a May 3 letter to his wife, Adele, Buckner appeared proud that his men had inflicted heavy losses on the enemy at a relatively low cost. "We have already killed 30,000 Japs that we know of," he wrote. "This is more than the total killed on Iwo Jima and our losses have been less than half those suffered in taking that island."

ALTHOUGH ADMIRAL NIMITZ SUPPORTED BUCKNER'S decision to not open a second front, Nimitz and some of his admirals were unhappy with the Tenth Army's slow progress. Admiral Raymond Spruance, commander of the Fifth Fleet, vented to his former chief of staff, Captain Charles Moore, on the subject. "I doubt if the Army's slow, methodical method of fighting really saves any lives in the long run. It merely spreads the casualties over a longer period," while increasing the number of Navy casualties from the prolongation of Japanese air attacks on American warships. "I do not think the Army is at all allergic to losses of naval ships and personnel. There are times when I get impatient for some of Holland Smith's drive," wrote Spruance, noting that Smith's Marines on Iwo Jima "finished it up in 26 days."

During an inspection tour of Okinawa on April 23, Nimitz read Buckner the riot act. The Pacific Fleet's commander-in-chief had flown in from Guam, where his headquarters was moved in January from Pearl Harbor

to be closer to the fighting. Nimitz demanded that Buckner speed up his campaign. Resenting Nimitz's intrusion on what he regarded as his turf, Buckner replied that ground operations were his concern, not Nimitz's.

The usually mild-mannered admiral bristled at this. "Yes, but ground though it may be, I'm losing a ship and a half a day," he said, and then sharply reminded Buckner who was in charge. "So if this line isn't moving within five days, we'll get someone here to move it so we can all get out from under these stupid air attacks."[54]

Nimitz's concern about his losses was understandable. Over the course of three mass *kikusui* attacks and other air assaults during April, kamikazes and conventional Japanese aircraft had sunk thirteen ships and damaged more than a hundred others, killing 956 sailors and wounding 2,650. Eight hundred ninety-seven others were listed as missing in action.[55]

DETAILS OF THE SECOND-FRONT DEBATE were leaked to the press, and correspondent Homer Bigart broke the story in the *New York Herald Tribune* on May 29. Of Buckner's frontal attacks, Bigart wrote, "Our tactics were ultraconservative. Instead of an end run we persisted in frontal attacks. It was hey-diddle-diddle straight down the middle."

David Lawrence jumped into the controversy in his syndicated "Today in Washington" column. Bigart's report, wrote Lawrence, confirmed persistent rumors in Washington that "American strategy has been faulty" on Okinawa. In fact, the columnist said in a burst of hyperbole, Okinawa might be "a worse example of military incompetence than Pearl Harbor." Lawrence declared that an island campaign "cannot be fought by massing artillery or deploying troops as would be done on a vast terrain in Europe." He suggested that someone more experienced in amphibious warfare than Buckner would have moved "aggressively and in less time." Lawrence proposed convening a panel of retired officers to conduct an investigation.[56]

Lawrence's column unfairly judged the tactical situation, overlooking the uniquely formidable Japanese defenses faced by the Tenth Army. But Lawrence's and Bigart's widely read dispatches ignited a firestorm that demanded an official response. Stepping up to answer the accusations, Admiral Nimitz staunchly defended Buckner, the man he had threatened to replace, and condemned Lawrence's report.

At a press conference on Guam, Nimitz told reporters that Buckner's tactical decisions "were his own, but they had my concurrence." The proposed

new landings, he said, would have had to be made over "unsatisfactory beaches against an alerted enemy defense. They would have involved heavy casualties and would have created unacceptable supply problems." He said Lawrence had no firsthand knowledge of what was happening on Okinawa and suggested "that he has been made use of for purposes which are not in the best interests of the United States."[57]

PROGRESS DURING THE APRIL 19 offensive was slow, but by the fifth day, April 23, the three-division assault had attained nearly every objective—with two exceptions. In the east, the 7th Division's 184th Infantry had crept within 230 yards of Hill 178's peak, where it was awaiting relief from the 17th Infantry.

And then there was the "Kakazu Pocket." It had defied capture by the 96th Division, and now was the nemesis of the 27th. Plastered by naval gunfire, artillery, and air strikes; repeatedly attacked by ground troops; and finally bypassed, Kakazu yet remained a Japanese stronghold.

To eradicate the stubborn obstacle, General Hodge organized a muscular special task force of four infantry battalions from the 7th, 27th, and 96th Divisions, to be accompanied by tanks, flame tanks, self-propelled guns, and chemical mortars. General William Bradford, the 27th's assistant commander, would lead the task force. It moved into position on April 23 and would jump off the next morning.[58]

That night, Japanese artillery pounded XXIV Corps's lines for six hours.

AT 7:30 A.M. ON THE 24th, the Bradford Task Force, which included four tank battalions, attacked after a short artillery barrage. To the attackers' amazement, no one opposed them; Kakazu Pocket was deserted, except for about six hundred dead Japanese soldiers who had been left behind.

Up and down the battle line, the story was the same. In the center, the 96th Division's six-battalion assault south from Nishibaru Ridge encountered only Japanese stragglers. The Americans quickly occupied Nishibaru Village, Tanabaru Escarpment, and Hill 143. In the east, the 7th Division's 17th Infantry replaced the 184th on the slope of Hill 178 during the night of April 23–24. Anticipating a hailstorm of gunfire when it stormed the hillcrest in the morning, it was met only by scattered artillery fire. When the Americans occupied the hilltop, they discovered that the Japanese had removed their weapons and supplies, and had buried most of their dead— evidence of a planned withdrawal.[59]

Tenth Army scouts discovered that the Japanese had pulled back to new defensive positions 1 mile to the south; its epicenter was Shuri Castle—General Mitsuru Ushijima's headquarters. As the Thirty-Second Army occupied the new line, it was joined by reserves that had languished for weeks near Minatoga to safeguard against a possible American amphibious assault. The 24th Division and the rest of the 44th Independent Mixed Brigade now moved into the Shuri Line. These units, if they had been inserted immediately into the first defensive line, might have put iron into the April 12 counteroffensive and helped achieve a breakthrough. That opportunity was now lost.

ALONG THE ABANDONED 5-MILE OUTER Shuri defensive ring, the enemy had suffered shocking losses—30,000 killed, according to Buckner's estimate, but probably far more—and, in places, its carefully built positions had been pulverized by the grinding XXIV Corps's offensive. Following the Japanese withdrawal, the Americans were left to marvel at the intricate defensive systems that had defied their best efforts.

The Thirty-Second Army's orderly withdrawal from the outer ring foreshadowed the great battle for the island that would be fought on the main Shuri Line. The movement of tens of thousands of Japanese soldiers to prepared positions a mile away bespoke careful planning and execution from a still-potent enemy, not a routed army. Buckner's Tenth Army was now entering a new, more dangerous battlefield.

EXCEPT FOR STRAGGLERS AND INFILTRATORS, the outer ring had been wholly abandoned everywhere but at "Item Pocket," a knot of intensive resistance on the 27th Division's right, a short distance north of Gusukuma Village and Machinato Airfield.

Four strongly defended low-lying coral and limestone ridges, separated by gullies and rice paddies, radiated from the center of the position. They overlooked Route 1 to the east, and coastal areas to the west and north. It was called "Item Pocket" because on maps its center was in Area 7777's "I" sector—"Item" in military argot.[60]

The area covering 2,500 by 4,000 yards had no readily apparent weaknesses. The defensive positions had been developed months before L-Day. In the hollowed-out hills were tunnels with narrow-gauge railroads, living quarters, and aid stations. The area was tenaciously defended by up to seven hundred Japanese soldiers from two companies of Lieutenant

Colonel Kosuke Nishibayashi's 21st Independent Infantry Battalion. The battalion included a machine-gun company, an antitank company, and assorted antiaircraft and mortar units. Okinawan auxiliaries augmented the Japanese regulars.

Surrounded by a minefield and a network of antitank trenches, Item Pocket bristled with heavy weapons: eighty-three light machine guns, forty-one heavy machine guns, sixteen grenade launchers, seven 47mm antitank guns, two 81mm mortars, two 70mm howitzers, and six 75mm guns. All of the positions were mutually supporting, and the entire area could be hit by pre-registered Japanese artillery fire from the south. The defenders had plentiful food, water, and ammunition.[61]

On April 20, the 27th Division's 165th Infantry was advancing toward Gusukuma and, beyond it, Machinato Airfield and Naha, Okinawa's capital city. Aerial reconnaissance of the area and maps revealed neither Japanese strength nor important terrain features, giving rise to a false sense of optimism.

The 165th's executive officer, Lieutenant Colonel Joseph Hart, was so confident that the regiment would quickly reach its objectives that he carried a bright-green sign bearing the words "Conroy Field," which he intended to put up at Machinato Airfield to honor Colonel J. Gardiner Conroy, the 165th Regiment commander killed in November 1943 on Makin Island. Hart also announced that the 165th would hold a dance in Naha on Saturday night.[62]

But the regiment walked into a Japanese buzzsaw north of Gusukuma. Rifle, machine-gun, and mortar fire converged on the infantrymen from concealed positions in the finger ridges and ravines, inside which tunnels and rooms had been carved out. The ridges, fanning out from a northwest-southwest axis, soon bore 27th Division-vernacular names: Potter's, Charlie, and Gusukuma Ridges, framed by Dead Horse Gulch to the south and Anderson Gulch to the north. A swath of Gusukuma Ridge was renamed Ryan's Ridge in honor of its eventual captor, Captain Bernard Ryan, commander of Company F of the 165th. Potter's Ridge was named for Captain John Potter, whose Company I finally seized it.[63]

On April 20, the 165th's 1st and 2nd Battalions proceeded south, with the 1st marching down Route 1 and the 2nd farther to the west. The Japanese permitted Company C of the 1st Battalion to reach Charlie Ridge's southern nose before cutting it off with machine-gun fire from multiple concealed positions throughout Item Pocket. Then, a torrent of mortar fire rained down

on the trapped men; within a few minutes, the company lost five killed and twenty-two wounded. The 2nd Battalion attempted to join the 1st on its left, but Japanese mortars on Ryan's Ridge thwarted the movement.[64]

Tech Sergeant Ernest Schoeff's platoon of the 2nd Battalion led Company E in an attack on Ryan's Ridge on April 21. Sheeting enemy fire from atop the ridge cut off the platoon from the rest of the company. Schoeff and his men crawled, crept, and dashed up the hill to a road cut while under relentless rifle, machine-gun, and mortar fire. At nightfall, with just nine men still able to fight, the survivors were attacked from three sides by fifty to sixty shouting Japanese soldiers who had crawled to within 40 yards of Schoeff's position before pouncing.

It was one of the campaign's wildest melees. The heavily outnumbered Americans, hunkered in foxholes, desperately fended off the attackers with grenades, bayonets, rocks, fists, and rifle fire. Private First Class Paul Cook fired four cases of ammunition before he was killed, after dispatching ten to twenty enemy soldiers. Schoeff broke his rifle over the head of an enemy soldier, snatched a rifle from another and bayoneted him, and shot a third one. Forced to retreat by the ferocity of Schoeff and his men, the Japanese left thirty-five bodies on the hillside. With just four combat-capable men remaining, Schoeff elected to withdraw. He rejoined the rest of Company E just before midnight.[65]

Creeping forward under heavy fire, the 165th double-flanked Charlie Ridge on April 21, but could not overcome the hornet's nest on the ridge crest.

When Japanese in Item Pocket frustrated an attempt to build a Bailey bridge over Anderson Gulch on Route 1 to resupply the 1st Battalion, a bulldozer began a bypass route.

The operator was killed, and Lieutenant Colonel Walter Anderson, commander of the 193rd Tank Battalion, took the controls of his only remaining bulldozer tank to attempt to complete the bypass. But a 47mm antitank round ended Anderson's life, and the bypass was not completed.

Consequently, no supplies reached the 1st Battalion, which still managed to push ahead to the outskirts of Gusukuma Village before a hurricane of machine-gun fire from the village and Item Pocket to its rear stopped its advance.[66]

Over the next three days, the 165th struggled to find the key that would unlock the pocket's cunningly placed interlocking firing positions that blocked all approaches. After the regiment cleared Potter's and Charlie

Ridges, on April 22 a heavy air strike walloped pillboxes inside the pocket and reportedly knocked out a 47mm gun. But this did not noticeably reduce the tenacious Japanese resistance.

Before daylight on April 22, Japanese soldiers discovered wounded Americans from Company K that had been abandoned in a gulch and caves when the company withdrew to the crest of Gusukuma Ridge during a Japanese counterattack. The Japanese forced the wounded men into the open with phosphorus grenades and smoke from bonfires. They then shot them all, killing twenty-five men and wounding thirty-one.[67]

The key was fitted into the lock on April 25. Captain Ryan of Company F had proposed an attack on Gusukuma Ridge at 2 a.m., but the assault was delayed until morning because of enemy counterattacks lasting all night. Low on ammunition and having gone without sleep for two days, Company F began the attack at 9 a.m., crossing 600 yards of open ground under fire.

Minutes later, thirty-one men reached the ridge crest, while Captain Ryan and the rest of the company remained pinned down by gunfire below. The Japanese counterattacked the ridgetop from spider holes and caves. During the twenty-minute hand-to-hand fight, the Americans ran out of ammunition and were compelled to use their rifles as clubs to repulse the attack.[68]

Other 165th Infantry units struck Item Pocket from all sides, and 1st Battalion troops pushed into debris-clogged Gusukuma Village, where it seemed that enemy soldiers were hiding behind every wall and tree. Private First Class Richard King of Company A killed a Japanese sniper who was tied in a tree, then sat on a limb beside the body and picked off ten enemy soldiers by nightfall.[69]

For several hours on April 25, division headquarters refused to believe that part of Ryan's company had gotten on top of the ridge, and the thirty-one men who had reached it—now reduced to twenty-four effectives—remained on their own.

Finally, at 3:50 p.m., Ryan was given permission to reinforce his men on the ridge, and he led twenty-three men to the crest. He and two volunteers went for more help, returning with Company K by midnight and increasing the American force to just over a hundred defenders. For the rest of the night, they repulsed Japanese counterattacks, and at dawn the two companies still clung to Ryan Ridge.[70]

Ryan's bold attack had cracked open all of Gusukuma Ridge, and on April 26, Companies F and K cleaned out caves on the ridge's western slope. By nightfall, the enemy-held area of the pocket had shrunken, Japanese positions that had commanded Route 1 were sealed off, the bridges were rebuilt, and tanks were able to operate with the infantrymen.

Most of the 27th Division bypassed the last Japanese holdouts and advanced to the Kuwan Inlet south of Machinato Airfield, leaving behind two companies to dig out the "bitter enders."[71]

The 27th's commander, General Griner, was dissatisfied with the chaotic deployment of the 165th Infantry units, and fired the regiment's commander, Colonel Gerard Kelley, on April 27. Griner replaced him with Kelley's executive officer, Lieutenant Colonel Joseph Hart, the man who had sunnily predicted April 20 that the 165th would hold a dance in Naha on the following night.[72]

The New York Division was withdrawn from the lines on April 30 and sent to northern Okinawa for occupational duty, replacing the 6th Marine Division. The 27th reported 2,661 casualties, including 316 killed, during its time in the lines between April 16 and 30. The division claimed to have killed more than 5,000 enemy soldiers.[73]

The bitter irony for the 27th was that it was turning over the mission of breaking the western Shuri Line to the Marines, the New York Division's harshest critics.

The Shuri Line

Okinawa is a valley and a ridge, a valley and a ridge, all the way to the end of the island.

—SERGEANT R. V. BURGIN OF THE 5TH MARINES[1]

It was an appalling chaos. It was such a jolt to leave the quiet, beautiful countryside that morning and plunge into a thunderous, deadly storm of steel that afternoon.

—PRIVATE FIRST CLASS E. B. SLEDGE, DESCRIBING THE DAY THE 1ST MARINE DIVISION REACHED THE SHURI LINE[2]

My grave will be the sea around Okinawa, and I will see my mother and grandmother again. I have neither regrets, nor fear about death.

—SUICIDE PILOT ENSIGN TERUO YAMAGUCHI IN A LETTER TO HIS FATHER[3]

THE 1ST MARINE DIVISION'S MONTH-LONG idyll in central Okinawa ended May 1, when the Marines boarded trucks. With a great clash of gears, the trucks rumbled south toward the battle lines a dozen miles away, stopping near Machinato Airfield. From there, the Marines proceeded south on foot, walking single file down the right side of the narrow, dusty coral road.

Sergeant R. V. Burgin of the 5th Marines could see the lay of the land ahead of them. "Okinawa is a valley and a ridge, a valley and a ridge, all the way to the end of the island."

General Simon Buckner had committed the III Amphibious Corps from northern Okinawa to the southern part of the island on April 26 after the Joint Chiefs of Staff canceled Phase III of Operation Iceberg: the planned invasion of Miyako Shima in the Sakashima Islands east of Taiwan.

The 1st Marine Division went south first, to take the place of the 27th Division on the western battle line. The division had spent its first weeks on Okinawa building gravel-pathed bivouacs equipped with showers and mess halls. In the evenings, the Marines sang popular songs, drank "jungle juice" made from rations, and attended outdoor movies. Many of them had pet ponies, goats, and rabbits.[4]

All too soon, these peaceful days would become a distant memory, for the Marines were marching to the sound of the guns. From the battle line ahead, they could hear the explosion of Japanese artillery and mortar rounds, and the sheet-tearing sound of machine-gun and rifle fire.

"I was filled with dread," wrote Private First Class E. B. Sledge, a mortarman with the 5th Marines who had fought on Peleliu the previous fall. There, the 1st Division had suffered heavy casualties while destroying the veteran Japanese 14th Division in cave defenses and pillboxes similar to those on Okinawa. Okinawa would exact an even higher toll on the division.

A column of men marched toward the Marines on the other side of the road: the 106th Infantry of the 27th Division, whose place in the line the 1st Division would occupy.

"Their tragic expressions revealed where they had been," Sledge wrote. "They were dead beat, dirty and grisly, hollow-eyed and tight-faced." A soldier's eyes locked on Sledge's and he said, "It's hell up there, Marine."

Indeed, the 105th and 106th Infantry had been so reduced by casualties that full-strength Marine companies replaced the decimated Army battalions along a line extending from Kuwan, southwest of Machinato Airfield, to Miyagusuku and Awacha to the east.

The 27th Division's downbeat appearance and comportment disgusted Marines lacking Sledge's empathy. "We encountered the sorriest bunch of soldiers coming our way I'd ever seen," said Sergeant Burgin, a mortar-squad leader. "They were what was left of the 106th Infantry of the 27th Division, and they were exhausted, dead on their feet." Burgin witnessed a soldier refusing to obey an order from a sergeant, a gross infraction that

would have earned a Marine brig time; the soldier was not punished. "There was no discipline whatever in the outfit. . . . We thought they were the pits."

Bob Craig of the 1st Marines said the 27th Division's "disorderly withdrawal" appeared to have "no organized line of march, many had no weapons at all, there were rifles and BARs all over the nearby ground." The Army division would hold northern Okinawa while the 1st and 6th Marine Divisions joined the main battle zone.

Sledge's unit left the road and "plunged once more into the abyss," racing toward a ridge with mortar and artillery shells of all calibers bursting around them, including 150mm howitzers, "what men called the big stuff."

"It was an appalling chaos," wrote Sledge. "It was such a jolt to leave the quiet, beautiful countryside that morning and plunge into a thunderous, deadly storm of steel that afternoon."[5]

Sledge and three other mortarmen were sent as stretcher-bearers to a road cut through a ridge to collect a wounded man, just as Marine riflemen who had advanced to that point were withdrawing at a gallop. They "all wore wide-eyed shocked expressions," Sledge wrote.

"It was traumatic," said Lieutenant Robert Crowton. It was his first time in battle. His platoon advanced 50 yards under heavy fire. "By the end of the day, we were back where we started, and with a lot more respect for the Army division that we'd relieved."[6]

Far worse lay ahead.

THE 1ST MARINES HAD REACHED the battle line the previous day, April 30. It dug in south of Machinato Airfield, Kuwan, and Miyagusuku, through which the 27th had pushed on the 29th.

Before beginning their withdrawal, Army battalion officers warned the Marines that some Japanese were still holed up in Miyagusuku. The 1st Tank Battalion entered the village with conventional and flame tanks to mop up, knocking down walls and houses that were still standing, and drenching it all in 300 gallons of flaming napalm. After the fires died down, 3rd Battalion infantrymen entered the town and were pounded by heavy mortar and artillery fire. Enemy troops began reentering the village, and the Marines withdrew for the night under a smoke screen.

Along the western battle line, the 1st Marine Division faced a tactical problem that would become a disconcerting feature of the Shuri Line: a cluster of enemy-held hills bristling with mutually supporting fortifications. An attempt to seize one hill instantly attracted heavy fire from its

neighbors. The solution, simple but extremely difficult, was to capture the hills simultaneously.[7]

In a driving rainstorm on May 2 that portended the onset of Okinawa's rainy season, the 1st Marines pushed south of Miyagusuku toward the Asa-Kawa Estuary. There they encountered "the first example of the enemy's mutually supporting positions"—heavy artillery and harassing fire from two directions that cut up Company C, leaving it in an exposed position with heavy casualties. The Marines withdrew. That black, rainy night, the Japanese attacked Company K with bayonets, hurling grenades. The Marines repelled them after twenty minutes of fighting with grenades and mud-clogged rifles that they used as clubs. It was the 1st Division's first close-combat action on Okinawa.

On the division left, the 5th Marines were pinned down by powerful frontal and flanking fire from the excellent Japanese defenses in the area that became known as Awacha Pocket, south of the town of Awacha and north of Dakeshi. "The advance was untenable and had to be withdrawn to initial positions," wrote Lieutenant Colonel Martin Roth.[8]

DISTINGUISHING HIMSELF DURING THE 5TH Marines' struggle for Awacha Pocket was a fifty-three-year-old University of Chicago economics professor, Major Paul Douglas, who was wounded while acting as a stretcher-bearer.

It would be a wild understatement to describe Douglas as a Marine Corps anomaly. Nationally known for his support of the New Deal and intervention in the European war, Douglas had run for Congress in Illinois and lost in 1942. Within days of his defeat, he enlisted as a private in the Marine Corps, although his age disqualified him from the draft. Moreover, he was a Quaker.

Assigned the rank of major and made an adjutant, Douglas energetically lobbied his superiors for permission to go to the front. On Peleliu—where he was described as "that old gray-haired fellow rushing around like crazy up there"—he won a Bronze Star when he was wounded while carrying flamethrower ammunition to the front.

On Okinawa, Douglas was shot in the left arm while carrying wounded men to safety. He spent fourteen months at Bethesda Naval Hospital learning to regain partial use of his arm. Resuming his professorship at the University of Chicago, Douglas in 1948 was elected to the US Senate from Illinois and served for eighteen years.[9]

BY THE END OF MAY 2, the 1st Division had lost 54 men killed in action, 233 wounded, and 11 that were listed as missing. Despite mud and rain, incessant machine-gun fire, and avalanches of enemy grenades, the 1st Marines' 3rd Battalion managed to advance 300 yards south of Miyagusuku to a small range of hills. The weather diminished the Marines' firepower. "Everybody's weapons were all muddy and had a hell of a time firing them," Private First Class A. R. Fournier wrote in his diary. During the nighttime, when the Japanese repeatedly counterattacked, many weapons were inoperable.

Company K reported 43 casualties on May 2. Three days later, the company was relieved by Company E after losing 14 killed and 120 wounded over four days, with no sleep for three of them. Everyone was exhausted. "Four men [passed] out while digging their holes," Fournier wrote.[10]

These first clashes with the Japanese on Okinawa impressed 1st Division Marines with the enemy's thoroughness in removing traces of their presence when they withdrew from a position. They left no trash, gear, empty cartridge cases, ammunition cartons, or even spent brass cartridges. Sometimes there were only bloodstains on the ground. "We got an eerie feeling," wrote Sledge, "as though we were fighting a phantom enemy."[11]

The 1st Division's battering attacks, in which a modest gain with moderate to heavy casualties was considered to be a good day, was representative of the grinding progress seen all along the Shuri Line. To the Marines' left, the 77th Division inched toward the Maeda Escarpment and its Hacksaw Ridge, and farther east, the 7th Division struggled to capture Kochi Ridge and Conical Hill.

Although it was not apparent amid the roar of artillery, mortars, and machine guns and the cries for corpsmen and medics, the adversaries were in temporary holding patterns while they both secretly laid plans that they hoped would tip the battle's fortunes their way. In preparation, the Tenth Army replaced exhausted units and attempted to straighten its lines, while the Japanese moved up fresh troops from the Minatoga area in southeastern Okinawa.

THE THIRTY-SECOND ARMY'S SENIOR OFFICERS celebrated the emperor's birthday at a sake-drenched banquet April 29 at their headquarters beneath Shuri Castle. During the dinner, General Isamu Chō, the Army's chief of staff, exuberantly proposed a new counterattack. He believed that the ongoing reinforcement of the bloodied 62nd Division by the relatively

unscathed 24th Division and 44th Independent Mixed Brigade guaranteed that the Army this time could crush the invaders.

The next day, the Thirty-Second Army's officers endorsed Chō's plan—all but Colonel Hiromichi Yahara. He reminded his peers of the failure of the April 12–13 counteroffensive, at a cost of nearly 1,600 dead. A second counteroffensive would also fail, Yahara predicted, because the Americans were more numerous, possessed massively superior firepower, and held the nearby high ground. A new counteroffensive would squander manpower that would better serve the Thirty-Second Army by continuing to bleed the Americans in attritional battles, argued Yahara.

Having lost the debate, Yahara, in his capacity as the division operations officer, began working on the attack plan. The counteroffensive would begin May 4, coinciding with a new mass kamikaze attack planned by the 5th Air Fleet and 6th Air Army.[12]

ON THE AMERICAN LINE'S EASTERN extremity, the 7th Division faced a fresh Japanese 24th Division unit—Lieutenant Colonel Masaru Yoshida's 22nd Infantry, which occupied 500-yard-long Kochi Ridge and the surrounding high ground. The 7th's 17th Infantry discovered that the Japanese had masterfully integrated Kochi's defenses with nearby supporting positions.

Colonel Francis Pachler's 17th Infantry reached Kochi's forward slopes with few losses on April 25. That was the easy part, for the Japanese held pillboxes and an elaborate trench system on the reverse slope. Artillery and mortar positions on hills nearby were zeroed in on Kochi.

Although just yards away from the Japanese, Pachler's men were pinned down by concentrated enemy fire for more than a week. US artillery fire and close-air support were of no help because the Japanese lines were too close to the American positions. Sometimes the Japanese serenaded the Hourglass men with peculiar insults. "They were yelling in a sort of sing-song voice, 'To hell with Washington, to hell with Lincoln, and to hell with Roy Acuff, too,'" said Sergeant Joe Joy.

Pachler's men attacked repeatedly from April 25 to April 29, but the Japanese repulsed every assault with machine-gun fire that came from three directions. During the night of April 29, the regiment briefly overcame its aversion to calling in artillery support so close to its own lines—with disastrous results: "friendly" 105mm fire landed amid Company G, killing five men and wounding eighteen.

The 7th's 32nd Infantry attempted to break the stalemate by attacking a ridge southeast of Kochi, but the situation did not change. The 17th Infantry advanced a short distance on May 1–2, but was unable to penetrate the curtain of intensive mortar fire that foiled its attempt to seize one of Kochi's four knobs.

On May 2, engineers bulldozed a road for tanks, but enemy antitank fire prevented the tanks and supporting infantrymen from using it. Lieutenant Roland Glenn, a platoon commander with the 17th Infantry, hugged the ground with his men as artillery and mortar fire exploded around them. The man beside Glenn was killed. "His head, snapped back by the force of the bullet, entering through the steel helmet and into his skull and out the back of his head, dangled like a rag puppet against my side."

Roaring Japanese artillery, mortar, and machine-gun fire stopped a coordinated, two-battalion attack on May 3, even though a flamethrower squad blasted every inch of ground, leaving "steaming, bloated bodies . . . seared black. . . . Eyes stared out of roasted swollen heads without hair."[13]

ON APRIL 29, THE 77TH Division had begun relieving the 96th Division in the center of the battle line. Before the 96th completely withdrew, however, the Japanese struck the center of the 383rd Infantry's lines through several deep draws during the predawn hours of April 30.

After intensive close-in fighting, the Americans repulsed the attack, describing it as "the strongest counterattack we were to receive on Okinawa." Two hundred seventy-three enemy soldiers were counted dead.[14]

Later in the day, the 96th's depleted regiments wearily boarded trucks bound for the rear. The 381st, the primary unit that had besieged the Maeda Escarpment, had suffered 1,021 casualties and was at 40 percent strength. The 96th would return in ten days to relieve the 7th Division on the eastern flank.

After Kerama Retto and Ie Shima, which the 77th had finished mopping up just three days earlier, this would be the veteran division's third operation of the Okinawa campaign.

The 77th's immediate objective was unmistakable, looming to the south of the division: the 4,200-yard-long Maeda Escarpment, which stood 500 feet high on the south side of an open, half-mile-wide valley. It was defended by a polyglot of Thirty-Second Army units led by a Lieutenant Colonel Kaya: remnants of the 62nd Division's 12th and 14th Battalions and of the 272nd and 273rd Independent Battalions as well as the 32nd Regiment's

Shimura Battalion—about 3,000 troops in all. Upon the escarpment's east end stood a tall, jagged prominence known as "Needle Rock." On the escarpment's summit stood Hacksaw Ridge, a 50-foot precipice that might be scaled only at its western end.[15]

Before the 77th relieved it, the 96th Division had tackled Maeda. It had first approached the escarpment April 24 following the enemy's surprise withdrawal from Kakazu. After a full day of concentrated artillery fire and air strikes, the Deadeyes attacked on April 26. Three companies of the 381st Infantry reached the escarpment's crest with relative ease—but then the Japanese counterattacked.

They swarmed out of hiding places before and behind the Americans—Maeda being literally honeycombed with tunnels, caves, and spider holes that were more elaborate than anyone imagined. It turned into a primal, all-night brawl with men ducking behind boulders and throwing grenades and fighting with bayonets, knives, and chunks of jagged coral.[16]

Across a 200-yard saddle from Hacksaw and the monolithic Needle Rock that rose from its eastern end stood Hill 150. On the 26th, a company from the 96th's 383rd Infantry poured crude oil and gasoline into caves from atop Hill 150, set the inflammables afire, and then slaughtered the Japanese when they poured out of the hill into the open; an estimated three hundred enemy soldiers died.

That same day, Private First Class Lee Moore climbed atop Needle Rock, whose defenders had warded off all efforts to capture it. Firing his automatic rifle from the hip, Moore shot Japanese soldiers swarming at the rock's base, then attacked a nearby cave with a flamethrower and grenades—killing twenty-four enemy soldiers in all.

When the attack resumed on the 27th, the 383rd's 1st Battalion swung around behind Hill 150 and, accompanied by tanks from the 763rd Tank Battalion, killed another three hundred Japanese on Maeda's reverse slope. The 1st Battalion's nighttime position atop the hill was "the worse [sic] I've ever seen," said Company B commander Captain John Byers, with "Japs all around us and our fields of fire were sharply limited. . . . There were snipers all over, and we're even getting ricochet machine-gun fire from our own units on the escarpment."[17]

At Needle Rock, Captain Willard Bollinger realized his Company F could not dig foxholes in the hard rock and coral around the Needle that would be deep enough to protect them from a counterattack. He had an inspiration, though: he placed his men atop the boulders surrounding the

Needle. That night, Japanese from the reverse slope charged Company F's empty foxholes, and the Americans above them on the boulders shot them down. Forty-seven bodies were counted the next morning.[18]

On the following day, April 28, undermanned Company K of the 381st attacked the enemy barracks southwest of Maeda. After being caught in a crossfire between the barracks and Hacksaw's southern slope, the soldiers became embroiled in a vicious hand-to-hand fight in a draw where they had sought cover.

When Lieutenant Colonel Daniel Nolan, the battalion commander, called the company commander, Lieutenant Albert Strand, to check on the situation, Strand remained optimistic—even though his original thirty-six-man force had been quickly reduced to twenty-four effectives. Strand reported to Nolan, "I can see more Japs in front of me than I have men of my own. I think I can advance."[19]

Atop Maeda, Captain Louis Reuter Jr.'s Company G crept into a cave that went straight into a cliff, and it glimpsed the amazing Maeda interior superstructure hewn by the Japanese. Approaching a beam of daylight visible deep in the cliff, they found a shaft that plunged three levels or more to the base of the escarpment. Below, they heard Japanese voices. Turning down a passage to the right, they discovered a room hollowed from rock that the Japanese had used as an observation post. From it, the Hagushi beaches were plainly visible, and every road leading to XXIV Corps's battlefront. Before leaving the observation post, Captain Reuter appropriated a Japanese telescope and a pair of binoculars.[20]

Japanese gunners manning a concrete bunker built into a cliff face on Hacksaw thwarted every effort to seize and hold the ridge, and withstood American attempts to neutralize it. Shells ricocheted off it; it resisted attacks by flamethrowers and satchel charges, even when the explosives ignited an ammunition dump inside the ridge with a thunderous, earth-rattling explosion. The bunker was continually replenished by replacement troops that reached it from tunnels inside the escarpment.

The 77th Division's 307th Infantry relieved the 96th Division's 381st Infantry on April 29, also the last day on the Maeda line for the 383rd Regiment. Before the 383rd withdrew, its Company G had crushed a headlong attack by Japanese soldiers armed with "everything from grenades to spears," killing 125 of them. On this day, too, the 383rd's 3rd Battalion reached the crest of Hill 138, less than 1,000 yards from Shuri Castle, before the 77th's 306th Infantry took over.[21]

Sergeant Bruce Chilcote, a mortarman with the 381st, watched the 96th's battered companies come off the front line. "I couldn't believe my eyes when our rifle companies . . . passed through our mortar firing area," he said. "Each company had only 10 or 12 men remaining," instead of their normal strength of 150 to 200 men.[22]

In spite of the 96th Division's progress at Maeda escarpment and its claims to have killed 2,500 enemy defenders, Hacksaw Ridge remained firmly in Japanese hands, as did the lofty concrete bunker.[23]

THE DAY AFTER RELIEVING THE 96th, the 77th's 307th Infantry scaled Hacksaw Ridge on four 50-foot ladders and five cargo nets borrowed from the Navy. At the edge of the cliff top, the assault troops were met by a wall of machine-gun and rifle fire from pillboxes and fire trenches; knee mortars; hand grenades; and artillery, antitank, and mortar fire coming from positions farther south. One infantryman described it as "all hell rolled into one." As darkness fell, the Japanese counterattacked, driving the Americans back down the cliff. As they hastily descended in the dark, several soldiers were wounded by their own comrades, or were injured when they fell to the cliff base.[24]

The Japanese fiercely clung to Hacksaw in the face of everything thrown at them by the 77th, which was exhausted and understrength after its six-day campaign on Ie Shima. At one point, Colonel Stephen Hamilton, commander of the 307th Infantry, reportedly told Colonel Michael Halloran of the 96th Division's 381st Infantry, "You can have this damn thing back anytime you want it."

The limits of American ingenuity were tested. "Eventually all sorts of tactics were used," wrote Captain Richard Spencer of the 307th's 1st Battalion. Engineers built a trough to funnel an oil-gasoline mixture across the ridge and into caves on the reverse slope, where the volatile fuel was ignited and satchel charges were hurled into the flames. On May 2, the 307th pulled back from the lip of the cliff top so that high-explosive mortar rounds, tank fire, and howitzers could hammer it. Six phosphorus shells fired into a cave in a fifteen-minute period produced white smoke seen wafting from more than thirty concealed openings in the ridge.[25]

The 763rd Tank Battalion pounded Hacksaw on May 2 until part of its upper levels was sheared off and crashed to the ground. "It was like a section of the Maginot Line as it had four floors, electric lights, and five feet of reinforced concrete covered with dirt and rip-rapped with blocks of coral,"

wrote Lieutenant Bob Green, who commanded a platoon of tanks. For the next two days, the Japanese stubbornly resisted from inside the exposed complex as tanks picked away at it with their guns.[26]

The 307th's 2nd and 3rd Battalions slipped around to the southern, reverse slope of the escarpment and began blowing up caves while the 1st Battalion waged a harrowing hand-grenade battle on the crest on May 3. As fast as they could pull the pins, the Americans threw grenades handed up from the escarpment base via a human supply chain. The Japanese replied in kind with grenades and knee mortars. Neither side gave ground. The grenade fight was so intensive, officers said, that men would leave the fight weeping and vowing to not return. But a few minutes later, they could be seen pitching grenades again.

FROM THIS MAELSTROM EMERGED THE unlikeliest hero of the 77th Division's siege of Hacksaw Ridge, Private First Class Desmond Doss, a conscientious objector medic attached to Company B of the 307th Infantry's 1st Battalion. Doss, a devout Seventh Day Adventist from Virginia, was drafted into the Army in April 1942, and had become infamous in the 77th Division for his refusal to touch a gun, or to work on the Sabbath, which Adventists observed on Saturday.[27]

At Guam and Leyte, Doss won two Bronze Stars with a "V" for exceptional valor. Throughout the Hacksaw battle, the lanky, soft-spoken Virginian repeatedly exposed himself to enemy fire while carrying wounded men to the edge of the escarpment and then lowering them by rope to the cliff base, seemingly oblivious to personal risk. By May 4, Doss's uniform was so caked with blood that his platoon leader "promoted" a clean uniform for him.

May 5 was a Saturday—which Seventh Day Adventists like Doss were supposed to spend in prayer. On this Saturday, Doss was Company B's only unwounded medic, and the company had been ordered to assault Hacksaw again.

When Doss overheard his company commander say that he did not want to ask Doss to break his Sabbath, Doss stepped forward and volunteered to go, if he could first read his Bible for a short time. While Company B waited, Doss read silently. After fifteen minutes, he raised his head, smiled, and said he was ready.[28]

Company B ascended the cliff and, after a bloody, close-in battle, was again driven off the summit with heavy casualties. Back at the cliff base,

the company reassembled and called roll. Doss was not present, and it was believed he had been killed or wounded on Hacksaw.

But twenty minutes later the infantrymen were astonished to see Doss wave to them from the cliff top, and signal that he was ready to begin lowering the wounded, "mountain style," on ropes. Ignoring an order to leave the ridge, Doss began evacuating the wounded men one by one to the base of the cliff, 40 feet below. Over three hours, Doss lowered more than fifty men from the cliff. Awarded the Congressional Medal of Honor, Doss was the first conscientious objector to receive the nation's highest military honor.[29]

FROM A HUGE CAVE ON the southern slope branched numerous tunnels and shafts, including a multileveled one at least 100 feet deep. The complex contained a makeshift elevator, a hospital, dormitories, ammunition and food storage, and water reservoirs. The Americans sealed the miracle of Japanese engineering with an enormous dynamite charge.[30]

After the 307's 1st Battalion had secured Hacksaw, it prepared to storm the reverse slope by hauling explosives, cases of grenades, satchel charges, and gasoline up the northern slope. Then, the men lined the escarpment's southern edge, each with a box of grenades. The signal was given, and Companies A and C began a furious, twenty-minute grenade barrage, followed by a race down the reverse slope, where they bombed caves, spider holes, pillboxes, and tunnel openings.

After the assault troops dropped a double satchel charge into a large cave, "arms, legs and bodies were blasted 20 feet into the air along with fragments of a machine gun and a field piece." At another cave, a satchel-charge explosion blew two enemy soldiers through a hole atop the cliff.

As the battalion swarmed the reverse slope, the origin of so many of its miseries during the past five days, it was joined by its two sister battalions. Together, they wiped out many of the last strongholds, repulsed a bloody nighttime counterattack, and occupied positions overlooking Japanese defenses stretching to the Shuri foothills.

The bitterly fought, twelve-day battle for Hacksaw and the Maeda Escarpment ended May 6 when the last Japanese defenders were killed or condemned to slow deaths inside caves sealed by dynamite. The battle had cost the 77th Division's 307th Infantry 503 casualties, and the 96th Division, 536 killed or wounded. Nearly all of the Maeda Escarpment's 3,000 unyielding defenders were killed.[31]

WHILE THE 77TH DIVISION WAS struggling to capture Hacksaw Ridge, the Japanese Thirty-Second Army was preparing its second counteroffensive, so vigorously promoted by the army's chief of staff, General Isamu Chō. It would be the Thirty-Second Army's greatest error of the campaign.

In a bitter irony, to Colonel Yahara, the lone objector to the counteroffensive on the Thirty-Second Army's staff, fell the task of planning the attack—just as he had planned the April 12 counteroffensive that he had also opposed, and which had failed as he had predicted.

The relatively intact 24th Division, with fifteen thousand men, would lead the primary attacks in the center and eastern sectors. The 24th Division's 89th Infantry would assault the US 7th Division. The operation's keystone would be the 32nd Infantry's seizure of the high ground around Highway 5, central Okinawa's main thoroughfare; the east side of the Maeda Escarpment; and the town of Maeda. The 44th Independent Mixed Brigade would exploit any gaps made in XXIV Corps's lines. Once it had penetrated the lines, the 44th would pile into the Marines' rear, sowing havoc and isolating the Marines.

Prefatory to the main attack, several hundred Japanese troops would carry out amphibious landings before daybreak on May 4—"X Day"—on both the east and west coasts. The battered 62nd Division remained in the western sector, where the 1st Marine Division had recently relieved the 27th Division.

Coinciding with the ground attack would be raids by the 6th Air Army and 5th Air Fleet on Kadena and Yontan Airfields during the night of May 3 to destroy the Marines' close-air support squadrons before they became airborne. On May 4, there would be a mass kamikaze attack—Kikusui No. 5—on US transports and cargo ships with the object of disrupting the supply line to Okinawa.[32]

Ushijima and Chō rightly believed that the Americans would not expect a major counterattack so soon after the Thirty-Second Army's withdrawal to the main Shuri Line. Their faith in a coordinated air, land, and sea attack's ability to destroy the Tenth Army was based more on hope than reality, though. While Generals Buckner and Hodge fully expected the Japanese to continue their defensive, attritional strategy and nothing more, that did not mean that the Americans had let down their guard.[33]

Before the counteroffensive, Ushijima, Chō, and the Thirty-Second Army's seven other general officers held a banquet at their headquarters beneath Shuri Castle. Chō's chef—Chō was a devoted epicure—prepared a

feast, and Ushijima provided scotch for the occasion. The generals congratulated one another on the victory surely to come.[34]

Kantarō Suzuki, Japan's prime minister of one month, at about this time
addressed a radio broadcast to Okinawa's citizens. The Japanese homeland was preparing to fight the Americans and win the war, he said, but "to
discourage America [from attempting invasion], it is necessary to win the
battle on Okinawa."[35]

On the eve of the counteroffensive, an 89th Infantry diarist doubted that
the hoped-for air support would actually materialize, but he wrote that it
didn't really matter to him. "I will fight fiercely with the thought in mind
that this war for the Empire will last a hundred years. I must fight to the
bitter end."[36]

A copy of the enemy attack plan, dated May 1 and captured during the
counteroffensive's first day, said that the 24th Division, "as the backbone
of the army [Thirty-Second Army] offensive will . . . after a speedy breakthrough of the enemy's first lines, annihilate the enemy with continuous
day and night attacks." "Each soldier will kill at least one American devil,"
the enemy orders read.

Most of the 24th Division was committed to the 77th Division front, and
the Japanese plan, later conceded a 77th report, showed a "good knowledge
of our weak points." They included Highway 5, which separated the 306th
and 307th Infantry, and a gap between the 77th and the 7th Division to
the east.[37]

THE COUNTEROFFENSIVE BEGAN DURING THE night of May 3–4. At
10 p.m., Japanese artillery fired heavy concentrations all along the front—
7,600 rounds of all calibers before the preliminary shelling ended—and
amphibious troops boarded watercraft to land behind American positions
on the west and east coasts.

The 26th Shipping Regiment and elements of the 26th, 28th, and 29th
Sea Raiding Squadrons—about six hundred troops in all—attempted to
land behind the 1st Marine Division lines on the west coast. But the landing
craft operators had trouble with the reefs and became disoriented. Rather
than land well in the Marines' rear at Oyama, the boats sailed straight to the
1st Marines' Company B encampment along a seawall south of Machinato
Airfield.

The Japanese announced their presence with shrill battle cries. As star
shells lit up the scene, the Marines opened up with machine guns and rifles,

and American ships poured on 20mm fire. When they fired into the open boats, Marine rifle grenadiers ignited roaring fires that further illuminated the area and killed scores of troops. Amtracs from the 3rd Provisional Armored Amphibious Battalion waddled offshore past the reef and fired on the enemy from seaward. Riflemen and machine gunners blazed away at bobbing heads in the surf in the flickering light of flares. One platoon burned out six machine-gun barrels and used fifty boxes of ammunition.

About 200 Japanese were killed on the reef; 150 survivors who reached shore were trapped in a pocket that was methodically eliminated the next day.

Others hid in nearby cane fields and were hunted down and killed by the division Reconnaissance Company and the 1st Marine War Dog Platoon. Sixty-five assault troops who landed where they were supposed to, 5 miles north, scattered inland, and most of them were killed over the next two days. An estimated five hundred enemy troops died in the debacle.[38]

The attempted enemy landing in the 7th Division sector behind Skyline Ridge on the east coast was equally catastrophic. Just after midnight, Navy patrol boats spotted vessels carrying the 23rd Shipping and 27th Sea Raiding Regiment. The patrol boats illuminated the area with star shells and opened fire. Ships anchored in Nakagusuku Wan joined the slaughter. A few boats were able to return to their staging areas, and some of the Japanese managed to reach shore, but most of them died when their boats were destroyed. At least four hundred enemy soldiers were killed.[39]

The disastrous landings along the Okinawa coastlines did not stop the Japanese from proceeding with the rest of the counteroffensive. Enemy aircraft bombed Yontan and Kadena Airfields during the night with little effect, but hit an evacuation hospital, killing thirteen patients and medical personnel and wounding thirty-six others.

At 4:30 a.m., the Japanese laced the American lines with an even heavier artillery concentration than the one six hours earlier—an estimated 8,600 rounds, plus a large volume of mortar fire. Large groups of men clad in field green appeared in the dim, gray light, determinedly approaching the American lines.

During the opening attack on the 7th Division, soldiers from the 89th Infantry charged through their own artillery barrage before being mowed down by Hourglass troops and a hurricane of American artillery and mortar fire. The 7th Division reported killing 1,051 enemy troops and taking 1 prisoner.

In the 77th Division sector, the shelling plastered Colonel Stephen Hamilton's 307th Infantry command post behind the battle line. "Except for that terrible barrage on the Champagne front in 1918, when the Germans tried to wipe out the French forces, last night was the worst shelling I have ever experienced," Hamilton said afterward.[40]

Harrowing though the bombardment was, it was one of the rare occasions during the campaign when Japanese artillery was moved into the open—and exposed to counterbattery and naval gunfire, and air attacks. The Americans made the most of it, destroying fifty-nine Japanese fieldpieces.

Two Japanese battalions from the 32nd Regiment attacked the 77th Division's 306th Infantry to exploit weak points that enemy scouts had identified. Japanese bayonet and grenade attacks achieved incremental gains before most of the attackers were wiped out.

Sergeant John Smith, manning a machine gun, was attacked from both the front and the rear. After killing those charging him frontally with his machine gun, he snatched up an automatic rifle and killed five enemy soldiers behind him.[41]

When an enemy platoon attempted to exploit a small gap between the 77th and 7th Divisions by creeping up a draw, riflemen lined the high ground above the Japanese, held their fire until the enemy bunched up, then raked them with M-1 and automatic-rifle fire "until the last enemy had stopped kicking." About the same time, artillery and machine-gun fire cut down Japanese soldiers attempting to withdraw from a failed attack on 306th Infantry troops on a ridge. More than one hundred enemy soldiers were killed.[42]

By nighttime on May 4, it was obvious that the counteroffensive had failed, but the 24th Division's commander, General Tatsumi Amamiya, refused to give up. He ordered the attacks on the 77th Division to continue.

Beneath a knoll between the 306th's 1st and 3rd Battalions, a five-man artillery observation team led by Private First Class Richard Hammond was busy identifying potential targets when they saw a column of Japanese advancing below. After notifying higher-ups, the five privates opened fire with rifles, pistols, and a machine gun, repulsing the enemy attack. They stopped a second attack just 5 yards from their position, but one of the American enlisted men died and the other four were wounded. During the third attack, the Japanese reached the knoll above the team's position and pelted the privates with grenades; they threw back most of them, but one exploded, adding to one private's wounds.

Then, Private First Class Raymond Higginbotham, armed with two pistols, attacked the enemy soldiers on the knoll and drove them away. At dawn on May 5, an American patrol relieved the beleaguered privates and reported finding the bodies of about one hundred Japanese.[43]

From 3 a.m. until daylight on May 5, two battalions of the Japanese 24th Division's 32nd Infantry, supported by tanks from the 27th Tank Regiment, repeatedly attacked the 77th Division lines.

The 306th's Company E was in the bull's-eye. The Japanese could not break through the company, and six tanks were destroyed. When the attackers attempted to withdraw, Company E harried them with local attacks and artillery concentrations until they were annihilated. Daylight found the ground in the company area covered with enemy dead, in places stacked three or four deep. More than four hundred bodies were counted.[44]

The 32nd Infantry's 1st Battalion, led by Captain Koichi Ito, laid claim to the counteroffensive's sole success. After slipping through a gap in the American line, the battalion reached a supply road between the 7th and the 77th Divisions. Ito's six hundred men then marched cross-country. One mile behind the 7th's lines, they attacked a supply depot and motor pool at the base of Tanabaru Escarpment. The Japanese wrested the escarpment from the Americans and mined the road it had traveled to get there.

The 17th Infantry's 2nd Battalion waged a furious battle to take back the escarpment, and over the next two days, it killed 435 enemy soldiers, finally reaching the crest under a creeping mortar barrage. Japanese survivors slipped away from Tanabaru during the night of May 6–7, moving into a valley near the 306th Infantry, with scouts leading the way with flashlights that cast a red glow. Flailed by American mortar, rifle, and machine-gun fire, just 230 of Ito's original force of 600 returned to the Japanese lines.[45]

The 77th reported that it killed more than 2,000 Japanese on May 4–5, wiping out roughly three-fourths of the 32nd Infantry's manpower.[46]

THE JAPANESE COUNTERATTACKS GAVE AMERICAN troops the rare opportunity of fighting from their own fortified positions against enemy infantrymen who had come into the open—the converse of the usual grinding American assaults on hills bristling with pillboxes and defenders in caves and tunnels.

In the 7th Division's eastern sector on the counteroffensive's opening day, two thousand men from the 89th Infantry maneuvered around the American units on Conical Hill, Chimney Crag, and Kochi before they were spotted in an open area by Lieutenant Richard McCracken,

commander of the 184th's Company A. Unable to raise an artillery liaison officer, McCracken contacted Lieutenant Colonel Daniel Maybury. The battalion commander said he was pleased with the course of the battle, but McCraken cautioned that he should not become complacent—because a large group of enemy soldiers was less than 100 yards from Maybury's observation post.

"Oh, no," Maybury said dismissively, "that's a patrol from Company K down there."

"I don't know who the hell it is," McCracken replied, "but there's a lot of them, and they've got two field pieces that are pointed right at your OP."

Indeed, the Japanese were busy unlimbering two 75mm guns. Other nearby US units, however, had also observed the activity. A few minutes later, tanks arrived and scattered the enemy soldiers, and artillery fire wiped out many of those who lingered.[47]

On the western battle line facing the 1st Marine Division, the decimated 62nd Division, at well below 50 percent effectiveness, fought a strictly defensive battle while awaiting a breakthrough by the 24th Division that would isolate the Marines. Only then would the 62nd join the counteroffensive. It never did.

The Marines launched an offensive of their own during the morning of May 4 in the hope of storming Shuri from the west. The Japanese had anticipated them. The leading platoons were raked by gunfire from multiple sides by 62nd Division units entrenched in caves, pillboxes, and fortified tombs. The Marines paid a heavy price for meager gains, although some units did reach the high ground on the northern bank of the Asa-Kawa River, where they awaited enemy counterattacks.[48]

About 2 a.m. on May 5, Japanese artillery shelled the 1st Marines' Company G, which was dug in on a hill north of Dakeshi. Shrapnel and pieces of shredded trees filled the air as the enemy attack began. Lieutenant Robert Crowton said Japanese troops froze when star shells illuminated the battlefield, then continued soundlessly approaching the Marines, who were throwing grenades.

An enemy soldier ran up to Crowton. "I placed the barrel of my carbine against his chest and pulled the trigger," he said. "The breath went out of him in a whoosh, he fell, and didn't move again."

Something exploded near Crowton, blowing away part of his face, and the lieutenant spent the rest of the night wedged against a tree, bleeding. At daybreak, after the Japanese withdrew, Crowton picked up the rifle of a

dead enemy soldier and returned to his company lines. Covered in blood and unable to speak—he would receive 40 stitches in his tongue—Crowton was identified by his dog tags, evacuated to Saipan, and thence to Hawaii.[49]

AS MAY 5 ENDED, GENERAL Ushijima gloomily conceded failure and recalled his battalions to their old positions. The great counteroffensive had been a debacle from beginning to end, costing the Thirty-Second Army 6,227 men killed. Half of its remaining artillery pieces had been destroyed or damaged. The 24th Division returned to its lines with effectives numbering just one-third of its original force. The 27th Tank Regiment would never fight again as a mobile unit; its half-dozen remaining medium tanks would be converted into pillboxes and stationary artillery.

The battered 24th Division and the 5th Artillery Command abandoned the offensive tactics that had decimated them and adopted the defense-oriented, attritional warfare waged by the 62nd Division in the west. "The battle plan in the Shuri area sector will be an attrition of enemy strength until he has lost his endurance," wrote Ushijima, who also began converting service units into combat units. "One man out of ten will continue his rear-echelon duties," one of his orders said. "The remaining nine men will devote themselves to antitank combat training."

If further proof of the effectiveness of Yahara's attritional strategy was needed, casualty figures alone supplied it. While the 24th Division had squandered thousands of men to inflict 714 casualties on the 7th and 77th Divisions, the 62nd Division, fighting defensively against the advancing 1st Marine Division, had killed or wounded 649 Marines.[50]

The Thirty-Second Army's losses, however, had severely crippled, even doomed, Yahara's attrition strategy. The Japanese counteroffensive was the most consequential action of the Okinawa campaign.

Afterward, Ushijima summoned Yahara to his office and, with tears in his eyes, pledged to henceforth follow the operations officer's advice on strategic matters, and not General Chō's counsel.

"But he knew that it was too late to make up for the lost battles," Yahara later wrote. "We had lost most of our elite veteran force and were out of artillery ammunition. . . . In a battle of attrition we could have saved at least one-quarter and perhaps even a third of our forces until the end of hostilities." Had it not been for the counteroffensive, he wrote, the Thirty-Second Army might have prolonged the Battle of Okinawa for an additional month.[51]

Chō's personal secretary, Akira Shimada, said the counteroffensive's failure crushed the usually ebullient Chō. "He abandoned all hope of a successful outcome of the operation and declared that only time intervened between defeat and the Thirty-Second Army."

A Japanese intelligence officer summarized the Thirty-Second Army's predicament: "The situation on Okinawa is believed to be hopeless."[52]

WHILE THE BLOODY COUNTEROFFENSIVE RAGED on the tablelands of southern Okinawa, 125 Japanese Navy and Army warplanes—conventional and kamikazes—mounted a mass air attack May 3 and 4 on the US fleet. Although Kikusui No. 5 had no discernible effect on the Thirty-Second Army's counteroffensive, it was the deadliest mass air attack since the first one, on April 6–7. Japanese pilots sank six ships, damaged twelve others, and inflicted 754 casualties, more than the total sustained by the 7th and 77th Divisions.[53]

At 8:25 a.m. on May 4, after the destroyer *Morrison* had survived a series of close calls, a flaming Zero chopped her after stack, and crashed into the base of the forward stack with a deafening blast. A boiler exploded, exposing the forward fire room to flooding, and the power failed. A second Zero smashed into the main deck, rupturing the bulkhead and flooding the engineering spaces.

Seven twin-float biplanes—Willow training aircraft whose top speed was just 132mph—slowly approached while just 10 to 20 feet above the waves. They were highly maneuverable and hard to shoot down; machine-gun bullets often passed through the wood-and-fabric planes without causing consequential damage, and proximity-fused shells did not detonate when fired at them. In addition, because so little metal went into their construction, they were virtually invisible to radar. Although repeatedly hit, one of the Willows plowed into *Morrison*'s two deck guns, igniting the gunpowder in an upper handling room. A "tremendous fireball" shot above the ship.

To shake pursuers, another twin-float biplane landed in the water 500 yards astern of *Morrison*, taxied, took off, and crashed into a 5-inch gun, igniting the powder in its upper handling room. The explosion blew a hole in the bulkhead, and two compartments flooded, trapping belowdecks personnel. An "abandon ship" order was broadcast just as two additional explosions occurred. *Morrison*'s stern listed, she rolled over, her bow lifted like a breaching whale, and she sank at 8:40 a.m., fifteen minutes after she was first crashed.

An hour later, *LCS (L)-21* began picking up survivors. "They had every kind of wound and burn," said Gunner's Mate W. H. Stanley. "I helped pull one aboard whose feet were blown off and when we laid him on the deck, I pushed his legs together because his guts were coming out." One hundred fifty-two of *Morrison*'s 331 crewmen died.[54]

Besides meting out terrible punishment to the radar picket ships, Kikusui No. 5 precipitated one of the campaign's greatest air battles. Naval intelligence intercepts had provided ample warning of the mass attack, and six divisions of Hellcats from *Yorktown*'s VF-9, and four divisions of land-based Corsairs from Okinawa—from VMF-323 and VMF-224—were dispatched to intercept the intruders.

Forty to fifty enemy planes attacked Radar Patrol Station No. 1 alone. The combat air patrol shot down twenty-five of them, and antiaircraft fire claimed nineteen more. But a few determined kamikazes slipped through to crash *Morrison* and two other vessels patrolling the radar station.

At 8:38 a.m., a Val struck the stern of the rocket-armed *LSM(R)-194*, on patrol with *Morrison*, which was then taking her final plunge. The crash ignited fires in the aft steering and engine rooms, and a boiler exploded. *LSM(R)-194* sank by the stern, taking down thirteen men with her.

A third ship at Station No. 1, the destroyer *Ingraham*, shot down four planes in rapid succession, but a fifth attacker crashed her port side at the waterline and its bomb went off in the forward diesel room. *Ingraham* managed to stay afloat, with a loss of fourteen crewmen.[55]

Luce, patrolling Radar Picket Station No. 12 on May 4, went to general quarters when her radar screens filled with bogeys that were closing from a distance of 50 to 60 miles. A day earlier, kamikazes sank *LSM-190* at Station 12; thirteen men were killed or reported missing. The USS *Luce*, launched two years earlier, was named for Stephen Luce, the admiral who in 1884 had founded the Naval War College at Newport, Rhode Island. *Luce* had seen service from the Aleutians to the Philippines.

At 7:50 a.m., a twin-engine Betty swooped down on *Luce*. It overshot her port side, landing 100 feet off starboard, and its bomb exploded, knocking out *Luce*'s power and most of her radar and gun settings, and ripping her starboard side "like a sardine can." Flames shot 200 feet into the air.

A second kamikaze, a Zero, came in low on *Luce*'s port quarter. Without power, the destroyer's guns had to be manually operated, and they could not be trained quickly enough on the attacker. The Zero slammed into the port stern's 5-inch guns, causing a magazine to explode. The blast

blew currency from the paymaster's safe all over the ship, and a hole in the ship's bottom. *Luce* shuddered and began settling in the water, listing to starboard.

Flying metal decapitated Baker 2/c Virgil Degner. Ship's Cook J. C. Phillips said Degner was shouting to him when "his head fell off at my feet. I looked down . . . and I believe his mouth was still trying to tell me something." Degner's body, still erect, began to quiver, and it then fell over.[56]

Within five minutes of the first crash, *Luce* rolled over and sank by the stern, her bow thrust in the air. Of her 335-man crew, 149 died, and 94 were wounded. "Most of our men were lost below decks . . . a horrible way to die, trapped below deck, no communication and unable to see what was happening," said Art Replogle, a supply officer. As *Luce* went down, her depth charges detonated; scores of men in the water suffered concussions.[57]

Radio Technician 2/c Joe Bille was in the water looking for a life preserver when he found what he thought was an empty one. "When I turned it to put on, there was a portion of a man's chest inside. I quickly let it go."

Japanese planes strafed survivors in the water, but Corsairs came to the men's rescue, shooting down the enemy planes, circling the survivors until the attacks ceased, and dipping their wings twice in salute.[58]

In the water, sharks were "hitting men left and right, just tearing them up," said Petty Officer 3/c Tom Matisak, a radioman. Lieutenant Cliff Jones saw them attack the ship's barber, who was bleeding. "Two sharks got him. It was an awful, bloody mess as they chopped him and pulled him under."[59]

Gilbert Fox, a lieutenant on *LSM-80*, watched a kamikaze crash the light cruiser *Birmingham* on May 4. "I think all of us started shooting at the kamikaze plane with everything we had. . . . All the metal that went up had to come back down. And it sounded like rain on our ship with all the metal coming down," he wrote. *Birmingham* reported that forty-seven of her crewmen were killed and eighty-one were wounded.[60]

The destroyer-minelayer *Shea* was cruising Radar Picket Station No. 14 amid the attacks when an approaching twin-engine Dinah bomber released an Ohka piloted by Sub-Lieutenant Susumu Ohashi. A Grumman FM-2 Wildcat pilot flying combat air patrol saw the cigar-shaped missile drop from the Dinah an instant before his comrades shot down the bomber. The Ohka's pilot fired up the craft's solid-fuel rockets, and it swiftly pulled away from the Wildcat at speeds exceeding 500mph—too fast to be shot down.

Shea crewmen saw the Ohka approaching just five seconds before it struck. With an ear-splitting crash, it pierced the starboard side of the

Shea's bridge superstructure, killing twenty-seven sailors and injuring ninety-one. The damage and casualties would have been much worse if the Ohka had exploded on impact, as it would have if *Shea* had been more heavily armored. The ship's light construction saved her. The Ohka roared through the destroyer without exploding, came out the other side, and blew up 15 feet from *Shea*'s hull.[61]

The carrier escort *Sangamon* was leaving Kerama Retto when a Nick two-seat fighter came in fast, dropped a bomb, and crashed the flight deck just behind the forward elevator. The bomb plunged through the flight deck to the hangar deck and exploded.

Seaman 1/c Howard Burke, who was at his 40mm gun, was blown into the air. Below him, on his ship, Burke saw "a mighty fire and explosion going on," before blacking out. When Burke regained consciousness, he was in the water, bleeding from his left hand and arm. Burke and some other sailors clung to a 100-yard marlin line that he had tucked into his back pocket. Burke tried to hold up a badly burned friend, but his skin sloughed off and "I had him by the bone. I soon had to let him go. I was sinking myself. I never saw him again."

After four hours in the water, Burke was rescued. *Sangamon* survived the attack and fires, but required extensive repairs. Her losses on May 4 totaled 46 killed and 116 wounded.[62]

The previous day, May 3, had been a costly one at Radar Picket Station No. 10. The destroyer *Little* and the year-old destroyer-minelayer *Aaron Ward* were targeted in a well-coordinated kamikaze attack beginning at 6:30 p.m.

Three bomb-carrying Vals crashed *Little* near her stacks on the port side. A boiler exploded, and the destroyer's keel broke in two. She sank fifteen minutes later, at 6:55 p.m., with thirty men killed and seventy-nine wounded. *Little*'s after-action report said there was close coordination among the attacking planes that combined low-level and glide attacks. "They certainly did not appear to be 'green hands,'" the report said.

Five planes crashed *Aaron Ward*, three of them carrying bombs that exploded. The suicide pilots, who were all "very young," wore parachutes and oxygen masks, although none of them survived, the after-action report noted. Without power or water pressure, *Aaron Ward* drifted in the dark as fires roared. In an improvised emergency station set up in the mess hall for burned and badly injured men, a doctor performed surgery with a shark knife.

LSM(R)-95, a rocket ship, was hit by a suicide plane and sunk while going to assist *Little* and *Aaron Ward*; eight men died.

LCS(L)-83 came alongside *Aaron Ward* at 7:35 p.m. and began taking aboard the wounded and putting out fires. Towed to Kerama Retto, *Aaron Ward* somehow survived the severe battering, at a cost of forty-five men killed. "We all admire a ship that cannot be licked," said a laudatory message from Admiral Raymond Spruance, the Fifth Fleet's commander.[63]

At the close of Kikusui No. 5, the Japanese and Americans both claimed victory. In truth, both inflated their accomplishments—the Japanese extravagantly so, declaring that they had sunk two US battleships, three cruisers, and five other vessels. Admiral Matome Ugaki, who commanded the 5th Air Fleet, said several of the phantom sinkings were seen from shore on Okinawa. "Thus we achieved a great deal of success," he wrote.[64]

For their part, Americans claimed to have destroyed 249 Japanese planes, a remarkable feat given the fact that just 125 enemy planes participated in Kikusui No. 5. However, it was not unusual in the swirl of aerial combat for two or more pilots to take credit for shooting down the same warplane. Okinawa-based flyers claimed 60 of the 249 total, with VMF-323 alone taking credit for twenty-four kills, a single-squadron record at Okinawa.[65]

THE SUICIDE ATTACKS OF APRIL and early May had begun to tax both the Japanese and Americans in ways surpassing the losses of lives, ships, and planes. The nerves of US sailors aboard ships around Okinawa were fraying because of the persistent fear that a suicide plane might smash their ship at any time.

Volunteers to fill the thinning kamikaze ranks became harder to find. They had eagerly stepped forward the previous autumn when the Special Attack Corps was established, but with hopes fading for a Japanese victory, volunteers were scarcer. Moreover, the appearance of parachute-wearing pilots during Kikusui No. 5 suggested that a new reluctance to throw away their lives had crept into the Special Attack Corps pilots. In May, Japan began to draft liberal-arts students from universities for kamikaze service— and to assign men in training and tactical units to the Special Attack Corps.[66]

Naturally, many of the conscripted kamikaze pilots deeply resented their plight. Abused during their inadequate training, they were then sent up in marginally aerodynamic Zeros. It was unsurprising that they often

flew to their deaths drunk and bitter. In a letter home, Norimasa Hayushi, a twenty-five-year-old university graduate, wrote, "We are all going to die. I will never fight for the Navy; I will fight for my country, but never for the Navy, which I hate!" One man strafed his own command post after takeoff.[67]

American pilots noticed that fewer skillful, veteran pilots were now flying the suicide planes. "They didn't know how to defend themselves," wrote Lieutenant Robert Bentley of VMF-422. "They didn't do any sort of a fighter weave protection or anything. They more or less just sat there and waited to be shot down."[68]

Yet, the majority of kamikaze pilots remained committed to sacrificing themselves for the emperor, as attested to by their poignant final letters to loved ones.

Weeks after Haruo Araki's marriage, he did not hesitate to go into action as a kamikaze pilot against the American fleet at Okinawa. He did not survive. His last letter to his bride, Shigeko, said, "The happy dream is over. Tomorrow I will dive my plane into an enemy ship. . . . When I think of your future, and the long life ahead, it tears at my heart. Please remain steadfast and live happily."[69]

In his final letter to his parents and siblings, Ensign Susumu Kaijitsu said his "greatest concern is not about death, but rather of how I can be sure of sinking an enemy carrier. . . . Do not weep for me. Though my body departs, I will return home in spirit and remain with you forever."

"My grave will be the sea around Okinawa, and I will see my mother and grandmother again," Ensign Teruo Yamaguchi wrote to his father. "I have neither regrets, nor fear about death."[70]

Admiral Spruance said the pilots' willingness to die sobered and unnerved the Americans, whose culture of individualism was the very antipode of mass suicide.

"The suicide plane is a very effective weapon, which we must not underestimate," Spruance wrote to a friend, adding with a tinge of bitterness, "It is the opposite extreme of a lot of our Army heavy bombers who bomb safely and ineffectively from the upper atmosphere."[71]

by being forced to remain in the vicinity of Okinawa," wrote Marine General Oliver Smith, the Tenth Army's liaison to III Amphibious Corps.[4]

Buckner and his staff believed that by attacking every Japanese strongpoint simultaneously, the Tenth Army could crack the 5-mile-long Shuri defensive line and destroy Ushijima's Thirty-Second Army. "It will be a continuation of the type of attack we have been employing to date," said Buckner. "Where we cannot take strong points we will pinch them off and leave them for the reserves to reduce. We have ample firepower and we also have enough fresh troops so that we can always have one division resting." Despite Buckner's confidence, the Okinawa campaign's bitterest fighting lay just ahead.[5]

The offensive was scheduled to begin at 7 a.m. on May 11. During the preceding days, the Tenth Army added the 6th Marine Division to its lines, and the other assault divisions advanced to their attack positions. At least 200,000 men from both armies, plus uncounted civilians, jammed the battlefront. It became so crowded that each 600-yard sector eventually held a thousand men, a greater density even than during World War I, when the average thousand-man battalion occupied 800 yards.[6]

In a steady downpour, the 1st Marine Division, which had aggressively advanced with high casualties along the western Shuri Line during the Japanese counteroffensive, began wresting a series of low coral ridges from the Japanese before the attack date.

On the right, the 1st Marines approached Hill Nan and Hill 60. Like so many enemy strongpoints the Tenth Army would encounter on the Shuri Line, the hills were mutually supporting and had to be taken together. On the left, the 5th Marines faced an equally difficult problem at Awacha Pocket, a deep draw where the enemy was burrowed in caves and pillboxes. They would have to be blasted out by "blowtorch and corkscrew"— Buckner's metaphors for flamethrowers and explosives.[7]

Hospital Apprentice 1/c Robert Bush was administering plasma to a wounded Marine at Awacha Pocket when the Japanese counterattacked. While holding the plasma bottle high, Bush emptied his pistol at the enemy, and then continued firing point-blank with a discarded carbine, killing six of the attackers. Shrapnel from a grenade destroyed his right eye and put a hole in his chest. Still able to see out of his left eye, Bush snatched up an M-1 and shot every enemy soldier who appeared—until none remained on the hill. After his patient was evacuated, Bush collapsed while walking to an aid station. He was later awarded the Congressional Medal of Honor.[8]

On May 8, the 6th Marine Division, relieved in the north by the Army's 27th Division, assumed responsibility for the western part of the Tenth Army's line, and the 96th Division prepared to relieve the 7th Division on the eastern side of the island. When the shuffling was completed, the divisions would be aligned, west to east: III Amphibious Corps's 6th Marine Division and 1st Marine Division; XXIV Corps's 77th Division and 96th Division—nearly 100,000 combat troops.

When the 6th Division was trading places with the 27th Division, the Marines' resentment of the New York Division boiled over as the divisions' truck caravans passed each other. Whenever the columns stopped, the Marines pelted the Army vehicles with rocks, C-ration cans, bullets—anything at hand. The reason was Saipan, where Marine General Holland Smith had blamed the 27th for delaying the Marines' advance, and had fired its commanding general. "We hated the 27th from Saipan and now this," wrote Marine Corporal William Pierce. "Us relieving them? We were really teed off."[9]

When the convoy traffic ground to a halt on the overcrowded road, Sergeant William Manchester of the 29th Marines left his truck and climbed a hill to view the battlefield ahead. "I lingered on that hummock, repelled and bewitched. It was a monstrous sight, a moonscape," he wrote. "There was nothing green left; artillery had denuded and scarred every inch of ground."[10]

The Tenth Army's divisions settled into place. The 96th Division, after relieving the 7th, was assigned to capture Conical Hill, which anchored the Shuri Line in the east. The 77th was ordered to seize the rising hills south of Maeda Escarpment that led directly to Shuri Castle. The 1st Marine Division's mission was to capture Dakeshi Ridge, Wana Ridge, and Wana Draw—all mileposts on a southeastern trajectory to Shuri Castle. The 6th Marine Division planned to cross the Asa-Kawa Estuary, turn east, and march into the Kokuba River valley behind the castle. On Tenth Army maps, these objectives seemed reasonable enough; in reality, the place names would become bywords for terror and death.[11]

From May 7 to May 10, the Americans inched forward in the rain and mud, each division attempting to capture as much territory as possible before the Tenth Army's offensive began on May 11.

BEFORE BEING RELIEVED BY THE 96th Division, the 7th Division captured the town of Gaja and pushed south. The 184th Infantry was supposed to lead the push to Conical Hill on May 8, but cold, steady rain stopped the

advance. On May 9, the 184th captured Easy Hill and William Hill, two of the approaches to Conical. But when it tried to capture Conical itself, enemy artillery and long-range machine-gun fire stalled the attack on the north side of the promontory, 1,000 yards from its crest.[12]

The 7th's 17th Infantry persisted in its efforts to seize Kochi Ridge, which the Japanese had made the keystone of their defense of eastern Okinawa. The enemy's 24th Division utilized its dense web of caves and pillboxes with maximum efficiency, defending Kochi with "a zest and determination unequalled in the 7th Division's zone during the entire campaign," according to the division history.

Inching higher on Kochi Ridge, snipers from the 17th's 3rd Battalion dug shallow tunnels near the ridgetop. Firing from inside of them, they began picking off an average of forty Japanese a day. Doubting the reports, Lieutenant Colonel Lee Wallace, the battalion commander, went out on the ridge to see for himself. Within fifteen minutes, he saw his snipers kill five Japanese soldiers.

After the Japanese killed a friend and mutilated his body, Private First Class William Scheuneman resolved to shoot as many Japanese as possible. While burrowed in one of the sniper positions, Scheuneman methodically killed forty-seven enemy soldiers. He remained at his post for three days and nights.[13]

Impatient with the 7th Division's slow progress, General John Hodge, the XXIV Corps commander, visited the division command post to prod it to move faster. He told the 7th's temporary commander, General Joseph Ready, that the division's casualties were lower than the Tenth Army's other divisions. "To me that means just one thing—you're not pushing," Hodge told Ready, pointing out that after eleven days, the division had managed to advance just a few hundred yards against Kochi.[14]

In response to Hodge's admonishment, the 17th targeted nearby Zebra Hill, Kochi's mutually supporting position. Seizing Zebra Hill would accomplish two things: weaken the defense of Kochi, and remove an obstacle to the advance on Shuri.

Delayed for hours, the attack on Zebra began May 7, supported by conventional and flame tanks. Japanese artillery, mortar, and machine-gun fire smothered the assault. On May 10, the 96th Division, after ten days in reserve, took over the Shuri Line's eastern sector from the Hourglass Division.

During forty days of continuous combat, the 7th Division had sustained 5,680 casualties, including 636 battle deaths, 2,817 wounded, and 16 missing. The rest were non-battle casualties, most of them combat fatigue cases.

The division claimed to have killed more than 9,700 Japanese. The Okinawa fighting was markedly more intensive than the 7th's Leyte campaign of 1944, when, during 110 days of combat, the division reported losses of 618 killed and 1,580 wounded.[15]

The rear-bound Hourglass troops wore the same uniforms that they came ashore in on L-Day; they were now tattered and encrusted with dried mud and blood. Their steady diet of K rations had made them thin. The infantrymen were also exhausted from long nights of waiting for infiltrators in the rain and mud—much of the time while being shelled.[16]

The fighting during the month of April had cost the Tenth Army 20,000 casualties. May would be worse.[17]

ON MAY 8, AMERICAN SOLDIERS, Marines, and sailors at Okinawa learned that Germany had surrendered; the European war was over. The news prompted no euphoria, for it was apparent that Germany's surrender half a world away would have no effect on Okinawa operations or on plans being developed for Japan's invasion.

"Nazi Germany might as well have been on the moon," wrote Private First Class E. B. Sledge. "'So what' was typical of the remarks I heard around me. We were resigned only to the fact that the Japanese would fight to total extinction on Okinawa, as they had elsewhere, and that Japan would have to be invaded with the same gruesome prospects."[18]

Nonetheless, the end of the European war was duly observed at noon when every gun ashore fired one round at the enemy and every fire support ship fired a salvo "as a complimentary and congratulatory gesture."[19]

ON THE WESTERN SHURI LINE, the 1st Marine Division captured Hills Nan and 60 simultaneously—the only way to counteract their mutual support of each other. The 1st Marines' 1st and 2nd Battalions, supported by flame tanks, took control of the hills on May 9, sealing numerous caves. That night they repulsed a series of Japanese counterattacks.

After a week on the front line, the nighttime attacks were nothing new to the 1st Marines. "Our regular dish was a grenade fight each night," said a Marine from the 2nd Battalion's Company G. Besides throwing grenades, the Japanese also crawled into the Marines' foxholes and slashed them frenziedly with bayonets and knives. "Before we could get all of the Nips, they were over the cliffs and under us again."[20]

Proof of the 1st Division's eight-day immersion in furious combat on the Shuri Line were the Congressional Medals of Honor awarded to four

Marines and two Navy corpsmen for their actions from May 1 to May 9. Just one of them lived long enough to receive his medal.[21]

After taking over the Shuri Line west of the 1st Division on May 8, the 6th Marine Division advanced to the Asa-Kawa Estuary. Crossing it would be the division's first objective during the coming offensive. Division engineers planned to build a footbridge, because the river was too deep to ford near its mouth, and its bottom too soft to support vehicles.

The 6th Marine Engineering Battalion began building the footbridge after dark on May 9, and before dawn the next morning, three companies of the 22nd Marines crossed to the river's south bank. At first light, a two-man Japanese suicide team armed with satchel charges threw themselves on the footbridge, destroying the bridge and themselves. Under continual gunfire from three directions all that day, the Marine companies that had reached the south bank were unable to expand their small beachhead.

That night, the engineers returned to the river and laid a Bailey bridge that could support tracked vehicles, while Marine infantrymen waded the river upstream. Japanese artillery fire harassed the engineers as they built the Bailey bridge, but they managed to complete it before noon on May 11.

By nightfall of the first day of the American offensive, the 22nd Marines had broken out of their beachhead and cleared away obstacles to the bluffs overlooking the ruined capital city of Naha. After two attempts, Company C seized a dominating ridge south of the Asa-Kawa.

Wresting the ridge from the Japanese required a combined arms effort: shellfire from the battleship *Indianapolis*; conventional and flame tanks that blasted tombs lining the hilltop, as well as caves and pillboxes; demolition teams; and near-suicidal infantry assaults culminating in "bitter, close-in fighting," according to the 6th Division's action report.

At day's end, eighty effectives remained in Charlie Company, which numbered more than two hundred men when at full strength. Just four of Charlie's sixteen flamethrower operators remained in action; the Japanese, cognizant of the flamethrowers' effectiveness in clearing caves and pillboxes with their gasoline-propane mixture, deliberately targeted the operators. The company clung to the ridge that night despite furious counterattacks by Japanese from the reverse slope. To honor the company's sacrifices in capturing the ridge, it was named Charlie Ridge.

The next day, the Marines discovered that the limestone ridge harbored a veritable small city: three levels of corridors and tunnels leading to defensive positions, walls lined with bunk beds, and even a Japanese automobile. There were also two 47mm antitank guns, thirteen Nambu machine guns, a

heavy fieldpiece that could be moved into firing position on railroad tracks, seventeen small ammunition dumps, and three large ones.[22]

The unexpected appearance of the 6th Marine Division on the heights above Naha inspired an Okinawa newspaper to write, "Among the badly mauled enemy, it is a tiger's cub and their morale is high. If we can deal the 6th Marine Division a mortal blow, we will probably be able to control the enemy's destiny."[23]

The 22nd Marines had intended to advance southeast to the Asato River, turn east, and move into the Kokuba River valley behind the Shuri defenses. But the regiment had not gone far when it encountered a maelstrom of enemy gunfire coming from three unremarkable-looking, but well-fortified, hills. Their guns were skillfully positioned so that each hill could aid in the defense of the other two. Moreover, they all lay well within range of heavy artillery and mortars located in the Shuri Castle area.

At 8 p.m. on May 12, Lieutenant Colonel Horatio Woodhouse, the 2nd Battalion commander, sent an ominous report to regimental headquarters. "Got as far as 7672 George. Took hill but casualties were so heavy that George could not hold it," he wrote, estimating that just seventy-five men remained in George Company. "7672 is tunneled and caved. Lost three tanks in that area. All wounded were evacuated. 3–4 dead were left behind."

It was the beginning of the ferocious battle for Sugar Loaf Hill. Woodhouse bestowed the name on 7672 George because of its unremarkable profile. In the days ahead, Sugar Loaf and its two neighbors, christened Half Moon and Horseshoe Hills, would become the 6th Marine Division's bête noir.[24]

BEFORE THE TENTH ARMY'S OFFENSIVE officially began, the 77th Division, operating on the south side of Maeda Escarpment and Hacksaw Ridge, tackled three ridges that together formed an *E* to the north of Shuri. As casualties mounted daily, General Andrew Bruce's veterans ground forward against clusters of densely fortified caves and pillboxes.[25]

On May 9, the 305th Regiment's Company I advanced on the middle ridge and wiped out a machine gun below the hillcrest with grenades. When the Americans reached the crest, they found the dead gunner still clutching his machine gun and wearing "glasses as thick as coke bottoms," wrote an infantryman.

Enemy soldiers suddenly materialized from spider holes and trenches, and counterattacked Company I. George Fairbanks, enraged when an enemy bullet pierced his helmet and another struck him in the forearm,

stood up and emptied his automatic weapon at the Japanese. Aided by comrades, Fairbanks wiped out the attackers. Fairbanks's company proceeded to kill entrenched Japanese troops atop the ridge with grenades, rifle and automatic-weapons fire, and bayonets, and captured the ridge crest.[26]

ANCHORED BY CONICAL HILL IN the east and Dakeshi and Wana Ridges in the west—along with the Sugar Loaf Hill complex—the Shuri Line bent, but did not break before the initial onslaught of General Buckner's grand offensive May 11 and 12. In the east, the 77th and 96th Divisions faced a Japanese 24th Division that was at full strength, while on the western Shuri Line the 1st Marine Division's adversaries were the 44th Independent Mixed Brigade, nearly at full strength, and the 62nd Division, whose six hundred surviving regulars had been reinforced by six thousand service troops.[27]

The massive Tenth Army attack against the 5-mile Shuri Line's jumbled terrain bore no resemblance to the panoramic battlefield spectacles that had sometimes unfolded on the plains of Europe. Southern Okinawa's hills, gullies, valleys, and escarpments did not permit assaults by tank columns under an umbrella of close-air support.

Instead, Buckner's offensive quickly became a series of autonomous attacks against key strongpoints. Their reduction, the four American division commanders hoped, would unlock General Ushijima's defenses, and open a corridor to Shuri Castle, the Thirty-Second Army's bastion. On a map table, the strategy might have appeared to unfold neatly and irrevocably, but the reality was often more akin to the troglodyte-like fighting of World War I in western Europe. Over ten days of intensive fighting, the Shuri Line would become a goulash of mud, blood, and dismembered corpses.

AROUND MIDNIGHT ON MAY 12, Japanese amphibious troops attempted a counter-landing in the 6th Marine Division sector on Okinawa's western shoreline. As a consequence of the thirty-minute Japanese bombardment of the shoreline from Asa-Kawa northward for a mile that preceded the attack, the Americans were ready when the raiders' barges were spotted 3,000 yards from the beach, approaching from Naha. Naval patrol boats and destroyers intercepted and sank two barges. Marines wiped out the thirty to forty survivors who reached the reef.[28]

ELIMINATING THE JAPANESE CAVE AND tunnel complexes was the Tenth Army's most difficult tactical challenge. The Americans now knew

that massive bombardments alone, utilizing their overwhelming superiority in artillery, ready access to naval supporting fire, and unchallenged air power would not crack the Shuri Line; its cave and tunnel defenses were largely impervious to massive bombardments.

During the enormous artillery barrage of May 10–11 prefacing General Buckner's offensive, Colonel Hiromichi Yahara, the Thirty-Second Army's operations officer, was in his army's headquarters deep beneath Shuri Castle studying his maps. "I heard the continuing roar of enemy artillery only as the steady hum of cicadas," he wrote.

Although the bombardments denied the Japanese freedom of movement aboveground, they merely waited them out, emerged when they ended, and met the Americans with mortar, artillery, and machine-gun fire. The Americans tried to counter this by having troops ready to storm the cave entrances the instant a bombardment ended. This tactic worked—until the Japanese began posting a dozen infantrymen in foxholes outside the caves during bombardments. If they survived the avalanche of metal, they might delay the onrushing Americans until comrades inside the caves could reinforce them.[29]

The light, fast M4 Sherman medium tanks, with their 500-horsepower Ford engines, were a great asset. Easily mass-produced, they were plated with armor up to 3 inches thick and armed with a 75mm cannon, two .30-caliber machine guns, and a .50-caliber machine gun atop the turret. Impressive though they could be under ideal conditions, the M4s alone were not particularly effective in the twisted ridge-and-valley terrain ascending to Shuri Castle. Later, when terrain favored their use, they were demonstrably the most important factor in battle. But for the time being, it came as a "great relief" to Colonel Yahara and other senior officers that the large-scale mechanized attacks of the European theater had not materialized on Okinawa.

The American tanks were targeted by four- to six-man Japanese suicide demolition teams that typically hid in a circle of spider holes covered by woven wicker near roads. They emerged from the holes when tanks approached and hurled themselves and their 40-pound satchels of yellow picric-acid explosives beneath the tank treads, blowing themselves to bits and disabling the tank. To counteract the suicide attacks, infantrymen began accompanying the tanks to kill the enemy soldiers before they could detonate their explosives.

Enemy 47mm antitank guns could knock out an M4 at close range with a direct hit on its vulnerable side armor. The problem was addressed by

adding a protective concrete layer to the sides of the tanks. The Tenth Army would lose 153 conventional and flame tanks on Okinawa—the apotheosis of tank-infantry warfare in the Pacific.

The pairing of tanks with infantrymen was just one element of a new combined-arms approach that the Tenth Army was developing: tank-infantry teams, supported by artillery and naval gunfire, and close-air support from Hellcat dive-bombers and Corsairs.

It was called "processing," and because there were no adequate training sites in the Pacific for its development and too little time before Operation Iceberg, it was necessarily introduced and fine-tuned under combat conditions.

THE AMERICANS' MOST RELIABLE TOOLS for eradicating enemy cave fortifications were the "corkscrew and blowtorch"—explosives and flame-throwers. The Japanese used picric acid–based explosives, but American satchel charges were rectangular blocks of C2 plastic explosives in olive canvas bags with carrying straps. When a soldier pulled the satchel's fuse, he had eight seconds to throw it and seek cover before it detonated.

The "blowtorch" element was a "Zippo" tank with a 75mm flame gun capable of firing a napalm-gasoline mixture at a cave mouth up to 100 yards away. To ignite the fuel, the gunner pressed a solenoid switch. Japanese caves typically had a sharp, 90-degree turn in the entry tunnel to prevent direct gunfire from reaching the interior chambers. However, flamethrowers and flame tanks were often able to bounce a stream of fire past the bend and into the deep recesses of a cave, killing everyone in its path, sucking oxygen from the interior chambers, and suffocating the occupants.[30]

When flame tanks could not be used to neutralize an enemy cave, infantrymen sometimes employed a novel tactic. They would climb above the cave entrance while their comrades attacked the cave mouth. When the Japanese attempted to counterattack from the cave, the American soldiers who were crouched above the entryway shot them and hurled satchel charges into the cave, sealing the survivors inside. The Japanese called it a "horse-mounting attack." Colonel Yahara, the Thirty-Second Army's operations officer, described it as a "double envelopment." It was, he said, cause for "the greatest concern" because nearby Japanese troops were reluctant to fire at the Americans atop the entryway, for fear of accidentally hitting the defenders, or revealing their own positions.[31]

The Americans did not have the option, as the Japanese did, of taking refuge inside hollowed-out hills and ridges from the voluminous enemy

artillery fire. During the May 4 counteroffensive, 14,000 enemy rounds fell in twenty-four hours. "This fire covered not only our front line area but also well back into rear areas, quartermaster dumps and the like," wrote Marine Captain Levi Burcham.

Japanese artillery batteries, fired from positions behind the battle line, and also from caves, at times transformed the Okinawa battlefield into a simulacrum of 1916 Flanders. Marine Corporal George Peto was awed by the sight of a 150mm cannon, destroyed by American gunfire and lying on its side next to railroad tracks that disappeared into a cave. "The thing was huge, like a locomotive with a massive barrel coming out of it," he wrote. Japanese artillerists apparently would move it on rails from behind two thick iron doors to the mouth of the cave, fire it a half-dozen times, and then wheel it back inside.

Unlike the Americans, the Japanese were handicapped by not having forward observers assigned to infantry units. They relied on field telephones and even runners to provide the artillery batteries with targets. The coordinates sometimes took several hours to reach the gun battery, rendering the information useless.[32]

THE NAVY, SUPPORTING XXIV CORPS from Nakagusuku Wan (later named Buckner Bay), fired so many shells at Conical Hill on the Shuri Line's eastern periphery that it acquired the nickname "Million Dollar Hill." Its 500-foot peak's cone shape had suggested the plain American name that appeared on Tenth Army maps; the Japanese called it Utanamori.

Whatever its name, Conical, defended by one thousand entrenched Japanese, had defied capture for weeks. After it relieved the 7th Division on May 10, the 96th Division, fortified with 2,600 replacements it had received while in reserve, assumed responsibility for capturing Conical and the jumble of adjacent hills that anchored the eastern Shuri Line.[33]

The day before the offensive began, two battalions of the 96th's 382nd Infantry seized nearby Zebra and Item Hills after hard fighting. Item wasn't altogether secured; six tanks were lost May 11 trying to finish the job. The hills' capture cleared the division's path to a series of clay hills around Dick and Oboe—Oboe being the tallest in the Shuri area. Dick was a ridgeline that contained five small peaks with the confusing names of Dick Able, Dick Baker, Dick Right, Dick Center, and Dick Left.

Before the 96th could tackle those hills, the Japanese counterattacked Zebra during the night of May 10–11, twice driving the 382nd's 1st Battalion from the crest. The Deadeyes got it back after killing 122 enemy troops.

On May 12, the 382nd used blocks and tackles to lift 37mm antitank guns to Zebra's crest to support the impending attack on Dick.

Advancing toward the Dick hills, soldiers from the 382nd's 2nd Battalion were shocked when they stumbled upon a dozen Okinawa civilians poisoned with strychnine by the Japanese. They were "on the ground, writhing in pain," wrote Private First Class Donald Dencker. Medics were able to save some lives by forcing them to swallow a soap solution that induced vomiting, but the rest were too far gone and died.

The hills and ridges surrounding Conical, Dick, and Zebra teemed with enemy soldiers from the 24th Division's 89th Infantry, the 27th Independent Battalion, and men from the 3rd Independent Machine Gun Battalion and 23rd Antitank Company. Gunfire from each hill, flashing from caves, pillboxes, and hidden gun positions, protected both that hill and its neighbors, making it extremely difficult to seize any particular hill.

While Sergeant Bruce Chilcote was acting as a forward observer for his mortar squad, an enemy round hit his radio, which blew up in his hand. The next day, when Chilcote was assigned to another forward observer position, a staff sergeant volunteered to go in his place because of the injury to his hand. Chilcote's replacement was killed by a direct hit from a white-phosphorus artillery shell. "That is why," Chilcote later said, "for the next 30+ years since Okinawa there was an Easter lily in our church in memory of Staff Sergeant Andrew Flatt."[34]

On May 13, the 382nd's Company B captured Dick Able, but then was nearly annihilated by a swarm of enemy artillery and knee-mortar fire coming from several directions. The survivors withdrew. Their sister Company A, however, captured Dick Baker after being repulsed during its first assault.[35]

GENERAL BUCKNER APPEARED AT THE observation post of Colonel Edwin May, commander of the 383rd Infantry, to watch May's 2nd Battalion attack Conical on May 13. May's men already had cleared away enemy obstacles in the village of Gaja and from Conical's northern approaches.

Buckner had made the attack this day's top priority. The capture of Conical would permit the 7th Division, now in reserve, to return to the area and drive down the east coast to Yonabaru, flanking Shuri's eastern defenses. The Hourglass Division could then turn west and secure the road behind Shuri that connected Yonabaru and Naha. If the 7th Division was able to accomplish that, the Tenth Army would have surrounded the Thirty-Second Army and cut off its path of retreat.[36]

It seemed at first that capturing Conical would be ridiculously easy. Company F, supported by two tank platoons, stormed Conical's crest from the northeast without any casualties; the men of the Japanese 27th Independent Battalion had hidden from the tank fire in caves on the reverse slope. Two Company F platoons dug in 50 feet below the hill's round peak.

Then, the Japanese awakened to the dire threat to the Shuri Line's right flank and counterattacked directly over the crest, supported by a blizzard of mortar, artillery, and machine-gun fire. Tech Sergeants Guy Dale and Dennis Duniphan and their platoons repulsed the company-strength attack. Then, the Japanese battalion's commander, Lieutenant Colonel Takehido Udo, ordered a second counterattack that targeted the Duniphan platoon's left flank. Duniphan snatched up a BAR, planted himself in their path, and from 10 feet away emptied the BAR into a flood of screaming Japanese, inspiring his men to beat back the attack.

Company E reinforced F on Conical's crest, and then a spotter plane called in a concentration of artillery and mortar fire that helped shatter the counterattacks. Company G ascended the crest and dug in beside its two sister companies.[37]

On May 15, two Company G platoons charged through heavy Japanese mortar fire to reach Conical's northwest spur. The maneuver isolated that part of the hill from strong enemy forces to the northwest—the area that the Japanese had mistakenly believed the main American attack would target and where they had prepared strong defenses. The Americans had confounded the Japanese tacticians by instead directing the main attack at Conical's northeastern face. Colonel May described Company G's dash through the mortar fire as "the greatest display of courage of any group of men I have ever seen."[38]

With a strong foothold on Conical Hill—although still subject to sporadic counterattacks—the 96th Division could shift its focus to the Dick Hill area, as well as to Oboe and Flattop farther west. Moreover, Conical's containment sharply reduced the ability of the Japanese to interdict movement along the eastern coastal plain. That meant that the 7th Division could now emerge from reserve and roll down the unprotected eastern coast to seize Yonabaru.

THE GRINDING CAMPAIGN TO CAPTURE the Dicks, Oboe, and Flattop reflected the primary difficulty that faced the Tenth Army up and down the Shuri Line: cleverly concealed positions inside nondescript hills that made it nearly impossible to attack one hill without drawing fire from its

neighbors, and powerful artillery counterfire from Japanese positions near Shuri Castle.

The Tenth Army renewed its offensive on May 14 with the object of securing the eastern and western approaches to Shuri. The 382nd Infantry's frontal attacks on the Dick hill complex proved costly; while attacking Dick Center on May 14, an Company L platoon that began the assault with twenty-three men returned with just two effectives.

A forty-man platoon reached the top of Dick Right with only fifteen men still able to fight. Machine-gun and mortar fire from nearby Flattop had cut down the other twenty-five; the fire was so intensive that the Deadeyes had to dig their foxholes while lying down.

Company E's mortar section, operating from the base of Dick Right, fired 1,400 rounds a day for three days, and sometimes 120 rounds in an hour, in attempting to dislodge the enemy from the reverse slope. Through the long nights, the combatants dueled with grenades, and the Americans flung 5-gallon cans of napalm onto the reverse slope, igniting them with phosphorus grenades.[39]

While advancing with the 96th Division, Lieutenant Bob Green's tank was stormed by a Japanese satchel-charge team. The explosion killed the enemy attackers and broke a tread on Green's M4 Sherman. Then, a second suicide team tried to hoist a 300-pound satchel onto the tank deck. A Japanese soldier got on the phone outside the tank and in English said, "Cease fire, please, cease fire, please." Responding to Green's frantic radio calls, tanks in the column behind Green charged up behind Green's tank and machine-gunned the enemy soldier. Luckily for Green and his tank crew, the huge satchel charge did not detonate.[40]

Earlier, Green had another close call while acting as a liaison between the 96th and the 763rd Tank Battalion. He was sharing a position with several artillery, naval, and air coordinators when two 155mm "friendly" rounds landed in the middle of the group. Green happened to be crouched at the bottom of a trench with his radioman when the deafening explosions rocked the ground. Shrapnel cut in two some observers standing in Green's trench. There were "terrible screams" from the wounded. Green recoiled in revulsion when what appeared to be a raw liver landed in his lap and a long piece of intestine ended up draped over his back, shoulders, and neck.[41]

The ferocious Japanese resistance from the Dick hills turned the American attackers into casualties by the scores. Private First Class Donald Dencker, an assistant gunner with a 382nd Company L mortar squad,

wrote on May 16, "The strength of Company L was ebbing with each day's action. We were down to about 79 men and woefully short of riflemen." As a consequence, an ammunition-bearer from each mortar squad was assigned to fill a frontline foxhole each night.[42]

On the western Shuri Line, things were no better. Marines were unable to penetrate the enemy lines west of Wana Ridge and Wana Draw, and northwest of Naha. Eighteen Marine tanks were destroyed or disabled by a cascade of Japanese antitank, mortar, and artillery fire, and by mines and suicide attacks.

WHEN THE OFFENSIVE BEGAN MAY 11, in the middle of the Shuri Line the 77th Division had advanced south toward the Shuri Heights down a mile-wide valley with Highway 5 on its west side. The 77th's three regiments had three objectives: Chocolate Drop, Wart Hill, and Flattop Hill. Chocolate Drop, bare and brown, rose from flat ground and had a slight peak on its crest. Barring the way were fiercely interlocking fields of machine-gun and mortar fire, as well as 47mm antitank guns—and the largest minefield on Okinawa, which severely hampered tank movement.

The 306th Infantry's 3rd Battalion led the initial thrust against Chocolate Drop and Wart Hill, which lay across a saddle and on a ridge that continued westward to Flattop. The battalion advanced just 200 yards before being swamped by artillery and mortar fire from Flattop and Ishimmi Ridge to the southwest. Then, machine-gun fire erupted from caves teeming with enemy soldiers at Chocolate Drop's base, making the hill's northern approaches a killing zone. Enemy gunfire also poured out of caves, pillboxes, trenches, and crevices higher on Chocolate Drop, and from the knolls and ridges paralleling the broad valley. The 3rd Battalion's advance stalled.[43]

On May 13, it was the turn of the 306th's 2nd Battalion; it led a combined arms attack on Chocolate Drop. Despite supporting fire from artillery, tanks, and self-propelled guns, three assaults ended in failure.

On May 14, the 306th's surviving riflemen comprised just a single battalion. Yet, it attempted once more to capture Chocolate Drop. Japanese antitank fire disabled six tanks, and the battalion-size regiment was flayed by gunfire. After the advance was called off, dead infantrymen lay on the ground in a windrow.

The fighting in the hills around Chocolate Drop continued day and night, often in driving rainstorms with bayonets and entrenching tools,

because the men were fearful of mistakenly shooting comrades in the thick gloom. "They would come over the hill, push us out of the reverse slope defenses we were in," wrote Captain Buckner Creel, commander of Company G. "Then we'd grenade and mortar them. Back over the hill they would go."

One night, Creel killed an Imperial Japanese Marine who assaulted him in the rain. Two rounds from his .45-caliber pistol "stopped him literally dead in his tracks."[44]

After marching south from Maeda Escarpment, the 305th Infantry's Company I had tackled the three ridges that formed an *E* before the Shuri Heights. Now the company was being ravaged by the enemy gunfire coming from west of Route 5. During morning roll call May 14, just two officers and forty-nine enlisted men were counted from a company that had once numbered more than two hundred men. The next day, Company I was given the job of cleaning out bypassed caves and trenches. Two days later, just thirty-four men remained in the company; twenty-nine of them were seasoned veterans who had been with I since it sailed from California.[45]

By May 15, the 307th—held in reserve by the 77th Division since the bloodbath on Hacksaw Ridge—took the lead from the 306th, and soon occupied a position just below Chocolate Drop's crest. The next day, the regiment ascended Flattop's summit, but was quickly driven back by Japanese soldiers on top hurling grenades and explosives. "Everyone, including the old-timers, was watching this horrible carnage and doing nothing," said Private First Class Larry Gerevas, a Company K rifleman.

Gerevas and others at the foot of the hill began firing at the enemy soldiers, driving them back from the crest. Gerevas's company then charged up the hill in a "suicidal frontal attack"—and was nearly wiped out before it was withdrawn.

A new officer arrived and ordered the survivors to attack again. When they refused, he threatened to court-martial them. "We told him to go to hell," Gerevas wrote. The officer left, and a short time later, what remained of Company K was sent to the rear after having suffered 85 percent casualties. Three more attempts by the 307th to capture Flattop failed.[46]

The 307th was now chewed up as badly as were its sister regiments. When Company E was relieved, it required an eighty-man litter team to bring out the dead and wounded. Of the company's original 204 men, 156 had been killed or wounded.[47]

The ubiquity of horror and death inspired some soldiers to seek religious solace, and others to spurn it. "I carried a New Testament but could

not read it," wrote Lieutenant Robert Roberts of the 307th. "It seemed obscene with the war going on." Roberts sought escape instead by sketching a plan for a home. "I would take [it] out from time to time and imagine life in it just for mental relief."[48]

Yet the bloody fighting was exacting an even greater toll on the Thirty-Second Army, although the intensity of its resistance had not noticeably decreased. "We have lost many elite troops," General Ushijima informed Imperial General Headquarters in Tokyo on May 16, adding that he had committed his last reserves and the Shuri Line was becoming weaker. He requested weapons for 25,000 men who lacked them, or fresh battalions of paratroopers. "We are surrounded by the enemy, but our fighting spirit remains strong," he wrote. "Please continue air operations to destroy all enemy naval forces in the Okinawa area." Imperial Headquarters replied that the Thirty-Second Army must do its best with its available resources.[49]

DAYS BEFORE USHIJIMA ASKED FOR a new mass air assault, 150 Japanese conventional and Special Attack planes had set upon the US fleet off Okinawa during Kikusui No. 6. Admiral Matome Ugaki, who had become the commander of the reorganized Japanese air force, "Ten Air Force," watched his pilots take off from a Kyushu airfield on May 11, the day that Buckner's offensive began. As the planes disappeared in the distance, he penned a melancholic poem honoring his kamikazes:

> *Flowers of the special attack are falling,*
> *When the spring is leaving.*
> *Gone with the spring*
> *Are young boys like cherry blossoms.*
> *Gone are the blossoms,*
> *Leaving cherry trees only with leaves.*[50]

Less poetic, but filled with raw pathos, were the pilots' own words to loved ones before their final missions. "I dreaded death so much," wrote Hayashi Ichizo. "And yet it is already decided for us. . . . Mother, I still want to be loved and spoiled by you. . . . I want to be held in your arms and sleep." Nakao Takenori said in his last letter to his parents, "Although I did not do much in my life, I am content that I fulfilled my wish to live a pure life, leaving nothing ugly behind me."[51]

Sailors at the Navy radar picket stations encircling Okinawa had grown weary of being targeted by kamikazes—to the extent, apocryphal or not,

that on the stern of a destroyer a large sign was erected with an arrow and the words "TO JAP SUICIDERS—CARRIERS ARE THAT WAY!"[52]

Most of the Kikusui No. 6 pilots evidently did not get the message; the fighter director for Radar Picket Station No. 15 reported five groups of enemy planes—more than one hundred in all—approaching RP 15's two destroyers and four patrol boats at various altitudes.

A handful of attackers, though, had gone trophy hunting and had found Admiral Marc Mitscher's fast carrier Task Force 58 flagship, *Bunker Hill*. Around 10 a.m. on May 11, two suicide planes burst through the clouds and crashed the carrier's flight deck. A Zero piloted by Sub-Lieutenant Seizō Yasunori hit first. Its 550-pound bomb plunged through the flight deck to the hangar deck and pierced the bulkhead before exploding outside the ship. The plane's momentum dragged part of a catwalk crowded with sailors overboard.

The second plane, a Zero flown by Ensign Kiyoshi Ogawa, struck minutes later, slamming into the base of the carrier island's command center. Its bomb blew a 50-foot-diameter hole in the flight deck, where thirty planes were being readied for takeoff, and penetrated to the hangar deck, where forty-eight more planes were being fueled and armed. The bomb's explosion ignited an inferno and wiped out a ready room full of pilots. The Zero's engine careered into the flag office, killing fourteen men on Mitscher's staff, but narrowly missing Mitscher and his chief of staff, Commodore Arleigh Burke.

Fires raged on five decks, incinerating the dead and sending thick, deadly smoke through the ventilator ducts, killing others. Scores of planes were destroyed. When shrapnel practically tore in half a Marine officer commanding a 20mm double Bofors gun, he ordered his men, who were trying to stanch the blood pouring from his lower torso, to remain at their guns, which they did until the guns quit functioning. He then requested an American flag, clutching it to his chest until he bled out and died.[53]

The fires radiated "tremendous heat," said Seaman 1/c Howard Jones, a 40mm gunner. "All the planes were just melted on the flight deck."[54]

Bunker Hill burned from amidships to her fantail, but the ship's damage-control parties, aided by crewmen manning hoses from the cruiser *Wilkes-Barre* and three destroyers, saved the ship. Her skipper, Captain George Seitz, swung the *Bunker Hill* broadside to prevent flames from being blown along the ship's length, and then ordered a sharp, 70-degree turn when gasoline pooled on the hangar deck so that the fuel would slosh overboard.

"It was an ugly, ugly sight," said Seaman 1/c Al Perdeck, who helped bring up the bodies from below deck. "They got mutilated, their arms with no flesh on them." Sailors laid the dead in rows and buried them at sea, wrapped in canvas, secured by cordage, and weighted by shell casings.[55]

The kamikazes killed 353 men and wounded 264 others. Forty-three more were reported missing in action.[56]

Sharks had trailed TF-58, feeding on discarded food, garbage, and the occasional Japanese corpse. When they surrounded a *Bunker Hill* survivor's life raft, the destroyer *Cushing* cleared a path to it with machine guns. Sharks followed *Bunker Hill* for days as it limped to repair facilities. The carrier did not return to action during the rest of the war.[57]

Mitscher transferred his flag to the "night carrier" *Enterprise*, the only US carrier deploying radar-equipped torpedo planes and Hellcat fighters for night operations. When he changed ships, Mitscher necessarily traveled light. Most of his staff, all of his clothing, and most of his files and personal letters had been destroyed on the *Bunker Hill*.

Enterprise's tenure as TF-58's flagship was destined to be remarkably short-lived.

On May 14, she was cruising the Philippine Sea southeast of Okinawa when twenty-six bogeys appeared on her radar screens. The combat air patrol rose to meet them and knocked down nineteen enemy planes. Anti-aircraft gunners claimed six more. That left one.

Around 7 a.m., the Zero, wreathed in flames, approached from the stern at an altitude of 200 feet. It rolled onto its back and dove into the flight deck near the forward elevator, its bomb exploding five levels below. The elevator shot 400 feet into the air before splashing into the sea.[58]

Mitscher's operations officer, Commander Jimmy Flatley, the much-decorated Navy pilot and squadron leader, was standing on the flag bridge with Mitscher and other officers as the Zero barreled toward the carrier. Flatley shouted for everyone to get down. After the plane crashed the flight deck, Commander Flatley raised his head and saw Mitscher still standing over the men sprawled on the deck, a frown on his face.

The admiral said, "Flatley, tell my task-group commander that if the Japs keep this up, they're going to be growing hair on my head yet."

The fires were quickly controlled. Strewn across the flight deck were parts of the plane, its pilot, and his personal possessions, including his wallet and some calling cards, which Mitscher and several officers kept as souvenirs.

The strike killed thirteen crewmen and injured sixty-eight others. It took *Enterprise* out of commission, requiring Mitscher to once more transfer his command of TF-58, this time to the carrier *Randolph*.[59]

THE STRUGGLE AT RP NO. 15 northwest of Okinawa on May 11 eclipsed all previous attacks on the picket ships. The enemy attackers swarmed the destroyers *Evans* and *Hugh W. Hadley*, and four smaller vessels: *LCS(L)*s 82, 83, and 84, and *LSM(R)* 193. The veteran fighter-director team, which had boarded *Hadley* at Ie Shima from another destroyer that had seen plenty of action, reported 156 attacks.

"It got to a point where this expert team of air controllers were helpless" to aid the overwhelmed fighter pilots, who were within visual range of all the attackers anyway, said Ensign Doug Aitken, a radar officer on *Hadley*. "There's nothing you can do but just let these guys fight it out."

When the attacks began at 7:40 a.m., twelve planes were on combat patrol. Another sixteen fighters were dispatched, but numerous enemy kamikazes were soon targeting each ship. The Corsairs splashed forty to fifty of them. They fired so many rounds that some of them ran out of ammunition and resorted to riding down the kamikazes into the water.

Two planes crashed *Evans* at the waterline, with one of its bombs exploding. A third plane struck the destroyer, and its bomb exploded in the forward fire room, causing both boilers to blow up. A fourth kamikaze crashed the main deck, starting fires. Japanese pilots' bodies were found in the galley and on the flight deck. The strikes left *Evans* dead in the water with thirty crewmen killed. Its gunners claimed to have shot down fifteen planes. Without power, crewmen battled the fires with portable fire extinguishers and bucket brigades. Their frantic efforts were successful; *Evans* survived and was towed into Kerama Retto for repairs.[60]

Three miles away, ten planes attacked *Hugh W. Hadley* at 9:20 a.m., and she knocked all of them down. Then, a streaking Ohka slammed into the destroyer at the waterline. When it exploded beneath the ship, the decks heaved 20 inches, breaking crewmen's ankles and bending the keel. A second kamikaze dropped a bomb just before it crashed the aft deckhouse and wiped out a 40mm gun crew. "There was nothing left of the gun and nothing left of them," wrote Aitken.

Fires sprang up, and the *Hadley* lost power and began to list. A third suicide plane shredded the ship's rigging and tore apart the ship's radio antennas before splashing into the water. Twenty-eight crewmen were killed.

Hadley's gunners claimed twenty-three kills. RP 15's landing craft ships lashed themselves to the *Hadley* so that she would not capsize, and towed her to the nearest port, at Ie Shima, for preliminary repairs.[61]

Around 7 p.m. on the day after the unprecedented attacks on RP 15, the *New Mexico* was sailing from Kerama Retto to the Hagushi anchorage when a Japanese George fighter made a strafing run on the battleship. When she returned fire, a shell from one of her 5-inch guns exploded beneath the plane, causing it to miss the stern, while detonating its bomb; shrapnel whizzed through the ship. Minutes later, a Frank fighter crashed amidships near the base of the stack, igniting fires. Crews extinguished the fires in thirty minutes, but the damage that had been done put the battleship out of commission. Fifty-four crewmen died.[62]

OKINAWA'S "PLUM RAINS"—A PERENNIAL SPRINGTIME event—began on May 7, two weeks late, according to Colonel Yahara. Rain fell nearly every day during the next three weeks. At its peak, about an inch of rain fell every day for two weeks, liquefying roads, hills, and valleys. The rain was "frequent and chilly," wrote E. B. Sledge of the 5th Marines. "It varied from drizzles to wind-driven, slashing deluges that flooded our muddy footprints almost as soon as we made them." The rain fell so hard at times that the Marines and soldiers sometimes had difficulty seeing their comrades in the foxholes next to them.[63]

"It was miserable, a sea of mud, with open stretches of water all over the place," wrote Corporal George Peto, a mortar squad forward observer in the 1st Marines. The Marines were attempting to reach Shuri Castle from the northwest, but were stalled before enemy strongpoints at Dakeshi and Wana Ridges. "We couldn't do much of anything, and neither could the Japs," said Peto. "After awhile, our ponchos were useless" against the drenching rains, and they had the drawback of restricting a man's movement. Some Marines elected to just get wet rather than wear the ponchos, and slung their rifles upside down to keep the bores dry.

Mortar squads set up in shallow depressions in 2-inch-deep water floating atop mud. "Each time we fired, they [the mortars] sank deeper into the muck," said Sergeant R. V. Burgin, a 5th Marines mortar-squad leader. "We shored them up as best we could with boards and stones."[64]

The red mud, usually knee-deep and sometimes waist-deep, mired jeeps, trucks, trailers, tanks, artillery pieces, bulldozers, and even tracked M29 Weasels—which had bested Leyte's mud, but not Okinawa's. "Some

of the Jeeps got stuck so badly that our tanks rolled right over them to keep going," said Tech Sergeant Porter McLaughlin of the 7th Division, but then the tanks bogged down, too. Soon, the roads were lined with steaming vehicles whose cooling systems had failed. There they remained until the ground became dry again.

The rain and mud slowed General Buckner's offensive nearly to a standstill, but he was able to joke about it in a letter to his wife. One of his generals had reported "considerable movement" along the front lines, he said. "Those on forward slopes slid forward, and those on reverse slopes slid back."[65]

Amphibious tractors laden with food, water, and ammunition managed to reach battalion supply dumps behind the front lines, but could go no farther. Troops hand-carried the supplies the rest of the way through the mud, sometimes for up to 2 miles. They slipped, slid, and sank beneath their burdens, with the mud sometimes sucking the shoes off their feet. They arrived at the front covered head to foot in mud.

Marine Corporal Robert Dunbar described the carrying parties as "beastly grueling work" in the rain and mud, with men sometimes having to lug boxes of .50-caliber ammunition weighing 110 pounds apiece. "Many of the men dropped from sheer exhaustion."

"It surpassed the drudgery of any working party I had ever experienced," wrote E. B. Sledge. Someone had the idea of using Okinawa ponies as pack animals—until they sank to their necks in the mud and had to be shot.[66]

The rain and mud frustrated the usual gravity-aided method of administering plasma from a container taped to a rifle stock, with the bayoneted rifle stuck in the ground. When the mud would no longer support a rifle, someone had to hold the rifle upright to dispense the plasma.

Jealous of their cigarettes, the Americans stored their tobacco and matches in a condom inside their helmet liners to keep them dry. Socks and letters from home had no such protection and often fell to pieces in a week. The incessant rain caused bullets in magazines to stick together, unless they were removed and individually oiled.[67]

Foxholes filled with water, forcing the men to use their helmets to bail. "I hated to do it so bad, I'd sometimes let it [the water] get to my knees before I'd do it," said Sergeant Joe Joy of the 7th Division's 32nd Infantry. "I just knew sometime one of us was going to raise up and a Jap would be standing there."

Indeed, that is what happened to Joy. One night, when he stood to empty his helmet, he saw a Japanese soldier standing six inches from his face. Unable to quickly reach his rifle under his poncho, Joy wrestled the enemy's weapon away from him and threw it down the hill. The Japanese soldier ran away.[68]

Private First Class Frank Graley of the 106th Field Artillery was literally washed out of his foxhole when its sides caved in. Sledge and his foxhole mate made a floor with ammunition crates, but they still had to bail.

"We had reinvented the equivalent of duckboards commonly used in World War I trenches," Sledge wrote. The surrounding landscape in fact closely resembled a Great War battlefield: rain pouring down, shellfire, muddy corpses crawling with maggots, discarded gear, disabled tanks and amtracs. "Utter desolation," wrote Sledge.[69]

It was nearly impossible to sleep in a driving rainstorm, and many soldiers stopped trying. Lieutenant Robert Roberts of the 77th Division's 307th Infantry said, "You sat on the side of your slit trench and let the water run off your helmet and poncho." One night, Roberts wrote, a landslide buried and suffocated two men in the 2nd Battalion message center before they could be dug out.[70]

Things were no better on the other side of the battle line, where the rain flooded the Japanese trenches, spider holes, pillboxes, and caves. "Brooks flowed in the tunnels," wrote Colonel Yahara. Japanese troops built dams and raised their beds out of the rushing water. In the headquarters cave beneath Shuri Castle, the accumulated rainwater was knee-deep.[71]

When the two-week rainfall ended and the heavy cloud cover lifted, the Tenth Army began air-dropping supplies to the 1st and 77th Divisions, bypassing the mud-clogged roads. Transport planes flew 327 sorties over two weeks, delivering 135 tons of ammunition, rations, and water; 28 miles of telephone wire; and field telephones. On Okinawa's east coast, when Highway 13 became impassable, landing craft delivered supplies to the 7th Division.[72]

The improving weather meant that the bloodletting could resume with even greater fury.

Red Flood Tide

[They] just cut us down like a mowing machine going through a hayfield.

—PRIVATE FIRST CLASS WENDELL MAJORS,
DESCRIBING HIS COMPANY'S ATTACK ON SUGAR LOAF HILL[1]

It was the most ghastly corner of hell I had ever witnessed. The place was choked with the putrefaction of death, decay, and destruction. . . . Every crater was half full of water, and many of them held a Marine corpse. The bodies lay pathetically just as they had been killed, half submerged in muck and water, rusting weapons still in hand.

—PRIVATE FIRST CLASS E. B. SLEDGE,
AFTER VIEWING HALF MOON HILL[2]

It was no longer a glorious man-to-man fight but a grotesquely one-sided process in which a gigantic iron organism crushed and pulverized human flesh.

—A JAPANESE SURVIVOR OF THE SUGAR LOAF HILL BATTLE[3]

GENERAL MITSURU USHIJIMA HAD COMMITTED the last of his reserves. There was no possibility of his Thirty-Second Army receiving replacements, or more food, weapons, or ammunition. Moreover, the American offensive was testing the Japanese defenses on Okinawa as never

before. Yet like a veteran crew on a doomed warship, Ushijima and his staff reflexively employed countermeasures to the mounting crises, while aware of their ultimate futility.

In the west, the 1st and 6th Marine divisions' battering assaults during May's first two weeks had worn the Shuri Line to paper-thinness, although the Marines observed no apparent diminishment in the fierceness of the enemy's opposition.

Behind the scenes, though, the Japanese were rushing reinforcements to shore up the disintegrating 62nd Division, which had been in continuous action for five weeks. Its 11th Independent Infantry Battalion had been annihilated, as had been most of its 21st and 23rd Battalions. Of the thousands of men who had served in the original 62nd Division, just 600 men remained fit for duty. Ushijima attempted to bolster the skeletal division with a new, 6,700-man 63rd Brigade cobbled from a suicide boat group, airfield construction troops, a machine-cannon unit, and the remnants of the 64th Brigade.

Ushijima dispatched units from the 44th Independent Mixed Brigade to Dakeshi Ridge and ordered them to defend this first doorway to Shuri Castle to the last man. "Hold without fail," Ushijima said.[4]

GENERAL BUCKNER'S MAY 11 OFFENSIVE had begun the most intensive ten-day period of combat of the Okinawa campaign, with the fighting raging along a 5-mile battle line. In action were more than one hundred thousand US combat troops from Conical and Dick Hills in the 96th Division zone; to Chocolate Drop and Flattop Hills in the 77th Division sector; to Dakeshi and Wana Ridges in the 1st Marine Division zone; and on to the Shuri Line's western end, where Sugar Loaf, Half Moon, and Horseshoe Hills would pose a supreme test for the 6th Marine Division.

On May 11, the 1st Division's 7th Marines seized the ridgeline that overshadowed Dakeshi Village—Dakeshi Ridge, the first of three sequential enemy defensive lines barring the northwestern approach to Shuri Castle. During the fighting on Dakeshi Ridge's eastern slope, a Marine was hit by a Japanese flamethrower and began shrieking as the flames engulfed him. Enemy snipers shot the man's comrades when they tried to go to his aid. A corporal who reached the man's side and attempted to smother the flames with his poncho was shot through the eye.[5]

Japanese soldiers in tunnels, caves, and shafts fiercely defended the small agricultural town of Dakeshi Village. Snipers fired on the Marines from

houses, from behind walls, and from inside wells and cisterns. When they tried to clear the town, the Marines were pinned down by fire from Dakeshi and Wana Ridges. George Lince, an assistant machine gunner, said some Marines were killed or wounded without having seen a live enemy soldier in the area.

In the village, the scene was chaotic. Corpsmen were shot while patching up casualties. A painfully wounded Marine begged to be shot, and when two comrades crawled to him, shouting for a corpsman, a Japanese grenade killed all three. So many corpsmen were killed or wounded that the division afterward began training infantrymen to take their places. More so than in other campaigns, Japanese soldiers on Okinawa deliberately shot corpsmen and medics. "You knew you were going to get hit. You just didn't know when or how," said Corpsman Bill Lynne. In some units, so many medics and corpsmen were shot that the Red Cross armband was discarded because "it made a good target"; instead, they were issued .45-caliber pistols for self-protection.[6]

The 7th Marines repelled two counterattacks and numerous infiltration attempts, all the while under constant artillery and mortar fire. They finally cleared the village of snipers and sealed Dakeshi Ridge's reverse slope caves, where the Marines uncovered the 64th Brigade's command post. The commander and his staff had fled to Shuri Castle.

Tank-infantry teams spent the next three days securing Dakeshi Ridge and its network of caves, tunnels, and underground firing positions, opening the door to the next hornet's nest on the way to Shuri Castle: Wana Draw.[7]

"The main enemy defenses of southern Okinawa radiated from Shuri like the spokes of a wheel," the 1st Marine Division Special Action Report said of this phase of the operation, "and the hub of that wheel was protected by some of the most rugged terrain encountered on the drive southward."[8]

THE 1ST MARINES, SUPPORTED BY tanks, seized Hill 55 at the mouth of Wana Draw on May 13, but were ejected by Japanese machine gunners and antitank guns fired from caves, plunging artillery fire from the Shuri Castle area in the 77th Division zone, and suicide squads hurling satchel charges. The Marines had pricked a nerve, foreshadowing the brutal struggle that lay ahead for control of Wana Draw.[9]

Through Wana Draw lay the path to Shuri Castle to the southeast that the 1st Marine Division had chosen to take. Fully cognizant of Wana

Draw's surpassing importance to Shuri's defense, the Japanese had transformed it into a lethal snare and intended to fight to the death defending it.

About 500 yards wide and 900 yards long, Wana Draw ran roughly
east to west, with a stream meandering along its floor and into the town of
Wana, located at the draw's mouth on the west end. Shellfire had reduced
the town to rubble.

Wana Ridge, a long coral spine extending to Shuri, comprised the northern wall of Wana Draw, rising 150 feet above the draw's floor. Both sides of
Wana Ridge were pitted with enemy-occupied caves, holes, and tombs that
they had converted to pillboxes. Wana Draw's south side was undefended,
as was the high vertical wall at the head of the draw to the east.[10]

The 1st Marine Division planned to attack the heights and the draw simultaneously with tank-infantry teams. It was here that the technique of
"processing"—tanks operating in close support of infantry—won an en-
thusiastic supporter in division commander General Pedro del Valle. He
became a believer when he saw tanks rolling ahead of his infantrymen to
batter fortified positions and disrupt enemy fire on his foot-bound troops.[11]

On May 17, a dozen tanks and four self-propelled M-7s tried to advance
with the 5th Marines, which had relieved the 1st Marines. Japanese gunners succeeded in separating the armor from the troops to better destroy
both—their answer to the American tank-infantry teams. Japanese 47mm
antitank guns knocked out two tanks, and mortar fire wreaked havoc on
the infantrymen accompanying them. The Marines withdrew with heavy
casualties, although the foray was not a complete bust; observers identified
two of the 47mm positions, and the battleship *Colorado* destroyed them.

FRONTLINE TROOPS SAW THE EFFECTS of naval gunfire support every
day. Naval forward observers, both on the ground and in spotter planes
launched from warships, relayed their coordinates to fire support ships offshore. Ground units also directly requested support from the battleships,
cruisers, and destroyers assigned to them. When intervening hills blocked
their targets, ships had the advantage over artillery of being able to move to
a place that gave them a cleaner shot.

Five-man artillery observer teams assigned to the infantry battalions
that they supported were in continual radio and wire telephone contact
with their batteries and with spotter planes overhead that could see targets
that the ground observers could not. While ground observers focused on
nearby enemy positions, airborne spotters picked out more distant targets;
the coordinates for both were sent to batteries in their respective sectors.[12]

THE 7TH MARINES ATTEMPTED TO advance along Wana Ridge's crest, but three days' effort had produced meager results. On May 19, the 1st Marines relieved the 7th, which had suffered 984 combat casualties since May 10. Company officers were especially hard-hit: there had been six command changes in Company I, five in Company K, and three in L.

After sixteen days on the battle line, George Lince, an assistant BAR gunner with Company A of the 7th Marines, was filthy and thin, his normal 30-inch waistline having shrunk to 27 inches. Traveling to the regiment's rest area after it had been relieved, Lince noted the "evidence of total war. The trees were all leveled, with blackened and smoking areas. The smell of death, from visibly rotting bodies and burned powder, supported the fact that there had been a hell created for mankind by men."[13]

The Japanese had thwarted every attempt to seize Wana Ridge's eastern approach, so the division tried to force a western entry; the approaches were flatter and better suited for armor. Tank-infantry teams entered Wana Draw from the west each day and began the slow process of neutralizing its reverse slope cave defenses with bazookas, flamethrowers, flame tanks, and grenades and dynamite thrown from close range. It was brutal, elemental combat prosecuted by corporals and privates. Enemy counterattacks and fierce 47mm antitank fire prevented the Americans from capturing Wana Ridge, or advancing into the draw more than a short distance. At one point, 47mm gunners on Shuri scored seventeen hits on eight tanks.

Sergeant Merlin Smidt of the 1st Marine Tank Battalion lost three tanks in Wana Draw to land mines and satchel charges. Smidt won a Silver Star when he left one of the tanks, crawled to the ridge crest while under heavy fire, and organized the evacuation of wounded men there while repositioning those still able to fight.

Each night, the Japanese sabotaged American tank approaches to the Wanas and replaced 47mm guns knocked out by American gunfire. Reports characterized the enemy resistance as the "frantic use of every possible weapon available to stop tanks." Indeed, General Ushijima said, "The enemy's power lies in its tanks. It has become obvious that our battle against the Americans is a battle against their tanks."

Despite the savage resistance, the Marine tank-infantry teams made steady progress through May 20. Tank crews and infantrymen improved their coordination daily. "Superb infantry, superb tankers," said Lieutenant Colonel A. J. "Jeb" Stuart, commander of the 1st Marine Tank Battalion. "The men had lived together, trained together. . . . They had complete confidence in each other."

On May 21, the 1st Marines' 3rd Battalion, after a heavy rocket-fire pre-lude, attempted to work its way along Wana Ridge's reverse slope on the north side of the draw to neutralize the cave defenses. The Japanese would have none of it; the after-action report said that in their "death struggle," the Japanese drove the battalion around the western nose of the ridge, all the way past Wana Village.[14]

There were nightly counterattacks. The sound of screaming and clang-ing metal awakened Corporal Kenneth Hebard of the 5th Marines, napping in his foxhole while his companion stood watch. Hebard saw two enemy soldiers leaping over his foxhole and a third one slamming a sword down on his comrade's helmeted head. "I grabbed my rifle, stuck it in the Jap's throat and pulled the trigger." He then shot the two Japanese who had jumped over him. His foxhole buddy evidently had had enough; he handed Hebard his rifle and left. Hebard used the two rifles and some grenades to kill ten enemy soldiers.[15]

Three armor-piercing antitank rounds slammed into Corporal Jack Armstrong's Sherman tank as it maneuvered through a narrow ravine. The driver, Corporal Harlan Stefan, his left arm blown off below the elbow, somehow steered the tank out of the draw one-handed as his stump spurted blood.[16]

The Marines nicknamed Wana Draw "Death Valley," and it was no mystery why. It would require more than a week of hard fighting and the spilling of an inordinate amount of blood to gain more than a foothold there and on Wana Ridge. "We ate and slept with the bloated bodies of Japs and our own men," said Private First Class Manuel Rivas of the 1st Marines, "and the only safe place to get any relief from the artillery fire was in the Okinawan tombs."

IN THE RELATIVE SAFETY OF the concrete tombs—after grenades had dispatched any Japanese soldiers inside—Marines and soldiers shared quarters with large jars of dried human bones. "The odor was terrible, it was musty. . . . The native women came to moan and weep at the tombs be-cause we desecrated their ancestors," said Pharmacist's Mate 2/c Bill Clark, a corpsman with the 22nd Marines.

In peacetime, relatives brought food and water to the tomb every day until the deceased's body decomposed, normally a three-year process. The remains were then removed from the tomb by relatives, who scraped the flesh from the bones before placing them in a large urn that was returned to the tomb.

The tombs might have provided protection from enemy gunfire, but they also harbored colonies of fleas. Marines and soldiers learned that once the fleas got under their field jackets and infested their fatigue shirts, it was nearly impossible to be rid of them. "Language is not adequate to describe the persistent annoyance of fleas," said Staff Sergeant John Holt of the 96th Division's 381st Infantry.[17]

But while "we were shot to pieces and beaten bloody," as Marine Corporal Melvin Grant described the fighting at Wana Ridge and Wana Draw, the Japanese were subjected to a howling cacophony of gunfire from tanks, artillery, and naval warships. The continual explosions for hours and days on end drummed into the Marines "a sense of stupefaction and dullness" beyond what even veterans of Peleliu had experienced, said E. B. Sledge, who had fought there. "A lot of fellows cracked up or close to it. They are laying in their holes shaking and are sick and weak," wrote Private First Class A. R. Fournier, a 1st Marines diarist.[18]

To kill Japanese defenders in their caves, Marines atop Wana Ridge lowered satchel charges by rope to the cave entrances. The Japanese, however, often pulled out the fuses before the explosives could be detonated. Demolition units solved the problem by attaching two fuses to each satchel charge.

To prevent enemy troops from scooping up live American grenades, which had five-second fuses, and pitching them back to the Americans, US troops habitually popped the handles and counted to two before throwing them. When replacement grenades with three-second fuses arrived, "not everyone was told" of the change, wrote Corporal Robert J. Sorenson of the 5th Marines. When men counted to two before throwing the new grenades, they sometimes went off in their hands, causing "friendly" casualties.[19]

GRAVES REGISTRATION TEAMS THAT ROVED the battleground, recovering and identifying bodies, witnessed horrors daily. Private Nils Anderson of the 29th Marines described a Marine's body that had swollen to twice its normal size. "His clothing was split and, of course, he was turning black and green." Nearby were the remains of three Japanese. "The skin [was] almost like a pool still attached to the skeletons . . . beneath the bodies," wrote Anderson. If a dead American still had his dog tags, one would be driven between his front teeth to accompany the body. If no dog tags were in evidence, someone had to be found to identify the body.[20]

Corporal Robert Sorenson, a 5th Marines machine gunner, stepped forward when an officer asked for two volunteers to help bury the bodies of

eight to ten Japanese soldiers. But when the men reached the site, there were two hundred bodies, not ten, belonging to Japanese soldiers killed that morning. The officer told Sorenson and his companion that they couldn't possibly bury them all. Instead, he tried burning them with gasoline. When the officer ignited the fuel, "their ammo started exploding and we had to run for cover," Sorenson said. The fire scorched, but did not destroy the bodies.[21]

Snipers plied their trade from inside the tombs on Wana Ridge; one enemy sharpshooter killed or wounded thirteen Marines. Private First Class Robert Milner of Company I of the 1st Marines was attempting to eliminate the prolific sniper when either he or another Japanese sniper shot Milner first. "I heard a roar, saw a huge purple flash, and blacked out." Shot in the head, Milner regained consciousness on a stretcher in a hospital tent, where a doctor was using forceps to remove pieces of helmet and bone from his head. Milner was flown to Guam for further treatment and survived.[22]

At 2 a.m. on May 22, up to two hundred Japanese attacked the 1st Marines' Company C on Wana Ridge. After an intensive grenade battle, the enemy troops occupied part of the ridge, until at dawn the Marines reorganized themselves and drove them away, leaving the ground littered with up to 140 enemy dead.[23]

Violently repulsed during repeated attempts to capture Wana Ridge, the 1st Marines in desperation called on the 1st Pioneer Battalion to pump napalm through a hose over the ridge's crest, so that they could then ignite it with phosphorus grenades. The tactic had worked when they were stopped on Peleliu.

But before the Marines could make use of the tactic, the torrential plum rains set in, and operations had to be suspended. Wana Draw became a swamp. Tanks and amphibian tractors attempted to churn through the mud and got stuck. With virtually all vehicle traffic halted, for days little food could be brought up, no fresh water reached the front, and the dead could not be buried. To slake their thirst, the troops drank putrid water from shell holes after purifying it with a few drops of iodine. The Marines' foxholes had to be bailed out constantly, and often crumbled and collapsed.[24]

Consequently, from May 24 until May 27 there was no change in the Japanese and Marine lines. But during the interregnum there was no letup in Japanese and US artillery and mortar fire, and fresh casualties occurred each day.

Weeks of rain and mud also spawned a host of physical problems for the Marines and soldiers—chief among them "immersion foot," or "trench foot" in World War I parlance. Without opportunities to don dry socks, the men noticed that when they walked or ran, their feet hurt, and their feet slipped around inside their boondockers. As a result of being wet all the time, their hands became wrinkled, their nails softened, and sores appeared on their knuckles and the backs of their hands.[25]

OCCASIONALLY, SOMEONE WHO BY RIGHTS should have been killed got lucky. Corporal George Peto, a forward observer for a 1st Marines mortar squad in Wana Draw, was struck in the right shoulder by a 2-pound Japanese knee-mortar round. It bruised him, but it did not explode. "The shell was laying there on the ground, the fuse sizzling," he wrote. He picked it up and threw it down the slope. It went off immediately after leaving his hand; Peto was unhurt.[26]

Peto went out with a patrol to find an injured Marine who had been heard shouting that he was being tortured. The patrol proceeded cautiously, fearful of walking into a trap. They found the man's battered body. "He was a helluva bloody mess," wrote Peto. "His face was really swollen from the beatings. . . . The Japs had also bound him tightly with dry rope, and then had poured water on it, making the rope shrink, and of course, causing the guy a lot more pain before he died."[27]

Every night, Japanese infiltrators lurked in the stygian gloom, and frequently the enemy activity coalesced into a shrieking counterattack. But sometimes the danger came from below.

Sergeant Vernon Taylor of the 7th Marines' Company I had just returned to his mortar squad from a Guam hospital when, during the night, "We were awakened by a trap door [opening] at our feet," he said. To the Marines' amazement, six Japanese deserters who had been hiding in a small cave beneath the Marines' position emerged. They were unarmed and wore only loincloths.

"They begged for mercy," Taylor said—and were justified in so pleading, for Taylor's company had yet to take a prisoner. This time, however, the Marines escorted the Japanese to division headquarters for questioning.[28]

AT THE OUTSET OF THE May 11 offensive, the 6th Marine Division's 22nd Regiment had crossed the Asa-Kawa, captured heavily fortified Charlie Ridge on the river's south bank, and reached the bluffs overlooking the smashed capital city of Naha. All appeared to be going well.

The 22nd's next move was to turn southeast and then east, with the object of slipping behind the Shuri defenses. There, the 22nd intended to maul the enemy's rear and sever his avenue of retreat to the south.

The Marines' planned envelopment made good tactical sense, but Ushijima and his strategists had anticipated it, knowing that this natural corridor from the west posed an existential threat to the Shuri Line. In acting to block it, the Japanese committed considerable manpower and resources—and transformed three hills in the area into bristling strongpoints.[29]

FIFTY FEET HIGH AND 300 yards long, Sugar Loaf Hill resembled a layer cake that had failed to rise. The Japanese called the undistinguished-looking mound of coral and red clay Hill 51.2. A quarter mile to the southeast lay Half Moon Hill, and 200 yards south of Sugar Loaf was Horseshoe Hill. The Marines automatically assumed that enemy troops would defend the triangular terrain feature, but they had no conception of the extent to which they would do so.

Tactically and strategically, the hills, although small in stature, occupied a dominant position—as befitted the western anchor of the Shuri Line. Although they covered a relatively small area, their close proximity to one another and the fact that they were mutually supporting endowed them with tremendous strength. If one were assaulted, gunners embedded in the other two could flail the attackers with mortar, artillery, and machine-gun fire. Tunnels and galleries connected the three hills. Moreover, from the Shuri Heights to the east, Japanese artillery could rain down metal on all three hills and their approaches. "It is hard to conceive a more powerful position than the Sugar Loaf terrain afforded," said the 6th Marine Division after-action report.[30]

The hills' two thousand Japanese defenders mainly belonged to the 2nd and 3rd Infantry Battalions of the 15th Independent Mixed Regiment, part of the 44th Independent Mixed Brigade. Okinawan conscripts augmented the force. A 75mm antiaircraft battery, 47mm antitank guns, and 20mm automatic cannons lent supporting fire. As the fighting intensified, three hundred naval troops would be sent up the Asato River corridor from the naval base on the Oroku Peninsula to reinforce the three hills.[31]

To thwart the Marines' envelopment of Shuri—which would be disastrous for the Japanese—Ushijima was committing some of his last reserves to what could be the pivotal battle of the Okinawa campaign. Colonel Hiromichi Yahara, Ushijima's operations officer, would describe the battle for Sugar Loaf Hill as "a mighty struggle."[32]

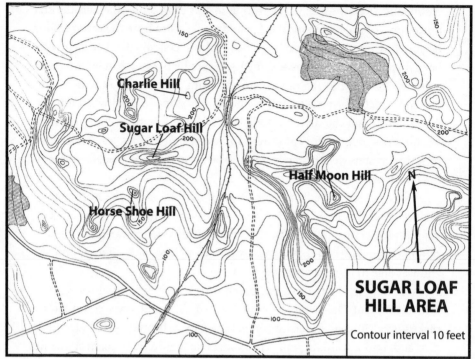

Map adapted from 6th Marine Division Special Action Report

GENERAL LEMUEL SHEPHERD, THE DECORATED Belleau Wood veteran who led the 6th Marine Division, had warned his officers that the fighting in southern Okinawa would be unlike anything that they had previously encountered. Outflank the enemy, he advised, rather than attempt to "outslug" him. Lest his officers mistake his admonition for softness, Shepherd told his officers to instill in their men the belief that "killing a Jap was like killing a rattlesnake." Above all, keep pushing. The 6th Division's experience since reaching the front line May 8 had borne out Shepherd's warnings of severe artillery bombardments, desperate counterattacks, and nearly nonstop mortar and machine-gun fire. Now, however, a quantum leap in the violence quotient awaited the Marines in the drab, nondescript hills just ahead.[33]

Approaching Sugar Loaf Hill on May 12, the 22nd Marines badly underestimated the dimensions of the threat that they faced, sending a small force—Company G and four Sherman tanks—to capture it.

Automatic-weapons fire blazed from gun slits carved into the hillside, and uncannily accurate knee-mortar fire and artillery fire from the reverse slope began churning the hill's approaches—whose coordinates had evidently been mapped to the inch by the enemy. Swept by the storm of gunfire, Marines fell moaning to the muddy ground with bullet wounds, and an amphibious tractor bringing reinforcements was stopped dead when a bullet whizzed through the driver's visor, killing him. Troops spilling from the tractor's rear ramp were cut down, and other amphibious tractors sent to pick up the men were immediately knocked out. Gunfire disabled three of the four tanks sent into the assault.

It was a scene of bedlam. Some men were undone by the hurricane of gunfire. Near Private First Class James Chaisson huddled a sergeant, "a big, rugged guy, crying like a baby." When the thirty-four-year-old Chaisson reminded the sergeant that he was supposed to lead, he composed himself and was able to resume his duties.[34]

Four George Company men somehow reached Sugar Loaf's low summit. Lieutenant Dale Bair, recently named the company's commander, picked up a .30-caliber machine gun, sans tripod, from two wounded gunners and fired it from his hip. "He looked like that Marine Corps statue we have at Parris Island [the Corps's South Carolina boot camp]," said Sergeant Ed DeMar—until Bair was hit by a swarm of bullets that also struck DeMar in the left thigh and arm.[35]

They could not hold the fire-swept hilltop. The survivors withdrew on hands and knees behind a curtain of smoke created by 140 smoke shells fired by the tanks. In a very short period, George Company had suffered eighty-six casualties, emerging from the disastrous first assault on Sugar Loaf with just seventy-five men. "We realized we were in great difficulty," understatedly remarked Lieutenant Charles Kirkpatrick, a forward artillery observer.[36]

The next day, May 13, Lieutenant Colonel Horatio Woodhouse's 2nd Battalion prepared to attack Sugar Loaf again after a heavy bombardment by artillery and naval gunfire, and close-air support strikes with bombs and rockets. The shelling and bombing had no discernible effect. When Marine tank-infantry teams began their assault, they were met by a storm of artillery, mortar, machine-gun, and small-arms fire. They made little headway.

The Japanese artillery fire was delivered with "sharpshooter precision" and was "atrociously effective," according to the 6th Marine Division historian. Its alarming accuracy gave rise to reports that a Japanese artillery

school in Naha had used the hill as a training ground "and that now the gunners were firing school problems."[37]

While the 2nd Battalion was pinned down on Sugar Loaf's approaches, the 22nd's other battalions destroyed some of the ruined villages on Naha's outskirts with tanks, bazookas, rifles, and machine guns. They were hoping to sever the Japanese resupply route to Sugar Loaf and its neighbors. After killing about seventy-five Japanese in Amike Village, the Marines withdrew. However, the enemy pipeline remained intact.[38]

On May 14, tank-infantry teams from the 22nd attempted to flank Sugar Loaf from the east and west, but were repelled by 47mm antitank fire. Company G tried again to reach the hilltop, only to be forced to withdraw with heavy casualties beneath a torrent of mortar fire from Horseshoe Hill.

When Lieutenant Colonel Woodhouse requested reinforcements for his battered battalion, down to 40 percent strength, he was given Company K from the 3rd Battalion and was told that Sugar Loaf had to be captured by that night, "regardless of consequences." Company F led the final attack, also a failure. They "just cut us down like a mowing machine going through a hayfield," wrote Private First Class Wendell Majors. Tanks moved in and laid down a smoke screen so that the wounded could be evacuated.

At dusk, plans were laid for a fourth assault—a rare nighttime attack to be led by Major Henry Courtney, the 2nd Battalion's executive officer. He had proposed "a banzai charge of our own!" The twenty-eight-year-old lawyer from Duluth, Minnesota, jokingly nicknamed "Smiley" because of his dour demeanor, always led from the front. Four days earlier, a shell fragment had sliced his right thigh, but he refused evacuation. Courtney had spent the day with his assault companies and was going back into action that night.[39]

ABOUT FIFTY MEN TRUDGED UP the steep, slippery slope in complete darkness, drenched by a wind-whipped cold rain from the East China Sea. Nighttime flares that had been fired every fifteen minutes, slowly descending on small parachutes, had now ceased, in order to protect the attackers from discovery. But lightning flashed, thunder pealed loudly, and rain pelted down, deepening the disturbing sense among the attackers that they were in the coils of a nightmare.

Their instructions were to "throw grenades as rapidly as possible" upon reaching the hilltop, and dig in. Courtney's tired, muddy shock troops included twenty-two volunteers from Companies G and F, along with

twenty-six others recruited from the replacements who had carried ammu-nition to the front.[40]

The unrecovered bodies of Marines killed during the earlier assaults lit-tered the muddy hillside. "I crawled over dead Marines and pieces of dead Marines all the way up the hill," said Corporal Ray Schlinder.

Around 11 p.m. the attackers halted just below the hillcrest, threw a vol-ley of grenades, and then stormed to the top. The Japanese threw grenades back at them, and enemy artillery fire began plastering the hilltop. Observ-ing Japanese preparing to counterattack from the reverse slope, Courtney launched his own attack, killing many of them and driving the others into caves. Courtney was roving the hillcrest, placing his men in strong defen-sive positions, when a mortar burst killed him.[41]

Captain Ed Pesley, the Company F commander, brought more am-munition on an amphibious tractor to the foot of Sugar Loaf, and hand-carried the ammo cases the rest of the way to the hilltop. The ammunition arrived just in time to stop a mass Japanese grenade attack. "We could see columns of Nips coming toward us," Pesley said. He called in artillery fire at ranges just 100 yards from the Marines. The Japanese taunted the Marines during the night, shouting, "Hey Marine, you're going to die! You're going to die by morning!" After Courtney's death, Pesley took command of the assault force.[42]

The 3rd Battalion's Company K, with 103 men, was dispatched to re-inforce Courtney's dwindling force at 2:30 a.m. on May 15. Upon reach-ing Sugar Loaf's summit, Company K came under withering mortar and grenade fire, and the new arrivals began falling with mortal or disabling wounds. Private First Class Jack Houston left the hillcrest and crawled be-hind a fallen tree, where four Marines sat silently, their "heads tipped for-ward as if sleeping." A shell landed nearby, "and they all pitched over like dominoes and I realized they all had been dead," said Houston.[43]

Corporal Schlinder threw about three hundred grenades before a frag-ment from a knee-mortar round sliced through his right lung and into his liver. All night, he lay where he had fallen while the fighting raged around him.[44]

Corporal Donald "Rusty" Golar, a self-described "glory hunter," fired his light machine gun near Sugar Loaf's ridge crest until enemy gunners on an adjacent hill zeroed in on him. Golar shifted his fire to them, shout-ing, "Yeah!" Using up all of his ammunition, he and two riflemen discov-ered they were the only ones from their squad still fighting on the hill; their comrades lay around them, dead or wounded.

Golar kept fighting. He emptied his pistol and hurled it toward the enemy. From the wounded he collected hand grenades and threw them. He found a BAR and fired it until it jammed. With nothing left to shoot at the Japanese, Golar, a brawny former longshoreman, picked up a wounded Marine to carry him off the hill. At that moment, Golar's luck ran out; he was hit by a sniper's bullet. He laid the wounded man on the ground and staggered to a ditch, where he sat down, tipped his helmet over his fore-head, and died.[45]

By dawn, just twenty survivors from Courtney's force remained on Sugar Loaf. A relief platoon from the 29th Marines' Company D, attack-ing with fixed bayonets, braved sleeting gunfire from three directions to reach the summit. The Japanese counterattacked at 8:30 a.m., but the Com-pany D platoon held, although by 11:36 a.m., just eleven of its original sixty men could still fight. Of Company K's 103 reinforcements, 30 effectives remained. Relentless mortar and antitank fire forced the survivors to with-draw later that day.

Colonel Yahara, the Thirty-Second Army operations officer, said the night attack on Sugar Loaf took the Japanese "completely by surprise." His men were accustomed to relaxing their guard at nighttime because the Americans they had fought previously had never launched a major assault after dark. A larger force might have broken through.[46]

Because of the heavy Japanese gunfire, the bodies of about a hundred Marines had been left behind on Sugar Loaf's northern approaches. Re-lieved by the 3rd Battalion, the 22nd Marines' 2nd Battalion went into reserve, having lost about four hundred of its nine hundred men in three days.[47]

Japanese losses had also been heavy. During the night of May 15, a com-posite force of service and support units reinforced the decimated 15th Independent Mixed Regiment on Sugar Loaf.[48]

THE 22ND MARINES' 3RD BATTALION assaulted Sugar Loaf again on May 16, while the 29th Marines' 3rd Battalion, supported by tanks, si-multaneously attacked adjacent Half Moon, from which Japanese gun-ners had smothered the Marines' previous attempts to storm Sugar Loaf. The 22nd reached the top of Sugar Loaf several times to engage in close-in fighting after braving hailstorms of grenades and mortar and automatic-weapons fire.

Then the Japanese hit the 22nd Marines with phosphorus shells. "The smell of phosphorous in human flesh was sickening, almost gagging us to

the point of vomiting," said Corporal Robert E. Lee Ferrier. Intensifying Japanese gunfire drove the Marines from the hill with heavy casualties.[49]

At the same time, the attack on Half Moon stalled, with the Marines huddling on the hill's northern slope beneath a shower of enemy grenades, mortars, and gunfire. "Oh man, they just slaughtered the hell out of us," said Private First Class Ed Soja. "We were literally getting blasted off of the hill with artillery and mortars," said Private Donald Honis. The battalion withdrew.

Wounded in the leg, Honis was loaded onto an amphibious tractor with about fifteen other wounded men. "The amtrac itself [was] like a slaughter-house," Honis said. "We're bleeding . . . and the blood is sloshing from side to side. Both guys on my left and right are bleeding on me."[50]

"This was the bitterest day of the Okinawa campaign for the 6th Division," said the division report for May 16. "Two regiments had attacked with all the effort at their command and had been unsuccessful."

The next day, the 29th Marines assumed responsibility for Sugar Loaf from the 22nd Marines, whose effectiveness had sharply declined as a result of its many casualties.[51]

MULTIPLE FRONTAL ASSAULTS ON SUGAR LOAF had failed, and now General Shepherd elected to follow his own advice to his commanders—to use maneuver to outflank the enemy and not attempt to "outslug" him.

On May 17, Shepherd sent the 29th Marines into a bowl that lay between Sugar Loaf and, to its left, Half Moon. From this point, two battalions struck Half Moon, while one battalion stormed Sugar Loaf. Company E advanced through heavy mortar fire and reached Sugar Loaf's crest, where it was driven off the hill by a furious banzai attack. Two more attempts failed, but on the fourth try the company repulsed a Japanese counterattack and held. But by then Company E had run out of ammunition and men—the company had suffered 160 casualties—and it was forced to withdraw.[52]

When the 29th first moved into the line between the battered 22nd Regiment and the 1st Marine Division, its men encountered a stream of casualties on their way to medical aid stations. They asked the wounded men, "How was it up there?" to which the wounded replied, "It could not be worse." "They told us good luck and God bless," said Corporal Hubert Welch of the 29th Marines' Company I.[53]

"The frustrating thing about those hills [Sugar Loaf, Half Moon, and Horseshoe] was that they looked like barren little humps covered with tree

The aircraft carrier *Franklin* burns after being bombed by a Japanese dive-bomber on March 19, 1945. The explosion and fires killed more than 800 crewmen. *National Archives*

Admiral Chester Nimitz, commander of the Pacific Ocean Area, pointing to Okinawa on a wall map. *Library of Congress*

Admiral Raymond Spruance, commander of the Fifth Fleet. *US Navy*

Admiral Marc Mitscher, commander of Fast Carrier Task Force 58, with Commodore Arleigh Burke. *US Navy*

US amphibious troops come ashore on Okinawa on L-Day. *Library of Congress*

Newspaper correspondent Ernie Pyle with 1st Marine Division troops beside an Okinawa roadside shortly after L-Day. *National Archives*

General Simon Bolivar Buckner Jr., commander of the invading US Tenth Army. *US Army*

General Mitsuru Ushijima, commander of the Japanese 32nd Army. *US Army*

General Isamu Chō, chief of staff of the Japanese 32nd Army. *US Army*

Colonel Hiromichi Yahara, the Japanese 32nd Army's operations officer and chief strategist.

Admiral Matome Ugaki, who commanded the Japanese Fifth Air Fleet and directed kamikaze attacks against US warships off Okinawa. He died in one of the last kamikaze missions. *Chiran Kamikaze Peace Museum*

Japanese schoolgirls scatter cherry blossoms in bidding farewell to kamikaze pilots departing on one of the first kikusuis.

American troops examine an Ohka kamikaze plane captured on Okinawa. *US Navy*

General Roy Geiger, commander of III Amphibious Corps on Okinawa. *US Marine Corps*

Army medic Desmond Doss, recipient of the Congressional Medal of Honor. *US Army*

Army medic Desmond Doss photographed while evacuating wounded men from atop Hacksaw Ridge. *US Army*

US Army troops with captured Japanese soldier on Okinawa. *US Army*

A Corsair fighter blasts
a target with rockets
during a close-air support
mission on Okinawa.
National Archives

A Japanese kamikaze goes down in flames off Okinawa. *National Archives*

The aircraft carrier *Bunker Hill* burns after being crashed by two kamikazes on May 11, 1945. *National Archives*

Smoke billows from the carrier *Bunker Hill* after it was crashed by two kamikazes on May 11, 1945. *National Archives*

The destroyer *Laffey* survived multiple bombs and kamikaze crashes while on picket ship duty off Okinawa on April 16, 1945. *US Navy*

The starboard side of the destroyer *Hugh W. Hadley* is badly damaged after being hit by Japanese kamikazes and conventional planes off Okinawa on May 11, 1945. *US Navy*

A Marine provides covering fire for a comrade during fighting on Wana Ridge.
National Archives

US troops battle on the Shuri Line. *US Marine Corps*

A Marine dashes for cover on the Shuri Line. *US Marine Corps*

Japanese POWS on Okinawa. *US Army*

General Lemuel Shepherd, commander of the 6th Marine
Division, studies a map near Naha. *Library of Congress*

American troops
mount an attack on
Japanese in a cave.
Library of Congress

Major Henry Courtney, who led the nighttime assault on Sugar Loaf Hill and was posthumously awarded the Congressional Medal of Honor.
Naval History and Heritage Command

Sugar Loaf Hill, a bump in the landscape that bristled with enemy defenses.
US Marine Corps

A 6th Division Marine scorches a Japanese position with a flamethrower.
US Marine Corps

Okinawa's nonstop "plum rains" and the ensuing mud paralyzed operations for days during May. *US Army*

Generals Simon Bolivar Buckner Jr. (r) and Lemuel Shepherd (l) watching the fighting in southern Okinawa. *US Army*

Marines aid an
elderly Okinawa
civilian.
US Marine Corps

Okinawa civilian
refugees on the move.

Japanese soldiers and
a civilian in captivity.
Library of Congress

The photograph of "the girl with the white flag," Tomika Higa, that appeared in newspapers across the United States. *US Army*

The last photograph taken of General Simon Bolivar Buckner Jr. (r) before he was killed on June 18, 1945. *US Marine Corps*

Mushroom cloud over Nagasaki after "Fat Man" was dropped on the city on August 9, 1945. *National Archives*

Japanese POWs listen as Emperor Hirohito's surrender announcement is read to them in August 1945. *National Archives*

stumps left by Navy gunfire," said Lieutenant Bob Scherer of the 29th Marines' Company F. "There was no outward indication of all the caves and tunnels inside."[54]

"It was back and forth, up and down, up and down and then all at once it began to rain, torrential rains," said Lieutenant Charles Kirkpatrick, a forward artillery observer. Foxholes began to fill with water. "Everybody was soaking wet, had mud all over you."

"All night, every night, shells erupted close enough to shake the mud beneath you at the rate of five or six a minute," wrote Sergeant William Manchester. "You could hear the cries of the dying but could do nothing," because the Marines were under orders to not leave their foxholes at night. "Any man who stood up was cut in half by machine guns manned by fellow Marines."

A Japanese soldier armed with a sword and a grenade attacked Sergeant Charles Miller and his squad, shouting, "Banzai!" He banged the grenade against his helmet to ignite the fuse. Instead of activating the usual seconds-long fuse delay, the grenade detonated immediately and blew off the soldier's head. "We started laughing," said Miller, "and said, 'Made in Japan! Made in Japan!'"[55]

THE STRUGGLE TO SEIZE SUGAR LOAF amid the storms of flying metal transformed the landscape into a muddy tableau of horror.

"All across the face of this hill . . . there were bodies, parts of bodies of the Japanese that had been blown up by artillery fire," said Kirkpatrick. "It had an awful smell and of course nobody got any sleep."

The dead, wrote combat photographer Alan Manell, "have a sweet smell that's something terrible."

"We were fighting and sleeping in one vast cesspool," wrote Sergeant Manchester. "Mingled with that stench was another—the corrupt and corrupting odor of rotting human flesh."

When the Marines ate their rations, "there was a horde of black flies that had been over eating those Japanese bodies. . . . You had your hand full of food you're trying to get in your mouth, [but] it's all covered with flies." On Sugar Loaf, Marines nibbled on fruit and chocolate D bars and, because of the stench and the buzzing flies, tended to eschew the K, C, and 10-in-1 rations that included hash and cheese, ham and eggs, powdered coffee, and biscuits. Widespread diarrhea and dysentery added to the shocking odor that permeated the area. On average, each man lost 15 to 20 pounds during

the fighting on Sugar Loaf Hill. Some men displayed symptoms of malnutrition, with sores appearing on their hands.[56]

"The sewage, of course, was appalling. You could smell the front long before you saw it," wrote Sergeant Manchester of the 29th Marines. "This, I thought, is what Verdun and Passchandaele [sic] must have looked like."[57]

"There were bodies everywhere," wrote Richard Whitaker of the 29th Marines. "The stench was incredible. The bodies were rife with maggots, and maggots mature into huge, ugly green flies. . . . They would light on your face and crawl into your nostrils, your mouth, and your eyes."[58]

Once when the battle line fell unusually silent, the Americans became aware of a sound they had not heard before, but which had probably always been in the background. "It seemed weird and eerie, it was a low moan rising and falling over the hills and valleys," said Private John L. Speheger of the 29th Marines. "It was a drone. The drone of trillions of flies that were hovering over the battle line, feeding on and laying maggot eggs on the corpses that covered the vast area."

The enormous flies, the swarming maggots, and the rotting bodies murdered appetite and nauseated the fighting men; Speheger, for one, was so repulsed that he could not bring himself to eat anything for three days. "If you were close enough, you could hear the mass of maggots working in the bloated body," he said. "They made a swash-swash sound. The stench was so terrible it was indescribable."[59]

Burial details interred Americans and Japanese alike—the enemy dead placed in shallow graves for the sole purpose of reducing the odor. But when it rained, the Japanese dead often reappeared. "You'd walk up and a hand would come up and feet and all covered with maggots," said Private First Class George Niland of the 22nd Marines.

Corporal Hubert Welch of the 29th Marines, standing in the rain in soft mud to his knees near Sugar Loaf Hill, was horrified when he realized that he was on top of a freshly dug Japanese grave. A decaying arm stuck out of the mud and the stench of rotting flesh assailed him—so powerful that it caused Welch to vomit.[60]

The Tenth Army's dead were gathered up and taken to Graves Registration sites for identification and burial. It was a thankless, stomach-churning job from beginning to end. Corporal Welch, assigned to collect dead Marines, at one point reached down to lift a body by the cartridge belt. To Welch's horror, "the body was so decayed that the belt just came right through him and I ended up holding the belt in my hand." The corpses

were carried on ponchos to amphibious tractors that took them to Graves Registration. A Marine who got in an amtrac to return to his unit quickly exited and walked back instead when he found it "was full to the top with bodies."

Private First Class Landon Oakes had a different reaction when his stretcher was placed atop another amtrac carrying sixty to seventy dead Marines to the rear. Wounded by shrapnel and shot full of morphine, Oakes felt something akin to a mystical experience. "That should have been a nauseating experience, but it was far beyond that," he said. "I think I was quite proud to leave the lines with those men. They gave their all."

Many of the dead had been blown to pieces, so it was a challenge to ensure that each set of remains contained a head, torso, two arms, and two legs, all laid out on a stretcher. "If they didn't match, we'd do that anyway, and Graves Registration could sort out the pieces later," said Marine Private Nils Anderson.[61]

DAYS OF BLOODY, FUTILE ASSAULTS on Sugar Loaf Hill caused many 6th Division Marines to wonder what it would take to capture the miserable little hill. And then, on May 18, the seventh day of the siege, the 29th Marines' Company D, led by Captain Howard Mabie, attempted a double envelopment with armor and two assault platoons—and the maneuver worked.

After one hour of intensive fighting, the Marines captured the malignant, body-strewn smudge of muddy red clay and coral. "Send up PX supplies," read the message to the regimental command post. "Sugar Loaf is ours."[62]

While a platoon led by Lieutenant Francis Smith had scaled Sugar Loaf's western slope, a second platoon had tackled the east side. Tanks from Company A of the 6th Tank Battalion made their way to the hill's southern, reverse slope. Smith's platoon reached the top on the west side, and his men hurled grenades down the reverse slope as the tanks fired into cave openings there.

The attack rousted the defenders from the caves—scores of enemy troops, many of them belonging to suicide squads and armed with satchel charges to hurl at the tanks. "The Japs came running down from the crest. There must have been 150 of them. We fired . . . and blew them all over the landscape" with machine guns, said Lieutenant Donald Pinnow, a tank commander.

Corporal Whalen McGarrity saw an enemy officer pointing with his saber to boulders for his men to take cover behind, and he aimed his tank's 75mm gun and fired, hitting the officer. "His sword went flying fifty feet through the air," wrote a witness.[63]

D Company dug in on Sugar Loaf's crest and braced itself for the expected Japanese counterattacks, which without fail came that night, along with the usual tempest of artillery fire. This time, after Sugar Loaf had changed hands eleven times, the Marines held.[64]

Said a Japanese survivor of the Sugar Loaf battle: "It was no longer a glorious man-to-man fight but a grotesquely one-sided process in which a gigantic iron organism crushed and pulverized human flesh."[65]

SUGAR LOAF'S CAPTURE MEANT THAT the Tenth Army had finally cracked the western Shuri Line, although Horseshoe and Half Moon Hills remained Japanese bastions. It was a major achievement, but ten days of fighting, from the crossing of the Asa-Kawa River until May 18, had been costly: the 6th Marine Division reported 2,662 combat casualties and 1,289 combat fatigue cases—almost all of them in the 22nd and 29th regiments. During roughly the same ten-day period, the 77th Division reported 1,467 casualties, and the 96th Division, 1,206.[66]

On May 19, the 6th Division reserve, the 4th Marines, relieved the decimated 29th Marines, which had earlier relieved the battered 22nd Marines. Private First Class Chris Clemenson said the survivors of Sugar Loaf in his Company E, which originally numbered about 225 men, were divided into two understrength platoons. "There was a corporal had one platoon. He had 18. I had 17," Clemenson said.

The Japanese immediately tested the 4th Marines with heavy counterattacks, but the 3rd Raider Battalion repelled the bloody assaults. During the fighting, a mortar round struck Joe McNamara's platoon sergeant in the head, spraying blood on everybody around him. It happened so quickly that the sergeant "was in the same position when I last saw him, but he didn't have a head," said McNamara. A corpsman who was also hit by the mortar round was "just a bundle of rags."[67]

"What was tough to take at this time of the battle was that we could not get our dead removed," said Trenton Fowler of the 4th Marines. "It was very hard on a person's morale to see a buddy's body decaying."[68]

A journal recovered from the body of an unidentified Japanese soldier on Sugar Loaf revealed the despair of hungry, doomed men who had "come

to [their] end in this despicable land." "Our forces are without planes, warships, or tanks. Because we are abandoned we have no hope other than to die resisting."[69]

The bloody siege of Sugar Loaf destroyed any remaining illusions about war that the Marines might have still held. William Manchester of the 29th Marines wrote, "On Sugar Loaf, in short, I realized that something within me, long ailing, had expired. Although I would continue to do the job, performing as the hired gun, I now knew the banners and swords, ruffles and flourishes, bugles and drums, the whole rigmarole, eventually ended in squalor."[70]

The *New York Times* reported, "The battle for Sugar Loaf Hill probably will go down in history as the bloodiest local battle of the Okinawa campaign."[71]

AT 7:19 A.M. ON MAY 18, the destroyer *Longshaw*, which had been acting as a fire support ship off Okinawa's west coast, ran aground on Ose Reef, 2,500 yards from shore, near Naha Airfield. The previous night, *Longshaw* had fired five hundred star shells to light up the Hagushi beachhead. But in the morning haze, the officer of the deck misjudged the distance to the coral reef, and the destroyer ran aground on it.

Lieutenant Commander Clarence Becker, the skipper, attempted to dislodge her, but failed. Then, the destroyer *Picking* tried to tow *Longshaw* off the reef; the cable parted. A fleet tug, *Arikara*, tried her hand, but before her efforts produced any results, a Japanese shore battery began firing on *Longshaw*. As the destroyer fought back, shore battery rounds landed amidships, hit the bridge, and finally the forward powder magazine, causing a massive explosion that blew off the bow.

Lying mortally wounded on the bridge, Becker issued the order to abandon the burning ship, but refused medical treatment and would not leave. Of the nearly three-hundred-man crew, eighty-six men, including Becker, were killed, and ninety-seven were wounded.

Later that day, US warships destroyed *Longshaw* with gunfire and torpedoes.[72]

TWO DAYS AFTER SUGAR LOAF'S capture, the 4th Marines' 3rd Raider Battalion attacked Horseshoe Hill. Mortars and light artillery from Horseshoe had helped crush the Marine assaults on Sugar Loaf prior to its capture on May 18. On that day, the 29th Marines' Company F had tried

to seize Horseshoe, and had climbed to the hill's forward lip, where the Marines saw a column of reinforcements from Naha reach the reverse slope.

Lieutenant Colonel Hiraga of the 6th Special Regiment had sent the soldiers from Naha to help carry out a night attack. A Thirty-Second Army staff officer described some of the reinforcements: "They each carried a pistol in the right hand, a canteen in the left, and wore a bag around their waist containing toilet articles. They really looked strange."

The enemy counterattack that night, supported by a heavy barrage of white-phosphorus shells, forced Fox Company to pull back. The 4th Marines relieved the 29th the next day.[73]

NOW, ON MAY 20, THE 4th Marines were taking their crack at Horseshoe. Supported by the 22nd Marines on their right, the 3rd Battalion attacked the western end of Horseshoe, with tanks blasting the cave positions that honeycombed the hill's forward slopes. By 4 p.m., the battalion was entrenching in dominating positions on Horseshoe's western side and anticipated a strong counterattack that night.

It began around 10 p.m. when a battalion-size Japanese force—four hundred to five hundred men—roared down on the 3rd Raider Battalion's K and L Companies. Pre-registered American cannon fire from fifteen artillery battalions pounded the attackers, but they kept coming. Flares fired by US naval ships continuously cast an eerie light over the frenzied melee that lasted more than two hours.[74]

"It was utter pandemonium," said Robert Powers. "They were mixing with our troops. They were in our foxholes. . . ." The attackers killed two of Powers's comrades with grenades and bayonets before Powers shot them with his rifle.

The Japanese ran through Company K. "For awhile, it was like a Wild West shootout, people were running all over the place," said Private First Class Paolo DeMeis. A bullet that hit one Marine ignited his three phosphorus grenades; his body burned until morning.

By midnight, the attack was over. Before dawn, the 4th Marines' Company B reinforced the beleaguered hilltop force.[75]

With daylight, a scene of utter desolation greeted the Marines who still clung to Horseshoe Hill's commanding western end. Bodies and body parts were scattered everywhere in the mud, along with pieces of weapons, bandoliers, and live grenades. The Company K area was so soaked in blood

that "it smelled like a hamburger." The bodies of 494 enemy soldiers were counted that morning.[76]

Later in the day, after touring the front lines, General Simon Buckner wrote in his journal, "An air of optimism exists in the front line divisions who seem to feel a slight weakening in the Japs before them."[77]

HOPING TO SUCCEED WHERE THE 29th Marines had failed on May 16, the 4th Marines' 2nd Raider Battalion tackled Half Moon Hill on May 20. But just as before, heavy mortar and artillery fire from the Shuri Heights and mortar fire from Half Moon's reverse slopes inflicted high casualties when the Marines reached exposed ground. The battalion was able to hold the western side of the hill, but could not reach the crest. Attempts to advance down the hillcrest were blunted by devastating artillery and mortar fire from the Shuri Heights.[78]

The 6th Marine Division commander, General Shepherd, decided to sequester but not capture Half Moon. After five days' of futility—each attack on Half Moon having been driven back by smothering artillery fire from the Shuri Heights—Shepherd concluded that it could not be taken without great loss. He sent the Fourth Marines southwest from Sugar Loaf and Horseshoe to the Asato River and Naha to continue the envelopment of the Shuri Line's west flank.

The 22nd Marines' 3rd Battalion moved to the Half Moon area to hold an eastward-facing line between the 4th Marines and the 1st Marine Division, which was pushing eastward from Wana Ridge toward Shuri. The 1st Division sent a battalion to occupy the 6th Division's eastern sector and the Half Moon battleground.[79]

E. B. SLEDGE OF THE 5th Marines' Company K dug in on Half Moon with his mortar squad, appalled by the gruesome artifacts all around him from the 6th Marine Division's furious battle. "It was the most ghastly corner of hell I had ever witnessed," said the Peleliu veteran. "The place was choked with the putrefaction of death, decay, and destruction. . . . Every crater was half full of water, and many of them held a Marine corpse. The bodies lay pathetically just as they had been killed, half submerged in muck and water, rusting weapons still in hand." It was "a stinking compost pile" of decomposing corpses and pieces of bodies.

Water had pooled at Half Moon's base because of the heavy rains. "We referred to it as the sea of death, because there were dead Marines laying

down there in that water," said Sergeant Harry Bender, a Company K comrade of Sledge's. From his foxhole, Bender could see the bodies of thirty-five dead Americans and Japanese. The rain also uncovered Japanese corpses buried in shallow graves.[80]

When a Marine slipped and slid down a muddy hill, which happened all too often, "he was apt to reach the bottom vomiting," said Sledge, and then stand up "horror-stricken . . . as fat maggots tumbled out of his muddy dungaree pockets, cartridge belt, legging braces. We didn't talk about such things. They were too horrible and obscene even for hardened veterans."[81]

As casualties severely thinned out the cadre of veterans, replacements were sent to the front—4,300 of them to the 1st Marine Division by the end of May. Some were long-serving, senior NCOs plucked from office jobs and unaccustomed to living in the field. Charles Kundert, a nineteen-year-old sergeant with the 4th Marines' 3rd Raider Battalion, said some of the replacements were nearly forty years old; one had six children.

But others were "green kids"—many of them draftees—who had been to boot camp and a few weeks of infantry training before being shipped to the replacement depot on Saipan. The veterans tried to help them stay alive, but "most of the replacements would be dead the next day," said Kundert. "You'd put them in the foxhole, and by the next day they were dead."

Thrown into the violent maelstrom of combat, they were understandably confused and terrified. Veterans described them as "fouled up as Hogan's goat," or "out of phase"—meaning that they were standing when they should have been down, and down when they should have been up and moving. Veterans sometimes had to coerce them into taking risks, such as helping to evacuate casualties.

Some of them died before their comrades could even learn their first names. Newly minted lieutenants were often killed while walking on the skyline. Some of the veterans avoided the replacements because, said Marine Corporal George Peto, "I did not want the pain of making new friends and then losing them the next day."

Forward artillery observer Paul Brennan said six replacements who arrived near Sugar Loaf one day, boasting about how many Japanese they planned to kill, all perished hours later during a sudden artillery barrage.

The attrition rate was cruelly high for all of the combat troops. Private John Speheger of the 29th Marines said there were fifty-four men in his platoon on L-Day. By the end of the campaign, just Speheger and one other Marine remained of the original fifty-four. Even with the ebb and flow of replacements, Speheger's platoon still numbered just fifteen.

Before the Okinawa campaign ended, XXIV Corps's four Army divisions would receive 12,777 replacements, and the two Marine divisions in III Amphibious Corps, 11,147. Of course, the Japanese Thirty-Second Army, isolated by the massive US naval and air forces surrounding Okinawa, received none.[82]

IN A LATE-MAY BROADCAST, TOKYO ROSE acknowledged the intensity of the fighting all along the Shuri Line and, in a rare gesture, recognized the sacrifices made by the Americans:

> Sugar Loaf Hill . . . Chocolate Drop . . . Strawberry Hill. Gee, those places sound wonderful! You can just see the candy houses with white picket fences around them and the candy canes hanging from the trees, their red and white stripes glistening in the sun. But the only thing red about those places is the blood of Americans. Yes, sir, those are the names in hills in southern Okinawa where the fighting's so close that you get down to bayonets and sometimes your bare fists. . . . I guess it's natural to idealize the worst places with pretty names to make them seem less awful. Why Sugar Loaf has changed hands so often it looks like Dante's Inferno.[83]

Some of the Americans had also begun to respect their enemy. "It was amazing how tough and disciplined the Japanese were," wrote Corporal Hubert Welch of the 29th Marines. "They could exist on very little food, were trained to take the hardest punishment, and were taught not to surrender." A report on enemy tactics by the 96th Division's 383rd Infantry noted the care taken by the enemy in selecting defensive positions that could mutually support their flanks and rear, and were accessible through tunnels, hidden paths, and entrenchments. "When it became apparent to him that our forces were closing in to clear and reduce these caves he would unhesitatingly resort to hand-to-hand combat, resisting and fighting to the last man."[84]

GENERAL SHEPHERD HAD CONCLUDED THAT capturing Half Moon Hill's reverse slope would be too costly. Half Moon's continued occupation by the Japanese, however, prevented the 6th Division from carrying out its plan to push directly eastward from the Sugar Loaf complex to Shuri.

Instead, the division marched south to the Asato River, with the intention of continuing to the capital city, Naha, and to the Kokuba River

bordering Naha on the south. At the river, the 6th Division intended to turn eastward and march into the Kokuba hills with the object of completing the encirclement of Shuri and severing the Thirty-Second Army's path of retreat to the south.

As the 4th Marines pushed down Sugar Loaf's southern slope and toward the Asato River, the losses quickly mounted amid the sheeting enemy gunfire. Corporal Melvin Heckt, a Company B machine gunner, described the reduction of his squad in disbelief: "Donvito was the first to be hit. Shrapnel in the hip. Durham was next. He received a concussion and possible broken collar bone. I couldn't believe he was hit. I just couldn't believe it. . . . Next, Ward Bowers was killed by Nip artillery."

Later, Heckt wrote, "Cullen was passing by with a piece of shrapnel in his back. Andriola was helping him walk back when a Nambu opened up and wounded Andriola in [the] buttocks and Cullen in [the] leg. Hassel was close to them and ran out to drag them out of the fire lane [and] was hit in [the] nose, mouth and arm."

Mortar fire caught three others unaware. "Poor Red McGee was blown all over the side of the hill. Only his red hair and scalp remained where he had been sitting," said Heckt.[85]

THE GREATER PART OF NAHA was now rubble. On October 10, warplanes from the Fast Carrier Force had destroyed roughly 90 percent of the city of 65,000 with conventional and incendiary bombs, and turned Naha's harbor into a shipping graveyard. Subsequent bombardments during Operation Iceberg had worsened the devastation.

Not knowing what might be in store for them in Naha, during the night of May 22–23 6th Marine Division patrols waded across the Asato River to reconnoiter the southern bank. When they encountered little resistance, early in the afternoon of May 23, two battalions from the 22nd Marines forded the river under a smoke screen and entered the city. They kept west of a 20-yard-wide north-south canal that bisected Naha and connected the Asato and Kokuba Rivers.[86]

East of the city, the 4th Marines suffered heavy casualties after crossing the upper Asato on May 23. Lacking tank support because of the mud, the regiment pushed into a flooded, gunfire-swept valley overlooked by a range of low clay hills held by the Japanese. The 3rd Battalion seized a north-south ridge and fended off a nighttime counterattack as losses mounted. By May 25, the 4th Marines' Company E had been whittled to forty men and

one officer. The 29th Marines took over from the 4th Marines on May 28 and advanced farther south, nearly to the Kokuba River.[87]

The city appeared deserted. In Naha's urban core, the 6th Marine Reconnaissance Company probed into the silent neighborhoods west of the canal and north of the Kokuba River, finding only demolished buildings and rubble-clogged streets. The 22nd Marines passed through the reconnaissance company and reached the Kokuba River estuary on May 28 without firing a shot.

Lieutenant Colonel Viktor Krulak, the division's operations officer, assigned the 6th Reconnaissance Company the job of defending western Naha, to free the 22nd for action in the Kokuba hills east of the city. In his message to the 6th Reconnaissance's commander, Major Anthony Walker, Krulak wrote:

> Reposing great confidence in your integrity and political ability, you are hereby named acting mayor of Naha. The appointment . . . carries all pay and emoluments accruing to office. To be collected from Imperial Treasury.[88]

During the night of May 28–29, engineers built three footbridges over the canal in a torrential rainstorm. Before dawn, the 22nd Marines crossed the canal into the eastern part of the city. Its first objective was Telegraph Hill, which bristled with radio antennas—and which was tenaciously defended by Japanese who had withdrawn from Naha to prevent the envelopment of Shuri. Also strongly defended was Hill 27, where Japanese machine gunners hidden in burial tombs swept the approaches, until tanks were able to bring direct fire on the tombs.[89]

Pushing eastward to complete the envelopment of Shuri, the 22nd and 29th Marines launched an assault into the Kokuba hills and fought a sharp battle on May 30 in a driving rainstorm. The immediate objective was Hill 46, which was in a range of small hills covered by windrows of stone rubble from demolished homes that provided the Japanese with good firing positions from which to sweep the bare open ground before them. Hill 46 fell June 1 after more than two dozen tanks ground through the mud to pulverize the enemy positions.[90]

Upon reaching the outskirts of Shikina, a village directly south of Shuri Castle and north of the Kokuba River, the 6th Marine Division had completed its role in the Tenth Army's plan to flank and encircle Shuri Castle.

The stubborn defenders of Half Moon Hill had blocked Shepherd's division from marching 1 mile east to Shuri from the Sugar Loaf Hill complex. Instead, it had embarked on a circuitous route covering 5 miles and roughly tracing the letter *c*. The division had marched southwest into Naha; then, southeast to the Kokuba River; and, finally, eastward toward Shikina, with the 1st Marine Division protecting its left flank. In that general area, the Marines anticipated meeting the Army's 7th Division on the Naha-Yonabaru highway.

In battling the 6th Marine Division at Sugar Loaf, Half Moon, and Horseshoe Hills, and outside Naha, the Japanese Thirty-Second Army had used up its last trained reserves. "All the key pieces of our game plan were spent in the emergency," wrote Colonel Yahara.[91]

WHEN THE 96TH DIVISION RETURNED to the front on May 10 to relieve the 7th Division in the east, the 383rd Infantry's first objective was Conical Hill, the eastern anchor of the Shuri Line. On May 15, Company G braved murderous mortar fire to reach and dig in just below Conical Peak. The position provided an excellent vantage point overlooking enemy positions between Conical and Shuri.

The 96th's mission had been to clear a path down the eastern coast for the 7th Division when it reentered combat so that the 7th could push on to Yonabaru to the south. Having failed to completely neutralize Conical to achieve that object, the 96th did the next best thing: it committed troops to secure the zone between Conical and the Pacific Ocean.[92]

The 381st Infantry attacked Sugar and Cutaway Hills, situated on a hogback extending southeast from Conical. The 381st captured both hills on May 21 while killing more than four hundred enemy troops. That opened a path for the 7th Division to push south down Route 13 to Yonabaru.

In the rain and mud, the 7th began marching southward on May 22, with the 184th Infantry's 3rd Battalion running interference ahead of Colonel John "Mickey" Finn's 32nd Infantry. Upon reaching the ruins of Yonabaru, the 3rd Battalion captured Chestnut Hill and several smaller nearby hills to the south and southwest, shoring up the 32nd's left flank as it turned west into the Yonabaru-Naha valley behind Shuri.[93]

Colonel Finn's regiment intended to blast the reverse slopes of the hills north of the road with tanks and flame tanks while advancing to its rendezvous with the 6th Marine Division in the Shikina area. On the 24th, the 32nd Infantry's 3rd Battalion led the western drive under a cloudless sky. Its three companies captured a handful of hills and covered about 1,000

yards along a thousand-yard-wide front, while the 184th pushed southward and overcame fierce resistance to capture Locust Hill, a black coral escarpment that stood on a 230-feet-high cliff.

Heavy rains resumed May 25—and would continue virtually without letup until the beginning of June—and Finn's 32nd Infantry met a strong defensive line of antitank guns, mortars, and automatic weapons that barred the way down the Yonabaru-Naha valley.

A platoon from Finn's 3rd Battalion attacked Duck Hill, reached the crest, and briefly held it until being forced back to the forward slope by machine-gun and mortar fire. A vicious hand-grenade battle ensued, and the Company I platoon was hit by enemy fire from three directions. Casualties were heavy.

Company I medic William Goodman was treating wounded men when five Japanese soldiers attacked him. With a pistol, Goodman killed them all, and then guarded his patients until they were evacuated. Finn pulled Company I back under cover of a smoke screen, leaving behind his dead.

The heavy rains transformed the roads into swamps, tanks and heavy assault guns could not be brought up, and the offensive stalled. A newspaper correspondent reported that at one point it took sixteen hours to travel 3 miles because of the mud.

Tanks and self-propelled guns, mired in 3-feet-deep mud, had to be pulled out by tractors or bulldozers. Supplies were hand-carried to the front lines. Three and a half inches of rain fell on May 26 alone, when the 32nd Infantry tried once more to break through the Japanese defensive line—and was repulsed with heavy casualties.[94]

On May 26, 27, and 28, the mudbound regiment reported no gains as torrential rains continued to lash the island. "Regiment again unable to use tanks due to boggy ground," the 32nd's report said. Furthermore, its right flank was dependent on the progress of the 96th Division to the north. The 96th, like the 7th Division, was paralyzed by the rains and limited its operations to patrols and artillery fire. May 29 found the 32nd Infantry in the same positions, while hitting the enemy with artillery fire and bringing up three-pack howitzers and new recoilless weapons.[95]

On May 30, the 32nd's attempted double envelopment of Mabel Hill failed after it encountered concentrations of Japanese tanks and troops.[96]

The Hourglass Division's westward advance had bogged down; it could not bridge the gap to the Marines south of Shuri and close the pincers around Shuri.

General Archibald Arnold had carefully plotted the moves that his 7th Division would make after reaching Yonabaru and pushing west to complete the envelopment of Shuri. To his great frustration, "the weather let loose and nullified all our plans and hopes."

The nearly daily downpours during the last ten days of May prevented the 7th Division from using tanks, and without armor to support its infantrymen, it waited out the rains.

Thus, there remained a 2-mile-wide gap between the 6th and 7th Divisions south of Shuri Castle—a gap that General Ushijima's Thirty-Second Army could exploit to withdraw to either southern Okinawa or the Chinen Peninsula southeast of Yonabaru.

"Without the rain, we could have moved considerably faster and caused the Japs a lot of trouble," lamented General Arnold. "Even so, we kept moving, which is remarkable enough in that mud."[97]

BY MAY 27, AMERICANS ON the battle lines were observing that while Japanese troops continued to stubbornly defend the northern approaches to Shuri Castle and the perimeters of the 2-mile gap to its south, other Thirty-Second Army units had disappeared. Then, resistance simply melted away before the 7th Division's 184th Infantry south of Yonabaru, and from the 96th Division on Conical Hill.

The rain and mud that had thwarted the Tenth Army's pincer movement around Shuri Castle had also curtailed American aerial observation flights. In the intelligence vacuum, the Japanese had begun retreating unseen to the south, forsaking the Shuri Line and the blood-soaked battlefields of Sugar Loaf, Horseshoe, and Half Moon Hills.

The final battle for Okinawa would not be fought at Shuri Castle after all.[98]

The Japanese Retreat from Shuri

What the troops accomplished here is a marvel. No harder battle or tougher defense fortifications have ever faced American troops in our entire military history.

—GENERAL JOHN HODGE, XXIV CORPS COMMANDER,
AFTER THE CAPTURE OF THE SHURI LINE[1]

The trip from Kochiada to Kiyan leaves an impression words are inadequate to describe. . . . Utter horror . . . dead every-where—everywhere . . . It was literally hell.

—TOKUYU HIGASHIONNA, A TEACHER,
DESCRIBING THE BLOODBATH THAT SHE WITNESSED
DURING THE THIRTY-SECOND ARMY'S RETREAT FROM
THE SHURI LINE TO THE KIYAN PENINSULA[2]

ON MAY 20, WHEN THE 4th Marines seized Horseshoe Hill, two days after Sugar Loaf fell following a furious, seven-day battle, the senior staff of the Japanese Thirty-Second Army conceded that the Shuri Line would very soon become "untenable."

The somber men had gathered inside the Army's command post be-neath Shuri Castle, a warren of caves where distant American tank fire from the crumbling western lines could be heard. Water from the drench-ing plum rains dripped and coursed down the walls, pooling on the cave floors. The air was thick, humid, and warm.

"We now realized that we were doomed," wrote Colonel Hiromichi Yahara, the Thirty-Second Army's operations officer.

Yahara had privately sketched a plan for the Thirty-Second Army's withdrawal to the Kiyan Peninsula, but had not yet shared the proposal with General Mitsuru Ushijima, or Ushijima's chief of staff, General Isamu Chō. But he realized that the time to act was at hand. "The pressure exerted upon the line from both Sugar Loaf and Conical Hill forced a decision as to whether or not to stage the last ditch stand at Shuri," Yahara wrote.

Yahara was aware that many officers—and particularly the ebullient General Chō—chafed at his attritional defensive strategy, even though the army's counterattacks on April 12 and May 4 had failed miserably. Thus, he knew that he had to tread lightly. He designated a staff officer to present his plan and two other options. By so concealing his authorship, the colonel hoped to avoid the automatic disapproval that he believed would likely greet his presentation of a withdrawal plan.[3]

The Army division's chiefs of staff braved heavy rain and enemy shellfire on May 22 to attend a nighttime meeting at the headquarters cave to decide the next course of action. "Everyone looked worn out," wrote Yahara, who chaired the meeting. "Staring a dark fate in the face, they treated each other with kind dignity and kept up an air of calm."[4]

Three options were presented: (1) fight it out at Shuri; (2) withdraw to the Chinen Peninsula southeast of Yonabaru; or (3) withdraw due south to the Kiyan Peninsula on Okinawa's southern coast.

If they elected to fight it out at Shuri, there would be no need to move troops or ammunition, but the shrinking defensive area would be increasingly vulnerable to attack, and the underground fortifications could not hold all of the remaining troops and artillery units.

Most important, a final fight at Shuri would not buy enough time for Japan to ready its defenses—the Thirty-Second Army's overarching mission. "It was recognized that to stay would result in a quicker defeat and consequently it was discarded in accord with the Thirty-Second Army policy of protracting the struggle as long as possible," Yahara wrote.[5]

Retreating to the Chinen Peninsula, attractive though it was for defense because it was protected by water on three sides, was rejected because of the poor roads and rough terrain between it and Shuri.[6]

All-weather Routes 3 and 7 linked Shuri to the Kiyan Peninsula, 11 miles due south, where the 24th Division had already prepared underground fortifications and stockpiled supplies and ammunition. Kiyan's 100-foot-high escarpments would also slow advancing American assault troops.

After Yahara finished ticking off the pros and cons of each option, there was no consensus among the officers about which to adopt. "In the end, each command insisted on sticking to its own territory." That left the decision up to Yahara, Chō, and Ushijima, who decided that the Thirty-Second Army would withdraw to the Kiyan Peninsula and make its last stand there.[7]

THE JAPANESE ATTEMPTED TO CONCEAL the withdrawal by counter-attacking along the western and eastern flanks as the Army pulled back elsewhere. Yahara estimated that the Thirty-Second Army had 40,000 effectives, just 36 percent of the 110,000 soldiers who were combat-capable on April 1.[8]

The much-diminished 89th Infantry, reinforced by engineers and heavy artillery troops, attacked the 7th Division positions near Yonabaru during the night of May 23 to draw attention away from the withdrawal. The attack failed when untrained reinforcements ran headlong into US mortar fire. Attacks during the following two nights also ended disastrously.

The withdrawal began during the night of May 22, when the 24th Transportation Regiment, which had been trained in night-driving while deployed in China, began moving wounded men and supplies to the south. Student nurses who had attended to the wounded men in the hospital caves beneath Shuri—often without any anesthetics to ease their pain—accompanied them on the journey south.

Hundreds of severely wounded troops were left behind in the caves and were given grenades or cyanide with which to end their lives. However, many could be seen crawling down the road and using shovels as crutches. As a further distraction from the retreat, two mass kamikaze attacks were hurled at the US Fifth Fleet.[9]

Mother Nature aided the Thirty-Second Army's retreat; downpours and low clouds limited American aerial observation on May 24 and 25. And what the pilots saw—groups of people in white civilian clothes seemingly traveling in every direction—did not necessarily suggest a troop withdrawal.

It was not until May 26 that weather conditions permitted an extensive survey of southern Okinawa. A spotter plane from the battleship *New York* lifted off after General Pedro del Valle of the 1st Marine Division reported that enemy soldiers had been seen leaving Wana Draw.

The observation plane broke through the rain clouds and the excited pilot reported jammed roads south of Shuri: three thousand to four

thousand troops on the march with tanks, trucks, and guns. Within minutes, warships began shelling the roads, followed by rocket and strafing runs by 50 Marine Corsairs that killed hundreds of soldiers and civilians, and left columns of burning vehicles along the roads.

Later in the day, a Japanese regiment was seen marching north from Makabe, in the extreme southern part of the island. The report muddled what had been an emerging picture of a general retreat. It was unclear exactly what was happening, except that the Japanese were on the move.[10]

The next day, May 27, 6th Marine Division patrols saw more evidence of an enemy withdrawal, and General Simon Buckner ordered his Tenth Army to apply "unrelenting pressure" on the Japanese. "Enemy must not—repeat—must not be permitted to establish himself securely on new position with only nominal interference," Buckner said.[11]

Buckner's order had come days late, though. The withdrawal of thousands of Japanese combat troops was well under way, and Thirty-Second Army officers were clearing out of the caves beneath Shuri Castle. Japanese combat units left behind 20–30 percent of their men to continue to engage American forces before also withdrawing.[12]

ON MAY 30, GENERAL JAMES BRADLEY'S 96th Division, stymied for nine days on Conical Hill and at the bases of Hen and Hector Hills, launched a full-scale drive toward Shuri Castle. The muddy ground was beginning to dry, and Japanese resistance had noticeably fallen off.

Between May 15 and 20, the 382nd Infantry had fruitlessly struggled to capture Dick Hill, and this battleground, like Sugar Loaf and Half Moon to the west and Conical to the east, reeked of decaying bodies, excrement, and bloody battle dressings.

The 382nd's attack began with encouraging gains. Company I stole a march on the Japanese on May 15, scaled Dick's eastern slope, and reached the skyline before the enemy reacted. But react they did: after a brutal hand-to-hand fight, Company I was forced to withdraw.

Thereafter, each charge to the hillcrest precipitated a hailstorm of machine-gun fire from neighboring Oboe and Flattop Hills, forcing the 382nd to withdraw to its former position. Enemy mortars on Dick's southern slopes hammered the Americans during the nighttime, when Japanese patrols probed the Americans' positions, igniting teeth-rattling rifle and machine-gun battles.

Finally, tank-infantry teams were able to push through a heavily mined road cut between Flattop and Dick Hills. Bomb squads had fed seven tons

of Bangalore torpedoes into the cut and detonated the mines so that the tanks could proceed. A 47mm antitank gun destroyed the first tank that entered the cut, but after the enemy gun was knocked out, tanks poured through the cut, and conventional and flame tanks blasted the reverse slopes of the two hills.[13]

ON MAY 21, THE 382ND began cleaning out pockets on Dick Hill. Private First Class Donald Dencker went looking for souvenirs on Dick Hill and instead found Japanese bodies in various states of decay. One corpse had "maggots crawling in and out of what had been his eyes, nose, and mouth." He stepped on another body thinly covered with dirt, and the remains oozed onto his boot. "I kicked off most of the muck and nearly threw up," he wrote.[14]

The 382nd shifted gears and tackled 500-foot Oboe Hill, charging through gunfire and grenades to reach its crest. Oboe was the dominant hill east of Shuri, and adjoined Hector and Hen Hills.

The Japanese did not give up Oboe easily. They immediately counterattacked, driving the five companies belonging to the 1st and 3rd Battalions from the hilltop. However, they clawed their way back up and fought all night to repel ceaseless Japanese counterattacks.

Recognizing the hill's importance to preserving the Shuri Line, the Japanese repeatedly stormed Oboe over the next three days. During the night of May 24, the attackers exploited a gap between two of the defending companies and at one point drove them to the bottom of the hill. The Deadeyes used thirty-five cases of grenades that night, and still clung to Oboe when morning came. The 383rd Infantry's 3rd Battalion was sent to reinforce the 382nd when it began using antitank teams and auxiliaries as infantrymen replacements.[15]

AMONG THE ALPHABET SOUP OF hills that stood between the 96th and the eastern outskirts of Shuri was Love, which abutted Conical. When a platoon from the 383rd's Company C attacked Love on May 16, fifty machine guns from Love, Conical, and three other hills eviscerated it.

Five survivors of the slaughter, trapped behind the Japanese lines, hid in a cave and tomb for three days and nights. Sergeant Donald B. Williams helped a man wounded by a grenade descend the hill as bullets spattered around them and struck the wounded man twice more in his arms. "I had to hold him to keep him from rolling down the hill," said Williams. He half-carried the man to another cave.

Although Japanese troops were all around them, Williams managed to scavenge a half-full canteen from a dead American for his wounded companion. The next day, US artillery and air strikes pounded the hill, but American infantrymen did not attack. Williams retrieved another canteen from outside the cave, but some Japanese spotted him and fired a bazooka round into the cave. The explosion knocked out Williams and wounded his companion yet again. Williams regained consciousness in time to see two Japanese crawling into the cave; he shot one and the other fled.

The other survivors hid in a tomb that they shared with four Okinawans; one of them refilled their canteens with water. The soldiers escaped when they heard Japanese troops singing and having a party nearby one night.

Williams, however, remained with his mortally wounded comrade for another day and night. When it became apparent that the man was near death, Williams, weak from hunger, crawled out of the cave and headed for the American lines, arriving at daybreak.[16]

THE 96TH CONTINUED ADVANCING WESTWARD toward Shuri, rolling up the eastern Shuri Line. Conical, however, remained a thorny obstacle, with enemy gunfire from the reverse slopes thwarting attempts to capture it and complicating efforts to seize the nearby hills. Gunfire from Conical and its neighbors had stopped the division for nine days northeast of Shuri at the base of Hen and Hector Hills, and steadily sapped the manpower of the 382nd Infantry's 2nd and 3rd Battalions. "When officers were hit, sergeants took over. When sergeants were wounded or killed, the Pfcs took charge," said George Brooks, a Company K rifleman. "There weren't enough replacements for all the platoon officers who were killed or wounded."[17]

Downpours made the roads impassable for tanks and trucks for a week beginning May 22. Like the Marines on the western Shuri Line, soldiers, covered head to toe in mud, hand-carried supplies and ammunition to the front through knee-deep goop.

During the three weeks that Private First Class Richard Book fought on Conical, his uniform never dried, and the 96th Division received no fresh clothing. "You had a poncho which was just a big sheet with holes in the middle. Where we dug in, we'd put those ponchos over the foxhole. We stayed like that for weeks," said Book. His unit did not take prisoners, but was instructed to "shoot them first, then you ask them who they were."

Despite being under fire and enduring the extreme discomfort of the constant rain and mud, "we knew we were going to win the war," Book said, "[but] we didn't know if *we'd* still be alive."[18]

Conical remained the sticking point. During the frenzied, close-range struggle, the Japanese resorted to jamming long sticks into the ground to catapult grenades over the hillcrest. On May 27, a Japanese company blundered in the dark during a rainstorm into the 381st's lines on Conical. The next night, the 381st repulsed a full-scale attack.[19]

But on May 30, to the surprise and relief of the 381st Infantry's 3rd Battalion, soldiers discovered that they could move down Conical's western slopes, denied to them previously by the Japanese 24th Division. The Japanese had gone, leaving behind the bodies of up to one hundred of their comrades.

As the 381st began to push west from Conical, the 96th's 382nd Infantry assaulted Hen and Hector Hills, which the Thirty-Second Army had not yet abandoned. The 2nd Battalion met fierce resistance when it attempted to capture the hills.

On Hen Hill, a former truck driver and recent replacement, Private First Class Clarence Craft of Company G, threw three cases of grenades over the crest while attempting to flush Japanese troops from a 6-foot trench high on the hill's reverse slope. He then shot an enemy soldier who poked his head above the rim. When these actions failed to dislodge the entrenched Japanese, Craft stormed the crest.

Standing at the edge of the trench, Craft fired his M-1 point-blank at the Japanese and charged into the trench, killing more of them. Ten enemy solders assailed Craft with spears, and he shot them down, one by one. Handed grenades and a satchel charge by his comrades, who supported his assault with automatic-weapons fire, Craft wiped out a machine gun and hurled the satchel charge into a cave. When it failed to detonate, Craft retrieved it from the cave, rearmed it, and threw it again. The explosion sealed the cave.

Lieutenant Roy Burns watched in amazement. "That damned fool is determined to get out of the Army, either [by winning] the Medal of Honor, or by death," he said.

Inspired by Craft's example, the rest of Company G sprinted to the crest of Hen Hill. Of the seventy Japanese who died there, twenty-five to thirty were killed by Craft.[20]

DURING THE THREE-WEEK AMERICAN OFFENSIVE that began May 11, the 96th Division suffered 2,074 casualties. The fighting decimated some units: the 382nd's Company L suffered 121 battle casualties and was reduced to 54 effectives, some of whom had been wounded previously. The

enemy suffered more, though: the division claimed to have killed 8,500 Japanese.[21]

In a letter home, Donald Dencker, serving with a Company L mortar squad, said that for weeks he had been lugging his forty-five-pound mortar through mud and up cliffs, along with his pack and cartridge belt. "In three days I've fired 1,000 rounds," he wrote. "Tonight, I have to sleep on ammunition cans. My blanket is soaked. What a desolate area this is. We have more dead Japs laying around than I can count. . . . Such is war."[22]

As the Deadeyes methodically cleared their sector, in one cave soldiers discovered several women, four small girls, two small boys, and a Japanese soldier, who quickly surrendered.

Given pencil and paper, one of the boys scrawled something on it, and a battalion interpreter translated it. "Have mercy on us," the message said.[23]

IN THE CENTER OF THE Tenth Army line, the 77th Division's southward drive toward Shuri was slowed to a snail's pace by a torrent of gunfire from the Shuri area and three hills: Flattop, Chocolate Drop, and Ishimmi, whose defenders were determined to fight to the death. "The enemy's stand is becoming more and more fanatical as we move forward into the main Shuri defenses," said the 77th Division operations report of May 21. Enemy mortars and machine gunners in caves, pillboxes, burial vaults, and hillside trenches bled the assault battalions during an all-day battle for Flattop's crest. When forced to withdraw at the end of the day, only thirty-four effectives remained in the 305th's Company I, and fourteen in the 306th's Company K.

When tank-infantry teams cleared the cut between Flattop and Dick Hills, the 307th's 3rd Battalion once more stormed Flattop, hoping for success after several failures. A chain of men snaking up the hill shuttled grenades to the men near the top, who threw them as quickly as the pins could be pulled. The tactic cleared the hilltop. The troops stormed Flattop's crest and continued down the reverse slope, blasting caves with flamethrowers and satchel charges. The Americans reported killing 501 Japanese who "resisted to the death."

Chocolate Drop defied capture for nine days. On the morning of May 16, when the 307th Infantry reported that the hill was "swarming with Japs," the regiment killed thirty-two enemy soldiers, and captured eight knee mortars and a prisoner who said the 32nd Infantry's 2nd Battalion had been wiped out. On May 17, Company G of the 307th reached the

summit but was forced to withdraw by "bitter hand to hand fighting" and "withering machine gun and rifle fire" from concealed positions on nearby hills. That night, the regiment surrounded Chocolate Drop and began sealing caves.

Lieutenant Bill Siegel of the 706th Tank Battalion said Chocolate Drop was his battalion's "worst experience" because of the mines that disabled many tanks. "Our vehicle casualties were very high." But the 77th Division managed to secure the hillcrest on May 20 after repulsing a counterattack by Captain Koichi Ito's battalion of the 32nd Infantry. The Americans annihilated the undersize unit; only Ito and twenty men survived.[24]

Based on identified enemy units, XXIV Corps estimated that 41,800 Japanese troops on Okinawa remained combat-capable; 32,954 had been killed. About 4,000 of the enemy survivors belonged to seven battalions—some at just 25 percent of full strength—that continued to face the 77th Division. The division had already destroyed five other battalions. In abetting the destruction of the Japanese defenders, the division's 302nd Engineer Combat Battalion had detonated, on average, 3,500 pounds of explosives per day, eliminating 925 enemy positions in three weeks.[25]

AT 3 A.M. ON MAY 17, the 307th's Company E silently approached Ishimmi Ridge under the eerie light of warship flare shells. After joining units of F and C Companies, the soldiers closed in on the ridge, 800 yards distant, reached the narrow ridgetop, and at 5:05 a.m. dug in there. Twenty-five minutes later, intensive mortar fire began falling, machine-gun and rifle fire swept the plateau from all directions, and Japanese artillery rounds from higher ground across the valley began landing among the attackers.

Then, enemy troops poured from caves and hit the Americans with knee mortars. Machine gunners and riflemen on a high ridge opposite Immini raked Company E. "Riflemen were blown to bits by these mortars and many were struck in the head by machine-gun fire," wrote Lieutenant Robert F. Meiser, a platoon leader. "The blood from wounded was everywhere; in the weapons, on the living, and splattered all around." American self-propelled guns, mortars, and heavy machine guns replied and broke up Japanese attacks before they began.[26]

With the approach of nightfall, the survivors withdrew to a perimeter around the company command post. All their water was gone; there were no rations left. Other units from the 307th's 2nd Battalion attempted to resupply the men atop Ishimmi, but were driven back by heavy machine gun

fire. All the while, artillery and mortar fire plastered Company E, keeping it
pinned to the ground. Ordered to hold "at all costs," the company prepared
for "a last ditch death stand."[27]

The next day, May 18, all of the medical supplies had been exhausted,
and the "moans and cries" of the wounded were now ceaseless. So were
the explosions of knee-mortar grenades from eight enemy launchers, fired
in pairs. The relentless mortar and artillery fire continued all day. "The
wounded were crazed for lack of medical care and water," wrote squad
leader Henry Lopez.

At 10 p.m. on May 18, litter-bearing teams suddenly appeared to carry
off the wounded. Eighteen badly wounded men were taken off the hill, and
several walking wounded hobbled away with them.[28]

Dawn of the third day, May 19, "found us hanging on only by our fin-
gernails, but there we were and more determined than ever to stay," wrote
Lieutenant Meiser. Throughout the day, the small band fought off Japanese
attacks with the aid of supporting arms. At 10 p.m., the 306th's Company L
began arriving to relieve the beleaguered troops. What remained of Company E—just 31 of the 129 infantrymen who had ascended Ishimmi early
May 17—returned to their former line of departure at 1 a.m. on May 20,
and slept for the first time in seventy hours. Of the 204 men who fought on
Ishimmi from May 17 through May 20, 156 were killed or wounded.[29]

On May 20, amid torrential rainfall, Company L showered Ishimmi's
southern and eastern slopes with grenades, using up boxes of them handed
up the ridge's north slope as quickly as they could pull the pins. They then
stormed the Japanese reverse slope positions with flamethrowers and
satchel charges. Ishimmi joined the growing list of formerly Japanese-held
ridges that were now in American hands.[30]

LUCK RAN OUT FOR PRIVATE First Class Desmond Doss, the indomita-
ble medic of the 307th's Company B who had single-handedly evacuated
more than fifty wounded men from a cliff on Hacksaw Ridge on May 5. On
that day, the devout Seventh Day Adventist had accomplished his singular
feat without being wounded himself. But on May 21, while under fire and
crawling to the aid of wounded men behind Flattop, shrapnel from a mortar sliced into both of Doss's legs. He treated his own wounds while waiting
for litter-bearers to reach him. It was a five-hour wait.

As they carried him to the aid station, Doss's stretcher-bearers came
under fire and took cover, leaving him on the ground on his stretcher. Doss
spied a seriously injured man nearby, rolled off the stretcher, crawled to the

man's side, and treated his wounds. As he waited for the litter-bearers to return, Doss was hit again, suffering a compound fracture to his arm. He splinted the arm with a rifle stock and crawled the last 300 yards to the aid station. The war was over for the doughty conscientious objector.[31]

THE 1ST MARINE DIVISION HAD attempted to eject the Japanese from Wana Draw and Wana Ridge with tank-infantry teams, flame tanks, mortars, bazookas, naval gunfire, and close-air support—and nothing had worked. On May 23, pioneers pumped napalm over the crest of Wana Ridge, and the 1st Marines ignited it with white-phosphorus grenades.

A torrent of enemy fire prevented the Marines from exploiting the potential weakness in the Japanese defenses. Then, four days of heavy rain had forestalled any movement in the battle lines.

On May 28, the rain relented, and the 1st Marines' 2nd Battalion attacked 110 Meter Hill. The objective marked the eastern edge of Wana Ridge and overlooked the northwestern outskirts of Shuri and part of the 77th Division zone. For these reasons, it was zealously defended. The assault troops reached the top of the hill, before heavy enemy fire drove them from it.

The 5th Marines' 1st Battalion, however, advanced 500 yards south and east of the Wanas without encountering opposition, and then with surprising ease seized part of Shuri Ridge, which had until then withstood days of artillery and naval gunfire, and air strikes. The high ground was just 800 yards west of what was left of Shuri Castle, which scouts said was lightly defended and would be the next day's objective.[32]

AND SO, ON MAY 29, the 5th Marines' 1st Battalion was poised to assault Shuri Castle—the coveted prize of the Tenth Army's two-month campaign. The four-century-old Ryukyu capital lay in the 77th Division sector, and before the battalion could cross into the sister division's zone, General Pedro del Valle had to give his approval. The 77th was grinding through the strong Japanese defenses north of Shuri, and del Valle reasoned that the division would not be able to reach the castle for at least two more days. The general green-lighted the 5th Marines' attack on the castle.[33]

The 77th Division was notified minutes before the Marines trespassed into its sector, and hastily called off scheduled air strikes and an artillery bombardment that would have struck Marines.

Led by Company A, the 5th Marines' 1st Battalion reached Shuri Castle at 10:15 a.m. and surprised the small garrison.

The company commander, Captain Julian Dusenbury, wanted to mark the signal achievement with a flag-raising. He did not have an American flag, but the Florence, South Carolina, native, had a Confederate battle flag in his pack. And so the "Southern Cross" was unfurled over the ruined castle. "All of us Southerners cheered loudly" upon learning about the flag-raising, wrote E. B. Sledge of the 5th Marines' Company K. An Alabama native, Sledge added, "The Yankees among us grumbled, and the Westerners didn't know what to do."[34]

Dusenbury's flag was replaced two days later by an American flag that the 1st Marine Division had flown at Cape Gloucester and Peleliu.[35]

General del Valle ordered two battalions of the 1st Marines to bypass Wana Draw, still held by the Japanese, and reinforce the Marines at Shuri Castle. The Marines formed a pocket inside the Japanese rearguard perimeter located on the castle's north side, creating the anomalous situation of enemy troops guarding the cave entrances beneath the castle while the Marines held nearby defensive positions. Muddy roads prevented supply trucks from reaching the Americans on Shuri, and food and ammunition had to be air-dropped or hand-carried by replacements.

Shuri Castle and its town, the Ryukyu Islands' capital that Commodore Matthew Perry had visited in 1853, was now a rubble-strewn ruin after two months of artillery and naval shelling and air strikes. Historian Roy Appleman estimated 200,000 rounds of artillery and naval shells; thousands of mortar rounds; and countless 1,000-pound bombs had pulverized the castle and town. The roofless walls of a church and school building remained upright, but nothing else. From the debris, the Americans exhumed two large, dented bells that had been cast in the sixteenth century. Little else was salvageable.[36]

SPEARHEADED BY STRONG COMBAT PATROLS, the 77th Division continued to inch southward toward Shuri. On May 29, in the hills before Shuri, twenty-five soldiers fought a brutal close-quarters battle with thirty Japanese near a cave complex. One US soldier entered a cave and with his rifle killed four enemy soldiers before being seriously wounded. When his rifle jammed, he used his helmet as a weapon to engage a saber-wielding Japanese officer until a comrade came to his aid and killed his antagonist. On the same day, a landslide killed three men and injured three others in the 77th Division zone.[37]

On May 30, the 77th advanced to Shuri's northeastern outskirts, where enemy resistance was described as "fanatical." After wiping out defenders

on the forward slopes and on the hilltop, the Americans pushed down the reverse slopes against heavy machine-gun and mortar fire.

With this effort, the 77th at last broke through the Japanese lines north of the castle. The 77th reported killing at least 53 Japanese and said that another 440 enemy soldiers were found dead in twenty-two caves. The division extended its lines southeast of Shuri and entered the stronghold on May 31.[38]

The 6th Marine Division, which had reached the Yonabaru-Naha road, still faced sporadic opposition from enemy units to its east. On May 30, Company C of the 29th Marines unknowingly entered a mined area and the Japanese electrically detonated a ton of explosives, wounding 25 Marines. Resistance in the Shuri area might have been ebbing, but deadly peril remained everywhere.[39]

AT A STAFF MEETING ON the 28th, General Buckner's intelligence officers had reported that, despite mounting evidence of an enemy withdrawal, it appeared the Japanese remained determined to defend Shuri Castle. Buckner expressed concern about a possible enemy counterattack on the 7th Division in the east. But after receiving new information the next day, the general concluded that the Japanese were indeed withdrawing to the south. Buckner insisted that Ushijima had waited too long to withdraw from Shuri. "It's all over but cleaning up pockets of resistance," Buckner told reporters. He was certain that Ushijima could not organize another defensive line.

But the general badly underestimated the Japanese. Colonel Yahara later said, "We were smarter than the enemy thought."[40]

AS WAS THE CASE ON Guadalcanal two years earlier, the Japanese withdrawal had caught the Americans off guard. In January 1943, Americans mistook an increase in nighttime landings on Guadalcanal of supplies and reinforcements for a prelude to a new Japanese offensive. It proved to be the very opposite. From mid-January to February 7, 1943, eleven thousand survivors of General Harukichi Hyakutake's 17th Army withdrew to Cape Esperance on the island's northwest tip. Destroyers ferried the men over three nights from Guadalcanal to the Shortland Islands.

In May 1945, there were no Japanese ships waiting off Okinawa to evacuate the Thirty-Second Army. But prepared fighting positions awaited General Ushijima's men on the Kiyan Peninsula, where they intended to further delay the American victory whose inevitability was apparent to even the lowliest Japanese private.

The Tenth Army command was slow to recognize that the Japanese had withdrawn from Shuri, but the American combat troops were aware of what had happened—and they were furious. "We all knew the Japs had outsmarted us again," said Sergeant Jack Armstrong of the 1st Marine Tank Battalion. "We were mad as hell that they'd been allowed to slip away . . . we were at the point where we really thought this thing was never going to end."[41]

Colonel Cecil Nist, XXIV Corps's intelligence officer, openly praised the Japanese achievement in his weekly summary. "Although the forces of General Ushijima are destined to defeat, his conduct of the defense of Okinawa has been such that his spirit can join those of his ancestors and rest in peace."[42]

TOO LATE, THE 7TH DIVISION'S 32nd Infantry captured Mabel Hill on May 31—after the departure of nearly all of its Japanese defenders, who had prevented the Thirty-Second from closing the 2-mile gap south of Shuri. As they climbed the hill, the Americans counted two hundred dead Japanese soldiers, killed by artillery and mortar fire over the previous six days. On the same day, the 32nd's Company I seized Duck Hill, formerly another fiercely defended strongpoint, with minimal casualties, and sealed caves with fifty to seventy-five enemy soldiers inside.[43]

Not every sealed cave remained so. At Dick Hill in the 96th Division zone, a surrendering enemy soldier said he had been sealed in a cave for five days, but had dug himself out. The thirty other soldiers in the cave did not survive, the prisoner said.[44]

At the end of May 31, forty-three days after the Tenth Army began its advance on Shuri Castle, it occupied the Shuri Line and the hills overlooking the Naha-Yonabaru road.

"What the troops accomplished here is a marvel," wrote General John Hodge, XXIV Corps's commander. "No harder battle or tougher defense fortifications have ever faced American troops in our entire military history."

Satisfying though that might have been, the battle for Okinawa was not yet over.[45]

THE BATTLE IN THE SKIES continued, although there was a two-week interval in mid-May between mass kamikaze attacks. Between April 6 and May 11, a *kikusui* targeted the US fleet at Okinawa every week without fail. But after Kikusui No. 6 on May 10–11, the Japanese 5th Air Fleet and 6th

Air Army were reeling from their staggering losses of planes and pilots—several hundred of each—and replacements from central and northern Japan were slow to arrive at the Kyushu air bases.

It also became more difficult to recruit kamikaze pilots. Many of the new pilots were not volunteers, but had been volunteered, and an increasing number was scarcely flight-qualified. Yet suicide attacks by pilots acting alone and in small groups continued almost daily.[46]

Two days after Kikusui No. 6, a Val dive-bomber crashed the destroyer *Bache* amidships while she was patrolling Radar Picket Station No. 9. Fires broke out, but crewmen brought them under control. Forty-one men died. Harry Gunther, *Bache*'s deck officer, said, "The amidships was a mess, with bodies and wreckage everywhere. I think we found the jawbones of the Val pilot. He had gold fillings in his teeth."[47]

Combat air patrol pilots went up every day to challenge the Japanese intruders between Kyushu and Okinawa. Captain Albert Wells of VMF-323, operating from Kadena Airfield, flew both combat air patrol and close-air support missions for Okinawa ground troops. There were frequent dogfights.

One day, Wells and his wingman climbed through overcast, breaking out into sunshine to see twenty-eight Zeros flying in formation 1,000 feet above them. In that situation, Wells said, "you just picked an airplane and just go after one airplane at a time instead of taking potshots at a whole bunch of different airplanes."

Wells shot down one Zero and found another adversary—one that proved to be adept at radical maneuvers that included rolls, a loop, and at one point approaching "nose to nose."

"He went so darn close over my head that I could see . . . the brass cartridges pouring out of the wing as he was shooting." The Japanese pilot performed the same maneuver at least six times. "He would always end up where he'd be coming down vertically on his back and I'd be going up almost vertically, not inverted, and we'd pass, real close."

At last, when they were roaring head-on toward each other, Wells kept firing until the last moment, when he "pushed the nose down as hard as I could so we didn't collide." As the Zero flew over him, Wells saw that "the cockpit . . . was full of flames. I rolled over and watched him go down" into the water, with a feeling of sadness. "I was sorry I didn't get to know the guy because he was good."[48]

Lieutenant Robert Klingman and his wingman were flying a combat air patrol mission over Ie Shima when they were informed that a twin-engine

Nick two-seater fighter was in the vicinity, flying at 25,000 feet. Klingman and Captain Kenneth Reusser fired off most of their ammunition to reduce their planes' weight so that they could climb higher. At 38,000 feet, Klingman got on the Nick's tail—and his guns froze, while the Nick's rear gunner riddled Klingman's Corsair. Reusser had exhausted most of his ammo shooting up the Nick's wing and left engine, so Klingman decided to take down the enemy plane with his propeller.

He bore into the Nick's tail, sawing into the cockpit of the rear gunner, whose guns had also frozen. In three passes, Klingman severed the rudder and stabilizer, and he then watched the Nick spin out and crash.

Although part of his propeller was gone, Klingman managed to return to Kadena Airfield, where he made a dead-stick landing.[49]

SINCE EARLY APRIL, THE 2ND Marine Aircraft Wing, better known as the Tactical Air Force, had carried out an array of missions from Yontan and Kadena Airfields. Besides flying combat air patrols to protect ships offshore, conducting sweeps to intercept air attacks from Japan, and providing close-air support of infantry operations on Okinawa, the TAF carried out bombing-strafing missions at the Japanese air bases on Kyushu. This was a new mission for fighter planes, and it marked the advent of the fighter-bomber age.

A night-fighter squadron later joined the hundred or so planes at the two Okinawa airfields. Army P-47 Thunderbolts began flying missions from Ie Shima in coordination with the TAF.[50]

The TAF had become fully operational on April 10. Led by General Francis Mulcahy, and later by General Louis Woods, it took over some close-air support duties, but not the majority of them, from carrier-based planes. Ironically, the land-based TAF pilots devoted most of their flying time to combat air patrols, while carrier-based pilots were responsible for most of the ground-support missions on Okinawa.

On Luzon, Air Liaison parties—forward observers on the battlefield—had begun communicating directly with close-air support pilots from Marine Air Group 24. The innovation saw limited use on Okinawa, because close-air support was just one of the combined arms weapons, along with artillery and naval gunfire.

Instead, the Landing Force Air Support Control Unit on Okinawa operated as an air traffic control center, linking infantry commanders and pilots, while coordinating large air strikes with artillery and naval gunfire.

This was a major improvement over the situation two years earlier on Guadalcanal, where close-air support tended to be ad hoc and informal, and thus tangential to ground operations. While close-air support had evolved considerably since then, it remained frustrating for ground commanders, with the chief problem being the delay between an air-strike request and its execution. Too often, the situation on the ground changed before the mission was carried out, or the mission was scratched.[51]

A 7th Marines after-action report bluntly stated, "Unit commanders lost faith in close air support as the operation progressed. There was too much 'red tape' in obtaining and clearing air missions." Scheduled missions were often canceled at the last minute or delayed indefinitely, placing the ground troops counting on air support at "a tactical disadvantage," the report said.

Other times, it said, inexperienced pilots requested large amounts of smoke to mark the front lines or their targets, and then "not infrequently [made] their strike in the wrong place, sometimes on our own troops." During the Okinawa campaign, 14,244 tactical sorties were carried out, more than during any other Central Pacific campaign. They included ten "bad drops" that were blamed for sixteen deaths and the wounding of fifty others.

In a freakish incident in May, US artillery apparently destroyed a Corsair providing close support near Shuri Castle. First Lieutenant Ed Murray was preparing to drop a 500-pound bomb when his plane "just disintegrated into powder," said Lieutenant Henry Brandon, who was flying about 1,000 yards behind Murray.

Enemy antiaircraft fire was initially blamed, but facts later emerged showing that an American 155mm gun crew in the area had just chambered a round when it was ordered to cease fire. Instead, the crew fired the chambered round. The gunners later reported seeing a bright flash— probably the round hitting the 500-pound bomb on Murray's plane.[52]

KIKUSUI NO. 7, WITH 165 Special Attack planes and 85 fighter escorts, scheduled for May 25, was to follow a commando raid on Yontan and Kadena Airfields to neutralize the squadrons based there. The Japanese believed the attacks would divert American attention from the Japanese retreat from the Shuri Line, and also deal a body blow to the Tactical Air Force.

In December on Leyte, Japanese paratroopers had conducted a similar attack against three US airstrips, blowing up planes and gasoline dumps.

However, enemy infantry who were supposed to march to the paratroopers' aid were unable to reach them, and the Americans regrouped and repulsed the attackers.[53]

Many nights, Japanese pilots strafed and bombed the airfields, or flew nuisance missions. The Marine pilots nicknamed the harassers "Washing Machine Charlie" and "Louis the Louse," the same names given to similar intruders on Guadalcanal in 1942. Their object was to disrupt the pilots' sleep, and at that they succeeded.

"We would have to run for our wet foxholes," when one of them flew over the airfield, wrote Lieutenant John Ruhsam. "There is hardly ever a morning that some snooper wouldn't wake us up." Returning to sleep after a flyover was difficult, he said. The harassing attacks prompted Marines to erect a sign at Yontan that read "WELCOME TO YONTAN—EVERY NIGHT A 4TH OF JULY."

Early in the campaign, enemy artillery hidden in caves shelled the airfields at night, until they were located and ferreted out.

But now, in late May, the Japanese intended to destroy the TAF planes and weaken American air power before the next mass kamikaze attack on the US task force east of Okinawa.[54]

On the clear, moonlit night of May 24, seven waves of Japanese bombers lifted off from Kumamoto Airfield on Kyushu on a mission to destroy the airstrips on Okinawa and Ie Shima. Four of the groups dropped bombs on Yontan and Kadena.

The seventh group, consisting of five low-flying "Sally" bombers, carried commandos. It arrived over Okinawa around 10:30 p.m. Antiaircraft batteries shot down four of them in flames near Yontan, but the fifth bomber penetrated the flak and made a wheels-up landing on one of Yontan's runways.

Nine commandos leaped from the plane and began hurling grenades and incendiaries at parked aircraft. "I couldn't believe what I was seeing," said Jack Kelly, a crewman with the 542nd Night Fighter Squadron. "Out came the Nips, loaded with incendiary devices, grenades and rifles." Kelly and his mates in their air-raid shelter were unarmed; their weapons were in their tent area. "All we had were screwdrivers and other assorted tools," he said.

Amid the confusion and gunfire on the airfield, the shock troops destroyed two Corsairs, four C-54 transports, and a seventh plane, and burned up to 70,000 gallons of aviation fuel. Twenty-six other planes were

damaged. The raiders killed two Americans and wounded eighteen others before service troops and reinforcements organized "search and kill" teams. The gun battle at the airstrip disrupted operations at Yontan for the rest of the night; planes returning from missions were redirected to Kadena Airfield.

At daylight on May 25, another commando emerged from the wreckage of the bomber that had crash-landed on the runway. He threw a grenade into a crowd of Marines, who riddled him with bullets while he held another grenade to his belly and blew himself 5 feet into the air. Three other dead crewmen, evidently killed by antiaircraft fire, were found inside the crashed plane.[55]

In all, the bodies of sixty-nine Japanese crewmen and shock troops were recovered from Yontan Airfield and from four nearby bomber crash sites.[56]

THE JAPANESE HAD HOPED TO meet weakened combat air patrols on May 25 as a result of the commando attack, but they instead encountered a sky full of American warplanes. Nonetheless, the Kikusui No. 7 Special Attack force, which included a large number of trainers because fighters were becoming scarcer, crashed a dozen ships. A Zero struck the radar picket destroyer *Stormes* after approaching from the stern, flying a parallel course, and then executing a wing-over. Its bomb exploded belowdecks. Twenty-one sailors were killed.

TAF Corsairs and Thunderbolts from Ie Shima shot down seventy-five enemy planes, the highest total claimed by TAF fighters in a single day of the Okinawa campaign. One of the downed planes was a former Luftwaffe plane with black swastikas painted on its wings. Carrier planes destroyed another 90 to 100 Japanese planes, raising enemy aircraft losses from Kikusui No. 7 to around 170.[57]

On May 26, the accumulated losses from the seven *kikusuis* prompted Japanese Imperial Headquarters to remove the 6th Air Army from the Combined Fleet's command and to assign it to homeland defense. The 5th Air Fleet was now solely responsible for attacking American ships around Okinawa.[58]

That same day, a kamikaze crashed the destroyer escort *O'Neill* while it was on anti-submarine picket duty, killing two crewmen and injuring seventeen others. Electrician's Mate 1/c Philip Farrand said the suicide pilot had sacks of rice in his plane, evidently to feed his soul after his death. "We had rice all over the ship," Farrand said. "It was scattered everywhere."[59]

Jack Govanus, a seaman on the destroyer *Anthony*, watched in horror at 7:45 a.m. May 27 as two Val Navy dive-bombers crashed the destroyer *Braine*. *Anthony* and *Braine* were patrolling Radar Picket Station No. 5, about 25 miles east of Okinawa, with four gunboats. One of the Vals struck *Braine* head-on, and the other crashed her amidship, plowing into the sick bay; its bomb exploded over the No. 3 boiler. The attacks ignited raging fires that made a shambles of the destroyer.

"The *Braine* had no bridge—no control—and it was circling to port with its engines running at standard speed," said Govanus. "Men were jumping off into the water on both sides of the ship, some with their clothes burning."

A third suicide plane splashed 50 feet away from *Anthony* and exploded, creating a towering geyser that carried the pilot's corpse, clad in a black funeral robe decorated with colorful dolls, onto *Anthony*'s deck with assorted engine parts from his plane.

Anthony caught up with *Braine* when she finally stopped circling, and her crew lashed the ships together for the trip to Kerama Retto for repairs. Crewmen boarded *Braine* to aid fire-control efforts and to carry wounded men to the *Anthony*, whose doctor had converted the wardroom into an operating theater. "The injuries are beyond belief," said Joe McNamara, an *Anthony* machinist who saw men with "eyes burned; both legs, both arms broken—all clothes burned off."[60]

Sharks swarmed some of the *Braine* survivors who had gone into the water, while crewmen on nearby gunboats opened fire on the predators with machine guns and rifles.

"We recovered one who had not made it, hanging pale and lifeless in his Mae West, a leg torn away, the other arm gone, gutted by the sharks," said John Rooney, a radioman on one of the gunboats. "We machine-gunned the sharks. In their mindless savagery they started tearing each other apart, this time turning the ocean crimson with their own blood."

"I looked back and saw a shark hit someone in the water and throw him into the air," said Walter Gaddis, a gunboat machinist's mate.[61]

Braine survived the disaster, but sixty-six of her crewmen did not, and seventy-eight others were listed as wounded.

KIKUSUI NO. 8 BEGAN ON May 27, when the Japanese sent 110 suicide planes and scores of escort fighters against the American fleet. They sank one ship and damaged six others—at a cost of 114 kamikaze and escort planes.[62]

Early on May 28, as Kikusui No. 8 began its second day, a pair of twin-engine "Frances" Navy bombers sank the destroyer *Drexler* at Radar Picket Station No. 15 in less than a minute, killing 158 crewmen and wounding 51 others.[63]

Six suicide planes had launched a coordinated attack on the radar picket station, patrolled by *Drexler*, the destroyer *Lowry*, LCS(L)-55, and LCS(L)-56. The combat air patrol shot down a Nick fighter as a Frances approached from starboard, appearing to take aim on *Lowry*, but passing over her and instead striking *Drexler*. The Japanese dive-bomber crashed *Drexler* between the main deck and waterline on the starboard beam, cutting steam lines and tearing a 40mm quad from its mount. *Drexler* lost power.

The crew quickly controlled the fires that broke out, and *Drexler* gunners, firing manually, splashed a second Frances that was diving on *Lowry*. At 7 a.m., a third Frances attacked *Drexler*. It missed on its first pass. Smoking and flying low, it circled, and approached *Drexler*'s bow. The Frances banked and crashed her port side, where its two bombs exploded. "There was a tremendous explosion which rocked the ship violently from stem to stern; parts of the ship were blown several hundred feet in the air," *Drexler*'s after-action report said.

Harold Tatsch, an ammunition handler, had returned to the ammunition room when the second plane crashed *Drexler*. "I'd just closed the latch and boy it flew open and there was steel and fire and everything where we were standing" moments earlier.

The explosion blew out the sides of the ship and ignited an oil fire that sent flames shooting several hundred feet into the air. Tatsch said men were going into the water as the ship turned onto her starboard side. He scrambled to the port side and jumped into the sea. Within seconds, *Drexler* rolled over entirely to starboard, her bow lifted high into the air, and she disappeared beneath the waves—in just forty-nine seconds.

It happened so quickly that scores of men were trapped belowdecks when *Drexler* sank, accounting for the high death toll.[64]

Drexler's skipper, Commander R. L. Wilson, praised the enemy pilots' skill and determination. "The pilots were not amateurs or hurriedly graduated students; they were good pilots and knew how to handle their planes," he wrote.[65]

James Vernon, a Hellcat pilot from the *Ticonderoga*, was on combat air patrol on May 28 over the radar pickets when rain and fog forced his group to land at Yontan instead of returning to their carrier. At Yontan,

the rumble of artillery to the south caused Vernon to compare his way of fighting the war to that of the ground troops.

"Ours was a clean, gentlemanly, impersonal mode of fighting, while living in comfortable quarters being well cared for and well fed. When we were on a mission, we either returned and continued as before, or we were dead."[66]

ALTHOUGH KIKUSUIS NO. 7 AND 8 and the daring attack on Yontan Airfield had not distracted the attention of the Tenth Army from the Japanese retreat from Shuri, torrential rains had shielded it from American eyes. When the Thirty-Second Army staff left Shuri, part of it moved several miles south to a temporary command post built at Tsukazan in 1944 by conscripted Okinawans using shovels and pickaxes. Colonel Yahara praised several girls who were busy repairing a water leak when the commanders arrived. "We'll do our best until the end," one girl replied.

Another command group went on to Mabuni in the Kiyan Peninsula, on Okinawa's southern tip; a cliffside cave there would become the final headquarters for Ushijima and his staff. After a two-day stay at Tsukazan, on May 29 Ushijima, Chō, Yahara, and their staff officers pushed on toward Mabuni, arriving before dawn on May 30.

They passed through a village devastated by artillery fire. "The stench of corpses stung our nostrils," wrote Yahara. "Many civilians were scattered on the ground, their belongings all around them."[67]

The Thirty-Second Army adopted the euphemism "*tenshin*" for the retreat, meaning "advance in different direction." Hashimoto Kichitaro, an Okinawan who fought with the Thirty-Second Army, was at the command post shelter when the withdrawal began. Unlike any movement that he had ever witnessed, this retreat was "chaotic. A defeated army on the run really has it tough. As the rain lashed down, we had no time to stop for a rest. We were under the gun so much that we even urinated on the move."[68]

Ushijima had urged all Okinawa civilians to go to the Chinen Peninsula on Okinawa's east coast—out of the path of the Thirty-Second Army's retreat to Kiyan. Few civilians heeded Ushijima's instructions. Neither did they follow instructions in the air-dropped American leaflets to stay away from Japanese soldiers, wear white clothes, travel in groups, and gather along the highway that ran down the west coast.

Instead, the civilians and their possessions mingled with the retreating army on the roads south of Shuri. "It was Japs and Okinawans and kids

and old people and ducks and dogs and cats," said a Marine who witnessed the exodus.[69]

The migration to the south was a hell for both civilians and soldiers. Japanese troops, Okinawan student nurses, and civilians emerged into the open after living for two months in spider holes, trenches, tunnels, and reeking, blood-soaked hospital caves—only to face a typhoon of steel sweeping down on them from the sea, air, and land.

US warships that cruised within easy gunfire range of the withdrawal route between Shuri and the Kiyan Peninsula shelled the troops, military vehicles, and civilians that jammed the roads. The Tactical Air Force based at Yontan and Kadena strafed and bombed them, and American artillerists participated in the carnage from the Shuri area.

The result was a bloodbath surpassing anything yet seen on the embattled island. In a little more than a week, an estimated 15,000 civilians were killed, along with more than 10,000 Japanese soldiers.

"The trip from Kochiada to Kiyan leaves an impression words are inadequate to describe," wrote Tokuyu Higashionna, a teacher, who saw dead children on the backs of mothers, and live children beside dead mothers. "Utter horror . . . dead everywhere—*everywhere* . . . It was literally hell."[70]

Sixteen-year-old Kikuko Miyagi of the Himayuri "Lily" Student Corps—one of the detachments that with the male Iron and Blood units had enrolled 2,312 Okinawa teenagers—was rousted from a Shuri hospital cave. She had attended to badly wounded soldiers there since her nighttime graduation ceremony March 24 amid a US bombardment. She had helped treat gas gangrene, tetanus, and brain-fever cases, and assisted during amputations. "Hands and legs were chopped off without anesthetic. They used a saw. Holding down their limbs was a student job," she wrote.

The Japanese dismissed the student nurses when they evacuated Shuri. Kikuko and her comrades were turned out of the hospital cave on March 25. During their last night there, the nurses watched soldiers prepare individual doses of powdered potassium cyanide mixed with glucose power. They were administered orally or by injection to patients who were too badly wounded to join the retreat.

After leaving the cave, Kikuko and her comrades for the next ten days journeyed through a Dante-esque landscape.[71]

"We'd become accustomed to the smell of excrement, pus, and the maggots in the cave, but the smell of death there on that road was unbearable," Kikuko said. During the daytime, the refugees hid in the fields. They

traveled by night down muddy roads "full of artillery craters with corpses, swollen two or three times normal size, floating in them."[72]

Kikuko was among the twenty-one survivors from the original 225 Himeyuri Student Corps nurses who were mobilized. The nurses had an unusually high mortality rate among the Okinawa youths between the ages of thirteen and eighteen who served in nursing and Blood and Iron boys' units. Of the 2,312 youths mobilized, 1,105 died in battle or from disease. They were fiercely patriotic, said Sesoko Seiken, the only survivor of twenty-two boys from the Prefectural Fisheries School who fought beside the Japanese. "We were consumed by a burning desire to offer our lives in defense of the nation," he said. "We had no fear of death whatever."

Before the Thirty-Second Army withdrew, Captain Hirose Hideo, a guerrilla warfare specialist, asked fifty-seven Okinawa teenagers who had been selected to become infiltrators when the Army relocated to Mabuni, "Will you gladly go to your deaths?" The young soldiers roared in reply, "Yes, sir!"[73]

ABOUT THIRTY THOUSAND MEN FROM the Thirty-Second Army reached the Kiyan Peninsula. Colonel Yahara listed twelve thousand survivors of the 24th Division, which had served as the army's rearguard; seven thousand from the 62nd Division; three thousand from the 44th Independent Mixed Brigade; three thousand artillerymen; and five thousand assorted troops.

Although more than half of their heavy weapons had been left behind at Shuri or discarded during the retreat, by June 4 the survivors held prepared positions along a new line, with the 44th IMB occupying the western line, the 24th Division in the center, and the 62nd Division on the eastern side.

Despite General Buckner's confident prediction that Ushijima could not organize a new defensive line, he in fact had done so, and now the US Tenth Army would have to crack it.

More bloody battles lay ahead.[74]

The Last Ditch

The Japs there began their heavenly ritual, "Harakiri," by blowing themselves up with grenades and demolition packs. One could see body parts flying up in the air and all over.

—CORPORAL FRANK KUKUCHKA OF THE 29TH MARINES, DESCRIBING THE MASS SUICIDES ON THE OROKU PENINSULA[1]

IT WAS FITTING THAT THE 4th Marines would spearhead what would be the Marine Corps's final contested amphibious operation of World War II, a landing on Oroku Peninsula. The 4th Regiment was the reincarnation of the unit of that name that was surrendered at Corregidor in 1942 and had ceased to exist. In February 1944, the regiment was reborn. On Okinawa, the 4th Marines and its parent 6th Marine Division captured Mount Yae-Take on the Motobu Peninsula, had fought on Sugar Loaf and Horseshoe Hills, and marched into bomb-shattered Naha, Okinawa's capital city.[2]

Just to the south of Naha, Oroku protruded from the island's west coast like a thumb and was defended by the Okinawa Naval Base Force commanded by fifty-four-year-old Admiral Minoru Ōta. So long as Oroku remained in Japanese hands, nearby debris-choked Naha harbor could not be cleared and transformed into a US port.

Admiral Ōta was one of the last surviving "*rikusentai*" commanders who had led the Japanese marines of the Special Naval Landing Forces. They were exceptional naval troops trained in infantry tactics and weapons. In 1943 on Tarawa, the 7th Sasebo Special Naval Landing Force fought

nearly to the last man against invading US Marines and soldiers who outnumbered them 8-to-1. That same year, Ōta's 8th Combined Special Landing Force had battled the 1st and 4th Raider Battalions on New Georgia.
But by June 1945, most of the Landing Force troops were dead or wounded;
now, reserves and service troops filled the Landing Force ranks for the
most part.[3]

On June 4, the 4th Marines boarded amphibious tractors in Naha and
crossed Kokuba Estuary with the 6th Marine Tank Battalion for a shore-to-
shore landing on Oroku Peninsula. Behind them were the 29th Marines.

Oroku was the Okinawa battlefield in microcosm. A jumble of fortified hills, caves, bunkers, and ridges in a 3-mile-by-2-mile area, the
peninsula was defended by largely second-tier troops determined to fight
to the death.[4]

Ōta's Naval Base Force was ordered by General Ushijima in late May to
withdraw from Oroku to the Kiyan Peninsula after destroying the weapons that they could not carry. But when the naval troops reached their new
positions near Nakagusuku to fight beside the Thirty-Second Army, the
younger officers implored Admiral Ōta to permit them to return to Oroku
and die fighting from the positions that they had prepared there. Ōta not
only consented to the unusual request, he in fact led about two thousand
men back to Oroku. There they rejoined the service troops, Okinawan conscripts, and administrative and construction troops that had stayed behind.

Because many of the Naval Base Force's weapons remained with the
Thirty-Second Army near Nakagusuku and the weapons they left on Oroku
had been destroyed, the returnees were obliged to arm themselves with a
hodgepodge of heavy weapons: two hundred machine guns and 40mm cannons salvaged from wrecked planes at Naha Airfield on Oroku's western
shore, and 200mm naval guns and antiship rockets.

Three-quarters of Oroku's defenders had never received ground-combat
training, but they prepared a credible defensive line along a southeast-
northwest ridge running the length of the peninsula, with Hills 57 and 62
forming the core of the Japanese defense. The defenders heavily mined the
roads, flatlands, and valleys, and covered all approaches with automatic
weapons concealed in camouflaged caves.[5]

Before the American assault, sixteen commandos from the 6th Marine Division's Reconnaissance Company crossed the Kokuba Estuary to
Oroku at night in rubber boats. They identified some enemy positions and
a gun battery. Their report concluded that Oroku was "lightly defended,"

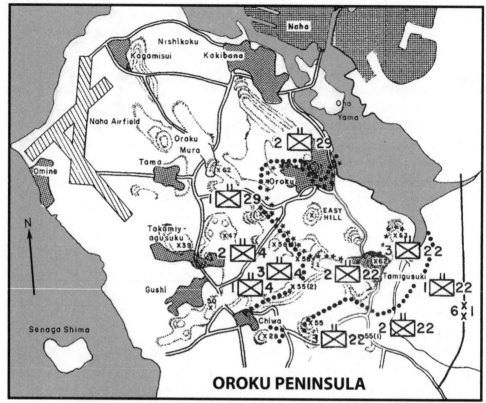

OROKU PENINSULA

Map adapted from The History of the U.S. Marine Corps in World War II, Volume 5, *by Benis M. Frank and Henry I. Shaw Jr. (Historical Branch, U.S. Marine Corps, 1968). Original map by T.L. Russell.*

suggesting that the commandos did not advance very far inland. Oroku, it would be seen, would exact a high price for a small gain.[6]

After an hour-long artillery bombardment in which 4,300 shells fell on the hills overlooking the landing beaches, at 5:51 a.m. on June 4 the 4th Marines' 1st Battalion, led by amphibious tanks, went ashore on Oroku's north point; the 29th Regiment landed four hours later. The Marines initially faced light, sporadic machine-gun and 20mm fire, but resistance steadily stiffened as they pushed farther inland, where they soon ran up against the familiar mutually supporting positions.[7]

Meanwhile, the 6th Reconnaissance Company and 708th Amphibious Tank Battalion assaulted Onoyama Island between Naha and Oroku and secured it, after killing twenty-five enemy troops. The Japanese had

destroyed the island's connecting bridges, and they had to be rebuilt. Engineers laid a Bailey bridge between Onoyama and Naha, and began as-
sembling a pontoon bridge between the tiny island and Oroku while being
harassed by machine-gun fire. They completed it by dark, and supplies and
more tanks rolled to Oroku.

A week earlier, the 6th Reconnaissance Company had carried out a mission that couldn't have been more different: it robbed the Bank of Naha.
Ordered to look for Japanese documents, the Marines blew the bank vault
with C-4 and Primacord. The explosion scattered Japanese yen everywhere;
the bank robbers discovered that the vault boxes had already been emptied.

Corporal Hubert Welch of the 29th Marines' Company I and his comrades had been warned about the existence of new, jet-propelled Japanese
rockets known as "locomotives from hell" because of the terrifying noise
that they made. Now, when they heard a high-pitched shriek, they knew
that one was on its way. "You could see the thing coming toward you," he
said. When it hit the ground, there was an interval of a few seconds before there occurred "the most terrible explosion you have ever heard." The
rocket attacks ended after only a few hours, when the Japanese rocketeers
either ran out of missiles or were overrun.[8]

The Marines advanced a mile inland on the first day, fanning out across
the heavily mined rice paddies and valleys while being subjected to concentrations of artillery fire. By June 5, the Marines began fashioning a noose
around Ōta's men in the hills. The admiral radioed General Ushijima that
day: "I will command my remaining units to defend Oroku Peninsula as
brave warriors unto death." Ushijima praised Ōta's fighting spirit, but
urged him to withdraw and join his men on the Kiyan Peninsula. He did
not wish "to see your forces perish alone."[9]

But by then, retreat from Oroku was impossible; the 1st Marine Division, advancing southward along Okinawa's western coastline, had sealed
off Oroku from the Okinawa mainland.

NAHA AIRFIELD FELL ON JUNE 6, but only after an enemy artillery
piece and a 20mm machine cannon on Senaga Shima, a small island 500
yards southwest of Oroku, were silenced by air strikes as troops stood
and cheered.[10]

Sergeant William Manchester was recovering from a gunshot wound
that he received June 2 in the Naha area when he went AWOL from the
hospital to rejoin the 29th Marines for the Oroku landing. On June 5, as he

and his comrades warmed their breakfast in a courtyard outside an ancestral tomb, he heard the familiar shriek of an incoming enemy round. Manchester instinctively ducked into the doorway of the tomb, even though the odds of being hit by a mortar fired over a hill were extremely low. Manchester's two companions, Izzy Levy and Rip Thorpe, ignored the sound and continued heating their food.

The shell landed in the exact center of the courtyard, beating the long odds. "Rip's body absorbed most of the shock," Manchester wrote. "It disintegrated, and his flesh, blood, brains, and intestines encompassed me. Izzy was blind."

Manchester was flung to the ground. Both of his eardrums were broken, shrapnel and fragments of Rip's bones had pierced his back and left side, and he had suffered a brain injury. Manchester rose to his feet, staggered blindly into the courtyard, and collapsed. Left for dead, he lay there for four hours before a corpsman saw that he was alive and administered morphine. He was evacuated to Saipan.[11]

Japanese firing from camouflaged caves in Hills 57 and 62 slowed the Marines' advance on June 7 and 8, and inflicted high casualties. "Blowtorch and corkscrew" tactics, aided by the 6th Marine Tank Battalion, methodically eliminated enemy resistance. General Shepherd committed his last regiment, the 22nd, to attack from the base of the peninsula to the northwest.

The Japanese were driven onto high ground near Tomigusuku, and the 6th Division compressed the pocket to an area of just 1,000 by 2,000 yards. On June 9, the 4th Marines made modest inroads. "Every Jap seemed to be armed with a machine gun," the regiment reported. It claimed to have killed more than 1,500 enemy soldiers, "and there were still plenty left."[12]

The 29th Marines entered Oroku Town on June 10. That night, the defenders counterattacked and were repulsed. In the morning, two hundred dead enemy soldiers lay before the Marine positions.[13]

Shepherd ordered an eight-battalion attack supported by tanks on June 11. It resulted in the capture of Hill 53 and the town of Tomigusuku on the south side of the pocket. On June 12, the converging regiments forced the defenders into the open. In a rice paddy between Oroku Town and Hill 53, many of them were killed, others blew themselves up with satchel charges, and eighty-six surrendered.

The Japanese made their last stand on June 13 in the southeastern corner of the peninsula at the incongruously named Easy Hill—the Naval Base

Force headquarters. The Marine attack on the hill was described in the division report as "slow, laborious and bitterly opposed."

As his company assaulted Easy Hill, Corporal Frank Kukuchka of the 29th Marines' Company I said, "The Japs there began their heavenly ritual, 'Harakiri,' by blowing themselves up with grenades and demolition packs. One could see body parts flying up in the air and all over." Eight hundred sixty-three Japanese died in this final battle—many by their own hand—and seventy-three were made prisoners.[14]

Admiral Ōta and five of his staff officers committed suicide by cutting their throats during the night of June 13. Their bodies were found in a tunnel, arranged with precision. Each officer, clad in a freshly pressed naval uniform, lay on his back with a saber on his belt; his hands were behind his head; and his feet pointed away from the wall. More than two hundred corpses were found in the underground headquarters complex, which included an infirmary with medical equipment.[15]

In his final message to General Ushijima, Admiral Ōta wrote: "Enemy tank groups are now attacking our cave headquarters. The Naval Base Force is dying gloriously at this moment. . . . We are grateful for your past kindnesses and pray for the success of the Army."[16]

Nearly 5,000 Japanese died defending Oroku. What began as a sideshow to the Tenth Army's drive to the Kiyan Peninsula proved costly for the 6th Marine Division, which reported 1,608 casualties during the ten-day operation.[17]

ON THE FOGGY MORNING OF June 1, the Tenth Army crossed the Yonabaru-Naha valley, hoping to overtake Ushijima's Thirty-Second Army before it could occupy a new defensive line in southern Okinawa. On the left was the 7th Division; the 96th Division advanced down the middle; and the 1st Marine Division, replacing the 6th Marine Division on the right flank, pushed southward along the west coast.

Enemy resistance was spotty—in general, the hills were lightly defended or not defended at all—a change from the intensely contested strongpoints the Americans had struggled for weeks to capture along the Shuri Line. Moreover, the Japanese defenders were often second-echelon troops lacking the battle skills of the frontline troops, most of whom lay dead along the Shuri Line.

More than sixty thousand American infantrymen slogged through standing water and mud up to 3 feet deep to meet the enemy at Operation Iceberg's last reckoning.

The roads were lined with the bloated bodies of Japanese soldiers and Okinawans who had perished in the blizzard of steel from US warships, warplanes, and artillery. Their lives had ended violently in especially large numbers at the bridges and crossroads targeted by US guns—at Madanbashi, Ichinchibashi, and Yamakawa Bridges, nicknamed the "Bridges of Death"; and at Haebaru Junction, which became known as the "Crossroads of Death."[18]

Heavy rains transformed roads into quagmires and halted tank and truck travel. XXIV Corps coped better with the situation than the 1st Marine Division, which was bogged down in the west and unable to get food, water, and ammunition to frontline units. What they did receive was lugged from supply depots by carrying parties of replacements, or parachuted to them from torpedo bombers. "Carrying parties of replacement troops formed an almost unbroken chain from the regimental dump at Jichaku [Jitchaku] . . . A large number of men dropped from sheer exhaustion," said a 1st Marines report.

XXIV Corps had learned on Leyte in the fall of 1944 how to operate in marshes and driving rains—by using bulldozers and winches to bring supply trucks forward. Early during the drive south, the 1st Division, its men on limited rations because of the collapse of its supply system, lagged a mile and a half behind the 96th Division's right flank. "For two-thirds of the distance of the drive our right flank was exposed," said the 383rd Regiment's report.[19]

Marine leaders who had deplored the 27th Infantry Division's slow pace on Saipan were now accused of the same sin. General Buckner wrote in his journal on June 3 that he'd told the III Amphibious Corps commander, General Roy Geiger, "to get the 1st Marine Division off its tails. Told him I was dissatisfied with its progress. Sent O. P. Smith (the Marine liaison between the Tenth Army and III Amphibious Corps) down to investigate."

Two days later, Buckner grumbled, "First Marine Division still trailing behind the 96th Division." General Hodge reassigned the 77th Division's 305th Infantry from mopping-up operations around Shuri to plug the gap. The 5th Marines narrowed it to 1,000 yards when it crossed into the 96th Division sector to attack through Tera and secure high ground south of Gisushi.[20]

IN THE EAST, THE 7TH DIVISION'S 17th Infantry captured Hills 75 and 72, and the 184th Infantry seized Hill 117, killing more than two hundred Japanese troops, and then proceeded to capture Hills 181 and 145.

Lieutenant Robert Faw led the assault platoons up Hill 117, where the enemy put six bullet holes in his field jacket; he was uninjured. Captain Herbert Reiman, the Company K commander, ordered a supply sergeant to bring a replacement jacket to Faw; the bullet-riddled one was "hard on his morale," Reiman said.

The 32nd and 17th Infantry swept through Chinen Peninsula without encountering organized resistance. Near Minatoga Estuary, the 17th Infantry's Company L discovered a massive cave teeming with frightened civilians and some Okinawan conscripts who had left the Japanese ranks. The Americans lured 250 people from the cave and sent them to an internment camp.

A platoon of the 184th Infantry's Company A was harassed by rifle fire while cleaning out the ruined village of Gushichan on the southeast coast. The soldiers found a way to determine where the gunfire was coming from: by planting small sticks in the holes made by the bullets in the town's soft rock walls. They then avoided those lines of fire.

By day's end June 5, a 400-foot-high plateau and a tall hill with cliffs 170 feet high loomed before the Hourglass Division—the Yaeju-Dake Escarpment and Hill 95, which constituted the eastern part of General Ushijima's defensive line. By June 8, the 17th and 184th Infantry had crowded forward to face the Japanese strongpoints across a green, mile-wide valley. The enemy fortifications could not be flanked; they would have to be stormed. That same day, Army engineers opened the port of Minatoga and crews began unloading supply ships, resolving the 7th Division's problem of bringing food and ammunition down flooded Route 13 to the division front lines.[21]

The 96th Division advanced steadily southward through the middle of the island. On June 2, the 381st Infantry's Company E wiped out nearly sixty enemy troops defending a hill, and Company A charged another strongly defended hill and killed forty-nine more. That night, Company A repulsed an enemy counterattack.

On June 5, a machine gunner on a bypassed hill near Iwa killed the 383rd Infantry's highly respected commander, Colonel Edwin May, described by General James Bradley, the 96th's assistant commander, as "the finest soldier I have ever known."

Before the Deadeyes rose the 300-foot-high Yuza-Dake, darkly characterized in the 383rd Infantry's report as "grim, desolate and foreboding."[22]

THE 1ST MARINE DIVISION HAD reached the East China Sea coastline on June 7, closing the last possible avenue of retreat from the Oroku Peninsula

for Admiral Ōta's force. The drive to Okinawa's west coast made it possible for the division to receive supplies by water, reducing its dependence on air-drops. On June 9, LVTs began landing supplies and evacuating the wounded.

After days of subsisting on reduced rations because of the impossibility of vehicle travel on the mud-clogged roads, the division was back on full rations. It advanced southward and captured Itoman. On June 10, the Marines reached the approaches to their new nemesis: Kunishi Ridge.[23]

WHAT REMAINED OF THE JAPANESE Thirty-Second Army had begun occupying caves and crevices on June 3 in the unbroken, 5-mile-long wall of coral looming before the Tenth Army. Ushijima had chosen his army's final battleground carefully. The 24th Division had skillfully readied the defensive positions in early April before leaving the area to join the army on the Shuri Line.

The coral barrier spanned the Kiyan Peninsula from Hill 95 on the Pacific coast in the east to Kunishi Ridge, which extended west for 1 mile before ending near the East China Sea south of Itoman. Between Hill 95 and Kunishi stood Yaeju-Dake, crowned by the "Big Apple," which stood 60 feet above the escarpment, and Yuza-Dake, which lay across a sprawling saddle from Yaeju-Dake. Before the Tenth Army could begin to assault the coral barrier hills and escarpments, it would have to make a perilous crossing over low, open ground under fire.

For the Japanese, there was no hope of further retreat. A Houdini-esque escape such as they had executed on Guadalcanal was an impossibility: hundreds of warships and thousands of carrier- and land-based warplanes patrolled every square mile of sea around the island.[24]

Of the Thirty-Second Army's remaining thirty thousand men, fewer than ten thousand were combat-trained infantrymen; the rest were service troops, Boeitai, and artillerists. The twelve thousand men in the largest intact unit, the 24th Division, were assigned to the primary defenses of Yaeju-Dake, Yazu-Dake, and Kunishi Ridge in the center and western parts of the peninsula, where they faced the 96th and 1st Marine divisions.

The 44th Independent Mobile Brigade's three thousand soldiers defended Hill 95 opposite the 7th Division, while the seven thousand men remaining in the decimated 62nd Division, once Ushijima's best division, were now in reserve at Makabe. The rest of the army—eight thousand men—possessed skills that the army no longer could use because of the loss

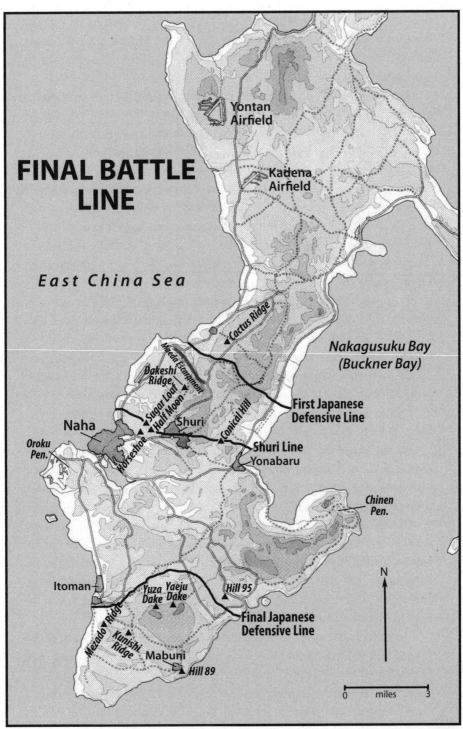

FINAL BATTLE LINE

Yontan
Airfield

Kadena
Airfield

East China Sea

Cactus Ridge

Naeda Escarpment

Nakagusuku Bay
(Buckner Bay)

Dakeshi
Ridge

Sugar Loaf
Half Moon

Shuri

Conical Hill

**First Japanese
Defensive Line**

Naha

Horseshoe

Shuri Line

Oroku
Pen.

Yonabaru

Chinen
Pen.

Itoman

Yuza
Dake

Yaeju
Dake

Hill 95

Mezado Ridge

Kunishi
Ridge

Mabuni

**Final Japanese
Defensive Line**

Hill 89

N

0   miles   3

Map adapted from Okinawa: The Last Battle *by Roy E. Appleman, et al.
(Center for Military History, 1948)*

of heavy weapons and equipment. These men were apportioned among the frontline units as replacement infantrymen. There were shortages of grenades, mines, and machine guns, but the 5th Artillery Command had managed to retain half of its guns, now positioned behind the escarpments.[25]

Although thinly deployed, the Thirty-Second Army appeared at first glance to still be capable of formidable resistance. But its assorted components were neither integrated nor coordinated. Moreover, veteran US troops quickly surmised that, with Ushijima's best troops dead on the Shuri Line, the enemy's combat skills had declined sharply. The half-trained rear-echelon troops and Okinawan homeguard replacements executed basic maneuvers poorly; their concealment was sloppy; they opened fire prematurely; and if flushed from a position, they simply ran until they were shot down.[26]

From his new command post inside Hill 89 at Mabuni, General Ushijima began directing his army's final dispositions. The complex's three openings provided views of Mabuni and the sea, and the escarpment to the west. Its central shaft connected passageways on multiple levels above and below. A path led from the cave mouth that looked seaward to a spring at the foot of the hill.

The new command post lacked the Shuri headquarters' amenities and was unpleasantly damp and odiferous; low-hanging stalactites dripped water and made it unsafe to walk without a helmet. It was crowded with teenage nurses and schoolboys from the Blood and Iron units, and lice were rampant. "It was an awful place," said Colonel Hiromichi Yahara. Water had to be carried up the cliff from the spring, a dangerous assignment, as evidenced by the corpses and canteens littering the ground near the aptly nicknamed "Spring of Death."[27]

Three days after Ushijima and his staff had settled into the new command post, US patrol boats appeared offshore and began firing at the cave entrance. An adjutant was wounded in the hand, and General Chō's uniform jacket, left outside when the shooting began, was torn by bullets. It was no longer safe to venture out of the cave during the daytime.[28]

BECAUSE OF THE DELAYS DUE to mud, rain, and flooded roads and streams, it had taken a full week for the Tenth Army to reach its new positions opposite the Thirty-Second Army on the Kiyan Peninsula. The three US divisions prepared to assault the towering escarpments before them, after first replenishing their stocks of food, water, and ammunition.

The plum rains ended June 5, and American patrols began probing the Japanese defenses. During the next days, the ground dried sufficiently to move up tanks and flame tanks with their 200-foot hose extensions. The first assaults on the Kiyan escarpments were planned for June 9 and 10.[29]

"But for the deluge, I feel that the enemy would by this time have been destroyed," wrote General Buckner. In attempting to mitigate the cost of permitting his quarry to escape, Buckner said that during their escape from Shuri, the Japanese had abandoned tanks and artillery that had become stuck in the mud. "We are pressing him as relentlessly as possible and are supplying our troops near the shores by water and those in the center by air."[30]

WHILE THE TENTH ARMY PURSUED Ushijima's Thirty-Second Army through the rain and mud to the Kiyan Peninsula, the Japanese Air Force launched another mass suicide attack on the US fleet. Kikusui No. 9, however, was a shadow of the earlier attacks in which up to seven hundred suicide and conventional planes had hurtled toward the radar picket stations surrounding Okinawa. Just fifty warplanes participated in Kikusui No. 9. Imperial Japanese Headquarters had begun hoarding planes and pilots for the homeland's defense. An estimated 10,700 planes, half of them kamikazes, reportedly remained available in Japan for combat.

During the attacks from June 3 to June 7, large formations were rare—and when they did occur, they were quickly broken up. On June 3, twenty-five Zeros were spotted near Radar Picket Station No. 15, and four Corsairs from VMF-323 took on twelve of them, shooting down nine.

The Fifth Fleet became known as the 3rd Fleet on May 27 as part of the routine rotation between the 3rd Fleet's admirals William Halsey and Admiral John "Slew" McCain, and the Fifth Fleet's admirals Raymond Spruance and Marc Mitscher. Spruance and Mitscher had respectively directed naval and air operations since January 26; Halsey and McCain were now in command. Also relieved was Admiral Richmond Kelly Turner, the acerbic amphibious force commander known as "The Alligator," whose prolific memos were known to subordinates as "snowflakes." Turner's successor was his antithesis, mild-mannered Admiral Harry Hill. The rotation did not affect ships' captains and crewmen, only the top echelon. Freed from their day-to-day responsibilities, Spruance, Mitscher, and Turner now concentrated on planning Operation Downfall, the invasion of Japan.

Kikusui No. 9 was a failure. Although there were close calls, no ships were damaged, and most of the attack planes were destroyed by shipboard

antiaircraft fire and alert combat air patrols of Corsairs, Hellcats, and P-47 Thunderbolts. The *kikusui* era was drawing to a close: one final mass attack, Kikusui No. 10, would be attempted on June 21–22.

A typhoon on June 4 and June 5 proved to be more destructive than the Kikusui No. 9 Special Attack planes. As the winds rose on June 4, the picket ships were recalled to their anchorages. The storm struck the 3rd Fleet east of Okinawa on June 5 and damaged thirty-four ships, including the battleships *Massachusetts*, *Indiana*, and *Alabama*; the carriers *Hornet* and *Bennington*; and escort carriers *Windham Bay* and *Salamau*—the carriers all sustaining flight-deck damage.[31]

The kamikaze attacks never wholly ceased. Between the mass attacks, suicide pilots in small groups and individually sacrificed their lives for the emperor.

During the morning of June 10, the destroyer *William Porter* was patrolling Radar Picket Station No. 15 with destroyers *Aulick* and *Cogswell* and four gunboats. Shortly after 8 a.m., a Val suddenly dove out of the overcast sky and attacked *Porter* head-on. It struck the water next to the ship's port side, and its bomb detonated beneath the ship. The explosion lifted *Porter* out of the water, and slammed it down violently. Sixty-one crewmen were injured, most of them suffering from badly sprained or broken ankles. *Porter*'s seams split open, her after engine room flooded, and she listed to starboard. To keep her afloat while crewmen were being evacuated, two gunboats lashed themselves to her. Then, at 11:19 a.m., *Porter*'s bow thrust into the sky and she sank beneath the waves.[32]

Early the next evening, June 11, two Val dive-bombers appeared again over Radar Picket Station No. 15. *LCS(L)-122* splashed one of them, but the second Val smashed into the base of her conning tower, and its bomb exploded. The plane struck just 2 yards from where the ship's commander, Lieutenant Richard McCool, was standing. McCool was knocked unconscious. When he came to his senses, although injured and bleeding, McCool took charge of firefighting efforts and helped rescue men from a blazing compartment, emerging with serious burns.

LCS(L)-122 survived. The Japanese pilot's remains, which were scattered all over the ship, were collected in a mailbag. Weighted with an old typewriter, the mailbag was dumped over the side.

McCool was awarded the Congressional Medal of Honor—the only Navy man on a ship to be so honored after L-Day. Four Navy corpsmen serving with Marine units also received the nation's highest military honor for their actions on Okinawa.[33]

THE 7TH DIVISION BECAME THE first Tenth Army unit to test the Japanese defenses on the Kiyan Peninsula. The 7th's commander, General Archibald Arnold, placed two tank companies in forward positions for the initial assault. In the open, flatter terrain and drier weather, conditions were better suited for deploying tanks than at any other period of the campaign.

At 7:30 a.m. June 9, the 32nd Regiment's 1st Battalion, led by Company C, went into action against Hill 95 and the coral hogback before it. On the right, the 17th Infantry prepared to tackle the east side of the 1,200-yard-long Yaeju-Dake Escarpment. Yaeju-Dake stood 400 feet above the valley to its north—the valley that the 17th Infantry needed to cross before attempting to scale the escarpment's heights.[34]

Machine-gun fire from caves in two coral knobs at the northern end of Hill 95 stopped Company C from seizing the forward hogback on June 9. The regiment replied with a deafening mortar bombardment of the hogback and an artillery barrage on Hill 95. After killing thirteen enemy soldiers in the caves and pinpointing the sources of the most concentrated Japanese fire, Company C withdrew for the day.[35]

AT YAEJU-DAKE, THE 17TH INFANTRY'S commander, Colonel Francis Pachler, held back his 1st Battalion on the right, where the preponderance of enemy machine-gun fire was concentrated. He elected to attack instead on the left, sending his 3rd Battalion against the more lightly defended southeastern side of the escarpment.

Company I's infantrymen belly-crawled through the muddy rice paddies toward the escarpment as enemy machine-gunners and snipers tried to kill them. The lead squad managed to reach the temporary shelter afforded by the cliff base and climbed to the rim. There, the Americans killed nine Japanese in ten minutes and seized a small corner of the escarpment, jumping into enemy holes where Japanese dead lay everywhere and using their bodies to reinforce the positions. To seem more numerous than they were, the Americans fired their rifles and continually threw grenades while they "yelled at the tops of [their] lungs just like [they] played soldier and injuns as kids," said Lieutenant Roland Glenn, the platoon leader. The ruse enabled Glenn's men to cling to their toehold until reinforcements could reach them.[36]

The Tenth Army had dented the Thirty-Second Army's final defensive line. The Japanese did not intend to give it up easily: eight men in another 3rd Battalion squad that reached the rim were caught in the crossfire of three machine guns and killed to the last man. However, other 17th Infantry

soldiers made the harrowing ascent unscathed, and by nightfall twenty of them held the sliver of escarpment. That night, with a light machine gun and automatic weapons they repulsed three Japanese counterattacks.[37]

STOPPED JUNE 9 BY MACHINE-GUN fire from the coral knobs on Hill 95, the 32nd Infantry resumed its attack on the hogback to the hill's north on June 10, with Company C in the lead once more. This time, artillery and naval gunfire, and machine guns blasted Hill 95's eastern side and summit as the Hourglass infantrymen climbed onto the hogback, wiping out the enemy defenders. The infantrymen advanced to the northeastern corner of Hill 95 and the enemy-held coral knobs and fortified caves that had thwarted them the day before.

During a brief lull in the fighting at midmorning, a large group of civilians descended a narrow path on Hill 95 and, with arms raised, entered the American lines.

A flame tank clanked up to the base of the coral knobs. Six-foot-five-inch Captain Tony Niemeyer, the commander of Company C of the 713th Armored Flamethrowers Battalion, attached a 200-foot extension hose to the tank's flame nozzle. Tank, mortar, and machine-gun fire suppressed enemy fire from the caves while Niemeyer, accompanied by a platoon of infantrymen, dragged the hose up the slope. From a spot near the caves, he sprayed them with napalm and gasoline, and they erupted in flames.

Up to forty panicked Japanese soldiers poured from the openings—and into a maelstrom of rifle and automatic-weapons fire. They were all killed. The burned bodies of forty more enemy soldiers were found in a gorge below the caves.[38]

Captain Niemeyer returned the next day with his flame-hose extension and led the assault up Hill 95's northwest slope. The daring captain was supported by an infantry platoon and intensive tank, artillery, mortar, and machine-gun fire. Over the course of forty-five minutes, Niemeyer burned his way to the top of Hill 95 as heavy-weapons fire pinned the enemy defenders.

Reaching the lip of Hill 95, Niemeyer sprayed the top with napalm and gasoline. When the 300-gallon fuel supply of the first tank was depleted, the hose extension was attached to a second flame tank, and Niemeyer continued his rampage.

The 32nd Regiment's 1st Battalion launched its decisive attack on Hill 95 on June 13, aided by a platoon of medium tanks and two flame tanks that burned a path ahead of the infantry. Four hundred sixty Japanese

defenders were killed. From the hilltop, the 32nd prepared to attack Hills 115 and 153. Ushijima's final defensive line had been breached.[39]

WITH ITS SISTER REGIMENT ATOP Hill 95, Colonel Pachler's 17th Infantry planned a rare night attack to seize the eastern side of Yaeju-Dake. The regiment's 3rd Battalion had captured a sliver of the southeastern part of the escarpment during its daylight attack on June 9, but there had been little progress since then. Pachler believed that a night attack would catch the Japanese unawares and succeed.

The assault was scheduled for 3:30 a.m. June 12—the very hour that the 1st Marine Division's 7th Regiment was planning to assault Kunishi Ridge on the western end of the enemy-held escarpment. It was coincidence rather than coordination, though. Colonel Pachler and Colonel Edward Snedeker, the 7th Marines' commander, planned their attacks independently; the regiments were miles from each other and under different commands. The Japanese command probably thought otherwise when the dust cleared.

To preserve the element of surprise, Paschler's attack would proceed without a preliminary artillery bombardment, aside from the usual harassing nighttime fire.

Late June 11, however, an intercepted Japanese radio message threatened to derail the night attack: it suggested that a night attack was imminent. However, the impending attack turned out to be a *Japanese* assault targeting the 7th Division's 32nd Infantry on Hill 95.

Indeed, the Japanese anticipated an assault on the escarpment on June 12, but not until 7:30 a.m., because the Americans usually attacked only during the daytime. The defenders had in fact evacuated the summit to avoid the expected American barrage preceding the attack; they planned to return to their positions before 7:30. By attacking hours earlier with no preliminary bombardment, Pachler caught the Japanese completely flat-footed.

Aided by heavy fog that reduced visibility to 10 feet, thereby concealing the men's movements and muffling the rattle of their weapons, Companies A and B of the 17th Infantry's 1st Battalion scaled the steep escarpment with ropes, reaching Yaeju-Dake's summit by 5:30 a.m. without a single casualty. The infantrymen had not fired a shot.

With daylight, however, small groups of enemy soldiers from the 15th Infantry, reinforced by service troops, emerged from caves in the center of

Company B's position—and were dispatched by rifle fire. That day, Company B killed sixty-three Japanese.

The 3rd Battalion's Company L had taken advantage of the fog and absence of enemy fire to seize a group of coral knobs to the south of the escarpment. The knobs were roughly 20 to 30 feet high and 40 feet across the base. They were "hollowed out and the place was alive with Japs," observed Captain Warren Hughes of the 17th Infantry. When about fifty Japanese soldiers approached in a column of twos, the Americans riddled the formation with rifle and BAR fire, killing thirty-seven men.[40]

From its new position atop the escarpment, the 17th was able to identify many Japanese artillery sites to the south. The Americans immediately exploited this advantage with a "time on target" burst on a battery of eight Japanese dual-purpose guns. One hundred forty-four artillery pieces were aimed at the same spot and fired at precisely the same moment. "The hills seemed to jump up, shake, and then settle again. . . . No more was heard from the Jap guns," wrote Captain Hughes.

The 17th Infantry extended its control to the entire Yaeju-Dake Escarpment by the next day, June 13, except for holdouts in caves. Less than a mile to the south was its final objective, Hill 153.

To the east, the 32nd Infantry defended Hill 95's summit against more than a dozen counterattacks on June 13, hurling back the Japanese each time with heavy losses.[41]

The last bastion of Japanese resistance was crumbling under the Tenth Army's hammer blows.

The Thirty-Second Army Collapses

The brigade is finished. Our right flank has collapsed. We can fight no more. I regret to report that unit command-ers are crying aloud as they watch their men dying in vain. Whatever we do we cannot stop the enemy.

—A JAPANESE FIELD OFFICER'S REPORT IN MID-JUNE[1]

The situation was one of those tactical oddities of this pecu-liar warfare. We were on the ridge. The Japs were in it, both on the forward and reverse slopes.

—GENERAL PEDRO DEL VALLE, DESCRIBING
THE 1ST MARINE DIVISION'S SITUATION AT KUNISHI RIDGE[2]

DIVE-BOMBERS, ARTILLERY BATTERIES, AND NAVAL guns pounded the 160-foot cliffs of Yaeju-Dake and Yuza-Dake for three days while the 96th Division, wedged between the 7th Division on its left and the 1st Ma-rine Division on the right, sorted itself into assault positions and then sat tight. On June 10, the Deadeyes swung into action.

Atop Yaeju-Dake stood the 60-foot "Big Apple," the 381st Infantry's objective. The 383rd would tackle Yuza-Dake, which lay southwest of Yaeju-Dake and on the other side of a broad saddle between the two es-carpments. One thousand yards of exposed ground lay between the 96th Division lines and the brooding heights.

When the attack began the morning of June 10, heavy enemy fire erupted from a ridge west of Yuza Town and from a strongpoint at the base of Yuza-Dake despite the naval gunfire, artillery, and air strikes showered upon the area over three days.

Failing to reach even the base of the escarpment, the 383rd veered toward Yuza-Dake's western end, next to the 1st Marine Division zone and the town of Yuza. On June 11, the 383rd's 2nd Battalion attempted to enter Yuza Town, but was met by a storm of gunfire from the rubble of the town and from Yuza-Dake, which loomed over the town's southern end. After hours of house-to-house fighting, the battalion withdrew from Yuza under intensifying enemy gunfire.[3]

IN APPROACHING THE BIG APPLE on June 10, the 381st first zeroed in on the saddle between Yaeju-Dake and Yuza-Dake. Companies B and C gained the saddle's lower level before dozens of Japanese machine guns stopped further advancement. A smoke screen was laid down so that men who were pinned down in the rice paddies below could reach the saddle step.

The Japanese, however, evidently concluded that the smoke screen was designed to conceal a withdrawal. When the smoke cleared, about one hundred enemy troops could be seen in the open changing into civilian clothing outside of a building. They apparently intended to disguise themselves as civilians in the hope of infiltrating the American lines that night. They never got the chance. Captain Philip Newell, the Company C commander, radioed the building's coordinates to the 361st Field Artillery Battalion, which obliterated it with a flurry of shellfire.

Early June 11, the rest of the 381st's 1st Battalion joined the two companies on the saddle's lower step. The battalion remained there throughout the day without attempting to advance while tanks, warplanes, and artillery plastered cave openings and pillboxes on the Big Apple.[4]

ON JUNE 12, THE 381ST'S 3rd Battalion shifted eastward to where the 17th Infantry early that morning had captured a larger area of Yaeju-Dake. The 381st's Company L then passed through the expanded 7th Division zone and drove west along the top of Yaeju-Dake toward the Big Apple, while its sister Company K worked along the escarpment base. Company L neutralized caves harboring enemy machine-gunners who had pinned down the 1st Battalion on the saddle, and the battalion advanced to a point

closer to the Big Apple. At 1 a.m. June 13, the Japanese counterattacked. The Deadeyes sent up flares.

"Whenever a flare would go up, the Japs would freeze," wrote a platoon leader, a Lieutenant Strand. "We'd run around like Indians, shooting to beat hell. When the flare went out, the Japs would start to run and we'd shoot anything that moved."[5]

Beginning their ascent of Yaeju-Dake from its base, Company K discovered a huge cave that the Japanese had made one of its strongpoints, with two entrances, two firing ports, two pillboxes, and at least three levels connected by ladders. The Americans attacked with automatic weapons, rockets, flamethrowers, grenades, and satchel charges, killing thirty enemy soldiers. Company K then joined Company L on the ridgetop. The 60-foot-high Big Apple loomed above them.

The Big Apple fell to the 381st Infantry on June 14, but Japanese machine-gun and mortar fire from nearby Hill 153 continued to harass the Deadeyes until the 7th Division captured it.

From Big Apple's summit, the end of the island was clearly visible 2 miles in the distance.[6]

WITH WARPLANES, ARTILLERY, AND NAVAL guns providing supporting fire for ground units, it was remarkable that there were not more "friendly fire" casualties than there were. When they occurred—artillerists shelling their own men, air strikes mistakenly targeting American units—they aroused rage and bitterness. A Corsair strafed a half mile of road clogged with American vehicles, killing three men and wounding fifteen. "No matter where the hell you are on this island, a guy isn't safe," said Sergeant Benjamin Capaldi of the 7th Division.

Sometimes, a single mistake led to unintended deaths. Corporal George Peto, a forward observer for the 1st Marines, saw a half dozen Marines hit by incoming mortar fire, and realized another FO had given a mortar squad the wrong coordinates. "He looked over at me and seeing the look on my face, quickly put two and two together. He broke down and cried like a baby," Peto said. "A day or so later, they took him away, shell-shocked, and I never saw him again."[7]

At other times, the circumstances were so bizarre that they left men speechless. Lieutenant Bob Green, whose 763rd Tank Battalion was attached to the 96th Division, had gotten out of his tank behind a hill, near where a mortar squad was shelling enemy soldiers on the reverse slope. A

low-flying Corsair suddenly appeared above the hill crest after completing a bombing run, and a mortar round struck it, blowing off one of its wings, which spiraled down amid shouts of "Heads up! Heads up!" Then, as Green watched in horror, the plane corkscrewed to the ground, and burst into flames. "I will never forget seeing the stricken look on the face of the pilot just before the plane crashed and he died," Green wrote.[8]

More than two months of continual combat had ground down the 96th Division's artillery. "The guns were so badly worn that they weren't accurate," said Private First Class Charles Moynihan of the 361st Field Artillery Battalion. Only one in twelve guns had "any kind of accuracy," he said. Further complicating the artillerists' task was a shortage of forward observers; operating on the front lines, their attrition rate was high. Corporals ended up leading FO sections, and "they were taking anybody they could get to go up there," said Moynihan.[9]

THE 1ST MARINE DIVISION HAD endured a week of misery on its march to southern Okinawa. The torrential rains had caused a breakdown in communications between ground units and their artillery and naval support. Because of the impassable roads, supplies failed to reach the infantry units. Above all, there was mud, mud, mud. At one point, the 1st Marines waded through calf-deep mud that tore the soles off their shoes. They went without rations altogether until the 96th Division's 383rd Regiment took pity on them and shared its K rations.[10]

On June 9, a 7th Marines company attempted to cross the deep gorge through which flowed Mukue Gawa, in order to reach the northern edge of Itoman. A storm of enemy gunfire forced it to withdraw under a smoke screen. Lieutenant Colonel Spencer Berger, who commanded the 2nd Battalion, observed the action from an LVT 100 yards offshore and tried another tack the next day.

Berger sent two companies over a 10-foot seawall. They waded 400 yards to the south across the river estuary, again scaled the seawall, and attacked the enemy-held ridge on Mukue Gawa's south bank. The Marines lost five officers in seven minutes while clearing the ridge and sweeping through Itoman.[11]

By day's end June 10, the 7th Marines occupied the high ground immediately south of the town. The vantage point provided an unimpeded view of the daunting objective before them: Kunishi Ridge, the western anchor of the Japanese defensive line.

On the same day that the 7th Marines seized the hills facing Kunishi, the 1st Marines captured the Japanese outposts to the east that were integral to their future assaults on Yuza-Dake and Kunishi. Lashed by rain, the 1st Battalion attacked Yuza Hill, immediately west of Yuza Town. To reach the hill, the Marines splashed through muddy rice paddies under withering machine-gun and artillery fire, and crossed railroad tracks and a stream, where the Marines hugged the bank to protect themselves from the flying metal.

Corporal Robert Sorenson, a Company C rifleman, recalled, "[I ran] as fast as I could, loaded down with equipment, and feeling like I was barely moving," as bullets kicked up dirt at his heels. "Fate and the long arm of God are really all that is between you and the enemy," he said.

Company C reached Yuza Hill's summit, but lost 70 of its 175 men getting there, including all of its officers, who were killed or wounded. The 1st Battalion's Company B joined it later that day. Mortar, artillery, and machine-gun fire from the Yuza-Dake escarpment plastered the Marine positions all night. At 4 a.m. on June 11, the Marines repulsed a Japanese counterattack, and Company C lost twenty more men. For the next two days, the 1st Battalion clung to Yuza Hill while under constant fire, until the machine guns and mortars on Yuza-Dake were finally silenced.[12]

West of Yuza Hill, the 1st Marines' 2nd Battalion captured another outpost, Hill 69 near Ōzato, and struggled to hold it for two days during furious, frequently hand-to-hand fighting. During the night of June 11–12, an attempt to infiltrate Company E atop the hill escalated into a chaotic counterattack, described in the after-action report as "one of the most exciting nights of the campaign for E Company."

Enemy soldiers had mingled with a large group of civilians who were attempting to pass through the battalion lines. The alarmed Marines discerned that about every fifth person was a Japanese soldier. Their cover blown, fifteen to twenty of them attacked the Marines with fixed bayonets and sabers.

Marine machine guns swept the attackers, eliciting "screams and shouts and general confusion." Company E's commander killed two Japanese soldiers while talking to superiors on a field phone. Two women were shot when they darted from a cave toward the Marines, and were found to be carrying grenades and satchel charges.[13]

AT KUNISHI RIDGE, THE 1ST Marine Division faced Ushijima's most effective remaining unit—the 32nd Regiment of the 24th Division. The

Japanese were entrenched in numerous fortified caves, pillboxes, and tombs on both the forward and reverse slopes of the rugged coral highland. To reach the foot of the escarpment, the Marines would have to cross an exposed 1,000-yard-wide valley of sugarcane fields and rice paddies.

When tank-infantry teams from the 7th Marines' 1st and 2nd Battalions attempted to cross the valley at midday June 11, they were met by a hurricane of direct fire from Kunishi Ridge and enfilading fire from nearby Hill 69. Accurate enemy artillery rounds crashed down on the tanks.

After two hours of futility, Colonel Edward Snedeker, the 7th Marines' commander, ordered a withdrawal. He sought a fresh approach to the familiar tactical problem that Kunishi posed, so much like the Shuri Line's labyrinthian system of mutually supporting positions.[14]

After the attack was suspended, tank driver Robert Boardman shut down his M4 Sherman for the night in a sugarcane field near Kunishi. But in the darkness, the Japanese quietly brought in 76mm antitank guns. At daybreak, "they let us have it, putting shells right through our tank," said Boardman. The ammo loader was killed. Boardman and the assistant driver dragged the wounded commander from the tank—and into a volley of rifle fire from enemy soldiers who had surrounded the tank. The three crewmen were all hit, but because of the enemy's poor marksmanship, they survived. "They were aiming for our heads but, thankfully, the Lord tipped their rifle barrels and the bullets went through our necks instead," said Boardman.[15]

Snedeker rode on an aerial reconnaissance flight later that day over Kunishi Ridge. Air strikes and artillery, naval, and mortar fire had proven ineffective in cracking the enemy strongholds, and the veteran of Guadalcanal and action in Haiti and Nicaragua was seeking creative solutions.

AT 5 P.M. ON JUNE 11, the battle line fell eerily silent. All along the front, American units had stopped firing as a result of a cease-fire ordered by the Tenth Army's commander, General Buckner. The previous day, copies of an appeal written by Buckner had been air-dropped behind Japanese lines. Buckner hoped that the message would persuade General Ushijima to surrender:

> The forces under your command have fought bravely and well, and your infantry tactics have merited the respect of your opponents. . . . Like myself, you are an infantry general long schooled and practiced in infantry warfare. . . . I believe, therefore, that you understand as clearly as

I, that the destruction of all Japanese resistance on the island is merely a matter of days. . . .

A committee of senior Tenth Army officers had gathered at a 7th Marines observation post outside Itoman to await Ushijima's response. Instead of a delegation of Japanese bearing white flags, the Japanese replied to the overture with a mortar barrage that landed on what would have been the surrender site. Hostilities resumed. Ushijima had in fact not received Buckner's letter; it would not reach his headquarters cave until June 17.

Colonel Hiromichi Yahara, the Thirty-Second Army's operations officer, later wrote that when General Ushijima did read the letter, he smiled broadly and said, "The enemy has made me an expert on infantry warfare." Staff officers were "unimpressed," and treated the communication "lightly," Yahara said. Buckner's appeal was "an affront to Japanese tradition"— meaning the samurai tradition that did not brook surrender. No response was sent.[16]

Even after three years of combat in the Pacific, US leaders yet believed that the Japanese on Okinawa, cut off from reinforcement and facing annihilation, might reasonably choose life over death. German and Italian soldiers had done so in the European theater, surrendering by the thousands.

The difference was cultural. Nippon's ancient Bushido code judged being taken prisoner on the battlefield to be an ignominious crime. Death in battle or by one's own hand was not only preferable, it was obligatory— the battlefield being a place only for the binary choices of victory or death.

This mind-set was ingrained in the Thirty-Second Army's men from General Ushijima down to the lowest private. Most of them, too, recognized the cold reality of their plight as the Thirty-Second Army's losses mounted week after week: that they were going to be sacrificed. The more perceptive understood why: to inflict heavy losses on the Allies and prolong the war, thereby compelling them to abandon their demand for unconditional surrender and to negotiate. Failing that, drawing out the campaign would at least buy time for Japan to prepare its mainland defenses for the anticipated massive Allied amphibious assault.

At the campaign's onset, Imperial Japanese Headquarters sent a message wishing the Thirty-Second Army "the best of luck in the coming battle and deeply regretting the fact that it as being forced to fight a large-scale action on such slender resources," said Akira Shima, General Chō's secretary. The message was received with "bitter amusement," he said.

The two Japanese counteroffensives caused excitement and hope to briefly flare in Tokyo. Emperor Hirohito sent a note of encouragement during the Thirty-Second Army's second counteroffensive on May 4: "We really want this attack to succeed." Like the April counteroffensive, it, too, failed.

For its part, the Thirty-Second Army faithfully radioed "battle lessons" to Imperial Headquarters. These were compilations of Thirty-Second Army and unit battle reports. Included were comments about the adversaries' tactics and suggestions on how to improve combat techniques, with the goal of helping Japan prepare for the mainland invasion.

But with one exception, "exhortations and encouraging words" were the extent of Tokyo's contribution to the campaign after it began. The 6th Air Army's unsuccessful airborne attack on Yontan Airfield on May 24 was the only tangible assistance provided. Ushijima's many appeals to Tokyo for more men and aid went for naught. A promise of six battalions of airborne infantry arriving by glider in early June—they never did—constituted the balance of Tokyo's contributions after the fighting began, said Shima.

Japanese prisoners also reported that Imperial Headquarters spoke of a two-division counterlanding on June 20 or June 23, supported by the Japanese Fleet and five hundred warplanes. The Japanese high command evidently hoped that this pipe dream would spur Okinawa's defenders to fight harder. Some Japanese soldiers might have believed it, but their commanders assuredly did not.[17]

In the meantime, the Kiyan Peninsula's defenders were facing extinction.

AFTER THE FAILURE OF HIS regiment's tank-infantry assault on Kunishi and his aerial reconnaissance flight, Colonel Snedeker recognized that flanking attacks would be of no use, and that a frontal attack would result in a bloody repulse. But he came up with another idea. When the 1st Marine Division's commander, General Pedro del Valle, came to Snedeker's command post later June 11 to discuss how to break through the Kunishi barrier, "stop our heavy losses and get on with the war," Snedeker recommended a night attack across the cane field. Del Valle liked Snedeker's daring plan.

The assault began at 3:30 a.m. June 12, the same hour that the 17th Regiment was attacking Yaeju-Dake's eastern extremity 2 miles away. Two 7th Marines assault battalions, the 1st and the 2nd, led respectively by Companies C and F, marched down both sides of a road that crossed the exposed

valley to the ridge. In the darkness, they were guided by the telephone poles bordering the road.

These Marines had never made a night attack, and many were extremely skeptical about whether it would work. "We thought someone had gone nuts," said rifleman Charles Owens. Lieutenant Winston Huff, the Company F commander, said, "From my jarhead worm's-eye view, it was a terrible idea." He later acknowledged that it turned out to be "a bright idea because it succeeded."

Moving in silence without artillery preparation and in complete darkness—flares and other illumination were prohibited—the two assault companies reached Kunishi's crest without encountering serious resistance.[18]

Problems developed when Companies B and G attempted to cross the wide, flat valley floor to reinforce the two assault companies. The Japanese spotted them at daybreak and pinned them down. As the day wore on, the reinforcements tried three times to reach the ridgetop under smoke screens. Every attempt failed.[19]

The two companies on the ridge were shelled and machine-gunned, and they began to run out of water and ammunition. Casualties mounted. Only a tank stood any chance of crossing the valley without being shot to pieces.

Tank-infantry teams being useless until the enemy's intensive gunfire could be suppressed, the 1st Marine Tank Battalion became a resupply-evacuation unit. Major Robert Neiman, the tank battalion's executive officer, supervised the transformation. Three crewmen were removed from each tank, leaving only the driver and the tank commander—and enough room for up to six infantrymen, and supplies, weapons, and ammunition.

With bullets and shrapnel from mortars and artillery pinging off their armored hulls, the M4 medium tanks trundled down the road across the exposed valley. Arriving at the escarpment, the reinforcements left the tanks through the belly escape hatches, where supplies were also unloaded. Wounded men crawled into the tanks through the belly hatches while the stretchers of the more severely wounded were lashed to the tank hulls behind sandbags to protect them from enemy snipers.

Nine tanks completed three runs on June 12, bringing fifty-four replacements to the front line. For an entire week at Kunishi Ridge, this was standard operating procedure, with the wounded evacuated along with many of the dead. Using a primitive airstrip near Itoman, VMO observation planes flew 641 Marines who had been wounded on Kunishi Ridge to rear-echelon hospitals. The flights lasted a mere eight minutes, eliminating

hours of jostling travel over bad roads in ambulance jeeps. The innovation improved upon Okinawa's already efficient system of processing and evacuating wounded men—a procedure that had reduced the campaign's mortality rate to half that of previous Pacific war battles, and nearly to the European theater's 2.8 percent rate.

The dead were deposited in a place behind the front lines. Rifleman Earl Rice helped carry his friend there. His body was laid on a pile of dead Marines. "The pile was over five feet, and at least up to my shoulders if not higher. It was a helluva feeling to put that guy on there."[20]

Under cover of darkness, large groups of reinforcements crossed the valley without drawing heavy enemy fire. More 7th Marines companies ascended the escarpment during the night of June 12–13.

DETERMINED TO REPAIR THE TENTH Army's breach of his last defensive line, General Ushijima dispatched two battalions of the 62nd Infantry Division—the Army's last reserves—to the shattered 44th IMB with orders to wrest the eastern part of Yaeju-Dake from the 7th Division. The 44th IMB's late commander, General Shigaro Suzuki, had said in his final message to army headquarters before he was killed:

Flowers dying gracefully on Hill 109,
Will bloom again amid the Kudan trees.[21]

In naming General Takeo Fujioka to command both the 62nd Division and the 44th IMB, Ushijima attempted to stiffen the spines of the men in those units. "The enemy in the 44th IMB sector has finally penetrated our main line of resistance," Ushijima's June 12 order began. "The plan of the 44th IMB is to annihilate, with its main strength, the enemy penetrating the Yaeju-Dake sector. The army will undertake to reoccupy and hold its Main Line of Resistance to the death."

To reinforce the collapsing eastern line, Colonel Hiromichi Yahara scraped the bottom of the barrel in order to send an assortment of men who nearly all lacked basic infantry combat training. They included two companies of the 36th Communications Regiment; two companies of artillerists; about one hundred construction workers; and the 11th Sea Raiding Squadron, supported by 1,500 Okinawa conscripts. The reinforcements totaled nearly six thousand men.

The local conscripts were armed with bamboo spears, ridiculous substitutes for the antitank weapons they were supposed to have. During their

first day in action, "all vanished like morning dew" amid the crash of gunfire from US ships, artillery batteries, and warplanes.[22]

"It was frustrating to see our men being killed by a well-equipped enemy, while we had nothing left to fight with," Yahara wrote later in *The Battle for Okinawa.*

Local commanders began to balk at orders to reinforce disintegrating units. Two days after being ordered to Yaeju-Dake, the 15th Independent Infantry Battalion had still not moved. "We can no longer hold our front line," said a Colonel Kidani, the 24th Division's chief of staff.

When Kidani tried to organize a counterattack that included the 15th Battalion, "they would not do it. This is totally incomprehensible!" General Ushijima intervened directly, ordering the 15th Battalion commander, Major Nagameshi, to "advance immediately . . . and take offensive action." Nagameshi's superior, General Suzuki, objected to the order, but made sure that it was carried out.[23]

The 24th Division's 89th Infantry, which had led the counteroffensive against the 7th Division in early May, was disbanded by its commander, Colonel Hitoshi Kanayama, when the regiment was ordered to join in an all-out counterattack. With fewer than one hundred men left, Kanayama burned the regimental colors and exhorted his men not to kill themselves, although Kanayama and his adjutant later committed suicide.[24]

A 44th IMB commander appeared unexpectedly before Yahara to report, "The brigade is finished. Our right flank has collapsed. We can fight no more. I regret to report that unit commanders are crying aloud as they watch their men dying in vain. Whatever we do we cannot stop the enemy."[25]

After-action reports showed that increasing numbers of Japanese soldiers were killing themselves, despite the Thirty-Second Army's efforts to discourage suicides and exhort troops to fight on. A captured document revealed this change. It instructed soldiers, if separated from their units, to fight to the death, killing as many enemy troops as possible—and to not take their own lives.[26]

THE 7TH DIVISION PUSHED BEYOND Hill 95 to Hill 153, described as "the essential point" of the Thirty-Second Army's last bastion on the eastern line. The 500-yard-long hill rose 30 to 50 feet above the surrounding terrain and stood in an open area. General Ushijima's command post inside Hill 89 was a short distance away and near Hill 115, a bulge on a mile-long ridge fiercely defended by the remnants of the 44th IMB and the 62nd Division.

Tanks and infantrymen began blasting and burning the Japanese from the hills' caves, crevices, and holes. Flushed from their hiding places, the enemy soldiers were machine-gunned.

The 32nd Infantry's Company G reached the summit of Hill 115 on June 16, but with just thirty-one effectives remaining. During the long night, they fended off repeated Japanese counterattacks from three sides. When reinforcements arrived at daybreak June 17, they still clung to Hill 115.

The June 16 journal entry of Sergeant Benjamin Capaldi described the shocking battlefield sights and smells that he witnessed while acting as a 32nd Infantry runner. "The smell is terrible, hundreds of dead Japs. Just stinking corpses with millions of maggots eating the flesh, whole bodies, half bodies, arms, pieces of hands and legs, even dead civilians who got in the way of this bloody battle," he said. Prolonged exposure to wholesale death made him fatalistic. "Bullets were flying around in every direction and after a while a guy doesn't even bother to duck anymore."

The 17th Infantry launched a two-battalion attack against Hill 153 on a 1,500-yard front early June 15. Led by two tank platoons, a platoon of assault guns, and three flame tanks, the 1st Battalion had little trouble advancing 900 yards under sporadic artillery and mortar fire. But Japanese gunners inside the coral heads stymied the 2nd Battalion with murderous rifle, machine-gun, and knee-mortar fire. The stubborn resistance prevented the 17th from capturing the hill until June 17.[27]

After Hill 153 fell, Ushijima ordered a battalion to retake it before morning June 18 while noting, "It is very painful to the Commanding General of the Army that the orders sent out from time to time . . . concerning that hill have been disregarded." But the 7th Division's 184th Infantry crushed the would-be counterattack before it began, destroying the assault force at the bottom of Hill 153. More than one hundred bodies were counted. In the personal effects of one of the dead soldiers, the Americans found a copy of Ushijima's attack order.[28]

For days, gunboats, artillery fire, and air strikes pounded on the door of Ushijima's headquarters inside Hill 89. General Buckner tersely noted in his diary, "Dropped 45 plane loads of napalm on reported location of enemy army CP." No safe havens remained for the Japanese as the American juggernaut swept down the island.[29]

THE 96TH DIVISION'S RELENTLESS ONSLAUGHT on Yuza-Dake ground down what remained of the Japanese 24th Division. "They did not

surrender, but died where they fought," Private First Class Donald Dencker of the 382nd Infantry wrote of the fighting on June 17. "All morning, we were shelling, burning, grenading, and blasting Japanese positions with satchel charges as we slowly advanced."

To conquer Yuza-Dake's western end, the 382nd's 1st Battalion had to first scale a 75-foot vertical cliff. Japanese defenders near the rim fired at the first two men who came over the top, but two companies reached the crest right behind them and killed about a hundred fleeing enemy soldiers. A man attempting to climb Yuza-Dake's southeast slope snagged a tripwire. A huge explosion injured twenty-seven soldiers.

Colonel Yahara wrote that three 24th Division regiments were caught in the Americans' pincers. "They fought to the last man, and the enemy captured the Yuza hilltop on June 17."[30]

Artillery spotters with the 96th Division observed a large number of enemy troops to the south in the village of Makabe. A "time on target" artillery concentration was ordered—using 264 guns from twenty-two Army and Marine batteries. It was believed to be the single largest concentration of the Pacific war. Two hundred sixty-four shells landed on the target simultaneously, wiping out the enemy soldiers, nearby civilians, and most of Makabe Village.[31]

The Thirty-Second Army was hemorrhaging a thousand men per day, and the toll was rising. The surviving troops were being squeezed into a smaller area at the island's southern tip, where American tanks forced them from cover to be killed. During the eight-day period from June 10 to June 17, the 7th Division claimed to have killed 4,288 Japanese soldiers.

There was no possibility of the enemy being resupplied or reinforced; US warships and aircraft had completely isolated the beleaguered defenders. The Thirty-Second Army still clung to important parts of the Kiyan defensive line, but the Tenth Army now occupied footholds on the escarpments, from one end of the island to the other.[32]

Although the Thirty-Second Army would never receive replacements, the Tenth Army was getting truckloads of them to offset its soaring casualties. Every week, green soldiers who had not yet been in combat took the places of veterans—with predictably tragic consequences. Lieutenant Robert Muehrcke, a platoon leader with the 383rd Infantry, described a new captain who arrived wearing an Army poncho over clean battle fatigues. "He was freshly shaven. The entire 1st Platoon was soaked and filthy."

"Where are the Japs?" the captain asked. Someone pointed the way, and the captain began walking in that direction.

"A single shot by a sniper killed him," said Muehrcke. "We never knew his name."[33]

TWO 7TH MARINES ASSAULT BATTALIONS were now atop Kunishi Ridge and engaged in "some of the worst, most vicious fighting we ever encountered on Okinawa," in the words of one Marine. Not helping was the fact that Japanese soldiers driven from Yaeju-Dake and Yuza-Dake by the 96th Division had joined the Kunishi Ridge defenders.

At 3 a.m. on June 14, assault companies from the 1st Marines began crossing the valley prefatory to joining the 7th Marines on Kunishi. However, flares fired by adjacent units illuminated the attackers, alerting the Japanese, who opened fire. Two Company E platoons managed to reach Kunishi's crest, where they, like their 7th Marines comrades, became dependent on tanks for water and to evacuate their wounded. After nightfall, Company F joined E on the ridge.[34]

Lieutenant Marcus Jaffe, commander of a 1st Marines company, described the carnage atop Kunishi Ridge in a letter home, adding, "Fortunately for my peace of mind (though the sorrow will exist for others), the personnel of this company and battalion has changed so much in the past month that very few of the dead are good friends of mine."[35]

General Pedro del Valle, the 1st Marine Division commander, was struck by the strangeness of the situation at Kunishi Ridge, "one of those tactical oddities of this peculiar warfare. We were on the ridge. The Japs were in it, both on the forward and reverse slopes."[36]

ON JUNE 16, THE 1ST Marines went into reserve for a needed rest. During twelve days of combat—at Hill 59, Yuza Hill, and Kunishi Ridge—20 officers and 471 enlisted men from the 1st Marines had been killed or wounded. During the first night at the Company K rest-area bivouac, all was relatively quiet—until an enemy soldier rolled a grenade down a hill into the encampment. When it exploded, three Marines were wounded. At first light, the injured Marines' angry comrades went hunting for the attacker. When they found him, "they riddled the shit out of him," wrote a Company K Marine.[37]

PRIVATE FIRST CLASS SLEDGE, A 5th Marines mortarman, was reminded of the coral ridges of Peleliu when his regiment marched south to Yuza-Dake. On their right was Kunishi Ridge; on their left, Yaeju-Dake,

where they heard sirens blaring from the Army tanks—an attempt to unnerve the Japanese. Sledge thought it ludicrous. "The Japanese rarely surrendered in the face of flamethrowers, artillery, bombs, or anything else, so I didn't understand how harmless sirens would bother them." Their wailing quickly became tiresome.[38]

Sledge's Company K was detached from the 3rd Battalion and temporarily transferred to the 5th Marines' 2nd Battalion, now on Kunishi Ridge. Company K crossed the open ground below the escarpment during the predawn hours of June 17, and the Cape Gloucester and Peleliu veterans didn't like it one bit. "We were stubborn in our belief that nobody but the Japanese, or damned fools, moved around at night." As they approached Kunishi Ridge crest, its silhouette against the sky reminded Sledge of Bloody Nose Ridge on Peleliu and "my knees nearly buckled."

For some Marines, Kunishi was one ridge too many. Sledge saw a distraught lieutenant, stroking his hair obsessively, telling his gunnery sergeant that he couldn't take it anymore. He saw a Peleliu veteran suddenly grab his rifle and, babbling incoherently, start toward the ridgetop. Certain that the man would be shot dead in seconds, Sledge and a sergeant tackled him. A corpsman led the man away, sobbing and trembling. Sledge's company lost 50 men in twenty-two hours on Yuza-Dake and Kunishi, leaving it with roughly 50 combat-capable men—21 percent of its normal strength of 235.[39]

"We were all thinking the same thing," said Sergeant R. V. Burgin, who was Sledge's mortar-squad leader. "If Okinawa was this bad, how bloody was it going to be fighting the Japs on their home ground?"[40]

MARINE TANKS THAT HAD GOTTEN behind Kunishi Ridge were shooting up the reverse slope as the 5th and 7th Marines began clearing caves with flamethrowers and satchel charges.

A troublesome Hotchkiss 88mm antitank gun that had been moved from cave to cave stymied the 1st Marine Tank Battalion's efforts. It was finally knocked out when an intelligence officer flying over the area in an observation plane spotted the gun after it had just fired, radioed tanks on the ground with its location, and marked the spot with smoke. A Marine tank company destroyed the gun. However, before the intelligence officer returned to base, a machine-gun burst from the ground hit him in the knee. The officer later lost his leg.[41]

Even after enemy gun positions in caves were wiped out, lone Japanese snipers concealed in piles of rocks remained a menace. One particularly

adept sharpshooter who had hidden himself well in a pocket atop Kunishi nicknamed "The Pinnacle" killed or wounded twenty-two Marines before he was located and killed.

Enemy fire from Yuza-Dake, which had not yet been secured by the 96th Division, harassed the Marines as they applied "blowtorch and corkscrew" methods to Kunishi's many caves and pillboxes.

After an interpreter failed to persuade enemy soldiers to leave a pillbox, demolition men with satchel charges were summoned. One of them crawled to the top of the pillbox and threw a satchel through the portal, flushing six Japanese. A Marine with a Thompson submachine gun killed them when they dashed into the open.[42]

On June 16, the 6th Marine Division's 22nd Regiment entered the 1st Marine Division lines preparatory to a major attack planned the next morning by III Amphibious Corps. The 8th Regiment of the 2nd Marine Division, which had been in reserve on Saipan since its feint toward the southern coast on L-Day, was attached to the 1st Division—the 2nd Division's first time in action on Okinawa proper.

During the furious battle for Kunishi Ridge, the 1st Marine Tank Battalion had carried 90 tons of supplies and 550 reinforcements to the front, and had returned with hundreds of wounded men. Flame tanks had expended 37,000 gallons of petroleum in scouring strongpoint caves and defensive positions. Japanese antitank guns and satchel charges, however, had taken a toll: twenty-two tanks had been destroyed or badly damaged.[43]

Shrouded in clouds of gun smoke from artillery and tank fire, air strikes, and mortar rounds, mile-long Kunishi Ridge had been the setting for Okinawa's last pitched battle. As fate would have it, the 1st Marine Division, the first American division to go into combat in World War II, would be the last to fight a major battle. Its five-day struggle to capture Kunishi Ridge cost the division 1,105 killed and wounded.[44]

AT 7:30 A.M. ON JUNE 17, the Marines advanced on some of southern Okinawa's last remaining Japanese bastions—Mezado Ridge 600 yards to the south of Kunishi Ridge, and the nearby town of Mezado. Japanese resistance was noticeably weaker, although stubborn pockets remained. The 7th and 22nd Marines seized Mezado Ridge and entered the town. Hills 69 and 52 also fell. A last-ditch Japanese counterattack failed and added a large body count to the staggering enemy losses. After Mezado's capture, the 8th Marines relieved the 7th.

AT THE END OF THE day on June 17, the Tenth Army held the Kiyan Peninsula's escarpments from the cliffs near General Ushijima's headquarters, to Yaeju-Dake, Yuza-Dake, and Kunishi Ridge in the west. The Americans occupied the heights overlooking the last 8 square miles of Japanese-held territory, including the towns of Medeera and Makabe. The Tenth Army could now clearly see the place 2 miles distant where Okinawa's southern tip met the sea.[45]

"We have passed the speculative phase of the campaign and are down to the final kill," General Buckner told newspaper correspondents on June 17.[46]

Its numbers melting away by the hour under the crash of American projectiles from the land, sea, and air—natives called it "*tetsa nobofu,*" or "typhoon of steel"—the Thirty-Second Army was finished as a fighting force. Lacking weapons and ammunition, some enemy soldiers were practically reduced to "indignantly assaulting enemy tanks with clenched teeth and naked fists," said a Japanese staff officer.[47]

The enemy's telephone connections were broken, and only occasional radio messages were getting through. That left messengers as the last option, meaning hours often elapsed between when an order was given and when it was delivered—if the runner survived the gantlet of gunfire.

Consequently, the Thirty-Second Army's leaders often learned long after the event of commanders killed and battalions wiped out. "It was grim and disheartening," wrote Colonel Yahara. When Yahara learned that US tanks had rolled into Komesu Village, south of Makabe, he conceded, "The collapse of our entire army was imminent."

"So much for that," was the reaction of General Isamu Chō, the Thirty-Second Army's chief of staff, when told that both flanks of his defensive line had collapsed. It was dismaying, but unsurprising to the Japanese commanders, who had expected their attritional strategy to bring them to this point.[48]

But spotty organized resistance persisted. As General Pedro del Valle had observed, while the Americans were *on* the escarpments, the Japanese remained *in* them—in pillboxes, crevices, and caves large and small that they shared with thousands of civilians.

The battle would continue until every last cave was neutralized or sealed with explosives.

The Civilian Tragedy

They were pitiful-looking people, half-starved, very little clothing, and very sick-looking.

—CORPORAL HUBERT WELCH OF THE 29TH MARINES,
DESCRIBING THE OKINAWA CIVILIAN REFUGEES[1]

Masses of wounded were lying all over the place, many of them covered in blood and crying for help. It was a scene straight from hell.

—SCENES WITNESSED BY TOMIKO HIGA DURING THE
EIGHT-YEAR-OLD'S ODYSSEY THROUGH SOUTHERN OKINAWA[2]

There wasn't anything easy about any of it. . . . Everything was compressed at the south end of the island and it was a slaughter.

—LIEUTENANT DAVID STRAUS OF THE
1ST MARINE DIVISION, DESCRIBING THE
FINAL WEEKS OF BATTLE IN SOUTHERN OKINAWA[3]

LARGELY IGNORING WARNINGS BY THE Americans and Japanese to seek the safety of the Chinen Peninsula—just thirteen thousand found their way there—or the island's west coast highway, many Okinawans had done exactly what they should not have: followed Ushijima's army to its last stand on the Kiyan Peninsula.[4]

Trapped between the furiously battling armies, they were killed in caves and shot while trying—too late—to flee to the northern part of the island. Civilian deaths soared in June as a consequence.

When the civilians first began attempting to slip through the American lines and leave the combat zone, US troops allowed them to pass. But when Japanese soldiers began dressing as Okinawan civilians and infiltrating the lines with concealed weapons, the lenient policy ended. Civilians were warned not to approach Tenth Army lines at night for any reason. When they did, they were killed by the score and by the hundred. They died, too, when the Japanese used them as human shields.

"Unfortunately, then we had to shoot them," Norris Buchter of the 29th Marines said. "That's when a lot of poor Okinawans got killed." When the Americans tried to hold their fire, the Japanese would sometimes force the issue by killing the civilians, igniting a firefight with the Americans that ended with most of the civilians dead.[5]

Japanese soldiers also weaponized the civilians by jamming primed grenades under their arms and forcing them to approach American soldiers. "They would come up to us and as soon as we got around them, they would raise their arms and those grenades would fly out and they would go off and they would commit suicide and they also would kill or wound the American soldiers," said Sergeant Raymond Maxwell of the 77th Division.[6]

When Joe Drago, a machine-gunner with the 22nd Marines, and his comrades seized two wagons filled with women's clothing and wigs, they fully expected Japanese soldiers disguised as women to attempt to infiltrate their lines. That night, someone shot an elderly man walking down the road toward the Marine positions. Then, scores of civilians approached. Drago and his squad leader jumped into the middle of the road with drawn .45s, ordering them to stop.

Someone in the crowd panicked and ran, and others raced after them. The Marines opened fire. Drago and his squad leader ran to their machine gun and directed a swarm of bullets at the fleeing civilians. Throughout the long night, screams and moans of pain were silenced by more gunfire. Daylight illuminated the result: hundreds of dead women, children, and old men. Drago and his comrades never discussed the incident.[7]

Patrick Almond's 4th Marines squad was camped on a road late one dark night when a large group of civilians approached. Behind them, Japanese soldiers in kimonos prodded the civilians toward the Marine lines.

Ordered to not let the group pass, the Marines opened fire. The enemy soldiers who attempted to return fire with rifles hidden under their kimonos were shot down. Wounded and dying civilians "were screaming and crying," wrote Almond. "There was a little baby strapped to a woman's back crying all night."

Under orders not to approach the wounded civilians in the dark, the Marines waited until daylight. They found about thirty civilians and ten Japanese soldiers dead in the road—and the baby alive in a shell crater that was half filled with water. "We all marveled at her," said Almond, "and someone gave her some candy."[8]

EIGHT-YEAR-OLD TOMIKO HIGA; HER TWO sisters, seventeen-year-old Yoshiko and thirteen-year-old Hatsuko; and their nine-year-old brother, Chokuyu, lived with their father on a farm near Shuri. Their father provided food for a Japanese signal corps unit. On the day of the massive US offensive, May 11, their father left home and never returned.

The four children, led by Yoshiko, headed south, traveling only at night. Death was everywhere. "Masses of wounded were lying all over the place, many of them covered in blood and crying for help. It was a scene straight from hell," wrote Tomiko.[9]

Eight days after quitting their farm, a stray bullet killed Chokuyu while he and Tomiko slept in a hole as shells and bullets fell around them. The older sisters buried him. Not long afterward, Tomiko became separated from her sisters in a group of refugees on the beach at Komesu. Tomiko was now alone.[10]

She awakened very hungry one morning, not having eaten in a day, and saw a line of black ants leading to a dead Japanese soldier. "His belly was swollen up like a balloon, and there was a terrible smell," she said. But in his haversack she found her favorite sugar drops. Thereafter, the eight-year-old routinely pillaged the packs of the dead, careful to first make sure they were indeed dead. "I always felt the dead soldiers were my friends," she wrote in her memoir.[11]

Along a riverbank, the girl saw many dead civilians, including mothers with dead children on their backs. Corpses floated in the water. Walking upstream, Tomiko passed "masses of corpses . . . There were people as far as the eye could see . . . they were all dead." When no more corpses were visible, Tomiko stopped and put her hand in the water for a drink. She recoiled; the water was infested with maggots. But she was thirsty, and

she parted the maggots with her hands and drank. When she had finished, "I wiped something away that was tickling my mouth and chin, and four or five maggots fell into the water."[12]

After wandering for weeks, the girl entered a cave. Inside were a man whose hands and feet had been amputated, and his blind wife. Tomiko cared for the elderly couple. When she told them that she wanted to die in the cave with them, they insisted that it was her duty to live. They fashioned a white flag from a torn loincloth, placed it on a stick, and ordered her to leave. She marched down a path with the flag toward some American soldiers. An Army combat photographer took a picture of her that was distributed to newspapers and magazines under the caption, "The Girl with the White Flag," dated June 25. At a refugee camp, Tomiko was reunited with her sisters.[13]

THE WAR DEPARTMENT HAD WARNED troops on their way to Okinawa that, because Japanese propaganda had turned public opinion against them, they should expect the island's civilians to be hostile and distrustful. The Army prepared as best it could to win over the large population of 450,000 civilians by training interpreters, assigning teams with water and medical supplies to combat units to care for sick and wounded civilians, and preparing to build refugee compounds. At the latter facilities, they envisioned mayors and village councils supervising sanitation, labor, food distribution, and land cultivation. But no amount of careful planning could undo the intensive propaganda that had made the civilians fear and hate the Americans.[14]

Indeed, the Japanese had convinced Okinawan civilians that the Americans would rape them, draw and quarter them, and crush their bodies with tanks. Death as a combatant, or by suicide, was preferable to becoming a prisoner, the Japanese told them.

Thousands of civilians burrowed into caves to escape the firestorm outside, but the caves proved to be as much prison as sanctuary. Often forced to share space with Japanese soldiers, the civilians were threatened with death if they attempted to surrender. Trapped between their fear of the Americans and the Japanese, they remained in the caves until hunger, gunfire, or explosives forced them into the open.[15]

During the campaign's early days, if an interpreter's shouted demand for surrender into a cave mouth was ignored, Americans followed up with explosives, flamethrowers, TNT, or gasoline. But when they realized that their "blowtorch and corkscrew" tactics were killing many noncombatants,

they tried harder to spare civilian lives—by using interpreters more often, and substituting smoke grenades for phosphorus grenades to empty out caves where civilians were believed to be hiding.[16]

During the attack on Ushijima's last defensive line, Marines asked Naha's former police chief to coax a Japanese schoolteacher and her Naha Primary School class from a cave near the capital where they had hidden for sixty days. The police chief attempted to reassure the schoolteacher that neither she nor the children would be harmed, but she refused to surrender unless either General Ushijima or General Chō gave his permission. Returning to the cave after the failed parley, the teacher detonated a powerful bomb that blew the top off the hill and sealed the cave with her and thirty children inside.[17]

Private First Class Jack London of the 7th Division's 17th Infantry crawled into caves occupied by civilians while telling them in a soft, soothing voice that they would not be harmed. Once he was inside the cave, "I would reach out to a child, coaxing it with a piece of candy to come to me," he said. "With the child in my grip, I would leave the cave, followed by the mother of the child. The other relatives would join the exodus." London used this stratagem repeatedly with great success.[18]

A boy of about seven and his younger sister summoned the courage to come out of a cave upon the urging of Corporal Dan Lawler, a 5th Marines machine-gunner. "They were both so scared they were shaking, and their clothes were streaked with dried blood," said Lawler. They refused Lawler's proffered K-ration chocolate bar, until he bit off a corner of it and chewed it. The boy took the chocolate, broke off a piece for his sister, and ate the rest. He shouted something into the cave, and up to eight Okinawans emerged. They, too, accepted chocolate—after the Marines reassured them by eating some of it first.[19]

Other efforts were less successful. Sergeant Benjamin Capaldi of the 32nd Infantry and some comrades crawled into a cave and encountered a woman of about twenty-five calmly smoking a cigarette. Her leg had been blown off at the knee. "She picked up her leg above her head and started jabbering in Jap," he said. "We left. There was nothing we could do."[20]

Dick Thom, the operations officer for the 96th Division's 381st Infantry, ordered a tank to fire its machine guns at fifteen people wearing tan uniforms in a rice paddy. They were all killed. "I found out they had been in the home guard, like Boy Scouts," said Thom. "They had all deserted, but they didn't know enough to discard the uniforms."[21]

In southern Okinawa in June, eighteen-year-old Howard Terry of the 29th Marines was spending a sleepless night alone in a water-filled hole when he saw a head pop up in front of him. Reflexively, "I blew it away, and the next morning I found to my dismay it was a little boy with a surrender ticket in his hand." The incident haunted Terry for decades.[22]

In the small town of Gushikami, 7th Division soldiers found a sick Okinawan girl in a courtyard and began bringing her food and water. They later learned that the girl was in fact a disguised Japanese soldier. "Someone quietly cut our prisoner's throat," said Lieutenant Donald Fitzgerald of the 184th Infantry.[23]

From the islet of Keise Shima, 11 miles southwest of the Hagushi beaches, Edmund Austin's 532nd Field Artillery battery supported the L-Day assault and the Tenth Army's advances southward. Austin and his comrades often occupied an observation post near a small shack that had been used by the Japanese. When they entered the shack one day, they saw a pan containing hot grease sitting on the stove.

Realizing that civilians were evidently using the shack, the Americans drew a clock on a surrender pamphlet to show that they would return at eight o'clock the next morning. They left the pamphlet in plain sight.

The next morning, four Okinawans were waiting for them. The artillerists escorted them to a truck that took them to a unit that received displaced people.

It was just the beginning. "It got to be quite a surrender place," said Austin. "The women were scared to death," but hunger compelled them to take their chances with the Americans.[24]

THE AMERICANS NICKNAMED THE GAUNT, impoverished civilian refugees "Okies," because they reminded them of the Dust Bowl migrants of the 1930s. Some were so weak from hunger or illness that they could not walk, but had to crawl on their hands and knees.

"They were pitiful-looking people, half-starved, very little clothing, and very sick-looking," wrote Corporal Hubert Welch of the 29th Marines. When coaxed into surrendering and taken to the barbed wire–enclosed compounds, they were given captured rice and K- and C-rations. *Time* magazine correspondent Robert Sherrod described what he saw when he toured one of the camps: "There were about 1,200 men and women and most of them were suffering from severe cases of malnutrition, which would take a lifetime to cure."[25]

THE 2ND DIVISION'S 8TH MARINES had arrived at Okinawa on May 30 after spending two months on Saipan. On L-Day, the 2nd Division had approached Minatoga's beaches in landing craft, but then had veered away without going ashore. The feint had kept the Japs guessing about the Tenth Army's primary landing place.

Later, the 8th Marines seized two small, unoccupied islands, Iheya and Aguni, north and west of Okinawa. Admiral Richmond Kelly Turner planned to establish radar warning stations on the islands, thereby reducing the number of picket ships positioned around Okinawa; picket ships had taken a beating from Japanese warplanes and kamikazes. Turner said that in the future outlying islands should be captured sooner to reduce ship losses.[26]

After landing on Okinawa, the 8th Marines were attached to the 1st Marine Division, to augment the division's depleted regiments. It was the first fresh infantry unit introduced into the campaign in two months.

By early June 18, the 8th Marines were poised to launch their first offensive on the island.[27]

At midday, General Buckner joined the 8th Marines' commander, Colonel Clarence Wallace, at the regimental observation post on Mezado Ridge, 600 yards south of Kunishi Ridge, to watch Wallace's regiment go into action. Tank-infantry teams were already crossing the valley south of Mezado in their attack on Ibaru Ridge.

Glinting in the sunlight on Buckner's helmet were three stars denoting his general rank. At the observation post, officers almost always wore helmet covers with their ranks painted on them in black, making them difficult for enemy snipers to see. On Ibaru Ridge, Japanese observers had undoubtedly discerned that a high-ranking officer was nearby. Buckner waved to some Marines from the South, who let out a rebel yell when they saw him, aware that Buckner's father had led Confederate troops at Fort Donelson, Perryville, and Chickamauga.

Wallace suggested that Buckner remove his helmet and put on a less-conspicuous one. He initially refused. Then, Wallace's radio operator said the regiment's operations officer had told him that the three-star helmet was plainly visible to anyone looking at the observation post. Buckner smiled, removed his helmet, and donned an unmarked helmet.

Two minutes later, a Japanese artillery shell exploded on a coral rock outcropping to Buckner's left. Shell and rock fragments struck Buckner in the chest, and he fell. Placed on a stretcher, the general held out his right

hand in a gesture suggesting he wanted to be helped to his feet. No one came forward.

Then, a company runner, Private First Class Harry Sarkisian, bent down and grasped the general's outstretched hand. Holding his hand tightly, Sarkisian repeatedly said, "You are going home, General; you are homeward bound." Someone began reciting the 23rd Psalm as Buckner died.[28]

When Buckner's death was reported to Thirty-Second Army headquarters, General Chō and the staff officers were elated, but General Ushijima was not. "He looked grim, as if mourning Buckner's death," wrote Colonel Yahara, the army's operations officer. "Ushijima never spoke ill of others. I had always felt he was a great man."[29]

General Roy Geiger, III Amphibious Corps's commander, a Marine for thirty-eight years, and a veteran of Guadalcanal, Bougainville, Guam, and Peleliu, became the Tenth Army's interim commander. On June 24, General Douglas MacArthur chose General Joseph "Vinegar Joe" Stilwell—so nicknamed because of his outspoken intolerance of failure and duplicity—to replace Buckner. Geiger's short tenure as Tenth Army commander marked the only instance of a Marine commanding a field army.[30]

Three days after Buckner was killed, the 8th Marines overran what remained of the Japanese lines on Okinawa's southern tip, eager to avenge the general's death. "We threw caution to the winds and rushed to smash those who had killed our commanding general," wrote Captain J. Fred Haley, who led Company A.[31]

The day after Buckner's death, General Claudius Easley, the 96th Division's assistant commander, was killed by machine-gun fire while making a daily inspection tour of the front lines. Minutes earlier, Easley's aide, Lieutenant John Turbeville, had been wounded by a hidden enemy machine gun, and Easley, as was his custom, had crawled to the top of a rise to try to locate its position. A burst struck the general in the forehead, killing him instantly.[32]

Easley's emphasis on marksmanship had earned the 96th Division the nickname "Deadeyes," and many of his men admired him for his approachability. But he was also known for aggressive tactics that some officers blamed for the division's large losses at Kakazu Ridge. "He was too damn brave, too gung-ho," said a 381st Infantry staff officer.

Buckner was the highest-ranking American general killed in action during World War II, and Easley was the last American general to die in combat during the war.[33]

FOUR DAYS BEFORE HE WAS killed, Buckner wrote to his wife, Adele, that the Tenth Army had trapped the Japanese at the southern end of the island on a plateau surrounded by cliffs. "They are likely at any time to try a last desperate counterattack which I would welcome as a quick way of ending the campaign." He went on to summarize his army's accomplishments: "It has been a tough one, but we still have a record of ten Japs killed for every one of ours and have broken the strongest defenses yet seen in the Pacific."[34]

The Tenth Army now occupied the 4-mile-long escarpment spanning the southern tip of Okinawa—the last Japanese bastion. From atop the escarpment, they could see the ocean 2 miles away and remind themselves that the long campaign was nearly ended. However, inside Yaeju-Dake, Yuza-Dake, and Kunishi Ridge were pockets of enemy soldiers in caves, tunnels, and crevices that had to be cleaned out or sealed.

Fresh troops relieved many of the depleted, exhausted combat units, which trudged to the rear for rest and re-equipping. In addition to the 8th Marines' relief of the 7th Marines, the 77th Division's 305th Infantry was sent southeast of Medeera to clear three hills ahead of the 96th Division's advance.

The frontline troops were grateful for the respite from combat. Lieutenant Robert Muehrcke, a platoon leader in the 96th Division's 383rd Infantry, and a fellow officer led the twenty-one survivors of Company F off Yuza-Dake on June 18 after thirty-nine days in combat. The Deadeyes had not shaved or bathed since going into action. Their fatigues were caked with dried blood from their comrades' wounds, or their own—each of the survivors had been wounded at least once.[35]

"There wasn't anything easy about any of it," said Lieutenant David Straus of the campaign in the south. The 1st Marine Division officer was in combat every day for a month without having eaten a hot meal. He slept on the ground when he slept at all. "Everything was compressed at the south end of the island and it was a slaughter," he said.[36]

Through the campaign's climactic final days, Americans continued to be killed and wounded. Crossing Mezado Valley as part of a tank-infantry team, Marine Captain Fitzgerald Atkinson's tank, hit by an antitank round, became inoperable. Atkinson was shot in the neck and riddled by shrapnel.

When he regained consciousness, seven Japanese soldiers were staring at him. Atkinson feigned death, and after the enemy soldiers departed, he escaped from his burning tank, rolled into an enemy trench, and was

eventually rescued. His many bullet and shrapnel wounds earned Atkinson the sobriquet "The Sieve."[37]

Even after the last escarpment fell to the Americans, fragments of the once-powerful Thirty-Second Army continued to fight. They often took American lives along with their own, despite the presence of flame tanks scorching their hiding places. "Fanatical Japs continue to cling to their rocky lairs and come out to fight again and again," said a report from the 7th Division's 32nd Infantry as it closed in on Ushijima's command post inside Hill 89.[38]

The defenders were dying in ever-larger numbers. During the first half of June, their casualties had averaged about a thousand a day. But the total continued to climb. On June 19, about two thousand were killed or wounded; on June 20, the total reached three thousand; and on June 21, four thousand Japanese casualties were recorded.[39]

Nearly all of Ushijima's best troops were dead, and most of those still fighting in southern Okinawa were support troops who had been thrown into the conflagration as infantrymen. Lacking combat skills, they faced veteran American soldiers who made quick work of them. With hope of victory gone, many blindly charged the American guns in order to die a samurai's death, or they took their own lives.

After months of watching comrades die in action and retaliating in kind, the Americans did not shrink from the bloody work. "The Japanese wanted to die for the Emperor, and we gave them the opportunity," wrote Private First Class Donald Dencker of the 96th Division's 382nd Infantry. "They had a chance to surrender and they didn't, so they were killed. 'Tough luck!' our men thought." On June 20 alone, the 96th Division killed a record 1,823 enemy soldiers, Dencker wrote.[40]

To the surprise of veterans of other Pacific battles, the number of Japanese prisoners taken soared in June. Previous island battles had produced small numbers of captives: 146 on Tarawa, 202 on Peleliu, and 216 on Iwo Jima.

Yet, on Okinawa, they were surrendering by the hundreds, convinced that Japan had lost the war. Historian Roy Appleman, in *Okinawa, the Last Battle*, wrote that during the first seventy days of the campaign, four Japanese surrendered daily on average. Between June 12 and June 18, the number rose to more than 50 per day. On June 19, 343 Japanese surrendered, and on June 20, nearly 1,000 prisoners were taken, the highest one-day total of the Pacific war.[41]

To roust the enemy from the escarpments, the 29th Marines employed a brutal tactic they had adopted during the struggle for Wana Ridge: pouring napalm from atop the cliffs into the vent holes of caves and igniting it with phosphorus grenades. This was one of the messages communicated to the enemy holdouts. Others were more ambiguous: while Navy ships cruised the coastline, broadcasting appeals to come out of the caves, sailors on deck shot Japanese waiting to surrender on the beaches.[42]

The situation was just as conflicted in the 96th Division sector, where the 381st Infantry was using a public address system to urge Japanese to leave their caves and surrender—and the 383rd Infantry's 3rd Battalion was shooting them when they emerged. The 381st's report writer suggested that someone "contact this unit and notify them that these Japs are surrendering." A postscript added, "3/383 notified."[43]

American planes dropped drums of napalm on Hill 89, from which Ushijima was presiding over the collapse of his Thirty-Second Army. The fuel seeped through the cave openings, caught fire, "and caused many casualties from burns and smoke inhalation," reported Colonel Hiromichi Yahara.

The command post cave, like many others, had already become a pesthole full of the sick and dying, lacking medicine and adequate food. Now it was also under siege by fire and by "time on target" artillery barrages in which shells from more than two hundred howitzers landed at the same instant. Five TOT barrages came one after the other on June 20; a huge cloud of dust hung above Hill 89. To its north, the town of Mabuni had been pulverized into a "wasteland" by two weeks of shelling and mortar and machine-gun fire, wrote Yahara.[44]

EACH NIGHT, JAPANESE SOLDIERS ATTEMPTED to slip through the American lines and escape the deadly trap on Okinawa's southern tip. A report from the 96th Division's 382nd Infantry said scores of Japanese were killed while attempting to breach the American lines, as their comrades harassed the Americans with small-arms and mortar fire. "Civilians came in throwing hand grenades in the morning," the report said. In two days, the 383rd Infantry claimed to have killed more than 300 Japanese soldiers, while the 382nd killed more than 150.[45]

The 1st Marine Division broke through the remaining Japanese defenses in Okinawa's southwestern corner and marched to the sea on June 19. Units of the 8th Marines also reached the beach.

The 5th Marines' tank-infantry teams assaulted Japanese strongholds on Hills 79 and 81 on the 1st Division's eastern flank, and crushed an attempted Japanese breakout to the north that night, shooting enemy troops advancing up a road. Its 3rd Battalion, which had reached the sea that day, lined up behind a stone wall along the beach by the light of flares, and picked off enemy soldiers attempting to swim away from shore in the dark.[46]

DENSELY POPULATED SOUTHERN OKINAWA HAD become a place where a man could lose his life in a hundred ways. One was by booby-trap. The Japanese sometimes used children to lure American soldiers into homes rigged with bombs.

In a smashed village, Lieutenant Roland Glenn of the 17th Infantry and his men approached a home whose front had been torn off by gunfire. Tied to a beam at the rear wall was a child screaming for his mother. She lay beyond his reach on her side, bleeding from a wound. When the mother saw the Americans approaching her, she waved them off. Suspecting that the home was wired with explosives, Glenn radioed for a demolition team. A careful search revealed that the Japanese had placed a trip wire and bomb beneath the woman, and the team disarmed it. The woman and child were removed from the home to receive medical treatment.[47]

US troops replied in kind by booby-trapping trails that ran along the southern cliffs with trip wires attached to powerful explosive charges. In the mornings, when they checked their trap lines for bodies, they sometimes discovered that an explosion had scoured all of the flesh from a victim's bones. With frontline gallows humor, someone would inevitably shout, "Soup bones today!"[48]

As the 5th Marines advanced south from Kunishi Ridge, Private First Class Sledge, who had seen practically everything during two hard campaigns, spotted a uniformed, fully equipped Japanese soldier lying dead in the middle of a road. Smashed into the mud by tank treads, the soldier "looked like a giant squashed insect," wrote Sledge. "It was a bizarre sight."[49]

ACROSS SOUTHERN OKINAWA, THE TENTH Army's hammer blows were shattering the remaining Japanese defenses. In the III Amphibious Corps sector, the 6th Marine Division's 22nd Regiment advanced rapidly down the western side of the battlefront, destroyed what was left of the Japanese 22nd Infantry, and began to encircle the 24th Division headquarters.

By June 20, just two pockets of strong resistance remained before III Corps. The 6th Division assaulted Kiyamu-Gusuku Hill, while the 1st Marine Division struggled to capture Hill 81. There, stubborn Japanese defenders withstood three days of intensive shelling by artillery, Navy warships, and tanks, and repulsed all of the 1st Division's attacks. Then, the enemy's defenses abruptly collapsed, and on June 21, III Corps pronounced organized resistance in its sector to be at an end.[50]

A Japanese prisoner led American intelligence officers to the enormous cave complex that was the 24th Division headquarters. A Nisei soldier broadcast a surrender appeal in Japanese. It did no good. General Tatsumi Amamiya, the 24th Division commander, had posted guards around the complex to prevent anyone from surrendering. Left with no other option, the 96th Division poured 1,700 gallons of gasoline into the main entrance and detonated 300 pounds of dynamite, entombing the holdouts.

When the cave was unsealed days later, Navy Lieutenant Frank Gibney described its interior as "one of the ghastliest sights I ever saw." About two hundred officers and men lay dead, all by their own hand and most of them by detonating grenades. The cavern's walls and floor were splashed with blood and body parts. Among the bodies that carpeted the cave floor was that of division commander Amamiya, who had chosen to die by a lethal injection.

There was one survivor. Amamiya had forbidden his orderly to kill himself; he was instructed to report to authorities in Tokyo how the 24th Division leaders had died. During the days following the mass suicides, the orderly had sustained himself on water from an underground spring and scraps of rations that survived the explosions.[51]

While atop the hills at land's end, Marines observed armed, uniformed Japanese soldiers below them on the beach carrying white flags. Disgusted that they had waited until the campaign's end to surrender, the Marines decided "the hell with those bastards" and opened fire on them, wiping them all out, said machine-gunner Dan Lawler, who claimed credit for most of the kills.[52]

SINCE THE 1930S, WHEN REPORTS reached the West of Japanese atrocities against Chinese civilians, Americans had reflexively deplored the inhumanity of their Japanese enemies. The feeling metastasized into hatred after the December 7, 1941, surprise attack on Pearl Harbor. The enmity deepened further during the early days of the Guadalcanal campaign, when

wounded Japanese soldiers killed American corpsmen attempting to treat them. For their part, the Japanese believed that Americans had abused and murdered African American slaves, massacred American Indians and stole their lands, and started a mid-nineteenth-century expansionist war against Mexico.

In the Pacific, during the American island-hopping campaign from 1943 to 1945, atrocities on both sides begot more atrocities. By L-Day, the Pacific war had become a war without mercy. Unlike the fighting in western Europe, in which the adversaries shared a common heritage and did not routinely kill prisoners, the Pacific war pitted two races against each other that shared only a common hatred, inspiring spontaneous massacres.

"We were losing the war" and wanted revenge, said teenager Taira Kichitoshi, a member of the Blood and Iron Student Corps who witnessed the harsh treatment meted out to American pilots captured on Okinawa. He watched as Japanese soldiers bound a wounded American pilot to a tree and left him there in the expectation the he would be killed by American bombs. Kichitoshi saw another pilot staked to the ground and used for bayonet practice. Japanese soldiers then began stoning him. "Everyone had gone crazy," said Kichitoshi.[53]

The tipping point for Private First Class George Niland of the 22nd Marines came when he saw the bodies of wounded American soldiers who, as they lay on stretchers, had been killed and mutilated by the Japanese. "I became just as blood thirsty as the Japanese," he conceded. "We all did . . . We showed no mercy. We never took a prisoner. We couldn't leave them there, we couldn't take them with us, and we couldn't send them back. So we interrogated them, and we killed them." But there were other Marines whose units did not kill prisoners, and they sometimes reported the murders of unarmed enemy soldiers by fellow Marines.[54]

THE 96TH DIVISION PUSHED SOUTH from Yuza-Dake to seize the towns of Aragachi and Medeera, still held by Japanese bitter-enders. The Deadeyes reached the hamlet of Ōzato first and found a dozen civilian women and children writhing on the ground. They had taken strychnine rather than fall into the hands of the Americans. Medics saved the lives of some of them, but others died.

Battalions from the 96th's 382nd Infantry and the 77th Division's 305th Infantry wiped out the last Japanese pocket on Yuza-Dake on June 19. The next day, three 96th Division battalions, led by conventional and flame

tanks, advanced over sugarcane fields and into Aragachi, with the infantry-men arrayed in a skirmish line, firing as they went.

Dencker of the 382nd's 3rd Battalion said his mortar section fired high-explosive and phosphorus rounds into the village, setting fire to the thatch-roofed houses and driving the Japanese into the open to be slaughtered. The Deadeyes killed 151 Japanese soldiers, took 2 prisoners, and interned 119 civilians.

In Aragachi as throughout southern Okinawa, death manifested itself in many gruesome varieties. Captain Donald Mulford said the thoroughly brainwashed Aragachi civilians "huddled in their holes, refusing to give up until burned or blasted out—some killing themselves and their children rather than face the horrors they had been led to expect." Afterward, "the sickly smell of death" permeated the rubble-strewn town, said Mulford. "One had to walk carefully, for the dead were everywhere."

The village's surviving old men and women wandered about numbly in tattered black kimonos. "Aragachi was a living, stinking testimonial to the horrors that war brings to a civilian population," wrote Mulford. Among the civilians herded to the rear there was "malnutrition everywhere," wrote Sergeant William Beckman of the 96th Division's 382nd Infantry.

An infant's naked corpse lay against the base of a stone wall. "No one seemed interested," wrote Captain Mulford, "except the hundreds of flies that swarmed over it."[55]

The 96th's 381st Infantry fought a block-by-block battle during its assault on Medeera, whose premises eventually compassed 1,347 Japanese dead—killed in action or by suicide. The Japanese fought desperately and without hope. A group of Japanese officers fought fiercely for a half hour before they all took their own lives.

In Medeera, the Deadeyes found air-raid shelters full of enemy soldiers who had to be blasted out with grenades, satchel charges, and flamethrowers. After two soldiers blew out a wall at the south edge of town with a satchel charge, two flame tanks roasted fifty-seven shrieking Japanese soldiers in a courtyard.[56]

THE FALL OF ARAGACHI AND Medeera left the Thirty-Second Army command post inside Hill 89 as one of two remaining Japanese strong-holds on Okinawa—the other was beneath Kunishi Ridge, where the cave strongholds of about four hundred troops of the 32nd Infantry were being systematically destroyed.[57]

On June 18, at what would be his last command post briefing, General Isamu Chō ordered four Thirty-Second Army staff officers to don civilian clothing and escape to the north, guided by Blood and Iron students. Two were to leave the island in a boat, fly to Japan from Tomino Jima, and deliver messages to Imperial Headquarters in Tokyo. The two other officers were to organize guerrilla fighters in northern Okinawa. Each officer carried two dried fish; a small bag of white rice; a two-day supply of dried bread, canned fish, and salt; and a first-aid kit. With American units tightening the noose around the command post by the hour, the plan was fantastical. Two officers were killed, and the fate of the other two was not known.[58]

With the end at hand, General Ushijima composed farewell messages to his superiors in Tokyo and to the troops who remained alive on Okinawa. In one message radioed to Imperial Headquarters, he pledged a final, last-ditch battle involving all of his surviving soldiers, "in which I will apologize to the emperor with my own death."[59]

Another farewell message to Imperial Headquarters said, "With a burning desire to destroy the arrogant enemy, the men in my command have fought the invaders for almost three months. We have failed to crush the enemy, despite our death-defying resistance, and now we are doomed." He added this postscript:

> Green grass dies in the islands without waiting for fall,
> But it will be reborn verdant in the springtime of the homeland.
> Weapons exhausted, our blood will bathe the earth, but the spirit
>   will survive.
> Our spirits will return to protect the homeland.[60]

On June 18, Ushijima ordered his remaining troops to make their way to northern Okinawa without engaging American combat units. They were to travel in twos and threes, wearing civilian clothing, and join the guerrillas in the north. En route, they were to destroy enemy installations with hand grenades. The attempts to infiltrate the US lines while avoiding confrontations failed dismally. In just one night, the 7th Division killed 502 Japanese soldiers trying to pass through its lines.[61]

A Thirty-Second Army staff officer penned Ushijima's final order to his soldiers:

My Beloved Soldiers:

You have all fought courageously for nearly three months. You have discharged your duty. Your bravery and loyalty brighten the future.

The battlefield is now in such chaos that all communications have ceased. It is impossible for me to command you. Every man in these fortifications will follow his superior officer's order and fight to the end for the sake of the motherland.

This is my final order.

Farewell.

To this, General Chō added in red ink: "Do not suffer the shame of being taken prisoner. You will live for eternity."[62]

BUT THIS WAS 1945, AND during the past year Chō's men had absorbed news of the losses of Saipan, Guam, Tinian, Peleliu, the Philippines, and Iwo Jima. Since April, the Americans had blanketed the island with surrender leaflets that averaged about fifteen per man. On May 9, US psy-ops technicians had announced Germany's surrender over Japanese tactical radio frequencies. Now patrol-boat loudspeakers blared surrender appeals daily.

Years had passed without even one important Japanese victory, and even the lowliest private could now see that the war was irretrievably lost. Now Japanese soldiers faced methodical annihilation by relentless, terrifying firepower, without hope of reinforcements.[63]

While most of the Thirty-Second Army's soldiers, drilled to automatic obedience, continued to follow orders to fight until they were killed, growing numbers of emaciated, filthy, often wounded enemy soldiers wearing loincloths and little else, emerged with their hands in the air from caves, crevices, and pillboxes. They capitulated in groups; one officer surrendered with thirty-seven of his men. Sometimes they were still shot by suspicious soldiers and Marines, but as the Americans grew accustomed to the sight of surrendering Japanese, most of them survived to receive medical care and food.[64]

THE 7TH DIVISION'S 32ND INFANTRY was approaching the Thirty-Second Army's command post inside Hill 89 on June 20 when up to seven hundred civilians suddenly appeared in front of the Americans, seeking

sanctuary. They crowded into the 32nd Infantry's front lines, and the attack was halted until the area was cleared. When it resumed, Company G reached Hill 89's crest by 3 p.m., and the rest of the 2nd Battalion stopped just 200 yards from the headquarters cave's main entrance.

That night, soldiers disguised as Okinawan civilians poured out of the hill, following their orders to infiltrate the American lines and make their way to the north. A fusillade of bullets cut them to pieces. In the morning, 424 bodies were counted. Many of the dead had killed themselves with grenades that they carried.[65]

The next day, the 32nd Infantry overran the enemy troops defending the cave openings, and secured the hilltop. They hurled a satchel charge down the main shaft, leaving a bloody pile of soldiers' bodies near General Chō's quarters. "The smell of blood was everywhere," wrote Colonel Yahara.

A short time later, grenades thrown by Japanese soldiers during a failed counterattack missed their targets and instead fell down the shaft and exploded, badly wounding two student nurses. Yahara watched as one nurse was given a cyanide injection that ended her life.[66]

Army engineers cut a road to the top of Hill 89, and conventional and flame tanks began roving the 400-yard-long hilltop, wiping out the suicidal resistance with flames and shells. When the 32nd Infantry's 2nd Battalion reached the northern cave entrance, it was driven back by a mortar barrage. The Japanese soldiers inside Hill 89 closed the cave entrance with explosives.[67]

By nightfall June 21, the Tenth Army held the summit of Hill 89 and every other important southern Okinawa stronghold. There remained what was euphemistically called "mop-up"—the dirty job of ferreting out the holdouts inside the hills, or entombing them with explosives. Every day, American units reported casualties inflicted by the cornered enemy survivors.[68]

AT SEA, SMALL GROUPS OF Japanese warplanes and lone wolfs continued to harry the Okinawa fleet after Kikusui No. 9's failure, and the Navy's picket ships remained on high alert.

On June 16, the destroyer *Twiggs*, back in action after being damaged by a kamikaze on April 28, was attacked as it left Radar Picket Station No. 2 at 8:30 p.m. to shell Japanese holdouts in Naha. A Jill torpedo bomber put a fish into her No. 2 magazine. The enemy plane then circled and crashed into the ship. Fires roared from bow to stern, and the after magazine

exploded. An hour after being torpedoed, *Twiggs* sank, taking 126 crewmen to the bottom, including Commander George Philip.[69]

The final Japanese "cherry blossom" attack, Kikusui No. 10, was launched on June 21 with forty-five kamikazes and about fifty conventional fighters. The assault began when an enemy fighter crashed the seaplane tender *Curtiss*. Its bomb exploded on the third deck and ignited a conflagration that gutted the ship, killed forty-one crewmen, and wounded twenty-eight others. Amazingly, *Curtiss* survived the disaster, and was repaired at Mare Island.[70]

The destroyer *Barry*, badly damaged by a kamikaze on May 25 northwest of Okinawa, had been towed to Kerama Retto and deemed unsalvageable. Late June 21, *Barry*, stripped of her gear and decommissioned, was being towed from Kerama Retto by the gunboat *LSM-59* to begin a new career as a kamikaze decoy when enemy planes crashed and sank both vessels.[71]

Previously, Japanese pilots had enjoyed success striking at night, because few American planes were aloft to challenge them. During Iceberg's first ten days, dusk was known as "children's hour for kamikaze kids" because they enjoyed free rein. Carrier fighters were not equipped for night missions and had to return to their flattops before darkness fell, and Yontan and Kadena Airfields were still undergoing repairs and were unready for land-based fighters.[72]

But the situation changed with the advent of night-flying, radar-equipped US combat air patrols, aided by a growing network of land-based radar stations on Okinawa and its surrounding islands that eventually totaled twenty-eight. Based at airfields on Okinawa and Ie Shima and on some carriers, night-flying pilots flew by instruments in darkened cockpits to protect their night vision, and were able to approach targets undetected—guided by six ground intercept stations dedicated to night missions. By day, the night fighters slept. At dusk, they began their missions, which lasted three to four hours.

Early June 22, the CAPs drove off or destroyed most of the Kikusui No. 10 attackers. Shortly after midnight, night-fighting F6F Hellcats destroyed four Bettys before they could strike the radar picket stations. Twin-tail, twin-engine P-61 Black Widows from the Ie Shima-based 548th Night Fighter Squadron added to the toll.[73]

Marine colonel Marion Magruder, a nighttime aviation pioneer and commander of VMF(N)-533, known as "Black Mac's Killers," shot down

a Betty at 2:45 a.m. on June 22 when a northern Okinawa radar station re-ported a Betty nearby, flying at 1,400 feet. Magruder crept up on it unseen and destroyed it. During its time in action, "Black Mac's Killers" claimed thirty-five kills, a record for night squadrons during World War II.[74]

Six Bettys in Kikusui No. 10 carried Ohkas in the expectation that the one-man, jet-propelled aircraft would have a chance to sink US ships. It was not to be. Two Bettys turned back before reaching the battle zone, two were shot down without releasing their missiles, and the other two got their Ohkas away, but neither struck a target—one went into the sea, and the other was last seen flying over Naha at great speed.[75]

As June and the Okinawa campaign ended, so did the mass kamikaze attacks. The Japanese were husbanding their remaining Special Attack forces for the defense of the home islands.

Between April 6 and June 22, Japanese 5th Air Fleet and 6th Air Army kamikazes conducted about 1,900 sorties, including the 1,465 attributed to the ten kikusuis. Hundreds of conventional bombers, dive-bombers, torpedo planes, and fighters also participated. It was estimated that 1,600 suicide and conventional planes were lost. Despite those losses, several thousand combat planes, trainers, and biplanes reportedly remained avail-able for special attack missions to defend Japan.[76]

Until the Navy refined its defenses against the suicide planes by flood-ing the battle zone with combat air patrols and introducing night-fighting, radar-equipped warplanes, Japanese pilots believed in the possibility of re-alizing the mantra, "One Plane, One Ship." The kamikaze ideal faded as the Navy's defenses became more sophisticated.

The US Strategic Bombing Survey reported that Japanese kamikazes sank 26 US warships—all destroyer class or smaller—and damaged 164 other naval vessels of the total of 36 ships sunk and 368 damaged during the Okinawa campaign by conventional and suicide planes. Naval person-nel losses in the fiery shipboard explosions were the highest of the Pacific war: 4,907 sailors and officers killed, and 4,824 wounded. The 807 sailors who died on the carrier *Franklin* constituted the single greatest naval loss of the Okinawa campaign. More than 750 US planes were lost near Oki-nawa and while bombing airfields on the Japanese mainland.[77]

GENERALS USHIJIMA AND CHŌ WERE at peace with their decision to not leave Hill 89 alive. On the night that they planned to commit hara-kiri, they held a banquet in the command post cave. Ushijima's cook, Tetsuo

Nakamuta, prepared a sumptuous meal of rice, potatoes, bean-curd soup, fried fish cakes, canned meats, pineapple, tea, and sake. There were "copious farewell toasts" made with sake and Chō's carefully hoarded last bottles of Black & White scotch, and the generals and their subordinates joined in singing the patriotic song "Umi Yukaba":

> *If I go away to the sea*
> *I shall be a corpse washed up.*
> *If I go away to the mountain,*
> *I shall be a corpse in the grass*
> *But if I die for the Emperor,*
> *It will not be a regret.*

During the early morning hours of June 22, the command post staff lined up to pay their final respects to Ushijima and Chō. Ushijima, in full dress uniform, and Chō, wearing a white kimono, walked to the cave mouth that overlooked the sea. At the base of Hill 89, a few dozen adjutants, soldiers, and engineers prepared to charge to the top and drive away the Americans. It was a hopeless mission. Yahara described it as "a cruel and heartless suicide attack." Indeed, a storm of American gunfire ended the assault before it really began.[78]

Inside the hill, the generals began their last journey. Chō volunteered to lead the way into the next world, "as the way may be dark," but Ushijima said that he would go ahead. The men exchanged poems. Chō's final lines read:

> *Bravely we fought for ninety days inside a dream;*
> *We have used up our withered lives,*
> *But our souls race to heaven.*[79]

The men stepped from their cave to a ledge overlooking the moonlit ocean. On the ledge, a white cloth had been laid over the quilt where they would die.

Yahara, ordered by Chō to infiltrate American lines and make his way to Japan, lingered to witness the ceremonial deaths. He and Ushijima's cook watched as the generals knelt on the cloth. On Ushijima's right stood his adjutant, Captain Sakaguchi, a master swordsman who had the great honor of decapitating the men with his razor-sharp saber after their

ritual suicides. On the back of Chō's white kimono was a poem that he had written:

With bravery I served my nation.
With loyalty I dedicate my life.

An aide handed Ushijima a traditional hara-kiri knife. With a shout, the commanding general made a deep vertical cut in his bared belly as Sakaguchi's saber flashed down on his neck. The process was repeated with Chō. Three orderlies buried them in shallow graves.[80]

In the span of just four days, the commanders of the two enemy armies and two other high-ranking generals had met violent deaths.

WITH THE CAPTURE OF THE Tenth Army's last objectives on June 21, General Roy Geiger, the Tenth Army's interim commander, announced that Okinawa had been secured and organized resistance was at an end.

Geiger's pronouncement notwithstanding, the roar of gunfire and mortar fire, and the clank of tank treads fitfully flared and echoed among southern Okinawa's hills and escarpments. Hundreds, if not thousands, of armed Japanese soldiers and thousands of civilians remained in caves and tunnels under the cliffs and hills. Those who could not be persuaded to surrender would be killed outright, or entombed in their hiding places.

Yet Geiger wanted closure before General Joseph Stilwell became the titular commander of the Tenth Army on June 23, and Geiger returned to the III Amphibious Corps.

At 10 a.m. on June 22, representatives from the Tenth Army's two corps and each of its divisions assembled to celebrate the American victory.

As a band played "The Star Spangled Banner," a color guard raised the American flag over Tenth Army headquarters.

Caught by a lucky breeze, the flag unfurled to its full length and breadth for all to see.[81]

The Battle Ends

All of nature, except for a few blackened trees, seemed to have been incinerated. So complete was the devastation that the most gifted poet could not have expressed the desolation of this Okinawa. It was beyond description or belief.

—COLONEL HIROMICHI YAHARA, DESCRIBING
OKINAWA AFTER THE BATTLE ENDED[1]

There was a fury, a storm of devastation, to the campaign on Okinawa that surpassed the ground fighting seen anywhere else in the war. The longer the conflict went on, the more terrible it became.

—GEOFFREY PERRET, A HISTORIAN OF
US ARMY OPERATIONS DURING WORLD WAR II[2]

[Okinawa was] a bloody, hellish prelude to the invasion of Japan.

—ADMIRAL RAYMOND SPRUANCE, FIFTH FLEET COMMANDER[3]

LIEUTENANT BOB GREEN OF THE 763rd Tank Battalion was ordered by headquarters officers to lead his tank platoon to a hill where Japanese holdouts were refusing to surrender. An infantry platoon and a POW with a loudspeaker accompanied Green's tanks while staff officers waited at the foot of the hill.

The infantry platoon's commander, whom Green identified as a Sergeant Constable, asked Green if he could ride in his tank. The sergeant, who was the platoon's fourth commander, had had a premonitory dream that he would die that day, and he believed that he would be safer in an armored vehicle. Green welcomed Constable inside his tank.

Green and Constable watched the POW persuade a dozen or more Japanese to leave the cave wearing only loincloths, their hands held high. The mission appeared to have been successful.

Constable leaned out of the tank to answer a question from one of his men when a shot rang out from the hill. Constable collapsed inside the tank, shot between the eyes, and died moments later.

As the tanks and infantrymen began returning with the prisoners to the staff officers at the hill's base, the soldier who had been talking to Constable shouted into the tank, "Did they just shoot old Constable back there awhile ago?" Green replied that Constable had been killed.

The infantryman told the others. Green then heard a sound coming from the soldiers much like "I would imagine the noise of many big zoo animals, such as a group of lions or bears, would make if they started growling together."

The growling was drowned out by the sounds of a BAR being fired on full automatic and shouting and screaming.

When Green looked out of his tank, all of the prisoners were dead. "The infantrymen stood over them and glowered at them," Green wrote.

The soldier holding the BAR told Green that the sniper had dropped his rifle and run down the hill with his hands up, joining the other prisoners. "We couldn't tell for sure which one it was that did it, after they all got mixed around down here, so we just shot the whole wad to make sure we got him."

The headquarters officers, "stunned and speechless" by what they had just witnessed, got into their jeeps with the POW and his loudspeaker and drove away. Green never heard a word about the incident.[4]

THE SOUTHERN ISLAND ESCARPMENTS WERE soaked in blood and death by the time General Geiger declared Okinawa secured, and yet the carnage went on, even though organized resistance had largely ended.

US troops killed Japanese infiltrators in large numbers along the front lines and near rear-area installations, which the enemy had been instructed to destroy with hand grenades.

During the mop-up phase, the Americans at times tried to pry the death-defying Japanese from their caves, crevices, and pillboxes with surrender appeals broadcast in Japanese by Nisei troops. Private First Class Taro Higa, reared in Hawaii by Okinawan parents and wounded in Italy while serving with a Nisei unit, coaxed many civilians and some enemy troops from their cave hideouts; he was fluent in English, Japanese, and Okinawan dialects.

But US troops often did not bother with translators or surrender appeals. "We killed them," said Private First Class Martin Allday of the 96th Division, usually by the stock-in-trade "blowtorch and corkscrew," Buckner's mild euphemism for the extreme measure of flamethrowers and explosives.

The neutralized caves were pestholes where dead Japanese soldiers, women, and babies lay in advanced states of decomposition. In the detritus the American troops sometimes found photos, notebooks, and rations taken from the packs of dead US soldiers.

IRONICALLY, JUST AS THE BATTLE was ostensibly winding down, the accumulated days and weeks of methodical killing were beginning to tip seasoned veterans into a numb madness. The incidence of battle fatigue rose sharply during June's last weeks.

Known as "shell shock" during World War I, battle fatigue often began manifesting itself after three or four weeks on the front lines, when a soldier might lose his physical edge and experience declining verbal ability and memory. The "thousand-yard stare," a sign that a man was unconsciously distancing himself from his surroundings, signified the next stage. The final symptoms, uncontrollable trembling and a descent into a vegetative state, usually landed the soldier or Marine in the hospital.[5]

"Some guys just went crazy and had to be dragged away," said Corporal George Peto. "Others went into shock and turned into zombies. Many just broke down." Peto approached a quietly weeping Marine in the throes of a breakdown beside a road and attempted to talk to the man, but his words made no impression. The man continued to cry, "tears rolling down his cheeks." A corpsman led him to the rear.[6]

In late June, Private First Class Sledge witnessed an attack by two sword-swinging Japanese officers. They were shot dead before they caused injury. Bullets tore off the top of the head of one officer, who was wearing his full-dress uniform, white gloves, and campaign ribbons.

The killing proved to be the final straw for one Marine, who stood over the dead enemy soldier with a dazed look on his face. Grasping his rifle with both hands, he "slowly and mechanically moved it up and down like a plunger" inside the officer's skull, wrote Sledge. "I winced each time it [the rifle] came down with a sickening sound into the gory mass. Brains and blood were splattered all over the Marine's rifle, boondockers, and canvas leggings."

The Marines' comrades grasped the man's arms and gently led him away with the wounded.

"This was the type of incident that should be witnessed by anyone who has any delusions about the glory of war," said Sledge.[7]

Corporal Kenneth Hebard of the 1st Marines reached the breaking point in late June after someone shouted that Japanese soldiers were running across an open field and Hebard reflexively shot several of them. To his horror, he discovered that they were Marines from another company. At that moment, a "friendly" mortar round landed 10 feet away from him and mortally wounded a friend. A corpsman attending to the dying Marine noticed Hebard's anxiety and sent him to a hospital.[8]

By the end of May, the hand-to-hand fighting and massive Japanese artillery and mortar fire had already taken a toll: the Army reported 7,762 non-combat casualties, and the Marines, 6,315. Most of them were classified as neuropsychiatric cases resulting from battle fatigue. A hospital dedicated to psychiatric cases was established behind the American lines near the Hagushi beaches.

Doctors developed a procedure for treating battle fatigue after a soldier or Marine was evaluated at the hospital. If the case was not too severe, the patient might be assigned to load supplies, rations, and ammunition onto trucks bound for the front. After several days, he might ride along with one of the shipments. Upon reaching the front, he often would rejoin his unit and perform ably. Most patients eventually returned to duty.

By late June, the Tenth Army reported 26,000 non-combat casualties.[9]

The large number of battle-fatigue cases was a consequence of the uniquely brutal character of the Okinawa battle. "There was a fury, a storm of devastation, to the campaign on Okinawa that surpassed the ground fighting seen anywhere else in the war," wrote Geoffrey Perret, a historian of US Army operations during World War II. "The longer the conflict went on, the more terrible it became. . . . In this total war between industrialized nations, a vortex of destruction was unleashed."[10]

In the aftermath of the Korean and Vietnam Wars, psychiatrists determined that battle fatigue might affect a veteran for the rest of his or her life, and trigger anger, depression, flashbacks, and suicidal thoughts. The condition was called post-traumatic stress disorder. In 1980, the American Psychiatric Association officially recognized PTSD as a mental disorder.

ON JUNE 22, THE DAY that Okinawa was pronounced secured, an estimated 15,000 to 18,000 Japanese troops were believed to be in hiding in southern Okinawa's caves, sea-cliff crevices, and ruined buildings, or were traveling northward to wage guerrilla warfare. Smaller numbers of Okinawan conscripts attempted to blend into the civilian population.

Hiroyuki Fukushima, an Okinawa Region Weather Observatory worker, had been wounded and was staying in a private home with other weather-station workers when he turned to one of them and said, "Depending on the way you look at it, it's better to die now while there are still people around to bury the bodies." While traveling on foot recently, Fukushima had seen enough decomposing bodies along the roads to know that he did not want to become one of them.[11]

The Thirty-Second Army dissolved the Blood and Iron for the Emperor Corps. Many of the teenagers had already deserted after concluding that the battle was lost, or they had stopped believing the Japanese propaganda about the supposedly bloodthirsty Americans, or they wished to return to their families, if they were still alive.

Those who remained with the Thirty-Second Army after the corps was broken up were ordered to slip through the enemy lines in groups of three, and travel to the north to fight as guerrillas. To prepare for their journey, the youths boiled rice in seawater, which everywhere along the coastline was stained red by the blood of floating corpses. The rice reminded some of the teens of "traditional festive red rice."[12]

Aboard US landing craft cruising offshore, Japanese war prisoners with bullhorns appealed to their comrades to strip to their loincloths, leave their weapons behind, and give up. Hundreds did. At other times, soldiers who emerged from caves were given cigarettes to take back to their comrades as tokens of goodwill.

XXIV CORPS AND III AMPHIBIOUS CORPS, which had driven all the way down the island to the sea, were given a new mission on June 23: to turn around, march northward in a long skirmish line, and kill or capture

any Japanese soldiers hiding in southern Okinawa. The operation, carried
out by the 1st and 6th Marine Divisions and the 96th and 7th Army Divisions, began at the very bottom of the island. To prevent enemy soldiers
flushed from hiding places from escaping to northern Okinawa, other
American units lined the Naha-Yonabaru road south of Shuri, barring
the way.

The soldiers and Marines ferreted out Japanese holdouts, buried the
dead, salvaged US and enemy equipment, and collected all brass shells
above .50-caliber, stacking them in neat piles. The soldiers grumbled about
the tedious, often dangerous work; it was an indignity to combat veterans,
they believed.[13]

"There are hundreds of Jap bodies all over our area and it is our job to
bury them," fumed Sergeant Benjamin Capaldi of the 32nd Infantry. "It's
a hell of a note to kill Japs for almost three months and then have to bury
them, too."[14]

Every cave was searched or neutralized by "corkscrew and blowtorch,"
and then sealed with explosives. Some Japanese soldiers tried to hide in the
grain and cane fields, but were flushed from their hiding places by flame
tanks. "It reminds me of quail hunting the way everybody moves through
the field behind the tanks, having a big time," wrote Lieutenant Bob Green
of the 763rd Tank Battalion, attached to the 96th Division.

Allday of the 96th's 382nd Infantry said that as flames crackled through
a dry grain field where a dozen Japanese were seen lying on the ground, the
Americans could hear grenades exploding as the soldiers killed themselves.
"I was glad they were doing it so that I didn't have to go in after them,"
said Allday.

Historian Roy Appleman described suicide by grenade as "a kind of
poor man's hari-kiri [sic]." Its victims were marked by torn bellies and
missing hands.[15]

Sometimes Okinawan civilians displayed the same strong aversion to
surrendering as did cornered Japanese soldiers. When Private First Class
Kenneth Portteus tried to persuade a woman with a baby on her back and
a five-year-old by her side to come out of a cave, the woman initially began
to come toward him. But people behind her shouted angrily, and she wa-
vered, and then returned to the cave. Seconds later, three explosions shook
the hillside. Inside the cave, Marines found ten shattered bodies, including
those of the woman and her children.[16]

THE MOPPING-UP BY THE AMERICAN divisions was completed in seven days instead of the anticipated ten. During the sweep northward, 8,975 Japanese soldiers were killed, and 2,902 soldiers and 906 labor troops were captured. Thousands of others were sealed in the caves. American casualties totaled 783.[17]

About 10,000 Korean men had been sent to Okinawa to become military laborers, and 600 to 800 Korean women served as the Thirty-Second Army's "comfort women." The Korean men received rudimentary infantry training, and many of them died fighting alongside the Japanese. More than 3,500 Koreans survived the campaign as war prisoners and detainees. They joined 7,401 Japanese soldiers and officers as captives. Okinawa's total of 11,250 prisoners surpassed all reported prisoner totals during the Pacific war.

Tenth Army intelligence officers' interviews with Japanese war prisoners revealed that their fear of being tortured and killed by the Americans—and not shame—was the underlying reason for their reluctance to surrender. But when they saw their comrades who had surrendered being treated fairly, and realized that their situation was hopeless, their inhibitions about becoming prisoners melted away.

Tenth Army leaders took pains to demonstrate their goodwill—to the extent of permitting a chaplain to marry an Okinawan girl and a captive Japanese officer as a shotgun-toting guard stood as a witness. A photographer recorded the unusual "Hollywood wedding," as reporters described it.[18]

A FEW ENEMY TROOPS ELUDED the Tenth Army dragnet and even managed to carry out their orders to damage or destroy American rear areas with grenades during their long infiltration to the north. When an ammunition dump erupted in a chain of explosions at 8:45 a.m. on July 5, Tenth Army officials suspected that it was the handiwork of a Japanese straggler with a grenade. The explosions at the dump continued for twelve hours, accompanied by billowing clouds of smoke.[19]

COLONEL HIROMICHI YAHARA, THE THIRTY-SECOND Army's chief planner and operations officer, was one of the Japanese soldiers captured at the end of the battle. On the eve of General Isamu Chō's suicide alongside General Ushijima, Chō had ordered Yahara to leave the headquarters cave beneath Hill 89, slip through the enemy lines, and report to Tokyo what had happened on Okinawa. Chō gave Yahara 500 yen for his journey.

After Ushijima and Chō took their lives, Yahara and several staff officers occupied a small cave near the main command post. They blocked the entrance with rocks and awaited their chance to escape. After dark, American soldiers with jackhammers began drilling into the rock above them, and the group left the cave and descended the cliff to another cave. They decided to split up and reunite later in northern Okinawa.

Yahara donned old civilian clothes, filled a pair of socks with cooked rice and tied them around his waist. Descending a footpath to the beach, he lost his footing and tumbled down Mabuni Hill, dropping his pistol, which discharged, drawing a fusillade of gunfire from all directions.

He hid in another cave, where a young soldier was sitting before a tiny fire with an Okinawan girl. Behind them were two soldiers—one of them wounded and the other dead, a suicide. As Yahara said a prayer over the dead soldier, the girl sobbed.

The next night, he and two other soldiers edged eastward past the "Spring of Death" and along a coral reef covered with decaying Japanese corpses. "A thousand faces of death appeared as we marched through this seaside graveyard," on their way to Gushican Cave, Yahara wrote.

They met a group of panicked, despairing soldiers who refused to budge from beneath an overhang, and a ranting, distraught man who shrieked at them before wandering off. Yahara and his companions entered a cave occupied by about fifty civilian refugees and remained with them for two days—until the cave came under air attack, and American soldiers appeared, ordering them to come out. Yahara led the refugees from the cave.

"A number of American soldiers now moved forward from their deployment positions and helped the refugees—taking an old man's hand, carrying children in their arms," said Yahara. "It was a touching scene. Hostility and fear were replaced by compassion."[20]

Yahara was classified as a civilian refugee and taken to a stockade. A few days later, the refugees were marched to the Chinen Peninsula and billeted in a house where thirty refugees were already staying. Yahara idled away weeks there before joining a work detail. Riding in a truck from Yonabaru to Naha, he passed through a battlefield where Japanese soldiers had fought so that the Thirty-Second Army could retreat from Shuri to the Kiyan Peninsula.

"All of nature, except for a few blackened trees, seemed to have been incinerated," he wrote. "So complete was the devastation that the most gifted poet could not have expressed the desolation of this Okinawa. It was

beyond description or belief." Hundreds of tents belonging to American servicemen covered the denuded hillsides.[21]

Three weeks after his escape from Thirty-Second Army headquarters, Yahara's captors discovered his true identity—that he had been the third highest-ranking enemy officer on Okinawa. Yahara was transferred to the Tenth Army headquarters camp and interrogated at length. He was plotting his escape when Hiroshima and Nagasaki were destroyed by nuclear weapons, and the war ended. Yahara was repatriated to Japan in January 1946.[22]

TENS OF THOUSANDS OF CONSTRUCTION troops—from the Army, the Navy, and the British Royal Engineers—had begun turning Okinawa into an immense air and naval base even as the armies fought along the Shuri Line and in southern Okinawa.

Planners envisioned Okinawa as the main forward base for the invasion of Japan, with eighteen airfields for B-29 missions. Four airfields for fighter escorts were planned on Ie Shima. Engineers also began rebuilding Yontan and Kadena Airfields, which the Tactical Air Force had hastily activated in April, but whose runways were thinly surfaced and poorly drained.

By the end of June, 95,000 construction troops commanded by Marine General Fred Wallace were at work transforming Okinawa. When completed, the airfield complex, with its component bases linked by a network of paved roads, would be able to accommodate the Eighth Air Force when it was redeployed from England to the Pacific. Living quarters were going up for nearly a half million soldiers, Marines, sailors, and airmen, and large areas were being cleared for bivouacs and supply and ammunition dumps.

By July, some of the airfields were completed, including six 10,000-foot bomber strips. Okinawa's airfields were later utilized for bombing missions during the Korean and Vietnam wars.[23]

During the drive north to the Naha-Yonabaru road at the end of June, E. B. Sledge of the 5th Marines marveled at the changed appearance of the places where he had fought just a month earlier. "We could barely recognize them," he wrote. "Roads that had been muddy tracks or coral-covered paths were highways with vehicles going to and fro and MPs in neat khaki directing traffic. We had come back to civilization. We had climbed up out of the abyss once more."[24]

The changes had occurred rapidly. As early as mid-May, General Buckner had written to his wife, Adele, that the rear areas in the throes of

construction had become almost unrecognizable. "It is remarkable what has been done in so short a time." By the end of June, there were 245,000 Americans on Okinawa and neighboring islands, and seven operational airstrips for fighters and bombers.[25]

SEABEES WERE BUILDING PORT AND cargo-handling facilities at White Beach on Nakagusuku Bay—renamed Buckner Bay following the general's death—to supplement the Hagushi beach sites, and at Kin Bay. Later, after it was cleared of debris, Naha Harbor would become a deep-water port.

Meeting the logistical needs of the Pacific war's biggest campaign had tested American capabilities, but it was just a precursor of the enormous task of supplying the divisions that would invade Japan.

Supplies and ammunition reached Okinawa from the Marianas, Ulithi, and Kerama Retto. Ships and LSTs initially landed the cargo at the Hagushi beaches, until new landing points were established along the west and east coasts during the Tenth Army's march southward: near Machinato and Naha on the west coast; and at Chimu Bay, Ishikawa, the Katchin Peninsula, and Kuba in the east. Between April 1 and June 30, an average of 22,200 measurement tons—a measurement ton equaled 40 cubic feet—was landed every day on Okinawa.[26]

For the first time, the Navy resupplied and refueled its task forces at sea. No such endeavor on this scale had ever been attempted; it was wildly successful. Supply ships delivered food, blankets, cigarettes, frozen provisions, and ammunition directly to the Fifth Fleet. New LST ammunition ships equipped with mobile cranes placed their cargo directly on the decks of surface warships while at sea. Fleet oilers refueled them while they were under way, obviating the need to put into port for supplies and fuel—a task that previously had sidelined them for ten days on average.

"For the first time in history a fleet steamed to the threshold of an enemy homeland and, with its own air force embarked, stayed there at sea for a period of months until our own land and air forces were firmly established on the enemy's doorstep," wrote Admiral Raymond Spruance, commander of the Fifth Fleet.[27]

The innovative naval resupply operation enabled the Fifth Fleet to shell Okinawa without remission from L-Day until the fighting reached the island's southern tip. In no other World War II battle did more naval gunfire bombard enemy positions—and with so little effect, because the

Thirty-Second Army was embedded so deeply inside Okinawa's hills and ridges. A fire-support ship was assigned to each frontline regiment and each division, while other vessels were given firing missions targeting areas behind the enemy's lines.

The barrage lasted from March until mid-June, when it was finally curtailed on the Kiyan Peninsula because of the risk of friendly fire casualties in the confined combat area. However, warships still fired star shells continually at night to foil enemy infiltrations. The Navy's meticulous record-keeping revealed that between April 1 and June 30 the fleet fired 23,210 shells of 12 inches or larger; 31,550 eight-inch high-capacity shells; 44,450 six-inch high-capacity shells; and more than 475,000 rounds of five-inch ammunition.[28]

KIKUSUI NO. 10 IN JUNE was the final mass suicide assault on the Okinawa fleet, but kamikaze attacks continued fitfully throughout July and into August.

During the early hours of the bright, moonlit night of July 29, the destroyer *Callaghan* was patrolling Radar Picket Station No. 9A with two other destroyers, *Pritchett* and *Cassin Young*, and three gunboats. *Callaghan*, due to be overhauled soon, was equipped with surface- but not air-search radar, which left her more vulnerable to air attacks.

An antique fabric-and-wood Willow biplane—difficult for radar to detect because it had few metal parts—suddenly appeared behind *Callaghan*. Lumbering along at about 60mph, the biplane was approaching the stern dead-on, making it nearly impossible for crewmen to train their guns on it.

The plane struck *Callaghan*'s starboard side near a rear gun mount, and its bomb plunged into the aft engine room and exploded, igniting antiaircraft ammunition. A red-orange flash blazed across the night sky. A fire sprang up in a gun mount, spreading below to its magazine, which exploded and "blew the ship in two almost," said Sonar Technician Wallace Brunton.

The order was given to abandon ship, and nearby picket ships picked up survivors while narrowly avoiding two other suicide biplanes. *Callaghan* sank at 2:34 a.m. July 29. Forty-seven crewmen died, and seventy-three were wounded.

Callaghan was the last US ship sunk by a kamikaze during the Pacific war.[29]

The next night, *Cassin Young*, which had been crashed by a kamikaze in April and had helped pick up *Callaghan* survivors, was patrolling the entrance to Nakagusuku Bay when it was struck by another wood-and-fabric biplane. She didn't sink, but twenty-two crewmen were killed, and forty-five others were wounded.[30]

THE JAPANESE DID NOT ACHIEVE their goal of trading one plane for one ship, and they lost sixteen ships of their own. US combat air patrols and naval gunners claimed to have shot down more than 7,700 enemy planes—3,900 of them suicide planes—during the three-month aerial onslaught, severely eroding Japan's ability to defend its homeland. A later analysis by the US Strategic Bombing Survey reduced the total from 7,700 to around 3,000. The survey said 18.6 percent of kamikazes hit their targets or caused damage by near misses. Just 1.8 percent of the suicide planes sank ships.[31]

Admiral Richmond Kelly Turner, the Joint Expeditionary Force commander, praised the radar pickets' effectiveness. They detected incoming raids at an average distance of 72 miles from Point Bolo, a few miles north of the Hagushi beaches. Less than 1 percent of the attackers were able to fly within 30 miles of the transport area undetected, said Turner.[32]

Yet, the Japanese pilots' eagerness to trade their lives and planes for an American ship sowed dread among the sailors off Okinawa, who feared an attack at any time. Crewmen with long service in the fleet periodically suffered from anxiety, loss of sleep, and no appetite because of the kamikaze threat.

THE AMERICAN B-29 BOMBING RAIDS continued against the Japanese mainland through May and June. On June 4, it was Kobe's turn. Kobe was Japan's main seaport and its sixth largest city. It had been bombed twice before. On this night, Kobe's steel plants were targeted by 450 to 500 of General Curtis LeMay's bombers, which dropped nearly 3,000 tons of incendiary bombs on a 10-mile area near Osaka Bay.

Two weeks later, 450 B-29s dropped incendiary bombs on four smaller cities: Kagoshima, Omuta, Hamamatsu, and Yokkaichi. A bombardier, Lieutenant Herman Blumenstock, watched bombs falling from the aircraft ahead of his, "and flames from below made them glisten like diamonds." Afterward, Lieutenant George Mott, the commander of the last plane over Kagoshima, said, "I think we can write off Kagoshima, for the city was blazing right to the waterfront."[33]

By late July and August, US bomber groups had done such a thorough job of destroying military targets on Kyushu that they had run out of them. The A-20 pilots of the Army Air Force's 3rd Attack Group were dismayed when they were sent to hit soft civilian targets, said Captain Howard Naslund, the group's assistant operations officer.

"Usually, after our previous strikes on purely military targets, such as ships or airfields, the crews talked excitedly about what they had seen, what they had hit," said Naslund. "But after these strikes, the men were absolutely silent, none of the usual talk."

During the group's final mission on August 12, Naslund's squadron, followed by two other squadrons, approached the city of Akume at nearly treetop level without being detected. "From our 40-foot altitude we could see residents in the streets, on sidewalks, looking in windows, paying no attention, until our combined eighteen Cal. 50 machine guns opened fire." When the three squadrons re-formed over the sea a short time later, flames from the distant city licked the sky.[34]

ACROSS OKINAWA IN JULY THERE lay a miasma of death and ruin. In Naha, just one building remained completely intact in the capital city that once was home to 60,000 people, but that was now abandoned; the rest of the city was "a mass of debris" with impassable, rubble-clogged streets. The Army Corps of Engineers began building coral roads to move traffic along.[35]

Elsewhere, the decomposing bodies of Okinawans and Japanese soldiers lay alongside the less-traveled roads, and in houses, fields, and shelters. Sealed caves held thousands more remains. Inside the Ufugusukumui Shelter near Itoman, which had been used as a command post and then a hospital, were three hundred to four hundred corpses. When the 32nd Infantry Brigade abandoned Ufugusukumui, potassium cyanide was administered to end the lives of the wounded that were left behind with the dead.

In the decades after the battle, farmers and construction workers across the island routinely unearthed the skeletal remains of dead civilians and Japanese soldiers and laid them beside the roads for removal.[36]

Admiral Raymond Spruance, the Fifth Fleet commander, said Okinawa was nothing less than "a bloody, hellish prelude to the invasion of Japan."[37]

GENERALS USHIJIMA AND CHŌ HAD ingeniously transformed Okinawa's corduroy-like rolling hills and valleys into a lethal defensive network that made the Tenth Army pay with blood for every yard of ground

captured. The decision to not oppose the Iceberg landings and to instead defend the southern island was an act of inspired fatalism. The Thirty-Second Army's senior officers never seriously believed that they would leave Okinawa alive; they believed that they had to hold out as long as possible to make America flinch from the bloody prospect of invading the Japanese mainland.

Chō's study of Russian tactics led to the Thirty-Second Army creating dense killing zones. The Japanese laced the hilltop approaches with land mines and tank traps, the forward slopes with trenches defended by machine guns and mortars, and the reverse slopes with mortars and light artillery. Spotters on high ground called down heavy artillery fire from the rear.

Artillery, mortar, and machine-gun fire from mutually supporting positions in nearly fireproof caves, tunnels, and ravines, and on escarpments made it impossible for General Buckner to execute a broad advance that would crush the enemy with one blow. Instead, Buckner's offensives became a series of smaller, close-in battles in which the Japanese fought from concealed positions that had to be approached from fire-swept open areas.[38]

Thwarted from maneuver by the dense, crowded terrain, the Americans learned to rely on tank-infantry teams and corkscrew-and-blowtorch tactics to blast their way through the interlocking defenses. It was so agonizingly slow at times that the Marines and soldiers sometimes felt they had been transported back in time to World War I, but against an enemy determined to fight to death.

YET, THE FIVE-WEEK BATTLE OF Iwo Jima was costlier than Okinawa in relative terms, with the ratio of American to Japanese deaths one to three, compared with Okinawa's one-to-ten ratio. In five weeks, Iwo Jima consumed 6,821 American lives, and accounted for 19,217 wounded, compared with 7,613 Tenth Army troops killed and 31,807 wounded during Okinawa's twelve-week battle.

The Japanese employed the same tactics on both islands. They fought from carefully prepared cave and pillbox defenses connected by elaborate tunnels, and they did not mount a water's-edge defense or launch massive banzai attacks as they did on Tarawa and Saipan. On both Iwo Jima and Okinawa, American forces destroyed the defenders with battering, head-on attacks.

The difference in the campaigns' casualty lists may have been due to the Tenth Corps's hybrid Army-Marine Corps composition, and the divergent

philosophies of its Army and Marine leaders. While Iwo Jima was almost entirely a Marine Corps operation led by an aggressive Marine general, an Army general commanded Operation Iceberg. The Army's XXIV Corps and the Marines' III Amphibious Corps operated independently of each other, and according to their respective cultures and traditions.

The Army sacrificed speed to minimize casualties—usually advancing with deliberation following heavy preparatory gunfire, ideally with the support of tanks. By contrast, the Marines sought to quickly reach their objectives, even if it meant forgoing supporting fire and accepting a steep "butcher's bill."

The deep-seated distrust between the two services was aggravated by the controversy that flared during the 1944 Saipan campaign. The Army resented the Marines' disparagement of the 27th Division for slowness and the dismissal of the 27th's commander for not moving faster. Many Marines believed the Army was too cautious; many soldiers thought that the Marines needlessly squandered men's lives.

Private First Class Richard Book, a 96th Division mortarman, had seen how Marine officers in southern Okinawa sent their men up a hill with "no softening fire, no artillery. . . . The Marines wouldn't soften up the place with machine gun fire, mortar fire, etc. It was just, 'Go take that hill.' The Japs up there just mowed the Marines down. . . . We [Army] had the type of training where you soften them up before you go charging."[39]

General Lemuel Shepherd, the 6th Marine Division's commander, attempted to temper his Marines' aggressiveness on Okinawa. The Corps's tactical approach on Iwo Jima under "Howlin' Mad" Smith had cost his V Corps's three Marine divisions and Army regiment more than 25,000 casualties in five weeks. Before Shepherd's troops went into the Shuri Line and attacked the Sugar Loaf Hill complex, Shepherd told his officers to outmaneuver the enemy, and to not try to "outslug" him.

But there were few opportunities for maneuver on the Shuri Line with its densely packed defenses, or on southern Okinawa's escarpments. Moreover, the Marines' eagerness to engage the enemy was deeply ingrained. Shepherd's division reported the highest number of battle deaths of the seven divisions that fought on the island—1,622, along with 7,000 wounded. The ten-day assaults on Sugar Loaf, Half Moon, and Horseshoe Hills were largely responsible for these casualties.

Like the 6th Division, General Pedro del Valle's 1st Marine Division had begun the campaign with more than 19,000 infantrymen. By the end of

the campaign, it reported 1,150 men killed in action, another 154 who died of their wounds, and 6,366 wounded. After going into action for the first time on May 1, it fought on the Shuri Line at Dakeshi and Wana Ridges, and Wana Draw. In June, it suffered major losses on Kunishi Ridge.

The 1st Division had received 5,000 replacements, but they were not enough to restore the most depleted units to full strength. The 5th Marines' Company K landed on Okinawa with 235 men, and during the campaign it received 250 replacements that theoretically would have raised its total to 485 men. Yet, at the end of June, just 50 Marines remained in Company K; 26 of them had come ashore on L-Day.[40]

A correlation might be seen between the Marines' tradition of tactical aggressiveness and the winners of the twenty-three Congressional Medals of Honor awarded for gallantry on Okinawa. Eleven of them went to the 1st and 6th Divisions, and three others to Navy corpsmen serving with those units. Four went to soldiers in the Army's 96th Infantry Division, which also reported the Tenth Army's second-highest casualty figure: 1,598 killed and 5,614 wounded. Two went to 77th Division soldiers, and a third was awarded to a medic attached to that division, Desmond Doss. The 27th Division earned one of the medals, and the other went to Navy Lieutenant Richard McCool, the commander of *LCS(L)(3)-122*, which was in action during Iceberg. Navy Chaplain Joseph O'Callahan and Navy Lieutenant Donald Gary received Medals of Honor for their actions aboard the *Franklin* before L-Day, and they were not included in the campaign total.[41]

In late June, General John Hodge, commander of XXIV Corps, complained to the new Tenth Army commander, General Joseph "Vinegar Joe" Stilwell, that the Marine Corps had unfairly received the lion's share of the credit for the Okinawa victory. Hodge said that he had even read news accounts "crediting them with moves actually made by my own divisions."

"I have been able to find but little mention of Army troops fighting their hearts out in the last twelve days of the 82-day battle," Hodge wrote. "The big picture and the overall result is that the American public thinks the USMC are the only good troops in the Pacific Area, that they do all the fighting, and that no one else can execute amphibious landings."[42]

THE CAMPAIGN CLAIMED THE LIVES of well over 100,000 Japanese soldiers and their Okinawan and South Korean auxiliaries. The Tenth Army's action report stated that there were 107,539 counted enemy dead, and estimated that another 23,764 enemy troops and auxiliaries had also died.

Undoubtedly, thousands of uncounted enemy dead lay moldering in the myriad caves sealed by American troops.

The ground campaign's bloodiest months were April and May, when 4,873 US soldiers and Marines were reported killed or missing in action, and 21,171 men were listed as wounded. The casualty total of 26,044 on May 31, with weeks of fighting ahead, was the highest of the Pacific war.[43]

During April and May, Okinawan historian Masahide Ōta wrote, 62,548 Japanese troops were killed, and an additional 9,529 were listed as missing—and later pronounced dead—for 72,077 total Japanese killed on the Shuri Line, Ie Shima, and the Motobu Peninsula. Thirty-five thousand more fell in June and during mop-up operations in July and August.

Those killed during April and May were the Thirty-Second Army's best combat troops. Second-tier enemy troops and the remnants of the 62nd and 24th Divisions and the 44th IMB continued to resist desperately, even fanatically, through June on the Kiyan Peninsula escarpments. They faced impossible odds against three combat divisions, and the onslaught of artillery, mortar, and naval gunfire, and air strikes.[44]

By the end of Operation Iceberg, 12,520 US soldiers, Marines, and air and naval personnel had died—7,613 from the Tenth Army, and 4,907 from the Fifth Fleet. More than 36,000 others were wounded during this first battle fought on Japanese soil.[45]

Believing that Okinawa merely foreshadowed exponentially heavier losses on the Japanese mainland, sailors, soldiers, and Marines were scarcely in the mood to celebrate their victory.

Dénouement

For the civilians trapped between the two armies, the Battle of Okinawa was like being "attacked by tigers at the front gate and wolves at the back."

—MASAHIDE ŌTA OF THE BLOOD AND
IRON CORPS AND FUTURE GOVERNOR OF OKINAWA[1]

Having a dream, I will go up into the sky.

—ADMIRAL MATOME UGAKI'S LAST MESSAGE BEFORE
LEAVING ON HIS SUICIDE MISSION ON AUGUST 15, 1945[2]

CERTAIN THAT THE AMERICANS WOULD rape, mutilate, and kill them if they were captured, a group of Okinawan schoolgirls and their teacher fled to a cliff overlooking the southern shoreline. Americans in a landing craft saw the girls and by loudspeaker urged them to go to the beach and come aboard, promising that they would be safe. To the girls, this was unthinkable.

"In our minds, it was as though the devil was inviting us into hell," said Kikuko Miyagi. "We were sure that if we were caught, we would be torn limb from limb."

Japanese soldiers had given the girls and their teacher a single grenade with which to take their lives. That night, they flung their belongings over the cliff into the sea, sang "Furusato" ("Hometown"), and wept. "I wish I

could meet Dad and Mom again before I die," a girl whispered to Kikuko as
they ate their moldy rice.

American soldiers suddenly appeared on the cliff and opened fire. The
girls dove into holes. Everybody around Kikuko was killed, but their bodies
shielded hers and she was unhurt. In another hole, ten of the girls and their
teacher detonated the grenade, and they all died. As Kikuko climbed down
the cliff, she saw friends' bodies along the way.[3]

ABOUT 80,000 SHELL-SHOCKED, HOMELESS CIVILIANS were persuaded to leave their hiding places in caves and crevices across southern
Okinawa in late June. But thousands of others lay dead, or sought death
rather than surrender.[4]

Civilians died in caves where the Japanese had ordered them to remain;
others were forced to jump off the southern seaside cliffs. A group of student nurses were among the jumpers—plunging to their deaths from rocks
high above the sea.[5]

In late June, Marines with flamethrowers killed nearly four dozen terrified student nurses in a cave where they were hiding from the Americans.
Hearing what they believed were Japanese voices inside the cave, the Marines had demanded through an interpreter that the occupants come out
and surrender immediately.

When the girls refused to leave the cave, forty-six of the fifty-one students and teachers were incinerated. The cave was a Japanese Army field
hospital staffed by young women from the Himeyuri Student Corps—
teenage girls from two high schools. The place where they died became
known as the "Cave of the Virgins." The Himeyuri Peace Museum was later
built at this site.[6]

Fourteen-year-old Shin'ichi Kuniyoshi was in a crowded cave with fifty
Japanese soldiers inside Hill 108 in southeastern Okinawa when American
soldiers lobbed grenades and a satchel charge into it. "I ended up being
pinned under the bodies of those killed and blown backward onto me by
the blast," he said.

Shin'ichi was unable to free himself from the crushing weight of the
bodies. But a wounded officer came to his aid. Covered in blood, his eye-
balls dangling from their sockets, and panting for breath, the Japanese officer lifted the bodies off Shin'ichi. The officer died of his wounds a short
time later.[7]

During the Tenth Army's sweep to cleanse southern Okinawa of Japanese holdouts, Marine George Peto's patrol entered a hamlet, where the people rushed to meet them, and then did something surprising.

"They all quickly lined up in formation on the road through the hamlet, unbuttoned their clothes, and dropped them to the ground," said Peto. The thirty to forty civilians stood at attention, "buck naked."

The Marines surmised that the Japanese had required the civilians to disrobe whenever they entered the hamlet, and that the villagers assumed that the Americans would demand likewise. "Maybe it was an act of forced humiliation," said Peto, "or maybe it was just to show that the villagers were not armed or carrying explosives."[8]

AS THE CAMPAIGN WOUND DOWN, the Americans redoubled their efforts to coax civilians from caves in the southern cliffs overlooking the sea.

One day, a 7th Division interpreter set up a loudspeaker atop a 200-foot cliff and spoke for more than ten minutes. At first, no one left the caves. Then, a man carrying a white cloth appeared on the strip of beach below. Others joined him, until the civilians numbered more than one hundred. A boy began to climb a trail winding up the cliff and the others followed him.

That day, the 7th Division detained between five hundred and six hundred civilians. Their numbers increased daily as the Okinawans realized that the Americans were not going to kill them. By the time that the island was secured, thousands of civilians were entering the 7th Division lines every day.[9]

Sergeant Everett Deiber of the 6th Marine Tank Battalion dismounted from his tank on a cliff overlooking Okinawa's southern shore. On the beach, Deiber saw a crowd of Japanese soldiers, civilian men, and women with children. Small boats plied the water, "out of rifle range, with talkers speaking in Japanese, imploring those on the beach to surrender."[10]

In its planning for Iceberg, the Tenth Army had anticipated that as many as 306,000 civilians would have to be fed, clothed, and housed by the Americans. During the operation's combat phase, each division was supplied with 70,000 civilian rations—mostly soybeans, canned fish, and rice—as well as medical supplies.

The Military Government Section overseen by General W. E. Crist expanded quickly behind the battle lines. Navy dispensaries and hospital units, military police, and civil-affairs personnel supported the refugee

camps. By the end of April, more than 125,000 civilians were staying in Military Government stockades and resettlement villages. Fewer than 30,000 additional civilians were captured in May during the intensive fighting along the Shuri Line, but by the end of June, 261,115 civilians were under the Tenth Army's care.[11]

MASAHIDE ŌTA, CONSCRIPTED AT AGE nineteen into the Blood and Iron Corps and later governor of Okinawa from 1990 to 1998, wrote that for the civilians trapped between the two armies, the Battle of Okinawa was like being "attacked by tigers at the front gate and wolves at the back."

The result was that about one of every three Okinawans living on the island on April 1 died during the three-month battle. Okinawa historians believe that civilian deaths, for which there is no exact count, totaled 120,000, but other estimates have ranged as high as 140,000.[12]

AT A MEETING IN TOKYO in February, Emperor Hirohito and seven senior statesmen had emphasized the importance of bitter resistance. What followed was General Tadamichi Kuribayashi's tenacious stand on Iwo Jima, and General Ushijima's masterful defense of Okinawa. With one exception, the emperor and his statesmen agreed that Japan must persevere until the Allies realized the futility of continuing the war and negotiated a peace. Prince Fumimaro Konoe, the lone dissenter, argued that if the war continued, the Soviet Union would ally itself with the Chinese Communists and Americans to drive the Japanese army out of China. The collateral damage might well be a Communist revolution in Japan, he warned.

Hirohito rejected Konoe's argument and insisted that a single decisive victory—delusional at best after three years of Japanese defeats—would compel the Allies to negotiate. Failing that, battles of attrition would so bleed American forces as to shock leaders and bring them to the bargaining table. The losses of Japanese soldiers, sailors, and airmen appeared to be of tangential concern to the emperor; Hirohito's first priority was to preserve his prerogatives as emperor.

But as casualties mounted on Okinawa and Allied bombings scorched more Japanese cities, Hirohito began to weigh a peace initiative in response to the Allies' demand for unconditional surrender. On June 22, the day that the Tenth Army officially secured Okinawa, Hirohito notified the Supreme War Leadership Council that he was ready to begin diplomacy to end the war.

Japanese overtures to the Soviet Union in the hope that Moscow would mediate negotiations with the Allies came too late. Japan and the Soviets had indeed signed a neutrality agreement in 1941, but the Soviet Union was now cooperating with the Allies, Japan's enemy. Since the Yalta Summit in February, the Soviets had been planning an invasion of Japanese-occupied Manchuria and Korea in August. Moscow now regarded the 1941 neutrality treaty as void, and was unresponsive to Japan's overtures.

The emperor's tardy contemplation of extending an olive branch was stunningly at odds with the galloping developments in Washington and New Mexico aimed at bringing the Pacific war to a violent conclusion.[13]

THE PACIFIC WAR, HOWEVER, ENDED because of neither negotiations nor invasion. Two weeks after FDR's death, War Secretary Henry Stimson had informed FDR's successor, Harry Truman, of the existence of an "immense project" involving a new explosive of "almost unbelievable destructive power."

"Within four months we shall in all probability have completed the most terrible weapon ever known in human history," Stimson wrote in the memorandum that he handed to Truman on April 25, "one bomb of which could destroy a whole city." This was indeed disturbing news to Truman, who had been vice president only since January 1945 after a decade in the US Senate, and who knew nothing about the top-secret Manhattan Project. Now Stimson summoned General Leslie Groves of the Army Corps of Engineers, who had been the project's director since 1942, to brief Truman about the breakthrough development of the first atomic bomb.[14]

Aside from a handful of Manhattan Project scientists and senior government officials, no one else had been apprised of the bomb, not even General Douglas MacArthur or Admiral Chester Nimitz. Planning for Japan's invasion was proceeding as if no such project existed. On May 25, the Joint Chiefs of Staff approved Operation Olympic, the amphibious assault on Kyushu tentatively scheduled for November 1, involving a dozen divisions, two others in floating reserve, and about 2,700 vessels—more than twice as many as had participated in Iceberg.

War Secretary Stimson expressed strong reservations. The invasion would be so bloody, he warned, that the United States should seek "any alternative" that would accomplish its goal of unconditional surrender. Olympic, to be followed by the Operation Coronet invasion of Honshu— the home island of Tokyo and Japan's other major cities—in the spring of

1946, would "leave the Japanese islands even more thoroughly destroyed than was the case with Germany," said Stimson. Although he concurred with his war secretary's gloomy assessment, Truman on June 18 reluctantly approved the two invasions of Japan's home islands, collectively known as Operation Downfall.[15]

AT THE ARMY AIR FORCE base at Alamogordo, New Mexico, at 5:30 a.m. on July 16, scientists detonated the first plutonium bomb, a nuclear device known as the "Gadget." General Groves's report about the so-called Trinity test said that the intense flash of light equaled "several suns in midday; a huge ball of fire was formed which lasted for several seconds," and was seen 120 miles away in Albuquerque, and at Santa Fe and El Paso. A billowing mushroom-shaped cloud rose to 41,000 feet. The explosion evaporated the steel tower on which the bomb was detonated. The test was a success.

The report on the Trinity test was read to Truman on July 21 while he was attending the Potsdam Conference in occupied Germany with Joseph Stalin and Winston Churchill. Truman was "tremendously pepped up" after hearing the report, wrote Stimson. Already, since Truman became president in April, US casualties in the Pacific had reached new heights.

The new weapon, Truman believed, would obviate the need for Operation Downfall and its projected Allied casualties of 250,000 to 1 million troops—in addition to enormous Japanese casualties. For a World War I veteran such as Truman who had seen wholesale carnage, saving lives was a powerful argument for using the bomb.

For Downfall, Truman had already authorized the movement of more than 1 million troops to the Pacific. More undoubtedly would be needed; the president believed that conquering the Japanese mainland would be tantamount to fighting "Okinawa[s] from one end of Japan to the other."

In that assessment, Truman was correct; the casualty estimate for Olympic was probably low. The Japanese reportedly were mustering more than six hundred thousand troops to repel the Kyushu invasion, albeit not all of them fully equipped, plus millions of civilians serving as an ad hoc fighting force.

Those projections worried some members of the Joint Chiefs of Staff. Blockade and massive bombing might be a more prudent strategy than invasion, they said. The invasion's massive casualties could erode civilian support for seeing the war through to Japan's unconditional surrender.

But JCS analysts argued that it would be better to invade quickly to stay ahead of the potential loss of public support. Since Germany's surrender, the American public had begun showing signs of war weariness, and it would lose patience with a siege of Japan by blockade and bombing, the analysts reasoned.[16]

Downfall's second phase, Operation Coronet, would be the main event: the attack on Honshu, Japan's largest, most heavily populated island whose cities included Tokyo, Kyoto, Osaka, Kobe, and Hiroshima. Tentatively planned for March 1946, Coronet's objective was to land twenty-five divisions—more than five hundred thousand men to be led personally by General Douglas MacArthur—that would march across the Kanto Plain to Tokyo and end the Pacific war within a year of the conclusion of the European war. Coronet's casualties would surely eclipse Olympic's, planners agreed.[17]

When Downfall commenced, it was likely that many of the most experienced troops and naval personnel would be missing from the invasion force. Historian Richard Frank wrote that many of them would probably be discharged by the fall of 1945 under the adjusted service rating score system. Points were awarded for months in service, months spent overseas, campaigns participated in, combat awards, and dependents living at home. A minimum eighty-five points were required for demobilization. The system did not apply to soldiers in specialties deemed critical.[18]

THE JAPANESE HAD CLOSELY WATCHED the preparations for these invasions that would dwarf the D-Day landings in Normandy. Japanese leaders had intensified their homeland defense measures early in 1945 under the banner of "Ketsu-Go" after the defeat in the Philippines, at the beginning of the assault on Iwo Jima, and with Okinawa's invasion imminent.

In late February, Japan had begun mobilizing its enormous home defense force, which combined with existing units would comprise 1.5 million armed men in fifty divisions and twenty-five independent mixed brigades—much larger than US intelligence estimates. Japan's plans emphasized defending Kyushu and Honshu's Kanto Plain, the Allies' primary targets. "The ground forces will win the final decision by overwhelming and annihilating the enemy landing force in the coastal area before the beachhead is secure," Japan's planners optimistically predicted.[19]

On March 10, the Japanese government announced that males between the ages of twelve and sixty and females aged twelve to forty were subject

to call-up for war production and home defense, an aspect of the overarching National Resistance Program. Public schools were closed, and children were sent to work in factories. The government began making special weapons for civilian use—bamboo spears and long bows for the most part, along with swords and light arms.

If, as Japanese leaders boasted, every mobilized citizen was prepared to fight to the death, the total might reach 28 million combat-capable civilians. They included specialized civilian militia units, such as a Patriotic Citizens Fighting Corps, and a kamikaze civilian ground force.[20]

American planners knew that thousands of conventional and suicide planes, many of them obsolete, had been reserved for the Japanese Götterdämmerung. In addition, the invaders would face suicide boats, manned torpedoes, and midget submarines. Japanese prison-camp commanders were under orders to execute all Allied war prisoners when the Americans landed.

The Joint Chiefs of Staff planners hoped to somehow limit the amphibious landings during Olympic and Coronet. During the Pacific war, amphibious operations cost 7.4 casualties per thousand troops per day on average, compared to 2.16 casualties for land operations in the European theater. It was unclear how the JCS planners intended to minimize amphibious operations while invading the Japanese islands.[21]

THE DECISION TO DROP THE bomb was made on July 24 at a meeting of Truman, Churchill, and the American and British chiefs of staff during the Potsdam Conference. The leaders agreed to deploy it within a few weeks. Truman told Stalin that America possessed "a new weapon of unusual destructive force," without providing details. Stalin showed "no special interest," Truman wrote.

General George C. Marshall, the US Army's chief of staff, later said a major factor in the decision was that "we had just been through the bitter experience of Okinawa." The president wrote to his wife, Bess, "I'll say that we'll end the war a year sooner now, and think of the kids who won't be killed! That's the important thing."

On July 26, the day that the cruiser *Indianapolis* delivered components of the uranium bomb known as "Little Boy" to Tinian in the Marshall Islands, the Truman administration released what became known as the Potsdam Declaration—a final warning to Japan. It demanded the unconditional surrender of Japan's military forces, with the alternative being "prompt and

utter destruction." It was broadcast on Japanese radio monitors, and B-29s dropped 7 million leaflets containing a Japanese translation onto Japanese cities. The leaflets read, "Today we come not to bomb you. We are dropping this leaflet in order to let you know the reply by the government of the United States to your government's request for conditions of surrender."

Japanese leaders did not respond to the Potsdam Declaration.[22]

SHORTLY AFTER 8 A.M. HIROSHIMA time on August 6, the B-29 *Enola Gay*, flying at 31,000 feet, dropped "Little Boy," a uranium bomb that was the first atomic weapon used in combat. It exploded 1,900 feet above the Shima Hospital courtyard with a tremendous explosion—whose power was estimated as being equivalent to 16,000 tons of TNT or 2,100 tons of conventional bombs. Two shock waves caused the plane to bounce and jump. Tail gunner George Robert "Bob" Caron shot photographs and described what he saw on the intercom: "a bubbling mass of purple-gray smoke and you could see a red core in it and everything was burning inside." About 140,000 Japanese citizens at Hiroshima died of bomb-related injuries and illnesses by the end of 1945.[23]

Three days later, the B-29 *Bockscar* dropped a plutonium bomb, "Fat Man," on Nagasaki. By the end of 1945, seventy thousand deaths were attributable to Fat Man.[24]

On August 10, Japan accepted the terms of the Potsdam Declaration, but only to the extent that it "does not comprise any demand which prejudices the prerogatives of His Majesty as a Sovereign Ruler." The Allies replied that upon agreeing to surrender, the Japanese government's prerogatives would be determined by the Allied powers.

Emperor Hirohito accepted the Allies' terms on August 14. In his unprecedented radio address to the Japanese people the next day, Hirohito said, in part,

> The war situation has developed not necessarily to Japan's advantage, while the general trends of the world have all turned against her interest. Moreover, the enemy has begun to employ a new and most cruel bomb, the power of which to do damage is, indeed, incalculable, taking the toll of many innocent lives. Should we continue to fight, not only would it result in the ultimate collapse and obliteration of the Japanese people, but also it would lead to the total extinction of human civilization. Such being the case how are we to save millions of our subjects or to atone

ourselves before the hallowed spirits of our imperial ancestors? This is the reason why we have ordered the acceptance of the Joint Declaration of the Powers.

The emperor's 100 million subjects had never heard his "jewel voice" until that day.[25]

GEORGE NILAND OF THE 22ND Marines said the news reached the 6th Marine Division on Guam, where it was preparing to assault the Japanese mainland. "I knew I was dead," wrote Niland, "because there was no way" that he expected to survive Operation Olympic. When he learned that a single bomb had destroyed Hiroshima, it was "the happiest day of my life . . . it was like getting a new life. Every day I have said a prayer for Harry Truman."[26]

Mortar platoon Sergeant R. V. Burgin of the 5th Marines was living in a camp for NCOs on the northern tip of Okinawa when he learned of Japan's surrender on August 15. A Corsair pilot celebrated the war's end by buzzing a nearby airstrip for spotter planes—upside down. The pilot, said Burgin, was flying so low that he "could have opened his canopy, stuck out his hand and dragged his fingers along the ground." After repeating the feat, the pilot gained altitude, performed several rolls, and flew away.[27]

E. B. Sledge and his comrades received word of Japan's surrender with "quiet disbelief" and "an indescribable sense of relief," after long believing that the Japanese would never surrender. "Sitting in stunned silence, we remembered our dead," Sledge wrote. "So many dead. So many maimed. . . . Except for a few widely scattered shouts of joy, the survivors of the abyss sat hollow-eyed and silent, trying to comprehend a world without war."[28]

The Tenth Army was scattered to the winds. The 2nd Marine Division and the 27th and 77th Army divisions were sent to Japan for occupation duty, the 1st Marine Division and most of the 6th Marine Division went to China, and the 7th Division embarked for Korea. The 96th Division sailed for the United States.

The 6th Division's 4th Regiment went to Japan instead of China, and became the first American combat troops to set foot on mainland Japan, where the fortifications were draped in white flags. The 4th Marines shared a steak dinner with the Bataan "death march" survivors of their namesake regiment, which had vanished from the rolls in 1942.[29]

IN THE RUINED COUNTRYSIDE OF southern Okinawa, pitted by deep shell holes and littered with smashed trees, several hundred Japanese soldiers from the 24th Division remained in caves, unaware that Hirohito had surrendered and that the Pacific war was over. Colonel Kikuji Hongo, commander of the 24th Division's 32nd Regiment, led the 55 officers and 342 enlisted men holed up in caves in the Itoman-Kunishi Ridge area. With an unofficial ceasefire in effect, neither side attacked the other. US planes dropped leaflets announcing Japan's surrender, but Hongo and his men did not believe them.[30]

On August 22, Captain Howard Moss, who was a language officer with the 7th Division, and a Japanese corporal approached the command post cave of the 32nd Regiment's 1st Battalion. Moss and the corporal told the battalion commander, Captain Koichi Ito, that the war was over. Unconvinced, Ito asked Moss for two days to absorb what Moss had said. Moss agreed to return two days hence. In the meantime, Ito visited Colonel Hongo, who instructed Ito to investigate what Moss had told him.

When Moss met again with Ito, he offered to take him to Kadena Airfield to hear a recording of Emperor Hirohito's radio message. After Ito had listened to the emperor's address twice, Moss took him to see Colonel Hiromichi Yahara, the Thirty-Second Army's former chief of staff and now a war prisoner. Yahara said it was true; the war was over.

On their trip back to Ito's cave at Kunishi, Moss showed him the place on Hill 89 where Generals Ushijima and Chō had committed suicide.

Ito told Hongo everything that he had heard and seen and, after discussing these matters with his staff officers, Hongo concluded that the emperor's instructions must be followed. Ito and Hongo burned the 32nd Regiment's colors, and on August 29, about 400 soldiers and 105 civilians emerged from their hideouts and surrendered to the Americans—the largest remaining group of Japanese holdouts.

Another three hundred Japanese soldiers surrendered after Ito convinced a friend, Captain Tsumeo Shimura, and the survivors of the 32nd Regiment's 2nd Battalion to surrender, along with a group of naval and air force troops that was preparing to slip into northern Okinawa to wage guerrilla warfare.[31]

For them, the Battle of Okinawa was now ended.

ONE HUNDRED THREE THOUSAND AMERICANS were killed while fighting Japanese forces from 1941 to 1945. Over half of the losses occurred

against increasingly frenzied Japanese resistance during the war's last year. Thirty thousand British, Indian, Australian, and other Commonwealth troops perished during the war. Japan, which in 1945 had 5.95 million men in uniform, reported 1.74 million military and 393,000 civilian deaths, with nearly all of the civilian deaths occurring after March 1, 1945.[32]

During the occupation of Japan after the war, Okinawa and the Ryukyus remained under US military authority. In 1951, the San Francisco Treaty restored autonomy to Japan, but not to Okinawa. In 1972, the United States returned Okinawa and the Ryukyus to Japan, but with the proviso that America would retain its military forces and bases on Okinawa as part of its defense treaty with Japan.

Today, 60 percent of the US bases on Japanese territory are located on Okinawa, as well as a large percentage of the 50,000 American personnel stationed in Japan. Yet Okinawa comprises less than 1 percent of Japan's land area. As subjects of Japan and, in a very real sense too, of the United States, Okinawans today have limited control over their island.

In recent decades, Okinawans have bridled at the oversize American presence. Islanders and Okinawa's governor have tried to block plans to move the Marine Corps Air Station from the more congested Futenma area to Camp Schwab in a less-populated area of Okinawa near Nago City. The United States has responded by returning nearly 10,000 acres in northern Okinawa to Japan, and announcing plans to transfer thousands of American servicemen from Okinawa to Guam.[33]

THE LAST KAMIKAZE WAS ADMIRAL Matome Ugaki, the commander of the Fifth Air Fleet. He blamed himself for the failure of his special attack pilots to crush the Americans. "I've never been so ashamed of myself. Alas!" he wrote.

On August 15, the day that Emperor Hirohito broadcast his surrender message, Ugaki elected to die as a samurai, while personally leading what was arguably the final kamikaze attack of the war. "I want to live in the noble spirit of the special attack," Ugaki wrote.

Ugaki rode from Fifth Fleet headquarters to Oita Airfield, where eleven Suisei dive-bombers of the 701st Air Group Special Attack detachment were warming up. The admiral's orders had stipulated that three bombers would carry out the attack, but the entire squadron insisted on going. Twenty-two airmen, each wearing a white headband with a rising sun in the center, stood in a line before their planes.

Ugaki's chief of staff and the air fleet's senior flight officer attempted to dissuade the admiral from carrying out the mission, but he told them, "This is my chance to die like a warrior."[34]

After boarding his plane, Ugaki was seen waving to people on the ground as the dive-bomber taxied down the runway.

En route to Okinawa, he sent a last message:

Despite brave fighting by each unit under my command for the past six months, we have failed to destroy the arrogant enemy in order to protect our divine empire, a failure which should be attributed to my lack of capabilities. . . . I am going to proceed to Okinawa, where our men lost their lives like cherry blossoms, and ram into the arrogant American ships, displaying the real spirit of a Japanese warrior. All units under my command shall keep my will in mind, overcoming every conceivable difficulty, rebuild a strong armed force, and make our empire last forever. The emperor Banzai!

Ugaki was never seen again. A last transmission from his plane at 7:24 p.m. said that it was going down on a target, but there were no reports of a kamikaze crashing a US ship. However, crashes of Japanese planes were reported August 15 on small islands off Okinawa. On Ie Shima, Americans in a jeep dragged away a body in a flying uniform, and a plane engine was later found.

Later, among the admiral's belongings, his staff found a note: "Having a dream, I will go up into the sky."[35]

Another group of kamikaze pilots had been waiting grimly at their base at Kanoya for the order to attack when they learned that the war had ended.

"I can remember the pale, drawn faces of the crew members," wrote Ensign Yukiteru Sugiyama, one of the pilots. "They were youths, their bodies were flowing with life. And they were waiting their turn to die. It was no longer possible to refuse to go. It was impossible to escape."

Then they heard the emperor's message. Surely to their great relief, they knew that they had been spared from making a futile attack on the US fleet with their flimsy, obsolete planes.[36]

ON THE SITE OF THE former Mabalacat Airfield, where Japanese Admiral Takijirō Ōnishi founded the first Special Attack Corps, stands a monument depicting a life-size kamikaze pilot on a pedestal. Erected in 2004, it

remains controversial today among Filipinos who remember their harsh treatment by the Japanese during the war.

ON SEPTEMBER 7, 1945, AT Kadena Airfield, Japanese commanders from the Amami and Sakishima island chains north of Okinawa formally surrendered the Ryukyus to American forces. The ceremony was held on a sunny day seventy-seven days after the conclusion of the Battle of Okinawa and five days after Japan's formal surrender on the USS *Missouri*.

Twenty-five tanks and a dozen 155mm self-propelled guns rumbled to the ceremony as a band played "Roll Out the Barrel" and "The Old Gray Mare."

An American flag snapped in the brisk northeastern breeze. It had flown above the Chungking headquarters of General Joseph Stilwell when he led Allied forces in China, Burma, and India before becoming the Tenth Army's commander.

A dozen Japanese senior officers arrived in a white plane emblazoned with green crosses. They joined Stilwell, General James Doolittle of the Eighth Air Force, General DeWitt Peck of the 1st Marine Division, and others at the surrender table. Stillwell arrived to the strains of "The General's March," and everyone present, including the Japanese, saluted.

General Toshiro Nomi, the Japanese commander on Sakishima, signed six copies of the document surrendering the Ryukyus to American forces. Stilwell, who had written the document, added his signature.

Formations of American bombers and fighters flew over the signatories.

When the ceremony ended and the Japanese officers were being led away, Stilwell caustically remarked, "There go the war lords of the Pacific."[37]

Epilogue

Never before had there been, probably never again will there be, such a vicious, sprawling struggle.

—*NEW YORK TIMES* CORRESPONDENT HANSON BALDWIN[1]

The strength and willpower, devotion and technical resources applied by the United States to this task, joined with the death struggle of the enemy, place this battle among the most intense and famous in military history.

—WINSTON CHURCHILL,
BRITISH PRIME MINISTER AND HISTORIAN[2]

THE BATTLE OF OKINAWA WAS neither the climax nor the resolution of the Pacific war, but its battle royale—fought by the United States with crushing power and ferocity, and by Japanese forces with calculation, abandon, and fatalism. The fighting left the once peaceful island a blood-drenched battlefield. At sea, the three-month siege of the US Fifth Fleet by Japanese kamikazes and conventional warplanes was unparalleled. The Battle of Okinawa stands as the longest sustained carrier campaign of World War II.[3]

"Never before had there been, probably never again will there be, such a vicious, sprawling struggle," wrote *New York Times* correspondent Hanson Baldwin of the Battle of Okinawa.[4]

It was the only World War II battle fought on Japanese soil. Its chief importance was its foreshadowing of the bloodbath that awaited when the Allies invaded mainland Japan. Even as fighting raged in the south, Okinawa, on Japan's doorstep only 350 miles away, was being transformed into the primary forward base for that invasion.

Beginning with the unplanned "meeting engagements" at Midway and Guadalcanal in 1942, US forces had stormed across the Pacific, wresting island after island from the Japanese. Each campaign was bloodier than the one before it, with the stubborn Japanese resistance intensifying and Americans utilizing their growing superiority in ships, planes, artillery, and manpower.

The Battle of Okinawa was the Pacific war's apotheosis. It was fought with stark ferocity in the air, on land, and at sea for three long months until the desperate Japanese defenders were crushed.

Of Okinawa, Winston Churchill said, "The strength and willpower, devotion and technical resources applied by the United States to this task, joined with the death struggle of the enemy, place this battle among the most intense and famous in military history."[5]

Then, in an instance of deus ex machina without warning or precedent, there came the atomic bombings of Hiroshima and Nagasaki. This secret new weapon of unimaginable destructive power killed more than 200,000 civilians, and ended the Pacific war with an emphatic bang, obviating the need to invade Japan's mainland.

Although Okinawa was the final major battle of World War II, it is often lost amid the crowded events that occurred during the spring and summer of 1945, and has not received the attention that it deserves. While the battle raged, there was the death of President Franklin Roosevelt, the only president many servicemen had known from childhood. The Third Reich collapsed and surrendered; Adolf Hitler took his own life. There were victory parades across the United States and in London and Paris. The Soviet Union emerged as a military colossus. Then, five weeks after Okinawa was secured, the mushroom clouds over Hiroshima and Nagasaki heralded the beginning of the atomic age.

The battle's great tragedy was the death of more than 120,000 Okinawa civilians. Their misfortune was not just inhabiting the final crossroads of the Pacific war, but living in a Japanese prefecture where they were regarded as disposable second-class citizens and were sometimes used as human shields. Equally dismaying, they too often appeared to

the heavily armed American soldiers and Marines to be "Japanese enough" to be killed.

The Okinawans died in exponentially greater numbers than did civilians caught in the line of fire between Japanese and Allied forces on any other Pacific island. Those who survived the storm of steel numbly crawled out of the caves and tunnels where they had hidden with their families and returned to flattened villages and homes.

THE AMERICANS WHO FOUGHT ON Okinawa would have difficulty recognizing the island today, or its 1945 battlegrounds—now covered by homes, car lots, fast-food franchises, and American military installations. Naha, which rose from its own ashes, is a sprawling city. Sugar Loaf Hill was remade during the 1990s into a small urban park known as the Sugar Loaf Peace Memorial Park/Water Pond Friendship Association. Surrounded by Naha, the place where the bloody, all-out battle took place looks nothing like it once did. Shuri Castle is now the headquarters of the University of the Ryukyus.[6]

The Cornerstone for Peace memorial, unveiled in Itoman in 1995 to commemorate the battle's fiftieth anniversary, honors those who died during Operation Iceberg. On its concentric arcs of black granite screens are etched the names of more than 241,000 men, women, and children who were killed during the campaign, or who died during the year following Japan's surrender in September 1945. The fifteen-month prolongation of Iceberg's casualty period resulted in 14,009 American names being inscribed on the monument, along with 149,329 from Okinawa Prefecture, and 77,380 names from the other forty-six Japanese prefectures.[7]

THE BATTLE OF OKINAWA WAS fought with the most lethal weapons of 1945. US battleships, close-air support attacks from carriers and airfields, tanks, artillery, and heavy mortars supported infantry attacks on hills and ridges. Japan deployed kamikaze planes, boats, swimmers, and the "forlorn hope" *Yamato* Task Force against the Fifth Fleet; infantrymen with satchel charges to knock out tanks; and ground troops who fought to the death with the tools of their trade: artillery, mortars, machine guns, rifles, and grenades.

In a twenty-first-century war against an industrialized nation, US amphibious and naval forces would find themselves on an entirely different battlefield than they did on 1945 Okinawa. Today's so-called anti-access/

area denial (A2/AD) weapons systems combine air defenses, short- and medium-range ballistic and cruise missiles, and counter-naval forces to deny access to an entire region. A2/AD is designed to cripple an adversary's maneuverability, and to make resupply efforts a nightmare. Non-forward-based units would have to run a gantlet of sophisticated defenses to even reach the battlefield, suffering high casualties before the battle was joined.

Although amphibious warfare, updated with twenty-first-century technology, remains a credible option in small-scale asymmetrical conflicts, today it is difficult to imagine hundreds of landing craft laden with infantrymen, tanks, and mobile guns bobbing in the surf off a major enemy-held island such as Okinawa.

In today's age of missiles and smart bombs, it is inconceivable that two massive armies, just hundreds of yards apart, would slaughter each other for weeks or months in the rain and mud, among the unburied dead.

Almost certainly, the Battle of Okinawa was the last battle of its kind.

One may hope so anyway.

Acknowledgments

THIS BOOK WOULD NOT HAVE been possible without the resources of research libraries in Virginia and the Washington, DC, area, and of the University of North Carolina libraries in Chapel Hill.

Senior reference specialist Megan Harris of the Veterans History Project at the Library of Congress's American Folklife Center was a great ally in my search for Okinawa veterans' stories. She sent a spreadsheet with details from the VHP database, and she made sure that transcripts from eighty-three Okinawa veterans' interviews were waiting at the Folklife Center when we began work. The VHP is an important resource for any historian seeking firsthand battle accounts from veterans.

At the Marine Corps History Division's Archives Branch in Quantico, Virginia, Dr. James Ginther, senior archivist, and historian Dr. Fred Allison aided me in locating battle reports, veterans' interviews, and other Battle of Okinawa–related material. Gray Research Center is an agreeable place to do research, with ample room to work and a helpful staff.

Nathaniel Patch, archivist at the National Archives in College Park, Maryland, pointed us to battle reports, memoirs, and communications related to the Battle of Okinawa, and led us through the necessary steps needed to bring the material to our worktable. The archives staff does an excellent job of safeguarding the priceless documents under its purview.

The National Museum of the Pacific War in Fredericksburg, Texas, has established a fine, user-friendly website with digitized veterans' interviews that were extremely useful.

During my research of the Battle of Okinawa, I read many unit and battle histories, memoirs, and oral accounts. Noteworthy were Roy Appleman's *Okinawa: The Last Battle*; Samuel Eliot Morison's *Victory in the Pacific 1945*; James and William Belote's *Typhoon of Steel: The Battle for Okinawa*; and Robin Rielly's *Kamikazes, Corsairs, and Picket Ships: Okinawa, 1945*—all valuable guides to the land and naval battles.

The account by the Japanese Thirty-Second Army's operations officer Colonel Hiromishi Yahara, *The Battle for Okinawa*, helped humanize the Japanese defenders, as did Thomas Huber's *Okinawa 1945*. E. B. Sledge's *With the Old Breed at Peleliu and Okinawa* is a classic wartime memoir that describes the horrors endured by combat infantrymen.

A heartfelt thank-you goes to my wife, Pat, who aided me greatly in conducting research and in reading the manuscript and offering good suggestions. Every writer should have such an astute in-house editor.

A special thank-you goes to Bob Pigeon, executive editor of Da Capo Press and one of the top military history editors in the country, for encouraging and supporting my efforts during the past several years. Because of changes in the publishing industry, the new Da Capo editorial/marketing/publicity team will not include Bob, and I will miss his guidance and critiques.

I am also grateful to Rachelle Mandik for her thoughtful, professional job of copyediting the manuscript, especially those challenging Japanese surnames.

Finally, Roger Williams of the Roger Williams Agency of New England Publishing Associates has my deep appreciation for representing me in the rough-and-tumble publishing world.

Notes

PROLOGUE

1. Richard Frank, *Downfall*, 89; Dower, 246–47.
2. Springer, 154–55; Satterfield, 58–68.
3. Satterfield, 62–65, 69–72; Springer, 189.
4. Orita, 294–95; Harris, 161; Foster, 35–36; Inoguchi and Nakajima, 4–7; Warner, 85; Hoyt, *How They Won*, 445; RG 38, Box 1504, NARA Task Group 58.1; Belote, 38–39.
5. Springer, 194–95; Rogers, *So Long*, 307–9.
6. *Franklin* Damage Report, Navy Library.
7. Springer, 211; Satterfield, 76–80.
8. Springer, 224, 243, 227.
9. Ibid., 206, 233–34, 239.
10. Springer, 177, 223; De Chant, 212–13; Foster, 37.
11. Satterfield, 25–30; Crosby, 229–30.
12. Crosby, 229–34; Springer, 254–57, 268; Belote, 41–42; Satterfield, 90, 121.
13. Springer, 302, 311; Morison, 98–99; Satterfield, 81–85, 99.
14. RG 38, Box 1504, NARA; World War II Diaries, *Wasp*, Box 1555, NARA: Springer, 236; Morison, 94–98; Grant Memoirs, 1–2, 4, VHP, AFC24631.
15. Buell, 346–47; Morison, 103–7; Foster, 76–77; Stafford, 446–49; Warner, 248; Gow, 66–67; Wright, 331–33; Gandt, 309.
16. Sakai, 317; Morison, 100.
17. *Ryukyu Shimpo*, xvi.
18. Rielly, *Kamikazes*, 100.

CHAPTER 1: THE ENEMY'S DOORSTEP

1. Geiger, USMC Archives, Box 6, Folder 106.

2. Morison, 3–5; Huber, 108.

3. Frank and Shaw, 12–13, 64.

4. Hayes, 687.

5. Gow, 21; Smith, 473.

6. Morison, 218–20.

7. Jomini, 121–22.

8. Dyer, 1064; Frank and Shaw, 65–66.

9. USMC Archives, *Third Amphibious Corps*, Box 4; Boomhower, 201; Ōta, 180; Hastings, 374.

10. Appleman, 7–9; Sherrod, 369.

11. Davidson, Williams, and Kahl, 88; M. D. Morris, 122.

12. Morison, 80–83; Gandt, 131; Appleman, 7–9; Hastings, 375, 370; Condit and Turnbladh, 292; Rottman, 10–16; Moskin, 376; Feifer, 61, 63; Kerr, 27–29; Yahara, xxiv, 5; M. D. Morris, 11; Dower, 46; Millot, 11, 13.

13. Kerr, 307–25, 335–42, 3–5; Feifer, 68; Toland, 800; Van der Vat, 12–13; Wolter, Ranzan, and McDonough, 60, 94–96; 183–84; M. D. Morris, 157.

14. M. D. Morris, 13; Kerr, 365–67, 376–78, 341–42, 389, 394–95, 399, 421–22, 461–63; Morison, 82.

15. Appleman, 44–45; Belote, 20–21; Yahara, 33; Dyer, 1066; *Ryukyu Shimpo*, 23–24.

16. Foster, 33; Rottman, 51; Appleman, 46.

17. Buell, 14, 16–22; Morison, 87; Harris, 160–61.

18. Harris, 107.

19. Ross, 99, 76, 80.

20. Frank and Shaw, 90–96; Sarantakes, 23–24.

21. Buell, 346–47; Morison, 103–7; Foster, 76–77; Stafford, 446–49; Warner, 248; Gow, 66–67; Wright, 331–33; Gandt, 309.

22. Edoin, 50.

23. Hoyt, *Inferno*, 10–22; Feifer, 15–16.

24. Time-Life, 154–56.

25. Edoin, 4, 6, 21, 37–38; Time-Life, 160; Hoyt, *Inferno*, 7–8.

26. Richard Frank, *Downfall*, 3–7; Warner, 174–75; Time-Life, 161–63; Edoin, 67, 69–74, 86, 103, 109; Hoyt, *Inferno*, 10–22; Cook, 344–49.

27. Edoin, 114–17, 130–33, 151–59.

28. Richard Frank, *Downfall*, 89; Dower, 246–47.

29. Ballendorf and Bartlett, 119–22, 141.

30. Taylor, 34; Halsey and Bryan, 56–60; Taylor, 304; Wheelan, 12.

31. Gow, 58–64; Breuer, 95.

32. Dyer, 1087; Carter, 311.

33. Rottman, 51–53; Alexander, *Storm*, 153–54; Wheeler, 96; Rielly, *Kamikaze Attacks*, 21–22; Kaplan Transcript, VHP, AFC33936; Gow, 67; Morison, 109–12, 134–35; Dyer, 1084–85.

34. US Army, *Ours to Hold*, 229; Morison, 117–19; Frank and Shaw, 104; Rottman, 54; Gow, 43, 66; Appleman, 57.

35. US Army, *Seventy-Seventh Infantry Division Operations*, RG 407, Entry 427, Box 9834, NARA; Morison, 120–21.

36. Gow, 58–60; Breuer, 120–21; Appleman, 60; Winton, 213; Rielly, *Kamikaze Attacks*, 73, 80–81.

37. US Army, *Ours to Hold*, 223–31.

38. US Army, *Seventy-Seventh Infantry Division Operations*, RG 407, Entry 427, Boxes 9835, 9836 NARA; Ōta, 14; Nelson, 198–99, 273; US Army, *Ours to Hold*, 233–34.

39. Ōta, 14; US Army, *Ours to Hold*, 232.

40. Dower, 248–49; Time-Life, 159, 169.

41. *Ryukyu Shimpo*, 31–37; Warner, 183–84; Pineau, 100.

42. US Army, *Ours to Hold*, 236; Appleman, 58; US Army, *Seventy-Seventh Infantry Division Operations*, RG 407, Entry 427, Box 9836, NARA.

43. Sherrod, 377; Minamoto oral history, National Museum of the Pacific War, OH01509; Appleman, 52, 60; Gow, 64–65; Morison, 122–23, 126–29, 133.

44. Rottman, 66.

45. Appleman, 57.

46. Gandt, 161–62; Sarantakes, 26–28; Geiger, USMC Archives, Box 6, Folder 106; Rottman, 33–34.

47. Pyle, 94–96.

48. Leckie, 64.

CHAPTER 2: L-DAY

1. Dyer, 194.

2. Miller, 415.

3. Rottman, *Okinawa*, 26; Gow, 71–77; Carter, 314; Moskin, 374; Morison, 90–91, 108–9.

4. Morison, 109; Sharon Lacey, 4; Appleman, 36; Frank and Shaw, 70–71.

5. Rottman, *Okinawa*, 54.

6. Frank and Shaw, 110; Leckie, 67–70; Rielly, *Kamikaze Attacks*, 21–22; Appleman, 63; Pyle, 98; Morison, 145–46, 151.

7. Appleman, 16; Morison, 136–37.

8. Frank and Shaw, 80–81; Appleman, 103.

9. Rob Morris, 168–69.

10. Manchester, 354; Morison, 144, 141; Pyle, 97–98.

11. Dyer, 194.

12. Morison, 148–51.

13. Pyle, 99–100; Gow, 80.

14. Spaulding interview, VHP, AFC431.

15. Frank and Shaw, 110; Love, *Hourglass*, 293–94.

16. Makos, 292; Sledge, 188.

17. Condit and Turnbladh, 289.

18. Macpherson oral history, VHP, AFC01975; Boomhower, 202–3; Miller, 415.

19. Wolf, 109; Rob Morris, 169; McMillan, 357–59; Frank and Shaw, 125; Pyle, 104; Buell, 349–50.

20. Sarantakes, 30; Alexander, *Storm*, 158; Fournier, *Journal*.

21. Sloan, *Their Backs*, 202–3.

22. Hallas, *Devil's Anvil*, 19; Moskin, 344–45; Newcomb, 9–12, 18; Yahara, 9; Rottman, *Japanese Pacific Island Defenses*, 5–8, 19–20; Breuer, 48.

23. Hayashi and Coox, 140.

24. Yahara, xiii; Sloan, *Ultimate Battle*, 298; Rottman, *Okinawa*, 57; Frank and Shaw, 120–21.

25. Huber, 17–18, 50–54; Williams, "Jap Tactics"; *Ryukyu Shimpo*, 14; USMC Archives, *Third Amphibious Corps*, Box 3, Folder 5; Rottman, 24.

26. Yahara, xi–xiii; Frank and Shaw, 56; Foster, 62.

27. Frank and Shaw, 54.

28. Morison, 154–55; Pase oral history, Natural Museum of the Pacific War, OH00133; Gow, 78; Frank and Shaw, 109–11.

29. Morison, 83; Love, *Hourglass*, 294; Pyle, 103, 107, 113; Pyle column, Genealogy Bank, Greensboro, NC, *Record*, April 12, 1945; Richardson, 128, 130.

30. Peto, 273.

31. Breuer, 48; Morison, 152–53; Love, *Hourglass*, 294–96; Wright, 204; Rottman, *Japanese Pacific Island Defenses*, 26–29; Appleman, 16; McClellan oral history, National Museum of the Pacific War, OH01509; Frank and Shaw, 115–17, 128.

32. Love, *Hourglass*, 297–98; Appleman, 76–77; McMillan, 362.

33. Lyle Green, 78; Richard Frank, *Downfall*, 72; Astor, 189.

34. Frank and Shaw, 77; Sarentakes, 54.

35. Richard Frank, *Downfall*, 72; Huber, 18–19; Ōta, 178–80; Belote, 185–89; Yahara, 219; Appleman, 417–19.

36. Frank and Shaw, 47; *Ryukyu Shimpo*, 4–5, 28.

37. *Ryukyu Shimpo*, 254–57.

38. Ibid., 46–47.

39. Kerr, 468; *Ryukyu Shimpo*, 40; Huber, 18–19; Frank and Shaw, 47; Gow, 21.

40. Frank and Shaw, 128–31; Sledge, 194, 196; Ōta, 48.

41. Frank and Shaw, 128–29; Appleman, 76–77.

42. Edoin, 23–24; Rottman, *Okinawa*, 60; Morison, 171–72; Bix, 493, 484.

CHAPTER 3: THE FIRST DEFENSIVE LINE

1. Hughes Memoirs, VHP, AFC01074, 79.

2. Davidson, Williams, and Kahl, 112.

3. Beckman oral history, VHP, AFC56196.

4. Bob Green, 112.

5. Morison, 218–20; Rottman, *Okinawa*, 59; Frank and Shaw, 162–66; Love, *27th Division*, 528–30.

6. Dyer, 1078; Gow, 40–41; Foster, 26–27; *Ryukyu Shimpo*, 220; Yahara, 19, 34; Rottman, *Japanese Pacific Island Defenses*, 49–50; Frank and Shaw, 46, 53–54; Alexander, *Storm*, 150–52.

7. Yahara, 19, 226; *Ryukyu Shimpo*, 241.

8. Hallas, 9; Warner, 318.

9. Gandt, 129.

10. Hallas, 5; Frank and Shaw, 48; Hastings, 369; Yahara, 11–14.

11. Gandt, 129; Yahara, xvii–xviii; Huber, 148, 24–25.

12. Yahara, xix, 34; Appleman, *Okinawa*, 95; Rottman, *Okinawa*, 47–48, 66; Huber, 20; Frank and Shaw, 43.

13. Rottman, *Pacific Island Defenses*, 25.

14. Morison, 92; Yahara, 216–18.

15. Huber, 9–11, 27.

16. McMillan, 370; Frank and Shaw, 188; Huber, 20–21; Rottman, *Pacific Island Defenses*, 24–30.

17. Frank and Shaw, 51; Appleman, 94–95, 250–53.

18. Huber, 66–67; Appleman, 87–91; Foster, 29; Hallas, 38–39; Peto, 375; Rottman, *Pacific Island Defenses*, 21; Rottman, *Okinawa*, 48–49.

19. Feifer, 45–49; Huber, 75; Frank and Shaw, 40.

20. Dower, 261.

21. Hastings, 377; Huber, 16.

22. Davidson, Williams, and Kahl, 90–93; Sharon Lacey, 178.

23. Astor, 190–91.

24. Sloan, *Ultimate Battle*, 85; Love, *Hourglass* 308–10.

25. Dencker, 188.

26. Appleman, 107–8; Gow, 84–86; Sloan, *Ultimate Battle*, 82–83; Rottman, *Okinawa*, 61; Fitzgerald oral history, VHP, AFC01488.

27. Hughes Memoirs, VHP, AFC01074, 79.

28. Dower, 105–6.

29. Gow, 86; Davidson, Williams, and Kahl, 100–1; Appleman, 110; Sloan, *Ultimate Battle*, 86; Beckman oral history, VHP, AFC56196.

30. Heinrichs, 388; Davidson, Williams, and Kahl, 95–100.

31. Appleman, 126–27; Davidson, Williams, and Kahl, 109–11; Beckman oral history, VHP, AFC56196.

32. US Army, *Ninety-Sixth Infantry Division Operations*, NARA, RG 407, Entry 427, Box 11563; Astor, 201–2; Davidson, Williams, and Kahl, 101–4; Sloan, *Ultimate Battle*, 123; Gandt, 220–22.

33. Davidson, Williams, and Kahl, 105–8; Sloan, *Ultimate Battle*, 121–22; Leckie, 99–103.

34. Astor, 204; Sloan, *Ultimate Battle*, 123–25; Davidson, Williams, and Kahl, 112.

35. Davidson, Williams, and Kahl, 111–12.

36. US Army, *Three Hundred Eighty-Third Infantry Regiment After Action Report*, NARA, RG407, Entry, Box 11566.

37. Appleman, 115–20, 124–29; Davidson, Williams, and Kahl, 113; Love, *27th Infantry Division*, 531.

38. Love, *Hourglass*, 300–5.

39. Ibid., 311; Appleman, 111–12.

40. Love, *Hourglass*, 312, 315–19.

41. Ibid., 319–22; Appleman, 139.

42. Love, *Hourglass*, 322; Warner, 189; Leckie, 105; Morison, 166; Nichols and Shaw, 85; Rottman, *Okinawa*, 34.

43. Love, *Hourglass*, 323; Fitzgerald oral history, VHP, AFC 01488.

44. Appleman, 129.

45. Love, *Hourglass*, 325.

46. Appleman, 103.

47. Beckman oral history, VHP, AFC56196.

48. Bix, 484–85.

49. Ugaki, 570–72; Huber, 36–39; Leckie, 109–10; Appleman, 131.

50. Yahara, 191–92; Frank and Shaw, 190.

51. Gandt, 245; Frank and Shaw, 190.

52. Walton, 63–64.

53. Appleman, 135–37.

54. Davidson, Williams, and Kahl, 112.

55. Love, *Hourglass*, 320; Gandt, 246–47; Huber, 32; Leckie, 110–13; Appleman, 123.

CHAPTER 4: THE KAMIKAZES

1. Warner, 242–43.

2. Ibid., 116.

3. Ōta, 143; Rielly, *Kamikazes*, 16–21, 91; Dower, 231–33; Kuwahara and Allred, 191; Warner, 227.

4. Gandt, 142–43.

5. Sakai, 317.

6. Millot, 229; Hara, 258; Inoguchi and Nakajima, 24–25.

7. Rielly, *Kamikazes*, 70.

8. Warner, 85.

9. Millot, 43–45.

10. Warner, 59.

11. Inoguchi and Nakajima, 4–13, 19; Isely and Crowl, 536; Hastings, 164–67; Warner, 94.

12. Millot, 51, 252–53; Dower, 231–33.

13. Richard Frank, *Downfall*, 179; Hoyt, *How They Won*, 445; Sheftall, 9; Warner, 116, 242–43.

14. O'Neill, 157; Heinrichs, 377; Inoguchi and Nakajima, 130–33; Moskin, 364; Richard Frank, *Downfall*, 180; Rielly, *Kamikaze Attacks*, 47.

15. Winton, 213–14.

16. Ibid., 213.

17. Ibid., 214–15; Astor, 177; Gandt, 134.

18. Morison, 200–2; PBS, "Sinking the Supership," Hiroto Takamoto; Yoshida, xv–xvi.

19. Stille, 131–41.

20. Hara, 269, 274.

21. Feiffer, 7–8.

22. Warner, 198.

23. Gandt, 133; Yoshida, 37.

24. Hara, 260–62, 284; Millot, 193.

25. Rielly, *Kamikazes*, 110.

26. Inoguchi and Nakajima, 200; Gandt, 217.

27. Rielly, *Kamikaze Attacks*, 22–23.

28. O'Neill, 144.

29. Inoguchi and Nakajima, 156; Frank and Shaw, 185–86; O'Neill, 160–62; Warner, 237–38; Rielly, *Kamikazes*, 53, 55.

30. Rielly, *Kamikazes*, 103–4, 205–6, 208.

31. Ibid., 108.

32. Ibid., 13–14, 18, 26–27, 34–35; Wolf, 86.

33. O'Neill, 163.

34. Ugaki, 572–73.

35. Gandt, 278.

36. Ford oral history, VHP, AFC76069.

37. Rielly, *Kamikaze Attacks*, 111–14.

38. *USS Bush After Action Report*, April 6, 1945; *USS Colhoun After Action Report*, April 6, 1945.

39. *USS Colhoun After Action Report*, April 6, 1945.

40. Rielly, *Kamikazes*, 119–21.

41. Jon Jones oral history, VHP, AFC85719.

42. *USS Emmons After Action Report*, April 6, 1945; Korney oral history, VHP, AFC82109; Warner, 193.

43. Boswell oral history, National Museum of the Pacific War, OH01317. When *Defense* crewmen recovered the mutilated body of one of the suicide pilots, Boswell scraped some flesh from a bone and put it in a cigar box, along with a large piece of a parachute. After the war, Boswell's mother made him get rid of the cigar box.

44. Ugaki, 576; Condon, 78; Gow, 192–93; Nichols and Shaw, 85; Gandt, 151, 225; Morison, 199.

45. Sarantakes, 36.

46. *USS Hancock Diaries*; *USS Hancock After Action Report of April 6, 1945*; Gandt, 206–7; Morison, 209.

47. Feifer, 20–21; Yoshida, xiv, xvii, 26, 35–36; Warner, 202–4.

48. Yoshida, 9–10, 18, 26–28.

49. Gandt, 135–37.

50. Feifer, 18–20; Morison, 202.

51. Gandt, 153; Morison, 203.

52. Sinking of *Yamato*, NARA, RG38, Box 216, Serial 00222; Millot, 197; Gandt, 110–11.

53. Gandt, 165; Foster, 18; Taylor, 199–200.

54. Morison, 204; Hara, 271–73; Gandt, 173–74.

55. Sinking of *Yamato*, NARA, RG38, Box 216, Serial 00222.

56. Morison, 205.

CHAPTER 5: SINKING THE BATTLESHIP *YAMATO*

1. Yoshida, 73–74.

2. Wukovits, 169–77.

3. PBS, "Sinking the Supership"; Taylor, 284; Warner, 207–9.

4. Hara, 287.

5. Ibid., 271; Yoshida, 47.

6. Ferry oral history, National Museum of the Pacific War, OH00022.

7. PBS, "Sinking the Supership"; Morison, 205; Ferry oral history, National Museum of the Pacific War OH00022; Condon, 78; Gandt, 187–88; Warner, 209–10; Hara, 276–79.

8. Yoshida, 73–74, 77.

9. Gandt, 176–77.

10. Yoshida, 79–83; Feifer, 25–26; Morison, 205–6.

11. Feifer, 26–28; Yoshida, 83–87.

12. Morison, 208; Gandt, 202–3.

13. Gandt, 188–89.

14. Yoshida, 61–62.

15. Feifer, 28; Hara, 283; Yoshida, 93–94, 102, 108–9, 140.

16. Yoshida, 114; Gandt, 137, 195–96; Feifer, 29–31. *Yamato*'s wreckage was discovered and confirmed in the 1980s, and surveyed in 2016 with digital video.

17. Gandt, 198–99; Yoshida, 144, 136–37.

18. Astor, 186–87.

19. Hara, 289; Gandt, 199.

20. Ugaki, 586.

21. Hara, 285.

22. Winton, 215; Van der Vat, 384.

23. Morison, 215.

24. Rielly, *Kamikazes*, 127.

25. Gandt, 223; Warner, 219.

26. Millot, 206; Sherrod, 380; Morison, 225–26.

27. Burrows oral history, VHP, AFC90365; Leckie, 118.

28. Ugaki, 580–83, 550.

29. Millot, 208.

30. Warner, 223; McWhorter, 184; Astor, 292; Rielly, *Kamikazes*, 146–49; Gandt, 228–31; Kalinofsky oral history, National Museum of the Pacific War, OH00048.

31. Inoguchi and Nakajima, 140–41; Rielly, *Kamikazes*, 29–30.

32. Inoguchi and Nakajima, 143–46; Morison, 108.

33. Warner, 225.

34. Gandt, 236.

35. Foster, 39; Springer, 26; Morison, 98–99.

36. Morison, 230–32; Warner, 114, 124; McWhorter, 178; *Plain Dealer*, April 15, and *San Francisco Chronicle*, April 13, Genealogy Bank.

37. Rielly, *Kamikazes*, 134.

38. Cooper oral history, National Museum of the Pacific War, OH00259.

39. Wukovits, 141.

40. Ibid., 142.

41. Ibid., 145.

42. Rielly, *Kamikazes*, 157–59; Gandt, 272.

43. Gandt, 280–82.

44. Wukovits, 148–60.

45. Ibid., 169–77.

46. Ibid., 178–79.

47. Rielly, *Kamikazes*, 162.

48. Wukovits, 190–204; Morison, 235–36; Gandt, 269.

49. Hallas, 1.

50. *USS Pringle After Action Report and War Diary*, April 16, 1945; Rielly, *Kamikazes*, 174–75, 171.

51. *USS Harding After Action Report of April 16, 1945; USS Bryant After Action Report of April 16, 1945*; Sherrod, 381–83.

52. Rielly, *Kamikazes*, 183–84; Morison, 244.

53. DeChant, 228–29; Wolf, 134–36, 140.

54. DeChant, 240; Sherrod, 407–8.

55. *US Strategic Bombing Survey*, 328.

56. Morison, 391.

57. Ibid.; Frank and Shaw, 73; Rielly, *Kamikazes*, 322–23.

58. Rielly, *Kamikazes*, 129, 132.

59. Ugaki, 596; Morison, 250.

60. Ugaki, 595.

61. Cook, 316–18; USMC Archives, *Third Amphibious Corps*, Box 4; Morison, 217–18, 389–91.

62. Alexander, *Storm*, 164.

63. Hannig, Memoirs, VHP, AFC74446; Foster, 65.

64. Rielly, *Kamikazes*, 155; Morison, 179; McWhorter, 190.

65. Morison, 389–91; Appleman, 102.

66. Carter, 337.

67. Gow, 138; Rielly, *Kamakazes*, 178; Edoin, 185, 199–200.

68. Hoyt, *Inferno*, 129; Harris, 163; Astor, 178; Potter, 371–72.

CHAPTER 6: THE DRIVE NORTH AND IE SHIMA

1. *Sixth Marine Division Special Action Report*, Box 7.

2. US Army, *Ours to Hold*, 271.

3. Frank and Shaw, 88; Hallas, 15, 216; Condit and Turnbladh, 241–42.

4. Nichols and Shaw, 91.

5. Astor, 213; Belote, 169.

6. Carleton, location 371.

7. Nichols and Shaw, 94, footnote.

8. Carleton, location 448; Dyer, 1100.

9. Frank and Shaw, 139.

10. Shepherd, "Battle for Motobu"; Appleman, 143; Kukuchka interview, VHP, AFC10513; Welch interview, VHP, AFC88352.

11. Belote, 169; Carleton, location 552.

12. Nichols and Shaw, 96, 102; *Sixth Division Special Action Report*, Box 7; Manchester, 357.

13. Nichols and Shaw, 97.

14. Carleton, location 650; Nichols and Shaw, 97–98.

15. Nichols and Shaw, 90, 98; Belote, 171.

16. Spaulding oral history, VHP, AFC431; Nichols and Shaw, 99; Belote, 171.

17. O'Donnell, 266.

18. Nichols and Shaw, 99.

19. Manchester, 357–58; Carleton, locations 835–37; Sloan, *Ultimate Battle*, 117–18; Nichols and Shaw, 101.

20. Leckie, 82; Ferrier oral history, VHP, AFC20811.

21. Belote, 172–73; Appleman, 148; Nichols and Shaw, 102–4; Carleton, location 1064.

22. Shepherd, "Battle for Motobu"; Frank and Shaw, 155; Belote, 173; Nichols and Shaw, 103–7; Appleman, 148; *Sixth Marine Division Special Action Report*, Phase III, Vol. III.

23. Frank and Shaw, 173–75; Nichols and Shaw, 106, 109.

24. Nichols and Shaw, 108.

25. Pyle, 120.

26. Appleman, 259–60; Astor, 217–21.

27. Astor, 224; Gow, 100–2; M. D. Morris, 71.

28. US Army, *Ours to Hold*, 255.

29. Sharon Lacey, 176.

30. US Army, *Ours to Hold*, 253–54; Sharon Lacey, 189–90; Morison, 176–77; Frank and Shaw, 166–67.

31. US Army, *Ours to Hold*, 256.

32. Ibid., 256–57.

33. Ibid., 258–59; Nichols and Shaw, 114; Appleman, 156–57.

34. Nichols and Shaw, 112; Nelson, 216–19; Gow, 108–9; US Army, *Ours to Hold*, 260, 280.

35. Nichols and Shaw, 116; Appleman, 162; Rottman, *Okinawa*, 69.

36. US Army, *Ours to Hold*, 279–80; Nelson, 219, 223; Levin oral history, VHP, AFC79217.

37. Morison, 240.

38. Nichols and Shaw, 116–17.

39. Nichols and Shaw, 117–18; US Army, *Ours to Hold*, 270–71, 273–74.

40. Appleman, 181.

41. US Army, *Ours to Hold*, 280–81.

42. Sherrod, 398–99; M. D. Morris, 71.

43. Miller, 407.

44. Ibid., 370–71, 391.

45. Ibid., 407, 411.

46. Pyle, 116, 130, 112.

47. US Army, *Ours to Hold*, 264; Astor, 233.

48. Miller, 424–28; Gandt, 289–90.

49. US Army, *Ours to Hold*, 265.

CHAPTER 7: THE APRIL OFFENSIVE

1. Gow, 119; Davidson, Williams, and Kahl, 114.

2. Potter, 374–75; Buell, 358.

3. Alexander, *Storm*, 166.

4. Sledge, 264–65, 312; Belote, 240; Sharon Lacey, 204.

5. Astor, 402–3; Peto, 285.

6. Sharon Lacey, 204.

7. Capaldi oral history, VHP, AFC97693.

8. Love, *27th Division*, 532–33.

9. Gandt, 252–53; Sherrod, 386.

10. Belote, 203; Gandt, 126–27; Sharon Lacey, 200.

11. Gow, 119; Davidson, Williams, and Kahl, 114.

12. Appleman, 184; Leckie, 126.

13. Appleman, 189.

14. Astor, 250–51.

15. Love, *27th Division*, 263–64, 331, 439–46, 520–23; Boomhower, 160; Sharon Lacey, 187.

16. Gailey, 322–23; Love, *27th Division*, 522–23. Later, an Army investigative board exonerated General Ralph Smith and criticized Holland Smith's management of the Saipan campaign. Neither Smith commanded men in combat again. Gailey, 224–25.

17. Astor, 260; Beckman oral history, VHP, AFC56196.

18. Appleman, 190–92; Love, *27th Division*, 523.

19. Appleman, 190–92.

20. Love, *27th Division*, 532–36.

21. Appleman, 192–93; Love, *27th Division*, 555–57; US Army, *Twenty-Seventh Infantry Division Operations*, NARA, RG 127, Box 258.

22. Frank and Shaw, 193–94; Davidson, Williams, and Kahl, 117.

23. Frank and Shaw, 193.

24. Ibid., 193–94; Foster, 100; Appleman, 194; *Tenth Army Operations*, USMC Archives, Box 13, Folders 1, 2.

25. Belote, 204.

26. Gandt, 253.

27. Alexander, *Storm*, 161; Appleman, 202–5; Sloan, 133; Belote, 210–11.

28. Belote, 211.

29. Ibid., 211–12; Love, *27th Division*, 180; Appleman, 205.

30. Davidson, Williams, and Kahl, 118–19; Appleman, 232; Gow, 130.

31. Davidson, Williams, and Kahl, 117.

32. Ibid., 114–17; Appleman, 197–98.

33. Love, *Hourglass*, 328–30.

34. Ibid., 333–35; Sloan, 132.

35. Love, *Hourglass*, 338–39; Appleman, 195–96.

36. Appleman, 207; Sarantakes, 42; Davidson, Williams, and Kahl, 117.

37. Appleman, 231–32; Davidson, Williams, and Kahl, 118–19; Belote, 215.

38. Appleman, 232.

39. US Army, *Three Hundred Eighty-Third Regiment After Action*, "Notes on the Enemy," NARA, RG407, Entry 427, Box 11566.

40. Davidson, Williams, and Kahl, 120.

41. Appleman, 238; Heinrichs, 394.

42. Love, *27th Division*, 561–62.

43. Ibid., 562.

44. Morison, 242–43.

45. Love, *27th Division*, 351; Belote, 214.

46. Belote, 215; Sloan, *Ultimate Battle*, 134.

47. Love, *Hourglass*, 343–48.

48. Alexander, *Storm*, 162; *Eleventh Marine Regiment After Action Report*, 4, NARA, RG 127, Box 260.

49. Gow, 123–24; Appleman, 241.

50. Huber, 44–46.

51. Sharon Lacey, 197.

52. Moskin, 383.

53. Hallas, 10; Frank and Shaw, 196; Belote, 212–14; Huber, 46–47; Moskin, 383; Vandegrift, 290; Alexander, *Storm*, 166; Astor, 277.

54. Sarantakes, 30, 51; Hoyt, *How They Won*, 481; Potter, 374–75; Buell, 358.

55. Morison, 389–91; Appleman, 102; Hallas, 10.

56. Sarantakes, 78; Genealogy Bank, Rockford, IL, *Morning Star*, May 31, 1945, and *Augusta Chronicle*, June 6, 1945.

57. Genealogy Bank, *Dallas Morning News*, Associated Press article, June 17, 1945.

58. Appleman, 243.

59. Davidson, Williams, and Kahl, 121; Appleman, 242–43, 247; Love, *Hourglass*, 353.

60. Appleman, 209–11.

61. Appleman, 209–10; Leckie, 136–38; Frank and Shaw, 49–50; Love, *27th Division*, 566–67.

62. Love, *27th Division*, 568; Appleman, 209–10.

63. Appleman, 209; Heinrichs, 395; Love, *27th Division*, 563.

64. Love, *27th Division*, 568.

65. Ibid., 571–72.

66. Ibid., 577; Appleman, 211.

67. Love, *27th Division*, 581, 583–84; Appleman, 213–18.

68. Love, *27th Division*, 593–94; Appleman, 217.

69. Appleman, 218.

70. Love, *27th Division*, 597.

71. Appleman, 219–19, 267.

72. Love, *27th Division*, 612.

73. Nichols and Shaw, 136.

CHAPTER 8: THE SHURI LINE

1. Burgin, 239.

2. Sledge, 205–7.

3. Millot, 251.

4. Burgin, 239; Frank and Shaw, 197; Leckie, 84.

5. Sledge, 205–7; Burgin, 231; McMillan, 341; Frank and Shaw, 199; Astor, 278.

6. Sledge, 210–11; Rob Morris, 170.

7. McMillan, 382–83; Frank and Shaw, 201.

8. McMillan, 375; Frank and Shaw, 202–3.

9. McMillan, 383–84; Moskin, 385.

10. Frank and Shaw, 202; Gow, 145; *First Marine Regiment After Action Report*, NARA; Fournier, *Journal*.

11. Sledge, 247.

12. Yahara, 38–39; Huber, 72, 75; Gandt, 298.

13. Belote, 225–26; Joy oral history, VHP, AFC 87853; Appleman, 269–72; Love, *Hourglass*, 360–84; Glenn, 104–5.

14. US Army, *Three Hundred Eighty-Third Regiment Operations Report*, NARA, RG 407, Entry 427, Box 11560.

15. US Army, *Ours to Hold*, 295–96; Davidson, Williams, and Kahl, 123, 130; Bob Green, 121; Astor, 335; Yahara, 53. It was said that the eccentric Kaya followed the example of a famous fourteenth-century samurai by dropping excrement on the heads of the Americans.

16. Davidson, Williams, and Kahl, 123–25.

17. Ibid., 123, 127–28.

18. Ibid., 128.

19. Ibid., 127–28.

20. Ibid., 129; Belote, 215–16.

21. Davidson, Williams, and Kahl, 130; Walton, 95.

22. Chilcote oral history, VHP, AFC 31046.

23. Sloan, *Ultimate Battle*, 147; Walton, 95.

24. US Army, *Ours to Hold*, 290, 298–99; Appleman, 278.

25. Davidson, Williams, and Kahl, 131; Frank and Shaw, 197–98; Spencer oral history, VHP, AFC 19082; US Army, *Ours to Hold*, 299–300.

26. Bob Green, 131–32.

27. US Army, *Ours to Hold*, 303–4.

28. Bradshaw, *The Faith of Desmond Doss*; US Army, *Ours to Hold*, 303–4.

29. US Army, *Ours to Hold*, 304; Astor, 335; Leckie, 177.

30. US Army, *Ours to Hold*, 301.

31. Ibid., 302–6; Frank and Shaw, 204; Davidson, Williams, and Kahl, 131; Astor, 335.

32. Yahara, 38–39; Gow, 142–43; Leckie, 149–50; Inoguchi and Nakajima, 151; Belote, 220–21.

33. Belote, 221.

34. Huber, 76–77.

35. Ōta, 118.

36. Belote, 222.

37. US Army, *Ours to Hold* 309–10; Appleman, 286.

38. USMC Archives, *Twenty-Fourth Corps After Action Report*; US Army, *Seventy-Seventh Infantry Division Operations*, NARA, RG 407, Entry 427, Box 9844; McMillan, 377–78; Astor, 327; USMC Archives, *Sixth Marine Division Special Action Report*, Vol. 2, Box 8, Folders 1, 2; Makos, 306–7; Leckie, 151; Nichols and Shaw, 146–49; Belote, 223.

39. Gow, 143; Appleman, 287–88; Love, *Hourglass*, 387; Gow, 143–44.

40. Benis Frank, *Okinawa*, 208; Love, *Hourglass*, 391; USMC Archives, *Twenty-Fourth Corps After Action Report*; US Army, *Seventy-Seventh Infantry Division Operations*, NARA, RG 407, Entry 427, Box 9844; Appleman, 297; Belote, 225; Gow, 143–44; US Army, *Ours to Hold*, 312.

41. Appleman, 295; US Army, *Ours to Hold*, 312–13.

42. US Army, *Ours to Hold*, 314.

43. Belote, 231.

44. US Army, *Ours to Hold*, 317–18.

45. Love, *Hourglass*, 393–96; US Army, *Ours to Hold*, 318.

46. US Army, *Ours to Hold*, 317–18.

47. Love, *Hourglass*, 389; Appleman, 290–91.

48. Frank and Shaw, 212–13.

49. Rob Morris, 172–74.

50. USMC Archives, *Twenty-Fourth Corps After Action Report*, 29; Yahara, 45–46; Appleman, 301–2; Frank and Shaw, 213.

51. Yahara, 191–92, 210, 46.

52. Yahara, 221; Rielly, *Kamikazes*, 235.

53. Inoguchi and Nakajima, 151; Sherrod, 391–92; Frank and Shaw, 208.

54. *USS Morrison After Action Report*; Gandt, 304–5; Rielly, *Kamikazes*, 213.

55. Rielly, *Kamikazes*, 212–14.

56. *USS Luce After Action Report*; Morison, 254–56; Astor, 297–98; Surels, 3–80, 116–30.

57. *USS Luce After Action Report*; Astor, 299; Warner, 241.

58. Surels, 140–59; Whitfield oral history, VHP, AF 106231.

59. Surels, 160.

60. Fox oral history, VHP, AFC 23056.

61. Gandt, 306–7; Morison, 391; Rielly, *Kamikazes*, 233–34.

62. Burke oral history, VHP, AFC 24259.

63. *USS Little After Action Report*; *USS Aaron Ward After Action Report*; Morison, 253; Warner, 238–40.

64. Ugaki, 604–5.

65. Sherrod, 391–92; Rielly, *Kamikazes*, 235.

66. Millot, 215–16; Rielly, *Kamikazes*, 91.

67. Warner, 217, 237.

68. Bentley oral history, VHP, AFC 23693.

69. Cook, 327.

70. Millot, 249, 251.

71. Buell, 358.

CHAPTER 9: THE MAY MUD OFFENSIVE

1. Manchester, 359–60.

2. Roberts oral history, 26, VHP, AFC 86156.

3. Sloan, *Ultimate Battle*, 264.

4. Hallas, 163.

5. *Ryukyu Shimpo*, xviii; Alexander, *Storm*, 166; Appleman, 312.

6. Manchester, 359.

7. Frank and Shaw, 214–18.

8. Bush oral history, VHP, AFC 89632; Medal of Honor citation.

9. Hallas, 18–19.

10. Manchester, 359–60.

11. Leckie, 168–69; Belote, 245–46.

12. Love, *Hourglass*, 297–99.

13. Ibid., 400.

14. Ibid., 401–2.

15. Ibid., 402–10.

16. Sloan, *Ultimate Battle*, 151.

17. Gow, 147.

18. Sledge, 223.

19. Morison, 268.

20. McMillan, 379, 382–83.

21. Ibid., 449–58.

22. Carleton, locations 1295–1346, 35%; Hallas, 27–28; *Sixth Marine Division Special Action Report*; Frank and Shaw, 222–23; Hallas, 34, 125–26.

23. Wheeler, 177; Carleton, location 1356, 36%.

24. Carleton, location 1368, 37%; *Sixth Marine Division Special Action Report*; Belote, 245–47.

25. Nelson, 237.

26. Ibid., 240–47.

27. Belote, 245–46.

28. *Sixth Marine Division Special Action Report* V, III, 3.

29. Huber, 60–62, 67–68; Yahara, 54.

30. *Okinawa: Marine Corps: Various*, USMC Archives, Box 13, Folders 1, 2; McMillan, 399–400; Moskin, 385; Yahara, 213; Huber, 115; Appleman, 256–57, 304–6; Sharon Lacey, 202–3; Neiman and Estes, 148; Bob Green, 67, 151–54; Dencker, 178; Astor, 265–26.

31. USMC Archives, *Okinawa: Marine Corps: Various*, Box 13, Folders 1, 2; Yahara, 214, interrogation, 64, footnote.

32. Walton, 43; Hastings, 377; Morison, 215; Heinrichs, 385; Appleman, 87–92; Dencker, 181, 186; Huber, 21–22, 69–70; Peto, 281–82.

33. Davidson, Williams, and Kahl, 131.

34. Chilcote oral history, VHP, AFC31046.

35. Dencker, 215–16; Davidson, Williams, and Kahl, 134–37; Appleman, 351–52.

36. Appleman, 356–57.

37. Ibid.; Belote, 269–70.

38. Appleman, 357.

39. Leckie, 179–180; Frank and Shaw, 237; Davidson, Williams, and Kahl, 142–45.

40. Bob Green, 155.

41. Ibid., 138–39.

42. Dencker, 222–29.

43. US Army, *Ours to Hold*, 325; Nelson, 240.

44. Astor, 367–68; Appleman, 338–40.

45. Nelson, 251–53.

46. Appleman, 341–42; Belote, 254–55; Astor, 370–72.

47. Roberts oral history, 29, VHP, AFC 86156.

48. Ibid.

49. Hallas, 148; Yahara, 62.

50. Rielly, *Kamikazes*, 239; Ugaki, 610.

51. Ohnuki-Tierney, 208–9.

52. O'Neill, 172.

53. Astor, 299; Gandt, 318–19; Rielly, *Kamikazes*, 267–70; Kennedy, 283, 287.

54. Howard Jones oral history, National Museum of the Pacific War, OH01819.

55. Wright, 230; Kennedy, 418, 424–26; Rielly, *Kamikaze Attacks*, 270.

56. Morison, 262–63.

57. Kennedy, 394, 426; Morison, 263.

58. Gandt, 320–21; Stafford, 464–65; Taylor, 297.

59. Stafford, 466; Morison, 263; Taylor, 297–98.

60. Rielly, *Kamikazes*, 242–46; Morison, 257–58; Aitken oral history, National Museum of the Pacific War, OH01497.

61. Rielly, *Kamikazes*, 247–48; Aitken oral history, National Museum of the Pacific War, OH01497; Warner, 254–60; Sherrod, 393.

62. Rielly, *Kamikazes*, 273.

63. Sledge, 235, 261.

64. Peto, 312–13, footnote; Manchester, 235; Leckie, 165; Burgin, 241.

65. Sarantakes, 64.

66. Manchester, 361; McMillan, 408–9; Nelson, 259; Love, *Hourglass*, 157–59; Dencker, 244; Sloan, *Ultimate Battle*, 175, 264; Dunbar oral history, VHP, AFC 31159; Belote, 262–63; Sledge, 223–24.

67. Manchester, 361; Nelson, 236; Leckie, 165.

68. Joy oral history, VHP, AFC 87853.

69. Graley oral history, VHP, AFC 02816; Sledge, 253, 261.

70. Roberts oral history, 26, VHP, AFC 86156.

71. Yahara, 82, 85.

72. Sherrod, 406; Belote, 263.

CHAPTER 10: RED FLOOD TIDE

1. Hallas, 64–68.

2. Sledge, 252, 260.

3. Hallas, 195.

4. Gow, 153–54; Appleman, 325.

5. McMillan, 387.

6. Lince, 114; McMillan, 391–93, 397; Rob Morris, 188–89; Aldrich oral history, VHP, AFC 107976; Speheger oral history, VHP, AFC 07192.

7. Frank and Shaw, 235–36; McMillan, 386.

8. *First Marine Division After Action Report*, NARA, RG 127, Box 252.

9. Frank and Shaw, 231–32, 235–36; Belote, 251; Leckie, 173–74.

10. Mason, "Battle of Wana Draw"; Burgin, 249.

11. McMillan, 398–400; Sloan, *Ultimate Battle*, 195.

12. Dencker, 217; Walton, 67–68, 89; Neufeld, 57, 208; Davidson, Williams, and Kahl, 199; Astor, 326.

13. Lince, 131.

14. Leckie, 173–75; *First Marine Division After Action Report*; McMillan, 394–98; Smidt oral history, VHP, AFC 92604; Sloan, *Ultimate Battle*, 195; Mason, "Battle of Wana Draw."

15. Hebard oral history, VHP, AFC 01520.

16. *First Marine Division After Action Report*; Sloan, *Ultimate Battle*, 165–67.

17. Clark oral history, 5–6, VHP, AFC 30617; Ferrier oral history, VHP, AFC 20811; Holt oral history, VHP, AFC 43172; Habern oral history, 4, VHP, AFC 02757.

18. Sloan, *Ultimate Battle*, 255–56; Sledge, 243–44; Fournier, *Journal*.

19. Sorenson oral history, VHP, AFC 12289.

20. Laura Lacey, 119–20; Belote, 242.

21. Sorenson oral history, VHP, AFC 12289.

22. Milner oral history, VHP, AFC 54694.

23. *First Marine Regiment After Action Report*, NARA, RG 127, Box 258.

24. McMillan, 400–1; Sorenson oral history, VHP, AFC 12289; *First Marine Regiment After Action Report*.

25. Sledge, 265.

26. *First Marine Regiment After Action Report*; Peto, 312.

27. Peto, 300.

28. Taylor oral history, 1, VHP, AFC 24731.

29. Williams, "Jap Tactics."

30. *Sixth Marine Division Special Action Report, Phase 3*, 5; Hallas, 37, 55; Manchester, 363.

31. Rottman, *Okinawa*, 79.

32. Yahara, 61.

33. Carleton, "Training Order No. 23–45" of May 6, in *The Conquest of Okinawa*, Location 1159.

34. Hallas, 37–46.

35. Carleton, location 1362; Berry, 334–39.

36. Hallas, 47–50; Kirkpatrick oral history, National Museum of the Pacific War, OH01506.

37. Carleton, location 1392; Hallas, 55.

38. Hallas, 57–59.

39. Hallas, 64–68; *Sixth Marine Division Special Action Report*, 5–6; Belote, 248; Sloan, *Ultimate Battle*, 179–81.

40. *Sixth Marine Division Special Action Report*, 5–6; Nichols and Shaw, 171; Sloan, *Ultimate Battle*, 180; Wills oral history, VHP, AFC 33968; Maxwell oral history, National Museum of the Pacific War, OH00282.

41. *Sixth Marine Division Special Action Report*, 6; Sloan, *Ultimate Battle*, 186; Medal of Honor citation. Major Courtney was awarded the Congressional Medal of Honor posthumously.

42. Laura Lacey, 90–93.

43. Hallas, 81–92.

44. Sloan, *Ultimate Battle*, 190.

45. Kogan, "Glory Kid."

46. Yahara, 214.

47. Sloan, *Ultimate Battle*, 193; *Sixth Marine Division Special After Action Report*, 6–7; Leckie, 171–72; Belote, 250.

48. Belote, 249–50; Hallas, 114.

49. *Sixth Marine Division Special Action Report*, 7; Ferrier oral history, VHP, AFC 20811.

50. Laura Lacey, 117–19.

51. *Sixth Marine Division Special Action Report*, 8.

52. Ibid.

53. Welch oral history, 31–32, VHP, AFC88352.

54. Sloan, *Ultimate Battle*, 194.

55. Hallas, 128.

56. Kirkpatrick oral history, National Museum of the Pacific War, OH01506; Hallas, 118; Sledge, 268; Laura Lacey, 60; Lince, 139.

57. Manchester, 359–60.

58. Laura Lacey, 110–11.

59. Speheger oral history, VHP, AFC 07192.

60. Hallas, 199; Welch oral history, 35, VHP, AFC 88352.

61. Laura Lacey, 121–22; Hallas, 112, 198; Welch oral history, 39, VHP, AFC 88352.

62. Leckie, 173.

63. *Sixth Marine Division Special After Action Report*, 9; Hallas, 166–70; Belote, 260–61.

64. *Sixth Marine Division Special After Action Report*, 9.

65. Hallas, 195.

66. Belote, 260.

67. Nichols and Shaw, 182; Hallas, 200–1; Gow, 152; O'Donnell, 270–72.

68. Fowler oral history, National Museum of the Pacific War, OH00006.

69. Hallas, 165.

70. Manchester, 382.

71. *New York Times*, TimesMachine, May 20, 1945.

72. Gandt, 323–24; Belote, 253–54.

73. Hallas, 171–74; Nichols and Shaw, 182; Yahara, 62.

74. Nichols and Shaw, 184.

75. O'Donnell, 274–75; Hallas, 185–87.

76. Hallas, 186–90; Nichols and Shaw, 184.

77. Sarantakes, 59.

78. Nichols and Shaw, 184; Carleton, location 2290.

79. Carleton, location 2290; *Sixth Marine Division Special Action Report*, 10–12.

80. Sledge, 252, 260; Makos, 312; Sloan, *Ultimate Battle*, 260–61.

81. Sledge, 260.

82. McMillan, 407–8; Spaulding oral history, VHP, AFC 431; Sledge, 301–2; O'Donnell, 277; Peto, 286; Hallas, 132–33; *Tenth Army Operations Reports*, Chapter 11, page 20; Speheger oral history, VHP, AFC 07192; Richard Frank, "The Pacific War's Biggest Battle."

83. Appleman, 343.

84. Welch oral history, 48, VHP, AFC88352; US Army, *Three Hundred Eighty-Third Infantry Regiment Operations Report*, Box 11560.

85. Hallas, 190.

86. *Sixth Marine Division Special After Action Report*, Phase 3, 11–15; Carleton, locations 122–36.

87. *Sixth Marine Division Special After Action Report*, Phase 3, 13–14; Appleman, 375–76.

88. *Sixth Marine Division Special After Action Report*, Phase 3, 14–15; Carleton, locations 122–36; Nichols and Shaw, 205.

89. Appleman, 375–76; Ōta, 155.

90. Appleman, 376–77; Nichols and Shaw, 205.

91. Nichols and Shaw, 212–13; Yahara, 75.

92. US Army, *Three Hundred Eighty-Third Infantry Regiment Operations Report*, Box 11560; Appleman, 357.

93. Davidson, Williams, and Kahl, 156–58; Appleman, 357–59.

94. USMC Archives, *Twenty-Fourth Corps After Action Report*, 30; Love, *Hourglass*, 420–26, 429–31; *New York Times*, TimesMachine, June 10, 1945; Appleman, 377–82.

95. Love, *Hourglass*, 429–30; *Seventh Infantry Division Operations*, Box 6208.

96. US Army, *Seventy-Seventh Infantry Division Operations*, NARA, RG 407, Entry 427, Box 9849.

97. Sloan, *Ultimate Battle*, 264.

98. USMC Archives, *Twenty-Fourth Corps After Action Report*, Campaign Overview, 30–31; Belote, 261–62; Love, *Hourglass*, 433–35.

CHAPTER 11: THE JAPANESE RETREAT FROM SHURI

1. Love, *Hourglass*, 537.

2. Belote, 290.

3. Yahara, 48–49, 68.

4. Ibid., 71, 210.

5. Ibid., 210.

6. Ibid., 210–11.

7. Belote, 277; Yahara, 68–72.

8. Yahara, 107.

9. Leckie, 183–84; Yahara, 76, 211; Hallas, 194, 205; *Ryukyu Shimpo*, 78–79.

10. Leckie, 185; Appleman, 389–91.

11. Hallas, 206; Appleman, 391.

12. Yahara, 211; *Sixth Marine Division Special Action Report*, 13.

13. US Army, *Ninety-Sixth Division Operations*, NARA, Box 11560; US Army, *Seventy-Seventh Infantry Division G-3 War Room Journal*, NARA, Box 9847.

14. Dencker, 249.

15. Davidson, Williams, and Kahl, 147–48, 160–61; Appleman, 349, 370.

16. Washington *Evening Star*, May 21, 1945, "Five Americans Reach Own Lines"; Appleman, 353–55.

17. Astor, 378.

18. Book oral history, National Museum of the Pacific War, OH00054.

19. Davidson, Williams, and Kahl, 157–61.

20. Ibid., 161–163; Sloan, *Ultimate Battle*, 269–70; Belote, 280–81 (Craft was awarded the Congressional Medal of Honor for his actions on May 30).

21. Davidson, Williams, and Kahl, 165; Dencker, 240–41.

22. Dencker, 246.

23. Belote, 267–68.

24. US Army, *Seventy-Seventh Infantry Division G-3 War Room Journal*, NARA, Boxes 9847 and 9848; Astor, 373; Heinrichs, 40–43; Appleman, 348–49, 338–41; US Army, *Ours to Hold*, 350; Yahara, 67; Belote, 256.

25. US Army, *Seventy-Seventh Infantry Division G-3 War Room Journal*; Huber, 115.

26. US Army, *Seventy-Seventh Infantry Division G-3 War Room Journal*, US Army, *Ours to Hold*, 341–42.

27. US Army, *Seventy-Seventh Infantry Division G-3 War Room Journal*, US Army, *Ours to Hold*, 343.

28. Astor, 373–76; US Army, *Ours to Hold*, 344.

29. US Army, *Seventy-Seventh Infantry Division G-3 War Room Journal*, US Army, *Ours to Hold*, 344–45.

30. US Army, *Ours to Hold*, 350.

31. Ibid., 352–53; Belote, 255.

32. Nichols and Shaw, 204; McMillan, 401–2.

33. Appleman, 396–97; Belote, 290, 293; Yahara, 105; Sloan, *Ultimate Battle*, 274; Leckie, 185–86; del Valle, "Old Glory."

34. Sledge, 274–76.

35. McMillan, 408; Benis Frank, *Okinawa*, 130.

36. *First Marine Regiment After Action Report*, Box 258; Appleman, 397, 402; Ōta, 146–47.

37. US Army, *Seventy-Seventh Division Operations*, Box 9848.

38. Ibid., Boxes 9848, 9849.

39. Ibid., Box 9849.

40. Gow, 171; Sloan, *Ultimate Battle*, 271; Yahara, 105.

41. Sloan, *Ultimate Battle*, 274.

42. Belote, 293.

43. Love, *Hourglass*, 436.

44. US Army, *Ninety-Sixth Division Operations*, Box 11560.

45. Love, *Hourglass*, 427, 438.

46. Leckie, 187–88; Appleman, 360.

47. Astor, 308.

48. Wells oral history, VHP, AFC 94616.

49. Sherrod, 392.

50. *Tactical Air Force Reports*, Box 15, Folder 13; Alexander, *Storm*, 159–60; Gandt, 275.

51. McFadden, 65.

52. DeChant, 223, 241–42; *Seventh Marine Regiment After Action Report*, Box 261, 17; Sherrod, 408; Wolf, 87–89, 163.

53. DeChant, 238; Breuer, 86–87, 91.

54. Sloan, *Ultimate Battle*, 241; Wolf, 110–11, 123.

55. Ugaki, 616–17; Ōta, 140–41; Astor, 319–20; Wolf, 170–71; Appleman, 361–62; DeChant, 236.

56. Sherrod, 402–3.

57. Ugaki, 617; Rielly, *Kamikazes*, 275; Sherrod, 407; DeChant, 238; Appleman, 362.

58. Hayashi and Coox, 143.

59. Farrand oral history, VHP, AFC 53286.

60. Govanus oral history, VHP, AFC 11729; Morison, 260; *USS Braine After Action Report of May 27, 1945*, NARA, Box 863; Astor, 394.

61. Rielly, *Kamikazes*, 279, 283.

62. Inoguchi and Nakajima, 151; Appleman, 362.

63. Morison, 261.

64. *USS Drexler After Action Report of May 28, 1945*, NARA, Box 954; Tatsch oral history, National Museum of the Pacific War, OH01546; Morison, 261.

65. Rielly, *Kamikazes*, 286–87.

66. Vernon, 145–48.

67. Yahara, 92, 98; Ōta, 146–47; *Ryukyu Shimpo*, 227–28.

68. *Ryukyu Shimpo*, 227–28.

69. Wright, 219; Belote, 279; Laura Lacey, 72.

70. Belote, 290.

71. Richard Frank, *Downfall*, 72; *Ryukyu Shimpo*, 25–26, 266; Cook, 354–56; Laura Lacey, 62–63.

72. Cook, 357.

73. Laura Lacey, 62; *Ryukyu Shimpo*, 25–26, 192.

74. Wright, 219; Yahara, 107–8, 211.

CHAPTER 12: THE LAST DITCH

1. Kukuchka oral history, VHP, AFC 10513.

2. O'Donnell, 261; Sloan, *Ultimate Battle*, 275.

3. Alexander, *Storm*, 206.

4. Leckie, 199–200; Belote, 292–93.

5. Gow, 172–74; Sloan, *Ultimate Battle*, 275; Belote, 292–93; *Sixth Marine Division Special Action Report*, 17–19; Appleman, 428–31.

6. Boan, 201–5.

7. Appleman, 431.

8. Nichols and Shaw, 220; Carleton, location 104; Boan, 183–85, 187; Welch, oral history, VHP, AFC 88352.

9. Yahara, 122–23.

10. Nichols and Shaw, 221.

11. Manchester, 383–84.

12. US Army, *Fourth Marines Special Action Report, Phase III*, USMC Archives, 12.

13. *Sixth Marine Division Special Action Report*, 20–22; Appleman, 432–33.

14. Kukuchka oral history, VHP, AFC 10513.

15. Appleman, 433; Welch oral history, 59, VHP, AFC 88352; Belote, 304.

16. Belote, 303.

17. *Sixth Marine Division Special Action Report*, 20–22; Ōta, 166–68.

18. Sloan, *Ultimate Battle*, 307; *Ryukyu Shimpo*, 221–22.

19. McMillan, 408–10; US Army, *Three Hundred Eighty-Third Regiment After Action Report*, Box 11560; *First Marine Division After Action Report*, Box 252; Sledge, 289; Appleman, 425.

20. Sarantakes, 72, 74; Appleman, 425.

21. Love, *Hourglass*, 440–47, 449–50.

22. US Army, *Ninety-Sixth Division Operations*, Box 11560; Davidson, Williams, and Kahl, 166; Belote, 306.

23. *First Marine Division After Action Report*, NARA, Box 252; Nichols and Shaw, 232–34.

24. Love, *Hourglass*, 439; Belote, 294–95, 305.

25. Yahara, 107; Belote, 295, 305; Huber, 85.

26. Sloan, *Ultimate Battle*, 280; Appleman, 455; Belote, 292.

27. Yahara, 100, 112–14, 222.

28. Ibid., 111.

29. Appleman, 434–36.

30. Belote, 305–6; Sarantakes, 66.

31. Sherrod, 417–18; Rielly, *Kamikazes*, 290–300; Inoguchi and Nakajima, 151; Orita, 312; Millot, 221; Gandt, 112, 327–28, 322.

32. Morison, 274; Rielly, *Kamikazes*, 304–6.

33. Rielly, *Kamikazes*, 308–11.

34. Belote, 296; Love, *Hourglass*, 456–57.

35. Love, *Hourglass*, 452–53.

36. Glenn, 120–21.

37. Appleman, 440; Love, *Hourglass*, 457.

38. Love, *Hourglass*, 454–55; Appleman, 441.

39. Love, *Hourglass*, 455–56, 465–66; Appleman, 442.

40. Belote, 299–300; Love, *Hourglass*, 458–60; *New York Times*, TimesMachine, June 13, 1945; Appleman, 446–47; Hughes oral history, VHP, AFC 01074.

41. Love, *Hourglass*, 460; Hughes oral history, VHP, AFC 01074; Capaldi oral history, VHP, AFC 97693.

CHAPTER 13: THE THIRTY-SECOND ARMY COLLAPSES

1. Yahara, 127.
2. Del Valle, "Southward."
3. Appleman, 443.
4. Davidson, Williams, and Kahl, 167–69; Belote, 310; Appleman, 443–45.
5. Davidson, Williams, and Kahl, 168–69, 171.
6. Ibid., 169–71.
7. Capaldi oral history, VHP, AFC 97693; Peto, 311.
8. Bob Green, 165.
9. Walton, 107, 110.
10. Frank and Shaw, 326.
11. Nichols and Shaw, 233.
12. Frank and Shaw, 332–35; Sorenson oral history, VHP, AFC 12289; Nichols and Shaw, 235; McMillan, 412, 414; Moskin, 393.
13. McMillan, 412.
14. Belote, 315; Appleman, 451; Nichols and Shaw, 337.
15. David Allen, "Battle of Okinawa Vet," *Stars and Stripes*, June 16, 2005.
16. Frank and Shaw, 338; Leckie, 200; Sarantakes, 77; McMillan, 415–16; Yahara, 132, 211.
17. Yahara, 223–24; Bix, 404–5; Davidson, Williams, and Kahl, 169.
18. Astor, 419–20; Frank and Shaw, 338.
19. Frank and Shaw, 339.
20. Neiman and Estes, 148–49; Frank and Shaw, 335; Astor, 420; Belote, 239; Alexander, *Storm*, 168.
21. Yahara, 125. Kudan is the site of the Yasukuni Shrine in Tokyo.
22. Appleman, 449–50; Yahara, 119, 126.
23. Yahara, 120–21.
24. Ōta, 168.
25. Yahara, 127.
26. *First Marine Regiment After Action Report*, A37–1, RG 127, Box 258.
27. Love, *Hourglass*, 463–64, 466–73; Capaldi oral history, VHP, AFC 97693.
28. Appleman, 456–58.
29. Sarantakes, 78.
30. US Army, *Ninety-Sixth Division Operations*, Box 11559; Dencker, 260; Davidson, Williams, and Kahl, 178–80; Yahara, 128.

31. Love, *Hourglass*, 180; Belote, 306.

32. Love, *Hourglass*, 474–75.

33. Astor, 405.

34. Makos, 323; McMillan, 418–20.

35. Frank and Shaw, 339–41; McMillan, 417–18; Moskin, 295.

36. Del Valle, "Southward."

37. Benis Frank, *Okinawa*, 340; *First Marine Regiment After Action Report*, Box 258.

38. Sledge, 294.

39. Ibid., 294–300.

40. Burgin, 260.

41. Astor, 417–18.

42. Makos, 328.

43. Del Valle, "Southward"; Belote, 304–5; *Third Amphibious Corps Action Report*, USMC Archives Phase II, 64–65; *First Marine Division After Action Report*, Box 252; Heinrichs, 409.

44. Astor, 413; McMillan, 420.

45. Appleman, 454–55.

46. Belote, 316.

47. Huber, 93–94.

48. Rottman, *Okinawa*, 16; Love, *Hourglass*, 463; Yahara, 129–30.

CHAPTER 14: THE CIVILIAN TRAGEDY

1. Welch oral history, 52, VHP, AFC 88352; Ōta, 50.

2. Higa, 43–48.

3. Straus oral history, National Museum of the Pacific War, OH00243.

4. Love, *Hourglass*, 451.

5. Holt oral history, VHP, AFC 43172; Laura Lacey, 66–67; Allen oral history, National Museum of the Pacific War, OH01297.

6. Maxwell oral history, National Museum of the Pacific War, OH00282.

7. Laura Lacey, 73–74.

8. O'Donnell, 265–66.

9. Higa, 43–48.

10. Ibid., 48–58.

11. Ibid., 58–60.

12. Ibid., 78–79.

13. Ibid., 80–118.

14. *Fleet Marine Force, Pacific, G-2 Observer's Report*. NARA, Box 11, Folder 25; M. D. Morris, 54.

15. Bob Green, 136–37.

16. Sloan, *Ultimate Battle*, 300; *Ryukyu Shimpo*, 454.

17. Laura Lacey, 71.

18. London oral history, 18, VHP, AFC 104717.

19. Sloan, *Ultimate Battle*, 304.

20. Capaldi oral history, VHP, AFC 97693.

21. Astor, 195.

22. Laura Lacey, 99.

23. Fitzgerald oral history, VHP, AFC 01488.

24. Austin oral history, National Museum of the Pacific War, OH01513.

25. Welch oral history, 52, VHP, AFC 88352; Ōta, 50.

26. Sarantakes, 71; Moskin, 395; Dyer, 1103; Rielly, *Kamikazes*, 344.

27. Nichols and Shaw, 243, 250.

28. Haley, "The Death of General Simon Boliver Buckner."

29. Yahara, 142.

30. Sarantakes, 87; Rottman, *Okinawa*, 34–35; Pineau, 141; Buell, 390. A friend of Admiral Raymond Spruance, Geiger came down with the mumps while on Okinawa. Geiger was embarrassed at having contracted a childhood viral infection and attempted to conceal it. But Spruance learned of Geiger's illness and he sent him a present: a diaper and safety pin. Geiger said he treasured the needling gift as a battle trophy.

31. Haley, "The Death of General Simon Bolivar Buckner."

32. Davidson, Williams, and Kahl, 183; Belote, 309.

33. Walton, 119.

34. Sarantakes, 79.

35. Nelson, 262; Astor, 424–25.

36. Straus oral history, National Museum of the Pacific War, OH00243.

37. Atkinson oral history, VHP, AFC 09332.

38. US Army, *Seventh Infantry Division Operations*, Box 6208.

39. Appleman, 465; Gow, 186–87.

40. Dencker, 267.

41. Appleman, 465.

42. Laura Lacey, 99–100.

43. US Army, *Ninety-Sixth Division Operations*, Box 11559.

44. Yahara, 131; Leckie, 199; Love, *Hourglass*, 478.

45. US Army, *Ninety-Sixth Division Operations*, Box 11559.

46. *First Marine Division After Action Report*, Box 252; Sledge, 305–6; del Valle, "Southward."

47. Glenn, 125–26.

48. Ibid., 132.

49. Sledge, 302.

50. USMC Archives, *Third Amphibious Corps Action Report*, Phase II, 64–65; *First Marine Division After Action Report*, Box 252.

51. Yahara, 195; Davidson, Williams, and Kahl, 190.

52. Makos, 330.

53. *Ryukyu Shimpo*, 281.

54. Laura Lacey, 102.

55. Davidson, Williams, and Kahl, 182–83, 188; Beckman oral history, VHP, AFC 56196; Dencker, 264–66.

56. Davidson, Williams, and Kahl, 190; Huber, 95.

57. Belote, 308.

58. Gow, 179; Yahara, 137–38, 222.

59. Astor, 428; Yahara, 219.

60. Inoguchi and Nakajima, 148–49.

61. *Ninety-Sixth Division After Action Reports*, Box 11552; Appleman, 458–59.

62. Yahara, 130.

63. US Army, *Tenth Army Section Reports*, USMC Archives, "Chapter 11, Psychological Warfare"; *Seventh Infantry Division Operations*, Box 6116; Morison, 276; Belote, 318; Frank and Shaw, 164.

64. USMC Archives, *Third Amphibious Corps*, Box 4.

65. Love, *Hourglass*, 478–80.

66. Huber, 98; Yahara, 144–45.

67. Love, *Hourglass*, 480–81.

68. Ibid., 481; Nelson, 268–71.

69. Rielly, *Kamikazes*, 352; Rielly, *Kamikaze Attacks*, 292; Morison, 275.

70. Warner, 263; Belote, 321; Inoguchi and Nakajima, 151.

71. Belote, 321.

72. Morison, 179.

73. Sloan, *Ultimate Battle*, 247; Rielly, *Kamikazes*, 314–15, 344; DeChant, 233; Belote, 321–22.

74. Belote, 322; Sherrod, 401–3.

75. Belote, 321–22.

76. Morison, 233; Belote, 313; Rielly, *Kamikaze Attacks*, 69; Dower, 331, 105*n*.

77. Gow, 195; Appleman, 489, footnote; Alexander, "Hellish Prelude"; Belote, 313; Inoguchi and Nakajima, 151.

78. Love, *Hourglass*, 481; Sheftall, 20; Belote, 317–18; Yahara, 147.

79. Yahara, 149–50.

80. Ibid., 149–51; Belote, 318; Huber, 100–2; Millot, 13–14.

81. Nichols and Shaw, 257; Belote, 310; Appleman, 471. After General Joseph Stilwell relieved Geiger as Tenth Army commander, he presided over a second end-of-campaign ceremony on July 2.

CHAPTER 15: THE BATTLE ENDS

1. Yahara, 181.

2. Perret, 527.

3. Alexander, *Storm*, 170.

4. Bob Green, 175–79.

5. Ōta, 98; Allday oral history, National Museum of the Pacific War, OH03776; Laura Lacey, 127–28.

6. Peto, 315.

7. Sledge, 306–7.

8. Hebard oral history, VHP, AFC 01520.

9. Astor, 363–64, 403; Appleman, 384; McMillan, 403; Hallas, 203; Alexander, "Hellish Prelude."

10. Perret, 527.

11. *Ryukyu Shimpo*, 355.

12. Ibid., 391; Hayashi and Coox, 53–54.

13. Sledge, 307–8.

14. Capaldi oral history, VHP, AFC 97693.

15. Bob Green, 169; Allday oral history, National Museum of the Pacific War, OH03776; Appleman, 467, 471–73.

16. Kogan, "Surrender or Die."

17. Appleman, 471–73; Sloan, *Ultimate Battle*, 327; Dencker, 270–72.

18. *Ryukyu Shimpo*, 432–33; *Tenth Army Operations Reports*, Box 13; Appleman, 467; Sloan, *Ultimate Battle*, 327; Hayashi and Coox, 51–55; Yahara, 193; Sarantakes, 49–50.

19. Sarantakes, 93.

20. Yahara, 155–70.

21. Ibid., 179–81.

22. Ibid., 186–89.

23. Belote, 319–20, 330, 184–85; Rottman, *Okinawa*, 88.

24. Sledge, 311.

25. Morison, 277; Sarantakes, 57; Appleman, 403, 420.

26. Appleman, 405–6.

27. Morison, 159–61; Leckie, 123–24; Carter, 311.

28. Morison, 246; Appleman, 253.

29. Morison, 280; Brunton oral history, National Museum of the Pacific War, OH02627; Warner, 267–68; Rielly, *Kamikazes*, 327; Millot, 224.

30. Morison, 280; Rielly, *Kamikazes*, 328.

31. Gandt, 345; Astor, 439; Hastings, 171; Appleman, 473; Leckie, 202, footnote; Richard Frank, *Downfall*, 182, 187.

32. Rielly, *Kamikazes*, 45.

33. *New York Times*, TimesMachine, June 5 and June 18, 1945.

34. Belote, 321–22, 332–33.

35. M. D. Morris, 53.

36. *Ryukyu Shimpo*, 271–73, 277; Hayashi and Coox, 50–51; Sloan, *Ultimate Battle*, 296.

37. Alexander, *Storm*, 170.

38. Gandt, 220; Huber, 60, 105–6; Williams, 43–45.

39. Book oral history, National Museum of the Pacific War, OH00054.

40. Alexander, *Storm*, 51; *First Marine Division After Action Report*, Box 252; Sledge, footnote, 268.

41. Davidson, Williams, and Kahl, 191; Medals of Honor list.

42. Sarantakes, 91–92.

43. *Tenth Army Operations Report*, Box 13, Folders 1, 2; Appleman, 384.

44. Ōta, 155; Gow, 166–67; Huber, 102, 104; Appleman, 383–84.

45. Morison, 282; Gandt, 345–46; Hastings, 402; Gow, 195; Astor, 439; Moskin, 397; Appleman, 473–74; Sledge, 312.

CHAPTER 16: DÉNOUEMENT

1. Mitchell, "Battle of Okinawa."

2. Ugaki, 665–66.

3. *Ryukyu Shimpo*, 332–37.

4. Appleman, 468; Sloan, *Ultimate Battle*, 310.

5. Yahara, 194; Millot, 220.

6. Manchester, 381; M. D. Morris, 45.

7. *Ryukyu Shimpo*, 164.

8. Peto, 358.

9. Love, *Hourglass*, 475–77.

10. Deiber oral history, VHP, AFC 32336.

11. Appleman, 35, 417; Frank and Shaw, 77.

12. Mitchell, "Battle of Okinawa"; *Ryukyu Shimpo*, 271–73, 277; Hayashi and Coox, 50–51; Sloan, *Ultimate Battle*, 296.

13. Bix, 487–94.

14. McCulloch, 376–78.

15. Pineau, 267–68.

16. Brower, 129–30, 133–34.

17. Belote, 324; Dyer, 1109; Richard Frank, *Downfall*, 117–18, 123, 194.

18. Brower, 136–38; Richard Frank, *Downfall*, 124; Alexander, *Storm*, 183.

19. US Army, *Reports of General MacArthur*, Vol. 2, Part 2, 591, 601–3.

20. Belote, 334; Warner, 175; Laura Lacey, 170–71.

21. Huber, 119–20; Fussell, 21; Laura Lacey, 170–71; Hayes, 702–3; Brower, 135.

22. McCulloch, 430–32, 437, 440–41, 447; Perret, 531–32; Bix, 500.

23. Rhodes, 709–11, 734.

24. Ibid., 740.

25. Ibid., 742–45; image of imperial rescript at http://ahoy.tk-jk.net/More-Images/JapaneseSurrenderProclamation.jpg.

26. Laura Lacey, 178.

27. Burgin, 266.

28. Sledge, 312–15.

29. Sloan, *Ultimate Battle*, 330.

30. Belote, 341; Ōta, 230–31.

31. Hirohito, Surrender Broadcast; Belote, 341–42; Ōta, 230–31.

32. Hastings, iii, 10; Dower, 297–98, 300; Hayashi and Coox, 55.

33. Chanlett-Avery and Mann, "US Military Presence on Okinawa."

34. Inoguchi and Nakajima, 164–68; Ugaki, 664–65.

35. Ugaki, 665–66; Warner, 316.

36. Warner, 216.

37. "Surrender of the Ryukyus," USMC Archives, Box 15, Folder 17; M. D. Morris, 39; Ōta, 231.

EPILOGUE

1. *Ryukyu Shimpo*, xviii.

2. Wright, 233.

3. Taylor, 279.

4. *Ryukyu Shimpo*, xviii.

5. Wright, 233.

6. Gow, 216; Hayashi and Coox, 56; Hallas, 218.

7. Mitchell, "Battle of Okinawa."

Bibliography

Alexander, Colonel Joseph H. *The Final Campaign: Marines in the Victory on Okinawa*, at: www.gutenberg.org/files/49119/49119-h/49119-h.htm.

———. "Hellish Prelude at Okinawa." *Naval History* 19, no. 2 (April 2015).

———. *Storm Landings: Epic Amphibious Battles in the Central Pacific*. Annapolis, MD: Naval Institute Press, 1997.

Allen, David. "Battle of Okinawa Veteran Shares Story of Courage Under Fire." *Stars and Stripes*, June 16, 2005.

Allen, Thomas B., and Norman Polmer. *Code-Name Downfall: The Secret Plan to Invade Japan—and Why Truman Dropped the Bomb*. New York: Simon & Schuster, 1995.

Angst, Linda. "Gendered Nationalism: The Himeyuri Story and Okinawan Identity in Postwar Japan." PoLAR 200, no. 1, 100–13. Also found at: www.anthrosource.onlinelibrary.wiley.com/do/pdf/10.1525/pol.1997.20.1.100.

Appleman, Roy E. *Okinawa: The Last Battle*. New York: Skyhorse Publishing, 2016. First published in 1949.

Astor, Gerald. *Operation Iceberg: The Invasion and Conquest of Okinawa in World War II*. New York: Donald I. Fine, Inc., 1995.

Ballendorf, Dirk Anthony, and Merrill Lewis Bartlett. *Pete Ellis, An Amphibious Warfare Prophet, 1880–1923*. Annapolis, MD: Naval Institute Press, 1997.

Belote, James, and William Belote. *Typhoon of Steel: The Battle for Okinawa*. New York: Harper & Row, 1970.

Bergerud, Eric. *Touched with Fire: The Land War in the South Pacific*. New York: Viking, 1996.

Berry, Henry. *Semper Fi, Mac: Living Memories of the US Marines in World War II*. New York: Arbor House, 1982.

Bix, Herbert R. *Hirohito and the Making of Modern Japan*. New York: Perennial, 2000.

Boan, Jim. *Rising Sun Sinking: The Battle for Okinawa*. Austin, TX: Eakin Press, 2000.

Boomhower, Ray E. *Dispatches from the Pacific: The World War II Reporting of Robert Sherrod*. Bloomington, IN: Indiana University Press, 2017.

Bradshaw, John. *The Faith of Desmond Doss*. Chattanooga, TN: It Is Written, 2016.

Breuer, William B. *Retaking the Philippines: America's Return to Corregidor and Bataan, October 1944–March 1945*. New York: St. Martin's Press, 1986.

Brower, Charles F. *Defeating Japan: The Joint Chiefs of Staff and Strategy in the Pacific War, 1943–1945*. New York: Palgrave Macmillan, 2012.

Buell, Thomas B. *The Quiet Warrior: A Biography of Admiral Raymond A. Spruance*. Boston, Toronto: Little, Brown and Company, 1974.

Burgin, R. V. *Islands of the Damned: A Marine at War in the Pacific*. New York: NAL Caliber, 2010.

Carleton, Major Phillips D. *The Conquest of Okinawa: An Account of the Sixth Marine Division*. Ebook. Pickle Partners Publishing, 2015, www.picklepartnerspublishing.com.

Carter, Admiral Worrall Reed (Ret.). *Beans, Bullets, and Black Oil: The Story of Fleet Logistics Afloat in the Pacific During World War II*. Washington, DC: Department of the Navy, 1953.

Chanlett-Avery, Emma, and Christopher Mann. "US Military Presence on Okinawa and Realignment to Guam." Congressional Research Service, June 14, 2017. Available at: www.fas.org/sgp/crs/row/IF10672.pdf.

Condit, Kenneth W., and Edwin T. Turnbladh. *Hold High the Torch: A History of the Fourth Marines*. Washington, DC: Historical Branch, G-3 Division, Headquarters, US Marine Corps, 1960.

Condon, John Pomeroy. *Corsairs and Flattops*. Annapolis, MD: Naval Institute Press, 1998.

Cook, Haruko Taya, and Theodore F. Cook. *Japan at War: An Oral History*. New York: The New Press, 1997.

Crosby, Donald F. *Battlefield Chaplains: Catholic Priests in World War II*. Lawrence: University Press of Kansas, 1994.

Davidson, Orlando R., J. Carl Williams, and Joseph A. Kahl. *The Deadeyes: The Story of the 96th Infantry Division*. Nashville, TN: The Battery Press, 1947.

DeChant, John A. *Devilbirds: The Story of United States Marine Corps Aviation in World War II.* New York, London: Harper, 1947.

Del Valle, General Pedro. "Old Glory at Shuri." *Marine Corps Gazette,* October 1945.

———. "Southward from Shuri." *Marine Corps Gazette,* October 1945.

Dencker, Donald O. *Love Company: Infantry Combat Against the Japanese, World War II. Leyte and Okinawa.* Manhattan, KS: Sunflower University Press, 2002.

Dower, John W. *War Without Mercy: Race & Power in the Pacific War.* New York: Pantheon Books, 1986.

Drea, Edward J. *Nomonhan: Japanese-Soviet Tactical Combat, 1939.* In *Leavenworth Papers No. 2,* 1981.

Dull, Paul S. *A Battle History of the Imperial Japanese Navy (1941–1945).* Annapolis, MD: Naval Institute Press, 1978.

Dyer, Admiral George Carroll. *The Amphibians Came to Conquer: The Story of Admiral Richmond Kelly Turner,* Vol. 2. Washington, DC: Department of the Navy, 1972.

Edoin, Hoito. *The Night Tokyo Burned.* New York: St. Martin's Press, 1987.

Eleventh Marine Regiment After Action Report, Okinawa. National Archives, RG 127, Box 264.

Feifer, George. *Tennozan: The Battle of Okinawa and the Atomic Bomb.* New York: Ticknor and Fields, 1992.

First Marine Regiment After Action Report, Okinawa. National Archives, RG 127, Boxes 252, 258, 260.

Fleet Marine Force, Pacific, G-2 Observer's Report, National Archives, RG 407, Entry 427, Box 11, Folder 25.

Foster, Simon. *Okinawa 1945: Final Assault on the Empire.* London: Arms & Armour Press, 1994.

Fournier, A. R. *"K" Company, 3rd Battalion, 1st Marine Regiment—Journal of Okinawa.* National Archives, RG 127, Box 260.

Frank, Benis M. *Okinawa: The Great Island Battle.* New York: Elsevier-Dutton, 1978.

Frank, Benis, and Henry I. Shaw Jr. *Victory and Occupation. History of US Marine Corps Operations in World War II, Vol. V.* Washington, DC: US Government Printing Office, 1968.

Frank, Richard B. *Downfall: The End of the Imperial Japanese Empire.* New York: Random House, 1999.

———. "The Pacific War's Biggest Battle." *Naval History* 24, no. 2 (April 2010).

Fussell, Paul. *Killing in Verse and Prose and other Essays.* London: Bellow Publishing, 1988.

Gailey, Harry A. *Howlin' Mad vs. the Army: Conflict in Command, Saipan 1944.* Novato, CA: Presidio Press, 1986.

Gandt, Robert. *The Twilight Warriors: The Deadliest Naval Battle of World War II and the Men Who Fought It.* New York: Broadway Books, 2010.

Genealogy Bank, www.genealogybank.com/explore/newspapers/all.

Gibney, Frank B. "Epilogue: The Battle Ended—Capture and Return." In *The Battle for Okinawa,* by Hiromichi Yahara, 193–99. New York: John Wiley & Sons, 1995.

———. *Sensō: The Japanese Remember the Pacific War.* Armonk, NY, London: M. E. Sharpe, 2007. First published in 1995.

Glenn, Roland. *The Hawk and the Dove: World War II at Okinawa and Korea.* Kittery Point, ME: Smith/Kerr Associates LLC Publishing, 2009.

Gow, Ian. *Okinawa 1945: Gateway to Japan.* Garden City, NY: Doubleday & Company, 1985.

Green, Bob. *Okinawa Odyssey.* Albany, TX: Bright Sky Press, 2004.

Green, Lyle D. *My World War II Experience Revisited.* Ann Arbor, MI: Proctor Publications, 1996.

Gunston, Bill. *Fighting Aircraft of World War II.* London: Salamander Books Limited, 2001.

Haley, J. Fred. "The Death of General Simon Boliver Buckner." *Marine Corps Gazette,* November 1982.

Hallas, James H. *The Devil's Anvil: The Assault on Peleliu.* Westport, CT: Praeger Publishers, 1994.

———. *Killing Ground on Okinawa: The Battle for Sugar Loaf Hill.* Westport, CT: Praeger Publishers, 1996.

Halsey, William Frederick, and Lieutenant Commander J. Bryan III. *Admiral Halsey's Story.* New York: Whittlesey House, 1947.

Hara, Captain Tameichi. *Japanese Destroyer Captain: Pearl Harbor, Guadalcanal, Midway—As Seen Through Japanese Eyes.* Annapolis, MD: Naval Institute Press, 1967.

Harris, Brayton. *Admiral Nimitz: The Commander of the Pacific Ocean Theater.* New York: Palgrave Macmillan, 2011.

Hastings, Max. *Retribution: The Battle for Japan, 1944–1945.* New York: Vintage Books, 2009.

Hayashi, Hirofumi. "Japanese Deserters and Prisoners of War in the Battle of Okinawa." In *Prisoners of War, Prisoners of Peace,* edited by Bob Moore and Barbara Hately-Broad, 49–50. New York: Berg Publishers, 2005.

Hayashi, Saburō, and Alvin D. Coox. *Kōgun: The Japanese Army in the Pacific War*. Quantico, VA: Marine Corps Association, 1959.

Hayes, Grace Person. *The History of the Joint Chiefs of Staff in World War II: The War Against Japan*. Annapolis, MD: Naval Institute Press, 1982.

Heinrichs, Waldo, and Marc Gallicchio. *Implacable Foes: War in the Pacific, 1944–1945*. New York: Oxford University Press, 2017.

Higa, Tomika. *The Girl with the White Flag. An Inspiring Story of Love and Courage in War Time*. Tokyo, New York, London: Kadansha International, 1991.

Hirohito. Surrender Broadcast. www.mtholyoke.edu/acad/intrel/hirohito.htm.

Hornfischer, James D. *The Fleet at Flood Tide: America at Total War in the Pacific, 1944–1945*. New York: Bantam Books, 2016.

———. *The Last Stand of the Tin Can Sailors*. New York: Bantam Books, 2004.

Hoyt, Edwin P. *Closing the Circle: War in the Pacific: 1945*. New York: Van Nostrand Reinhold Company, 1982.

———. *How They Won the War in the Pacific: Nimitz and His Admirals*. New York: Weybright and Talley, 1970.

———. *Inferno: The Firebombing of Japan, March 9–August 15, 1945*. New York: Madison Books, 2000.

Huber, Thomas M. *Okinawa 1945*. Havertown, PA: Casemate, 2004. First published in 1990 as *Japan's Battle of Okinawa, April–June 1945*.

Ienaga, Saburo. *The Pacific War: World War II and the Japanese, 1931–1945*. New York: Pantheon Books, 1978.

Inoguchi, Captain Rikihei, and Commander Tadashi Nakajima. *The Divine Wind: Japan's Kamikaze Force in World War II*. Annapolis, MD: Naval Institute Press, 1958.

Isely, Jeter A., and Philip A. Crowl. *The US Marines and Amphibious War: Its Theory, and Its Practice in the Pacific*. Princeton, NJ: Princeton University Press, 1951.

Ito, Masanori. *The End of the Imperial Japanese Navy*. New York: Jove, 1984. First published by W. W. Norton in 1962.

The Japan Times. Tokyo: The Japan Times, Ltd., Daily newspaper, 1897–.

Jomini, Antoine-Henri. *Jomini and His Summary of the Art of War*. (Condensed). Edited by General J. D. Hittle. Harrisburg, PA: Military Service Pubishing Co., 1958.

Kennedy, Maxwell Taylor. *Dragon's Hour: The Story of the USS Bunker Hill and the Kamikaze Pilot Who Crippled Her*. New York: Simon & Schuster, 2008.

Kerr, George H. *Okinawa: The History of an Island People*. Boston, Rutland, VT: Tuttle Publishing, 2000. Originally published in 1958.

Kogan, Herman. "Glory Kid," *Marine Corps Gazette*, September 1945, 60–61.

———. "Surrender or Die." In *The Leathernecks*, edited by Karl Schuon, 214–16. New York: Franklin Watts, 1963.

Kuwahara, Yasuo, and Gordon T. Allred. *Kamikaze: A Japanese Pilot's own Spectacular Story of the Famous Suicide Squadrons*. Clearfield, UT: American Legacy Media, 2007.

Lacey, Laura Homan. *Stay Off the Skyline: The Sixth Marine Division on Okinawa—An Oral History*. Washington, DC: Potomac Books, 2005.

Lacey, Sharon Tosi. *Pacific Blitzkrieg: World War II in the Central Pacific*. Denton, TX: University of North Texas Press, 2013.

Leavenworth Papers. Fort Leavenworth, KS: Combat Studies Institute, US Army Command and General Staff College. 23 Vols.

Leckie, Robert. *Okinawa: The Last Battle of World War II*. New York: Viking Penguin, 1995.

Lince, George. *Too Young the Heroes: A World War II Marine's Account of Facing a Veteran Enemy*. Jefferson, NC: McFarland & Company, 1997.

Love, Edmund G. *The Hourglass: A History of the 7th Infantry Division in World War II*. Nashville, TN: The Battery Press, 1988.

———. *The 27th Infantry Division in World War II*. Nashville, TN: The Battery Press, 2001. Originally published in 1949.

Makos, Adam. *Voices of the Pacific: Untold Stories from the Marine Heroes of World War II*. New York: Berkley Caliber, 2013.

Manchester, William. *Goodbye, Darkness. A Memoir of the Pacific War*. Boston, Toronto: Little, Brown and Company, 1999.

Marine Corps Gazette. Quantico, VA: Marine Corps Association. Monthly magazine, 1916–.

Mason, A. T. "Battle of the Wana Draw," *Marine Corps Gazette*, October 1945.

McClain, S. *Navajo Weapon*. Boulder, CO: Books Beyond Borders, 1994.

McCullough, David. *Truman*. New York: Simon & Schuster, 1992.

McFadden, Brian S. *Marine Close Air Support in World War II*. Theses to the faculty of the US Army Command and General Staff College. 1986. www.dtic.mil/dtic/tr/fulltext/v2/a369287.pdf.

McMillan, George. *The Old Breed: A History of the First Marine Division in World War II*. Washington, DC: Infantry Journal Press, 1949.

McWhorter, Hamilton III. *The First Hellcat Ace*. Pacifica, CA: Pacifica Military History, 2000.

Mersky, Peter. *The Grim Reapers: Fighting Squadron Ten in World War II*. Mesa, AZ: Champlin Museum Press, 1986.

Miller, Lee G. *The Story of Ernie Pyle*. New York: Viking Press, 1950.

Millot, Bernard. *Divine Thunder. The Life and Death of the Kamikazes.* New York: Pinnacle Books, 1970.

Mitchell, Jon. "The Battle of Okinawa: America's Good War Gone Bad," *The Japan Times,* March 30, 2015, www.japantimes.co.jp/community /2015/03/30/issues/battle-okinawa-americas-good-war-gone-bad/# .W9sr90Wow—u.

Moore, Bob, and Barbara Hately-Broad, eds. *Prisoners of War, Prisoners of Peace: Captivity, Homecoming and Memory in World War II.* New York: Berg Publishers, 2005.

Morison, Samuel Eliot. *Victory in the Pacific 1945.* Vol. 14 of *History of United States Naval Operations in World War II.* Edison, NJ: Castle Books, 2001. First published in 1960 by Little, Brown and Company.

Morris, M. D. *Okinawa: A Tiger by the Tail.* New York: Hawthorn Books, 1968.

Morris, Rob. *Untold Valor: The Second World War in the Pacific.* Charleston, SC, Oxford, UK: Foothill Media, 2014.

Moskin, J. Robert. *The United States Marine Corps Story.* New York, San Francisco: McGraw-Hill, 1982.

National Museum of the Pacific War. Online oral history transcriptions, at: www.digitalarchive.pacificwarmuseum.org.

Naval History. Annapolis, MD: US Naval Institute. Bi-monthly magazine, 1987–.

Neiman, Robert M., and Kenneth W. Estes. *Tanks on the Beaches: A Marine Tanker in the Pacific War.* College Station, TX: Texas A&M University Press, 2003.

Nelson, George R. *I Company: The First and Last to Fight on Okinawa.* Bloomington, IN: 1st Books Library, 2003.

Neufeld, William: *Slingshot Warbirds: World War II US Navy Scout-Observation Airmen.* Jefferson, NC, London: McFarland & Company, 2003.

Newcomb, Richard F. *Iwo Jima.* New York: Bantam Books, 1982. First published in 1965 by Holt, Rinehart and Winston.

New York Times archives online. TimesMachine. At: www.timesmachine .nytimes.com/browser.

Nichols, Chas. S., Jr., and Henry I. Shaw Jr. *Okinawa: Victory in the Pacific.* Washington, DC: Historical Branch, G-3 Division, Headquarters, US Marine Corps, 1955.

Nimitz, Admiral Chester W. *Command Summary of Fleet Admiral Chester W. Nimitz, USN. Nimitz "Graybook," Vol. 6, 1 January 1945–1 July 1945.* Washington, DC: Naval History and Heritage Command, 1946.

O'Brien, Francis A. *Battling for Saipan*. New York: Ballantine Books, 2003.

O'Donnell, Patrick K. *Into the Rising Sun: In Their Own Words, World War II's Pacific Veterans Reveal the Heart of Combat*. New York: The Free Press, 2002.

O'Neill, Richard. *Suicide Squads: Axis and Allied Special Attack Weapons of World War II: Their Development and Their Missions*. London: Salamander Books, 1981.

Oberg, Tanney Edward. *Lucky Sweetbrier: Coast Guard Cutter Survives World War II, Okinawa Kamikazes, Typhoons and More*. New York: IUniverse, 2005.

Ohnuki-Tierney, Emiko. *Kamikaze Diaries: Reflections of Japanese Student Soldiers*. Chicago: University of Chicago Press, 2006.

Orita, Zenji, with Joseph D. Harrington. *I-Boat Captain*. Canoga Park, CA: Major Books, 1976.

Ōta, Masahide. *The Battle of Okinawa: The Typhoon of Steel and Bombs*. Tokyo: Kume Publishing, 1984.

Perret, Geoffrey. *There's a War to Be Won: The United States Army in World War II*. New York: Random House, 1991.

Peto, George, with Peter Margaritis. *Twenty-Two on Peleliu: Four Pacific Campaigns with the Corps. The Memoirs of an Old Breed Marine*. Philadelphia, Oxford, UK: Casemate, 2017.

Petty, Bruce M. *Voices from the Pacific War: Bluejackets Remember*. Annapolis, MD: Naval Institute Press, 2004.

Potter, E. B. *Nimitz*. Annapolis, MD: Naval Institute Press, 1976.

Public Broadcasting System (PBS). "Sinking the Supership," on *Nova*. S33E02. Destruction of the battleship *Yamato*.

Pyle, Ernie. *Last Chapter*. New York: Henry Holt and Company, 1946.

Rhodes, Richard. *The Making of the Atomic Bomb*. New York: Simon & Schuster, 1986.

Richardson, Robert C., Jr. *Participation in the Okinawa Operation by the United States Army Forces, Pacific Ocean Areas, April–June 1945*. Vol. 1. Washington, DC: US Army, 1946.

Rielly, Robin. *Kamikaze Attacks of World War II*. Jefferson, NC, and London: McFarland & Company, 2010.

———. *Kamikazes, Corsairs, and Picket Ships: Okinawa, 1945*. Philadelphia: Casemate, 2010.

Rogers, Jerry L. *So Long for Now: A Sailor's Letters from the USS Franklin*. Norman, OK: University of Oklahoma Press, 2017.

Ross, Bill D. *Iwo Jima: Legacy of Valor*. New York: The Vanguard Press, 1985.

Rottman, Gordon L. *Japanese Pacific Island Defenses, 1941–45.* Oxford, UK: Osprey Publishing, 2003.

———. *Okinawa 1945: The Last Battle.* Oxford, UK: Praeger, 2002.

Ryukyu Shimpo. Descent into Hell: Civilian Memories of the Battle of Okinawa. Translated with commentary by Mark Ealey and Alastair McLauchlan. Portland, ME: Merwin Asia, 2014.

Sarantakes, Nicholas Evan, ed. *Seven Stars: The Okinawa Battle Diaries of Simon Boliver Buckner Jr. and Joseph Stilwell.* College Station, TX: Texas A&M University Press, 2004.

Sassoon, Siegfried. *Memoirs of an Infantry Officer.* New York: Coward, McCann, 1930.

Satterfield, John R. *Saving Big Ben: The USS Franklin and Father Joseph T. O'Callahan.* Annapolis, MD: Naval Institute Press, 2011.

Schom, Alan. *The Eagle and the Rising Sun: The Japanese-American War, 1941–1943.* New York, London: W. W. Norton & Company, 2004.

Schuon, Karl, ed. *The Leathernecks. An Informal History of the US Marine Corps.* New York: Franklin Watts. 1963.

Seventh Marine Regiment After Action Report, Phase III. National Archives, RG 127, Box 261.

Sheftall, M. G. *Blossoms in the Wind: Human Legacies of the Kamikaze.* New York: New American Library, 2005.

Shepherd, General Lemuel C. "The Battle for Motobu Peninsula." *Marine Corps Gazette,* August 1945.

Sherrod, Robert. *History of Marine Corps Aviation in World War II.* San Rafael, CA: Presidio Press, 1980.

Sinking of the Japanese Battleship *Yamato.* April 7, 1945. National Archives, RG 38, Box 216, Ser00222.

Sledge, E. B. *With the Old Breed at Peleliu and Okinawa.* New York: Ballantine Books, 2010. First published in 1981.

Sloan, Bill. *Their Backs Against the Sea: The Battle of Saipan and the Largest Banzai Attack of World War II.* Boston: Da Capo Press, 2017.

———. *The Ultimate Battle: Okinawa 1945—The Last Epic Struggle of World War II.* New York: Simon & Schuster, 2007.

Smith, Robert Ross. *The Approach to the Philippines,* from the series United States Army in World War II. Washington, DC: Center of Military History, US Army, 1996.

Springer, Joseph A. *Inferno: The Epic Life and Death Struggle of the USS Franklin in World War II.* St. Paul, MN: Zenith Press, 2007.

Stafford, Edward P. *The Big E: The Story of the USS Enterprise.* New York: Random House, 1962.

Stille, Mark E. *The Imperial Japanese Navy in the Pacific War*. Oxford, New York: Osprey Publishing, 2013.

Stockman, James R. *The First Marine Division on Okinawa: 1 April–30 June 1945*. Online only: Pickle Partners Publishing, 2014. First published in 1946. www.picklepartnerspublishing.com.

Surels, Ron. *DD522: Diary of a Destroyer*. Plymouth, NH: Valley Graphics, 1994.

Taylor, Theodore. *The Magnificent Mitscher*. New York: W. W. Norton, 1954.

Time-Life Books Staff, eds. *Japan at War*. Alexandria, VA: Time-Life Books, 1980.

Toland, John. *The Rising Sun: The Decline and Fall of the Japanese Empire*. New York: Bantam Books, 1981.

Toll, Ian W. *The Conquering Tide: War in the Pacific Islands, 1942–1944*. New York, London: W. W. Norton, 2015.

Tuchman, Barbara W. *Stilwell and the American Experience in China, 1911–45*. New York: Bantam Books, 1980.

Ugaki, Matome. *Fading Victory: The Diary of Admiral Matome Ugaki, 1941–1945*. Translated by Masataka Chihaya. Pittsburgh: University of Pittsburgh Press, 1991.

United States Army. *Ours to Hold It High: The History of the 77th Infantry Division in World War II*. Washington, DC: Infantry Journal Press, 1947.

———. *Reports of General MacArthur: Japanese Operations in the Southwest Pacific Area. Vol. 2, Part 2*. Washington, DC: Department of the Army, 1950.

United States Army Reports at the National Archives.

———. *Ninety-Sixth Division After Action Reports*. RG 407, Entry 427, Box 11563.

———. *Ninety-Sixth Division Operations*. RG 407, Entry 427, Boxes 11559, 11560.

———. *Ninety-Sixth Infantry Division*. RG 407, Entry 427, Box 11552.

———. *Seventh Infantry Division Operations*. RG 407, Entry 427, Boxes 6116, 6208, 9844.

———. *Seventy-Seventh Infantry Division After Action Report*, April 25–June 30, 1945. National Archives. RG 127, Box 258.

———. *Seventy-Seventh Infantry Division G-3 War Room Journal*. RG 407, Entry 427, Box 9847.

———. *Seventy-Seventh Infantry Division Operations, April 1945–October 1945*. RG 407, Entry 427, Boxes 9814, 9834, 9835, 9836, 9844, 9847, 9848, and 9849.

———. *S-3 Periodic Reports, April–June 1945*. RG 407, Entry 427, Box 6208.

———. *Three Hundred Eighty-Third Infantry Regiment Operations Report and After Action Report, 96th Division.* RG 407, Entry 427, Boxes 11560, 11566.

———. *Twenty-Seventh Infantry Division Operations Report, Nansei Shoto Phase I.* 4, RG 127, Box 258.

United States Marine Corps. Archives Reports, World War II, COLL/3720.

———. *Fourth Marines Special Action Report, Phase III.*

———. Geiger, General Roy. *Papers.* Marine Corps Archives, Box 6, Folders 106–9 (March–June 1945).

———. *Okinawa: Marine Corps: Various.* Boxes 11, 13, 33.

———. *Sixth Marine Division Special Action Report, Okinawa Operation, Vol. 3, Phase 3.*

———. "Surrender of the Ryukyus." Box 15, Folder 17.

———. *Tactical Air Force Reports, Tenth Army.* Box 15, Folder 13.

———. *Tenth Army Operations Reports, 1945.* Box 13. Six folders.

———. *Tenth Army Section Reports*, Chapter 11, "Psychological Warfare."

———. *Third Amphibious Corps Action Report of Okinawa Operations, Phases I and II.*

———. *Third Amphibious Corps, Tenth Army, Okinawa Operation 1945.* Boxes 3, 4. Folders 2, 5, 9, 10, 11.

———. *Twenty-Fourth Corps, Tenth Army, Operations and After Action Reports, Phases 1 and 2.* Reports, 1945, Box 14, Folders 1, 2.

———. *US Army Forces in the Pacific Area: Participation in the Okinawa Campaign.* Box 15, Vols. 1 and 2, Folders 14, 15, 16.

United States Strategic Bombing Survey. *Campaigns of the Pacific War.* Washington, DC: US Government Printing Office, 1946.

USS *Aaron Ward After Action Report of May 3, 1945.* NARA, RG 38, Box 794.

USS *Bryant After Action Report of April 16, 1945.* NARA, RG 38, Box 870.

USS *Braine After Action Report of May 27, 1945.* NARA, RG 38, Box 863.

USS *Bush After Action Report of April 6, 1945.* NARA, RG 38, Box 920.

USS *Colhoun After Action Report of April 6, 1945.* NARA, RG 38, Box 920.

USS *Drexler After Action Report of May 28, 1945.* NARA, RG 38, Box 954.

USS *Emmons After Action Report of April 6, 1945.* NARA, RG 38, Box 964.

USS *Harding After Action Report of April 16, 1945.* NARA, RG 38.

USS *Hancock After Action Report of April 6, 1945.* NARA, RG 38, Box 1018, Serial 0236.

USS *Hancock Diaries*, NARA, RG 38, Box 922.

USS *Little After Action Report of May 3, 1945.* NARA, RG 38, Box 1151.

USS *Luce After Action Report of May 4, 1945.* NARA, RG 38, Box 1265.

USS *Morrison After Action Report of May 4, 1945.* NARA, RG 38, Box 1254.

USS *Pringle After Action Report and War Diary*, April 16, 1945. RG 38, Boxes 1336, 1352, Serial S-34.

Vandegrift, A. A., and Robert B. Asprey. *Once a Marine: The Memoirs of General A. A. Vandegrift, Commandant of the Marine Corps in World War II*. New York: Ballantine Books, 1964.

Van der Vat, Dan. *The Pacific Campaign, World War II: The US–Japanese Naval War, 1941–1945*. New York: Simon & Schuster, 1991.

Vernon, James. *The Hostile Sky: A Hellcat Fighter in World War II*. Annapolis, MD: Naval Institute Press, 2003.

Veterans History Project. *Transcripts*. American Folklife Center at the Library of Congress.

Walton, Rodney Earl. *Big Guns, Brave Men: Mobile Artillery Observers and the Battle for Okinawa*. Annapolis, MD: Naval Institute Press, 2013.

Warner, Denis, and Peggy Warner. *The Sacred Warriors: Japan's Suicide Legions*. New York: Van Nostrand Reinhold Company, 1982.

Washington Evening Star. "Five Americans Reach Own Lines After Four Nights Behind Japs," May 21, 1945, 13.

Wheelan, Joseph. *Midnight in the Pacific: Guadalcanal, the World War II Battle That Turned the Tide of War*. Boston: Da Capo, 2017.

Wheeler, Keith. *The Road to Tokyo*. Alexandria, VA: World War II Time-Life Books, 1979.

Williams, Thomas. "Jap Tactics on Okinawa." *Marine Corps Gazette*, October 1945, 43–53.

Winton, John. *ULTRA in the Pacific: How Breaking Japanese Codes & Cyphers Affected Naval Operations Against Japan, 1941–45*. Annapolis, MD: Naval Institute Press, 1993.

Wolf, William. *Death Rattlers: Marine Squadron VMF-323 Over Okinawa*. Atglen, PA: Schiffer Military History, 1999.

Wolter, John A., David A. Ranzan, and John J. McDonough. *With Commodore Perry to Japan: The Journal of William Speiden Jr., 1852–1855*. Annapolis, MD: Naval Institute Press, 2013.

Wright, Derrick. *Pacific Victory: Tarawa to Okinawa, 1943–1945*. Gloucester, UK: Sutton Publishing, 2005.

Wukovits, John. *Hell from the Heavens: The Epic Story of the USS Laffey and World War II's Greatest Kamikaze Attack*. Cambridge, MA: Da Capo Press, 2015.

Yahara, Hiromichi. *The Battle for Okinawa*. New York: John Wiley & Sons, 1995. First published in Japanese in 1973.

Yoshida, Mitsuru. *Requiem for Battleship Yamato*. Seattle: University of Washington Press, 1985.

ORAL HISTORIES FROM VETERANS HISTORY PROJECT, AMERICAN FOLKLORE CENTER, LIBRARY OF CONGRESS

Aldrich, Army Asst. Surgeon Eugene. VHP, AFC, LOC, No. 107976.

Atkinson, Marine Captain Fitzgerald. VHP, AFC, LOC, No. 09332.

Beckman, Army Sergeant William. VHP, AFC, LOC, No. 56196.

Bentley, Marine Lieutenant Robert. VHP, AFC, LOC, No. 23693.

Burke, Navy Seaman 1st Class Howard. VHP, AFC, LOC, No. 24259.

Burrows, Navy Lieutenant Charles. VHP, AFC, LOC, No. 90365.

Bush, Navy Hospital Apprentice 1st Class Robert. VHP, AFC, LOC, No. 89632.

Capaldi, Army Sergeant Benjamin. VHP, AFC, LOC, No. 97693.

Chilcote, Army Sergeant Bruce. VHP, AFC, LOC, No. 31046.

Clark, Navy Pharmacist's Mate 2nd Class Bill. VHP, AFC, LOC, No. 30617.

Deiber, Marine Sergeant Everett. VHP, AFC, LOC, No. 32336.

Dunbar, Marine Corporal Robert. VHP, AFC, LOC, No. 31159.

Farrand, Navy Electrician's Mate 1st Class Philip. VHP, AFC, LOC, No. 53286.

Ferrier, Marine Corporal Robert. VHP, AFC, LOC, No. 20811.

Fitzgerald, Army Lieutenant Donald. VHP, AFC, LOC, No. 01488.

Ford, Navy Gunner's Mate Floyd. VHP, AFC, LOC, No. 76069.

Fox, Navy Lieutenant Gilbert. VHP, AFC, LOC, No. 23056.

Govanus, Navy Seaman Jack. VHP, AFC, LOC, No. 11729.

Graley, Army Private First Class Frank. VHP, AFC, LOC, No. 02816.

Grant, Aubrey. Memoirs. VHP, AFC, LOC, No. 24631.

Habern, Marine Sergeant Frank. VHP, AFC, LOC, No. 02757.

Hannig, Navy Lieutenant Frank. Memoirs. VHP, AFC, LOC, No. 74446.

Hebard, Marine Corporal Kenneth. VHP, AFC, LOC, No. 01520.

Holt, Army Sergeant John. VHP, AFC, LOC, No. 43172.

Hughes, Army Captain Warren. VHP, AFC, LOC, No. 01074.

Jones, Navy Electrician Mate 2nd Class Jon, Jr. VHP, AFC, LOC, No. 85719.

Joy, Army Sergeant Joe. VHP, AFC, LOC, No. 87853.

Kaplan, Navy Petty Officer Arthur. VHP, AFC, LOC, No. 33936.

Korney, Navy Water Tender 3rd Class James. VHP, AFC, LOC, No. 82109.

Kukuchka, Marine Corporal Frank. VHP, AFC, LOC, No. 10513.

Levin, Army Sergeant Jerry. VHP, AFC, LOC, No. 79217.

London, Army Private First Class Jack. VHP, AFC, LOC, No. 104717.

Macpherson, Marine Corporal David. VHP, AFC, LOC, No. 01975.

Milner, Marine Private First Class Robert. VHP, AFC, LOC, No. 54694.

Roberts, Army Lieutenant Robert. VHP, AFC, LOC, No. 86156.

Smidt, Marine Sergeant Merlin. VHP, AFC, LOC, No. 92604.

Sorenson, Marine Corporal Robert. VHP, AFC, LOC, No. 12289.

Spaulding, Marine Corporal Roger. VHP, AFC, LOC, No. 431.

Speheger, Marine Private John. VHP, AFC, LOC, No. 07192.

Spencer, Army Captain Richard. VHP, AFC, LOC, No. 19082.

Taylor, Marine Sergeant Vernon. VHP, AFC, LOC, No. 24731.

Welch, Marine Corporal Hubert, Jr. Memoir "Now Hear This!" VHP, AFC, LOC, No. 88352.

Wells, Marine Captain Albert. VHP, AFC, LOC, No. 94616.

Whitfield, Carley Mills, Motor Machinist Mate 3, VHP, AFC, LOC, No. 106231.

Wills, Marine Sergeant Ernest. VHP, AFC, LOC, No. 33968.

ONLINE ORAL HISTORIES FROM THE NATIONAL MUSEUM OF THE PACIFIC WAR

http://digitalarchive.pacificwarmuseum.org/cdm

Aitken, Doug. Oral history. OH01497.

Allday, Martin. Oral history. OH03776.

Allen, Charles. Oral history. OH01297.

Austin, Edmund. Oral history. OH01513.

Book, Richard. Oral history. OH00054.

Boswell, James. Oral history. OH01317.

Brunton, Wallace. Oral history. OH02627

Cooper, Bert. Oral history. OH00259.

Ferry, Francis. Oral history OH00022.

Fowler, Trenton. Oral history. OH00006.

Jones, Howard. Oral history. OH01819.

Kalinofsky, Hank. Oral history. OH00048.

Kirkpatrick, Charles. Oral history. OH01506.

Maxwell, Raymond. Oral history. OH00282.

McClellan, Bill. Oral history. OH01507.

Minamoto, Yoshihiro. Oral history. OH01509.

Pase, Charles. Oral history. OH00133.

Straus, David. Oral history. OH00243.

Tatsch, Harold. Oral history. OH01546.

Index